Women and International Human Rights Law

D0861466

This book presents the findings of the first comprehensive study on the most recent and most unique and innovative method of monitoring international human rights law at the United Nations. Since its existence, there has yet to be a complete and comprehensive book solely dedicated to exploring the Universal Periodic Review (UPR) process. *Women and International Human Rights Law* provides a much-needed insight to what the process is, how it operates in practice, and whether it meets its fundamental aim of promoting the universality of all human rights.

The book addresses the topics with regard to international human rights law and will be of interest to researchers, academics, and students interested in the monitoring and implementation of international human rights law at the United Nations. In addition, it will form supplementary reading for those students studying international human rights law on undergraduate programmes and will also appeal to academics and students with interests in political sciences and international relations.

Gayatri H. Patel is a Lecturer in International Human Rights Law at Aston University, UK.

Routledge Research in Human Rights Law

For more information about this series, please visit:

www.routledge.com/Routledge-Research-in-Human-Rights-Law/book-series/
HUMRIGHTSLAW

Women and International Human Rights Law

Universal Periodic Review in Practice

Gayatri H. Patel

Routledge
Taylor & Francis Group
New York London

First published 2020
by Routledge
605 Third Avenue, New York, NY 10017

and by Routledge
2 Park Square, Milton Park, Abingdon, Oxon OX14 4RN

First issued in paperback 2021

Routledge is an imprint of the Taylor & Francis Group, an informa business

© 2020 Taylor & Francis

Publisher's Note
The publisher has gone to great lengths to ensure the quality of this reprint but points out that some imperfections in the original copies may be apparent.

Library of Congress Cataloging-in-Publication Data
Names: Patel, Gayatri H., author.
Title: Women and international human rights law: universal periodic review in practice / Gayatri H. Patel.
Description: Abingdon, Oxon; New York, NY: Routledge, 2020. |
Series: Routledge research in human rights law | Based on author's thesis (doctoral - University of Leicester, 2015) issued under title: How 'universal' is the United Nations' universal periodic review process?: an examination from a cultural relativist perspective. | Includes bibliographical references and index.
Identifiers: LCCN 2019039671 (print) | LCCN 2019039672 (ebook) | ISBN 9780815376941 (hardback) | ISBN 9781351235105 (ebook) |
Subjects: LCSH: Women's rights. | International law and human rights.
Classification: LCC K3243 .P38 2020 (print) | LCC K3243 (ebook) |
DDC 341.4/858–dc23
LC record available at https://lccn.loc.gov/2019039671
LC ebook record available at https://lccn.loc.gov/2019039672

ISBN 13: 978-1-03-208283-7 (pbk)
ISBN 13: 978-0-8153-7694-1 (hbk)

Typeset in Galliard
by Deanta Global Publishing Services, Chennai, India

Dedicated to my beloved Husband, Hiten R. Patel

Contents

Illustrations

Figures

Tables

Preface

One of the most daunting, mundane, or possibly irritating questions that may wander into one's conscious, or unconscious, thoughts during the study of international human rights law is: 'Does international human rights law make a difference?'[1] Professor Douglass Cassel emphasises that the importance of this question is obvious due to the fact that 'the institutions of international human rights law deserve our energetic support only to the extent they contribute meaningfully to protection of rights'.[2] Such a promise of improving the human rights situation on the ground,[3] in all member states,[4] through the promotion of universality of all human rights[5] was made in the establishing resolution of the United Nations (UN) human rights monitoring mechanism, the Universal Periodic Review (UPR) process in 2008. The UPR process is employed by the UN Human Rights Council with an ultimate aim to 'improve the human rights situation in all countries and address human rights violations wherever they occur'.[6] Every member state of the UN is reviewed once in a cycle of four years under the same uniform procedure.[7] It was during the end of the first cycle of review that this project was conceptualised in the form of a PhD investigation of the first cycle of the UPR process, which was extended to the second cycle of review for the purposes of this book.

Amongst the growing body of literature, which is predominately a technocratic analysis of the process, this book will stand alone as the first comprehensive analysis of the UPR process through an exploration of the discussions held amongst state representatives during state reviews. The primary focus of this book falls at the heart of the UPR process, which is the review's central, yet, ambitious aim to promote and protect the universality of all human rights, through the work and operation of the process. Drawing upon the most pertinent challenge to any universal claim of human rights: the theory of cultural relativism, I have drawn upon the scholarly works of the most enduring debates on international human rights law, between universalism and cultural relativism, to inform the analysis of this investigation. To provide further depth and focus to this investigation, of the 55 different human rights issues that have been raised in the UPR process, I have selected to focus on women's rights, as it was the issue that was raised more frequently from session to session, as well as being one of the most contentious issues raised in the UPR process, to date. On more theoretical grounds, despite the wide-ranging jurisprudence on these areas of women's rights under international human rights law, there is a continued discrepancy between domestic laws and practices in relation to issues specifically experienced by women, and the protection guaranteed to women and their rights. This can be explained as being due to the inherent relationship between women and culture, whereby issues and concerns are more susceptible and fragile to regulation and justifications based on cultural norms. This increased susceptibility of women's rights issues to cultural justifications makes it an ideal selection as a focus of this study. This new lens of examining the UPR process is compelling and pertinent as it raises the question of whether a voluntary, non-coercive universally applied human rights initiative such as the UPR can actually generate positive results, or whether it represents an 'emperor-wears-no-clothes' feel-good exercise devoid of substance. This case study captures the essence of what occurs when states, representing the full range of attitudes and approaches to women's rights issues, participate in a collaborative setting.

As we come close to a decade in the existence of the UPR process, despite extensive optimism during its initiation, the book strikingly reveals how the attractive simplicity of the process claim on universality of human rights veils the multifaceted issues and concerns that are embedded in the interpretation and implementation of the selected women's rights issues. Based on the findings of this project, the book suggests that not only does this pose a serious and significant challenge in fulfilling the core aim of the process, causing irrefutable damage to the process' creditability, but it also has much wider ramifications for the project of international human rights law. Whilst not taking away from boasting an exclusive universal participation by all UN members states for over a decade, this book suggests that a sustained unchecked challenge to the universality of international human rights law that is voiced on the platform of the UPR process can potentially hinder the implementation of rights in the domestic context, and pave the way to shake the very infrastructure of the United Nations and its role in protecting and promoting the universality of international human rights law.

Notes

1 Professor Douglass Cassel, 'Does International Human Rights Law Make a Difference?' (2001) 2 *Chicago Journal of International Law* 121. On the importance of implementation for improvement in human rights protection see Rachel Murray and Elizabeth Mottershaw, 'Mechanisms for the Implementation of Decisions of the African Commission on Human Rights Peoples' Rights' (2014) 36 *Human Rights Quarterly* 349, 350.
2 Ibid.
3 UNHRC 'Res 5/1 Institution-building of the United Nations Human Rights Council' (18 June 2007) Annex A/HRC/RES/5/1, para 4 (a) (A/HRC/RES/5/1).
4 A/HRC/RES/5/1, para 3 (c).
5 A/HRC/RES/5/1, para 3 (a).
6 Office of the High Commissioner for Human Rights, 'Universal Periodic Review' <www.ohchr.org/en/hrbodies/upr/pages/uprmain.aspx.> accessed 28 August 2019.
7 UNGA 'Human Rights Council' (15 March 2006) A/RES/60/251 para, 5(e). (A/RES/60/251). On the importance of active periodic monitoring of human rights obligations, see Rachel Murray and Debra Long, *The Implementation of the Findings of the African Commission on Human and Peoples' Rights* (Cambridge University Press, 2015) 30.

Abbreviations

CAQDAS	Computer Assisted Qualitative Data Analysis
CAR	Central African Republic
CEDAW	Convention on the Elimination of all Forms of Discrimination against Women
EEG	Eastern European Group
FGM	Female Genital Mutilation
GRULAC	Latin American and Caribbean Group
HRC	Human Rights Council
ICCPR	International Covenant on Civil and Political Rights
ICESCR	International Covenant on Economic, Social and Cultural Rights
NGO	Non-Governmental Organisation
OHCHR	Office of the High Commissioner for Human Rights
QCA	Qualitative Content Analysis
UAE	United Arab Emirates
UDHR	Universal Declaration of Human Rights
UK	United Kingdom
UNESCO	United Nations Educational, Scientific and Cultural Organization
UPR	Universal Periodic Review
US	United States of America
WEOG	Western European and Others Group

Acknowledgements

Contrary to the commonly held perception of a monograph journey being one of solitude, I have been fortunate enough to be surrounded by many kind hearted people that have provided me with the required support over the years. I would like to begin by thanking Aston University, Faculty of Law, for providing me with research leave to enable me to undertake the research and complete this monograph. In particular, I would like to thank my colleagues: Ryan Murphy, Robert Goddard, and Odette Hutchinson for their support and understanding during the writing process. I owe them more than they will ever take credit for, thank you.

On a personal note, I would like to express my heartfelt gratitude to my brother, Nikil, for his support and guidance for the research and writing of this project, but also for many other aspects of my life. Nikil's sheer professionalism, integrity, and modesty are just a few of the many reasons why he is my inspiration. I should thank him, more often. My deepest gratitude in writing this monograph, and numerous other things in my life, is owed to my beloved parents: Prakash and Sadhna, by birth; and, Ramesh and Sushila; by marriage. Your combined unconditional love, boundless encouragement, and pride will always play a huge part in all of my life endeavours.

Finally, the most heartfelt and deepest gratitude is owed to my husband, Hiten. It is an understatement to say that this book, and many other wonderful things that have happened to me, would not have been possible without his enduring support, compassion, and generosity. I am forever indebted to his kindred and playful spirit, in particular his endearing dimpled smile, which has immersed me in an incommensurable amount of joy and fulfilment in every aspect of my life. Words cannot express how thankful I am to my husband, but as words are all I have to offer here, it is to my precious and adored husband, *Hiten*, that I dedicate this book.

1 A New Kid on the Block: What Is the Universal Periodic Review, and Why Was It Established?

Introduction

The Universal Periodic Review (UPR) is the most ambitious and intriguing development in the monitoring of international human rights law, in recent memory. Before embarking on the merited detailed examination of the mechanics and modalities of the UPR process, it is important to understand the historical context in which it was established to facilitate a fuller appreciation of the purpose, aim, and objectives of the review process, and, more importantly, to understand the impetus behind devising the UPR in the first place. To help illustrate this, the focus of this section is to briefly discuss the manner in which the human rights monitoring mechanisms operated under the predecessor to the United Nations (UN) Human Rights Council: the Commission on Human Rights ('Commission').[1] The first section will provide a historical account of the human rights monitoring undertaken at the predecessor to the United Nations Human Rights Council: United Nations Commission. The section will illustrate how the Commission undertook the task of monitoring human rights, which was one of the most significant contributions to its demise. A challenge is put forward to the preconceived notion that the demise of the Commission was solely due to the 'politicised' manner in which the monitoring of human rights was undertaken, and rather suggests new avenues of exploration to possibly explain the abolition of the Commission. Asking this new question in relation to old explanations on the reasons behind the abolition of the Commission is important to be able to assess the successes of the new human rights monitoring mechanism with a fresh perspective, which is not tarnished with the pre-existing measures of failures that had tarnished the Commission leading to its abolition. The second section will provide details of the mechanics and modalities of the UPR process. The third section will explore how the UPR process is tasked to give effect to the principle of universality, which is based both on the universal applicability of the process, but also to give effect to the normative claim of universality of international human rights norms. This embedded principle of universalism will be discussed with the aim of illustrating the primary focus of this investigation.

Asking a New Question in Relation to Old Explanations: A History of Human Rights Monitoring at the United Nations

In 1946, one of the first acts of the newly formed UN was to establish the Commission on Human Rights. Established under the auspices of Economic and Social Council (ECOSOC), the Commission was devised with the intention to create a body with the capacity to oversee one of the fundamental pillars of the new international legal orders under the UN Charter: the promotion and realisation of human rights.[2] The newly constituted Commission set forth a vision of an international bill, which consisted of three parts: a declaration of moral principles; legally binding obligations in the form of treaties; and measures of implementation. The Commission fulfilled the first two elements of its vision in the first 20 years, as its work primarily centred on the development of international human rights standards, with the drafting of the Universal Declaration of Human Rights, as its first task.[3] The Commission was the principal forum for international human rights discourse, as well as initiating and drafting various normative instruments, which later materialised as key international human rights treaties, which collectively were known as the international bill of rights.[4] This era of the Commission's work has rightfully been praised for its inspirational human rights movement in establishing a solid normative foundation in the UN's history.[5] Nevertheless, the same period has also been criticised for its failure to take action in response to conscience-shocking human rights atrocities that demanded immediate action,[6] demonstrating that the measures for implementation were proving to be far more difficult to conceptualise and establish.

The Commission's failure in taking action in relation to implementation stemmed from the ambiguity in its 1946 establishing resolution in relation to the body's mandate to respond to complaints of human rights violations received from individuals against their respective states, euphemistically labelled as 'communications'. In this way, it was unclear as to whether the Commission had the mandate to monitor human rights records of member states.[7] In addressing this ambiguity, and adopting the position that the body was to prioritise promotion over protecting human rights, the Commission in 1947 issued a statement that it had 'no power to take any action in relation to communications received by individuals'.[8] Despite this declaration, the Commission continued to receive an annual figure of 25,000 complaints of human rights violations.[9]

After a period of 20 years, and largely due to the wave of decolonisation that significantly changed the composition of the UN, the newly independent states pushed for establishing procedures to respond to human rights violations and thereby bringing the Commission's 'doctrine of no action' to an end in 1967.[10] The efforts of the newly independent states set the foundations for the procedures and mechanisms that were later developed to respond to human rights violations on an annual basis in any part of the world. This initiative established a form of human rights monitoring at the Commission in response to violations, which involved: debates on human rights norms and violations, establishment of working groups and rapporteurs, the adoption of resolutions of concern and condemnations on issues and situations, as well as generation of technical advice and support to countries. The irony is that these very procedures and mechanisms to respond to human rights violations, which were established with the most noblest of intentions were the most significant contributors to the demise of the Commission.

In 1967, based on the resolution 1235 (XLII) of the ECOSOC, the members of the Commission, or the Sub-Commission, could publicly mention violations of human rights that were brought to its attention through the complaints it had received. This initial debate could lead to the adoption of resolutions or the establishment of a special procedure, which could either focus on human rights situations in specific countries under the rubric of providing technical advice (country based procedures) or a specific human rights issue that may cover a number of different countries (thematic procedure). Later in 1970, ECOSOC adopted the resolution 1503 (XLVIII), which established a confidential procedure to respond to the individual complaints that were received by the Commission. The adoption of the 1503 procedure was a product of state delegates with the aim of competing objectives and goals, who sought to keep the language of the procedure as open ended, flexible, and ambiguous as possible. In this way, both the resolution and the criteria for the use and operation of the procedure were 'perfect case studies in ambiguity'.[11] Although adopted after the 1235 procedure, and built upon it, the 1503 confidential procedure developed at a more rapid pace, and has often been used as a precursor for the public procedure. The resolution provided the mandate to the Commission to examine complaints pertaining to 'situations which appear to reveal a consistent pattern of gross and reliably attested violations of human rights requiring consideration by the Commission'.[12] The complaints must originate from a person, or a group of persons, who can be clearly identified as being victims of the claimed violations. The complaint must not be politically motivated, the language must not be abusive or insulting to the state to which the complaint is issued against, and all domestic remedies must have been exhausted. A Working Group of five members examines the communications and decides whether they appear to reveal 'a consistent pattern of gross and reliably attested violations of human rights and fundamental freedoms'. The UN Secretariat constructs a summary of all the complaints received, and forwards a copy of each complaint to the governments concerned, who are requested to respond. Once a response has been received, one of the following actions may be taken: discontinue the consideration of the matter; keep the situation under review with the possibility of appointing an independent expert; or, the most serious outcome – take up the matter under public procedure, where by its very nature the issue and the procedure are no longer confidential.

Whilst the procedures are still in existence today, the method of operation under the Commission formed one of the major contributors to the body's demise. One of the major criticisms of the 1503 procedure was that the nature of its operation was shrouded in secrecy, leading to accusations of it being used in concealing the occurrence of widescale human rights violations, rather than protecting and promoting it.[13] From 1978 to 1985, 29 countries were considered under this procedure. During this period, whilst some states such as South Korea and Iran were considered, others requiring similar attention, such as North Korea and some Arab countries received no consideration.[14]

The lack of response to gross human rights violations was similarly made against the 1235 procedure. In particular for its lack of action between the years of 1976 and 1977, where the Commission notably failed to publicly respond to violations under several regimes, including Pol Pot's Democratic Kampuchea (Cambodia), Amin's violations undertaken in Uganda, Bokassa's Central African Empire, and the military's action in Argentina and Uruguay.[15] Over the years, the Commission faced heavy criticism for the manner in which the procedure was operated. One such criticism was that the Commission was highly selective when reviewing the human rights records of states under the 1235 procedure, as it was accused of disproportionately targeting the human rights records of non-western states.[16] Wheeler and Lauren's assessment of the 1235 procedure concludes that the less dominant and politically powerful states were more readily targeted due to the lack of support in the Commission.[17] In addition, it was noted that regional solidarity and strong political and economic clout ensured that some states were immune from scrutiny for their human rights records under the procedure despite serious human rights concerns.[18] Even the thematic procedures were not immune from the criticism of being used a politicised manner. This is because the thematic procedures were so specifically initiated, that the procedure became very similar to the country specific investigations.[19] For example, it is argued that the United States supported the creation of a Special Rapporteur on Religious Tolerance in order to focus attention on East European and Islamic states.[20] Similarly, at the Commission's 49th session in 1993, due to the support of the majority of the western states, a Special Rapporteur on the promotion and protection of the right to freedom of opinion and expression was appointed, despite strong opposition from non-western countries.[21]

The criticism of the Commission gathered particular momentum at the beginning of the twenty-first century when accusations of political bias were at its peak.[22] It was alleged that states sought membership of the Commission not to advance the promotion and protection of international human rights, but rather to protect themselves, or their allies, from being targeted by the Commission for their human rights records. The critics highlighted the selective nature of the Commission's work, which singled out some countries for criticism, whilst ignoring grave violations of human rights abuses in countries such as Sudan, Cuba, Iran, and Zimbabwe. The Commission began gaining a reputation for using the human rights rhetoric as a vehicle to advance the political agenda of the groups of states that had representation or allies on the Commission. This selective nature of the monitoring procedures at the Commission led to some describing the Commission as a 'sinking boat' as the selective nature of the monitoring procedure led to the body's work lacking in creditability.[23] In this way, the reasons behind the failings of the Commission which range from abusing the membership of the body to avoid criticism,[24] to its work being described as 'politicised',[25] and 'lacking in creditability'.[26]

The majority of the scholars that have written on the failings of the Commission argue that the politicisation of the human rights monitoring procedures were a major, if not the sole, contributing factor that led to the body's abolition. Whilst there is no denying of the existence of political horse trading at the body, accusing an inherently intergovernmental organisation, such as the Commission as being 'political' is a misnomer. Other international bodies, such as the UN Security Council and the General Assembly, both suffer from various degrees of 'politicisation', yet have not been subject to the same rigorous criticism as the Commission with calls to be abolished.

Scratching beneath the surface of the reasons provided in the existing literature on the failings of the Commission, there is a case to suggest that there is an unappreciated dimension in the assessment of the failings of the body, which explores the reasons why states adopted political tactics in the first place, which eventually resulted in the Commission losing its reputation as a credible human rights body. The existing literature on the criticism of the Commission fails to explore the role of cultural politics in the monitoring of human rights under the Commission, and how it had a possible influence over both the operation of the body and its role in contributing to the body's demise.

The relationship between culture and the discourse of international human rights law is both inherent and long standing, which is explored in greater depth in the next chapter. For the present purposes, an examination of the reports produced as part of the monitoring mechanism under the Commission reveals that when monitoring women's rights, the notion of culture was discussed in an exclusively condemnatory in nature.[27] For example, a report issued by the Commission provided that some violations of women's rights resulted from 'cultural prejudices … are incompatible with the dignity and worth of the human person and must be eliminated'.[28] A similar pattern can be seen in the reports issued following country specific investigations. Following a mission to Afghanistan, it was stated that 'discriminatory traditional and cultural laws and practices' act as a barrier to women accessing rights such as employment, food, land, and social security.[29] In a similar vein, a country report following an investigation to Mexico explicitly criticised the machista culture for relegating women to a subordinate role in their family and community and describing the values held in the machista culture as causing or perpetuating high levels of violence against women.[30] Likewise, a report on the state of Lebanon held that 'strong social and cultural taboos and a fear of ostracism' prevent victims from reporting sexual abuse.[31] A report following an investigation on Russia emphasised the 'traditional patriarchal norms of family honour' which perpetuate violence against women and ostracise those women that report domestic violence.[32]

First and foremost, it is undeniable that the practices referred to in the reports examined were grave violations of women's rights. However, what is notable is the consistently condemnatory rhetoric issued on the relationship between women's rights and culture. All the references to culture in the reports produced as part of the monitoring mechanism under the Commission noted how cultural norms acted as a hindrance to women's rights protection with a reoccurring recommendation that such cultural norms and practices should be eliminated. It is by no means suggested that the relationship between culture and such violations should not be discussed, rather violations of women's rights should be appropriately addressed, and there is merit in reflecting as to what the precise expectations and effect is of the tone of criticisms in relation to culture and the violations. In fact, such brash and repeated criticisms of cultural norms in the monitoring of women's rights beg the question as to the purpose, expectations, and the effectiveness of such criticisms. Can the claimed practices that are embedded in culture *simply* be eliminated? In light of this, the persistent condemnatory nature of criticisms at the Commission under its monitoring mechanism is superficial at best, and ethnocentric at worst. In fact, going further, such demonisation or isolation of culture presents a serious risk that the notion of culture may be adopted by repressive regimes to carry out violation of human rights under the guise of culture. More importantly, it is notable that there is no evidence in the monitoring of reports produced under the Commission whereby culture is incorporated into the discourse of human rights in a positive manner by recognising it as a possible vehicle to facilitate reforms to address violations in the domestic context. Incorporating the notion of culture in this way is likely to trigger discussions that directly engage with the violations in questions, with the aim of providing meaningful reforms. In contrast, the blanket cultural condemnation adopted at the Commission in its monitoring mechanism resulted in a lack of a fruitful dialogue on how best to address the violations followed by the issuance of superficial recommendations being made to eliminate practices embedded in culture which fails to take into account the very significant nature of culture and cultural norms.[33] Glimpses of frustrations of the lack of cultural sensitivity in the monitoring of human rights was evident in the 56th Commission session report, where a representative of Saudi Arabia argued that 'it was a matter of concern that some members of the international community appeared to have difficulty in understanding human rights within the context of Islam'.[34]

Whilst there is not sufficient space, nor indeed the purpose for this investigation, to undertake a study on the role of culture in the monitoring of the Commission, suffice it to state here that there are sufficient grounds to suggest that there is an unexplored dimension on the role of culture and how it is was utilised in the monitoring of the Commission. At the risk of speculation, the repeated condemnation of the notion of culture with its superficial recommendations may have contributed to the lack of effectiveness of the Commission in monitoring rights. Moreover, the frustration with the lack of cultural sensitivity in the monitoring of rights may be one possible explanation as to why some states opted to become defensive in the monitoring of human rights by adopting political tactics, rather than engaging in dialogues for facilitating meaningful reforms on violations that were claimed to be embedded in cultural norms and practices.

From this, it becomes apparent that the lack of cultural sensitivity adopted when monitoring human rights records of states in the monitoring mechanisms is a factor that has been underappreciated in the literature discussing the reasons that led to the failure and eventual demise of the Commission.

Establishing the UN Human Rights Council and the UPR Process

In the face of heavy criticism directed at the Commission, the United Nation's reports by Panyarachun in 2004[35] and Annan in 2005[36] laid down the foundations for replacing the Commission with a new Human Rights Council (HRC).[37] The most significant addition to the Human Rights Council, in comparison to the Commission, was to give effect to the principles of 'universality' of human rights through the Universal Periodic Review process. With the intention to address the strong criticism of the Commission's selectivity and political bias of the human rights monitoring procedures under the Commission, the former UN Secretary General Kofi Annan proposed that the new body on human rights should have a 'peer review function … to evaluate the fulfilment by all states of their human rights obligations'.[38] Accepting these proposals, the General Assembly, in the same resolution that established the HRC, required the body to undertake:

> [a] universal periodic review, based on objective and reliable information, of the fulfilment by each State of its human rights obligations and commitments in a manner which ensures universality of coverage and equal treatment with respect to all States; the review shall be a cooperative mechanism, based on an interactive dialogue, with the full involvement of the country concerned and with consideration given to its capacity-building needs.[39]

Based on these objectives, the Ambassador of Morocco, Mohammed Loulichki, was given the responsibility in the first session of the HRC to assist the working group to develop the details on the modalities of the process.[40] However, it was not until 2007 that members of the HRC agreed on the 'institution building package' providing the details on the modalities of the review process,[41] which have since been adapted.[42] The Universal Periodic Review is a peer review mechanism, whereby all member states human rights records are reviewed on a periodic basis on how the state is meeting all of its international human rights obligations. The first cycle of the review was undertaken between 2008 and 2011; and the second cycle was slightly lengthier at four-and-a-half years, which took place between 2012 and 2016; the third cycle is scheduled to take place between 2017 and 2021. During the first cycle of review, a total of 48 states are reviewed each year, in three two-week sessions, with 16 states being reviewed in each session. Due to the changes in modalities with extension of six months per cycle, in the second cycle 42 states a year were reviewed, with a reduced number of 14 states being reviewed at each session. In this way, every member state of the United

Nations will be reviewed every four years. The HRC Resolution 5/1 provides details on the primary objectives of the UPR system as:

(a) The improvement of the human rights situation on the ground; (b) The fulfilment of the State's human rights obligations and commitments and assessment of positive developments and challenges faced by the State; (c) The enhancement of the State's capacity and of technical assistance, in consultation with, and with the consent of, the State concerned; (d) The sharing of best practice among States and other stakeholders; (e) Support for cooperation in the promotion and protection of human rights; (f) The encouragement of full cooperation and engagement with the Council, other human rights bodies and the Office of the United Nations High Commissioner for Human Rights.[43]

The establishing resolution states that all reviews should be based on an interactive dialogue, which is undertaken in a 'non- selective', 'non-confrontational', 'non-politicised' manner.[44] Thus, it gives the opportunity for member states to share best practices, and the challenges faced, in the promotion and protection of human rights.[45] The UPR process is distinctive for its universality (all states are subject to review within a set cycle), its egalitarian nature, and its holistic orientation (as all human rights are addressed).

Whilst the universal applicability of the process may, in theory, prevent the selective nature of human rights monitoring that occurred under the Commission, it would be delusional to take the proclamations of the UPR process as to the nature of its operation in its establishing resolution very literally. The UPR process, after all, is a peer review mechanism and therefore by its very nature will retain at least some degree of politicisation. In fact, the UPR process cannot be presumed to provide independent and authoritative judgements on violations of human rights, primarily due to its governmental composition.

Nevertheless, the UPR process does provide value to the broader international human rights system at the United Nations. Its introduction was essential to diffuse the crisis of confidence that the pre-2006 human rights system was facing under the Commission. Despite its inherent political nature, the universal applicability and the diplomatic approach of the peer review process may be more amenable to state representatives when accepting recommendations for reforms. The UPR system's cooperative approach aims to achieve compliance with international human right norms through positive encouragement, assistance, and incentives.[46] In fact, Elvira Domínguez-Redondo points out that successes in raising controversial human rights issues in the UPR process are, in some instances, linked to the political and cooperative nature of the process.[47] In this way, the UPR process adds a practical value to the system of human rights at the United Nations as it applies pressure on states to commit to human rights improvements in relation to specific issues and concerns in their domestic context. It is very difficult for states under review to publicly assent to human rights norms through accepting or making recommendations, to then justify their own noncompliance or reject the very norms.[48] Thus, whilst the UPR process is more likely to be subject to politicisation due to its very nature, contrary to commonly held belief that politicisation limits the function of human rights monitoring, in fact, the politicisation in the UPR process can be more positive as the increased likelihood of being politicised, is likely to lead to more actual compliance.[49] The UPR platform provides an invaluable opportunity for all states to be made aware of human rights issues and policies on human rights across the different countries. In this way, the UPR process is a soft global governance mechanism,[50] with at its heart an audit process that is a notion of learning and sharing best practices through peers, working towards a collaborative project of improving human rights.[51] This is in sharp contrast to the human rights monitoring mechanism under the Commission that was shaped by the notion of 'naming and shaming'. It is important to note that the UPR's promises do not lie in enforcing human rights norms or providing adjudication on factual claims within a country in relation to violations. Rather, the UPR process provides a more unique promise in the human rights monitoring of disseminating best practices.

Aside from the practical benefits of the process, from the normative perspective, the UPR process adds value as it provides a platform to reveal where the areas of concern lie and highlights areas where there are genuine normative disputes that persist in contemporary international human rights law. In this way, the UPR process provides invaluable normative value to the identification and development of international human rights law. As the former facilitator for negotiating the details of the UPR process, Ambassador Mohammed Loulichki, famously stated that the 'faithful implementation of the principles of the UPR ... will serve, in the end, the authority and creditability of the Human Rights Council'.[52] In this way, the UPR with its transnational, universal, and political nature bears significant expectations of the human rights system and successful operation at the United Nations.

The Stages of the UPR Process

Each of the reviews of the 193 states are conducted by the UPR Working Group, which is chaired by the President of the Council and is composed of the 47 member states of the HRC.[53] A group of delegates called the troika, which consists of three member state representatives, provide general assistance with the reviews.[54] The review is undertaken by representatives of peer states, who assess the compliance of the state under review with the following: the Charter of the United Nations 1945, the Universal Declaration of Human Rights 1948, the human rights instruments to which the state is a party, any applicable international humanitarian laws and any voluntary pledges made by the states.[55] This broad scope of assessing compliance with human rights instruments means that even if a state had not ratified a human rights treaty, it is presumed that the human rights obligations that derive from the membership of the UN, UDHR, and the UN Charter, and customary international law are expected to be realised and states would be held accountable to them in the UPR process. Those states that are a member of the Council are required to be reviewed during their term of membership, in particular, those elected for one or two review terms are to be reviewed first.[56] During the three UPR Working Group sessions, 42 states are reviewed each year, with each session dedicated to reviewing 14 states each.

It is clear that the UPR process differs substantially from the 1235 and 1503 procedures on one important matter: universal application. All 193 UN member states have their human rights records subject to review in the UPR process using the same uniform procedure, thereby significantly reducing the possibility of political manoeuvring by states to avoid their human rights records being reviewed, as was the case under the Commission. Furthermore, unlike the monitoring procedures under the Commission, the review of states under the UPR process is not restricted to particular human rights issues, as it can hold the state under review accountable on any human rights issue that is of concern.

The UPR process is broadly divided into three stages: (i) the preparation for the review, (ii) the interactive dialogue, and (iii) the follow-up process to the second cycle of review.

Preparation of the Review

There are three main documents that form the basis upon which member states' human rights obligations are reviewed. The first is a National Report, which is no more than 20 pages in length and provides an outline of the human rights situation and concerns in the country. It is drafted and submitted by the state under review.[57] The second report is prepared by the Office of the High Commissioner on Human Rights (OHCHR). The report should be a maximum of ten pages, and is a summary of the information submitted by treaty bodies, special procedures, and other human rights entities in relation to the state under review.[58] The final document is a summary of the information submitted by civil society and non-governmental organisations (NGOs), which is again prepared by the OHCHR and is no longer than ten pages.[59] The comprehensiveness of the reports has been applauded by authors such as Vega and Lewis, who write 'that this is the first time that the human rights picture on the ground for all nations will be formally documented for all to see'.[60] The collection of data in the form of reports that are prepared for the UPR process has enhanced the information that is available on human rights situations around the world.[61]

Collectively, these reports form the primary body of information that will be used as the basis to undertake state reviews. Once these reports have been prepared and circulated, any state of the UN can provide notice of its intention to raise concerns, ask questions, or issue recommendations to the state under review during the interactive dialogue session.

The Interactive Dialogue Session

The interactive dialogue session of the UPR system is the 'core element of the entire process'.[62] The review itself takes place in the Human Rights and Alliance of Civilizations Room, Palais des Nations, under the magnificent ceiling sculpture by prominent contemporary Spanish artist Miquel Barceló. It is one of the largest conference rooms at the United Nations Office at Geneva, and has the facility to webcast all the interactive dialogues, in real time, from the UN website.

The delegation of the state under review, chaired by the President of the Human Rights Council, provides a presentation of its National Report, relaying the countries' human rights situations, concerns, and issues to the UN member states of the UPR Working Group, and other participating governments, which lasts for approximately 30 minutes. After this, the interactive dialogue session is formally opened. Whilst the review is primarily conducted by the UPR Working Group, composing of all 47 member states of the HRC, during the interactive dialogue stage, any one of the 193 member states of the UN present at the review can take the floor to ask questions and make recommendations on any aspect of human rights concern in relation to the state under review. A randomly assigned group of three states (known as the troika) facilitate the state review, and prepare the Final Outcome Report. The list of designated speakers is projected on a large video screen, with a digital clock counting down. Within the allocated time of two to three minutes, the state representative of the participating state will read out a short prepared statement, which can be a combination of comments, greetings, questions, and recommendations to the state under review.[63] Periodically, the statements issued by the participating governments are paused so that the state under review can provide response to the questions drawing upon expertise from the different ministers from the government.[64] The observer states then resume for another batch of statements, before the state under review is given another opportunity to respond. This lasts for approximately three-and-a-half hours (the length of time was increased by 30 minutes from the first cycle), with the state under review providing the final closing remarks for the interactive dialogue stage.[65]

What makes the UPR process unique is that rather than focussing on legal technicalities of international human rights norms, the UPR process provides a forum for a discourse to be undertaken on human rights issues amongst states.[66] Moreover, it is the first forum at the UN that enables an interactive dialogue to be undertaken between states in a format that allows for instant responses and feedback.[67] The discussions held during the interactive session tend to focus on a whole array of human rights issues, as opposed to one specific human right. The instantaneous and cooperative nature of the UPR process can be utilised to discuss human rights issues that would otherwise be too controversial, and risk confrontation amongst states on an international forum.[68] In this regard, it is likely that some of the human rights issues raised during the reviews may have a cultural dimension to them, which makes the interactive session in the UPR process a good platform to addresses the aims and objectives of this investigation.

At the conclusion of the interactive dialogue stage, the members of the troika prepare a document containing the summary of the discussions held in an 'Outcome Report'.[69] This report is then adopted at the Working Group Session held a few days after the interactive dialogue session. A few months later, the report is adopted at a plenary session of the HRC, which lasts for up to an hour. Time is allocated for further comments by the states under review, other states, or the civil society.[70] At the conclusion of the plenary session of the HRC, a Final Outcome Report for the state under review is produced. The report contains all the comments, questions, and recommendations made by the observer states, as well as the responses and comments made by the state under review.[71] Those recommendations that have not been responded to by the state during the oral review are required to be responded to in writing in the 'addendum'.[72] The recommendations that enjoy the support of the state under review will be identified as being 'accepted', and those recommendations that are not accepted will be 'noted'.[73] In this way, formally, no recommendations are recorded as being 'rejected' by the state under review in the UPR process.

The broad mandate of the UPR process is that, together with the various sources of information upon which the review is based, the UPR process is a soft law method of monitoring human rights. It provides a platform to showcase and share best practices of human rights protections, as well as an agenda setting tool to facilitate transnational communications on key human rights issues to improve the human rights implementation in states. In fact, the UPR process can be a source of international customary law precisely because of the high end involvement.[74]

A purely technocratic analysis of the procedures and the nature of recommendations of the UPR process can breed a scepticism in relation to the effectiveness of the UPR process. Moving away from this technocratic analysis, the focus of this book is on the impact of the UPR process more broadly for the system of international human rights law. The UPR process is as much as an international human rights policy as well as a national process, as the fundamental aim is to bring about changes in the domestic context.[75] In meeting this aim, the interactive dialogue session is the most significant aspect of the review, which is based on a plethora of reports from a variety of UN agencies, and information presented by the civil society and National Human Rights Institutions (NHRIs). Indeed, the discussions held at the sessions based on this information become significant catalyst for social changes and reforms in the domestic context. The nature of discussions held in the interactive dialogue can set the tone and inform national debates and awareness raising campaigns, and facilitate national public debates on the issue. This influence is further propounded by the fact that in the implementation of recommendations from the second cycle onwards, whilst it is primarily of the state's concern, states are encouraged to conduct broad consultations with all stakeholders. Many existing studies on the UPR process focus on the 'politicisation' of the procedure: some focus on member state experiences of the review; others on modalities and participation; whilst some assess the implementation of the recommendations. In this way, the focus of the studies on the UPR has largely been on the functioning of the UPR process, and is therefore technocratic in nature.

In line with the evolutionary character of the UPR process,[76] a review of the modalities was undertaken following a period of five years. As part of this review, it was recognised that the key outcomes of the review were that the focus of the second cycle, and subsequent cycles, will be on the implementation of the accepted recommendations in the previous cycle, and the development of the human rights situation in the state.[77] As a result, states during their review are under an obligation to report on the action it has undertaken in relation to the implementation of the recommendations in its National Report.[78]

The Follow-up Period

The period between the first and the second cycle of state reviews in the UPR process is called the 'follow-up' period.[79] The state under review has the primary responsibility for the implementation of the recommendations that were issued to it in the Final Outcome Report, which is to be undertaken during the follow-up period.[80] The progress on the implementation of the recommendations will form the focus of subsequent reviews.[81] In addition, the states that have been reviewed are encouraged to submit a mid-term report on the progress of the implementation of the accepted recommendations.

The Embedded Universalism of the UPR Process and Emerging Questions

The establishment of the UPR process was received with great optimism amongst key political figures and scholars alike. For instance, the UN Secretary General Ban Ki-Moon, who described the process as having 'great potential to promote and protect human rights in the darkest corners of the world'.[82] The process was described as a 'breath of fresh air' and a 'genuinely innovative, positive, and encouraging monitoring mechanism'.[83] At the first session of the Human Rights Council in 2006, the UPR mechanism was applauded as 'one of the most important and innovative features and mechanisms of the Council'[84] and recognised as 'a significant value-added to the Council'[85] that will greatly influence the credibility and future standing of the Human Rights Council.[86]

This optimism surrounding the review process is based on a significant trait of the UPR process, its *universal* nature. The UPR process is the most significant addition to the mandate of the Human Rights Council, with the principal aim to give effect to the principles of universality. The aim of furthering the principles of universality through the UPR process is based on two grounds. First is the universal applicability of the UPR process, whereby all 193 member states of the UN are periodically reviewed under the same uniform process.[87] Moreover, each state under review is subject to strict formality requirements before, during, and after the review to 'ensure equal treatment for every country when their human rights situations are assessed'.[88] The success of this aspect of the universal claim is evidenced by the complete participation and review by all member states of the United Nations, to date.

The second ground upon which the principle of universality is grounded upon is more normative in nature. One of the fundamental principles provided in establishing resolution of the UPR process is to 'promote the universality, interdependence, indivisibility and interrelatedness of all human rights', based on an interactive dialogue and equal treatment.[89] Indeed, unlike any other monitoring mechanism at the United Nations, the state's human rights record is reviewed against a plethora of international human rights instruments, including the Charter of the UN and of the UDHR; the process draws upon a comprehensive set of human rights obligations that form part of the formal standards according to which the states will be reviewed. This is particularly significant during the reviews of those states that have low ratification rates in respect of international human rights obligations. In this way, states undertaking the reviews in the UPR process are not restricted to discussing or making recommendations on international human rights norms to which the states under review have specifically adopted.[90] In this way, by enlisting a comprehensive set of human rights obligations as the foundation of the review process, together with its ultimate aim of promoting universal human rights norms through the reviews of states, a normative form of universalist claim on human rights can be seen to be embedded in the work and functions of the review process.

It is important to note that the promises of universality of the UPR process lie beyond the merely practical bureaucracies in ensuring that all states are monitored under the process. Rather, the aim is far deeper and ambitious which is to give effect to the principle of universality through the work and operation of the UPR process. By no means is the UPR process an enforcement mechanism to ensure that the universal principles of international human rights norms are met. Instead, the aim is to give effect to the principles of universality of international human rights norms through monitoring the states' human rights records and engage in a dialogue to best implement human rights norms as part of the work and operation of the UPR process.

This normative aim of giving effect to the principle of universality of international human rights norms through the work and operation of the UPR process is at the heart of this investigation. The aim of this investigation is to answer the following question: has the claim of promoting and protecting the universality of human rights been met, or challenged, during state reviews in the first two cycles of UPR process? To ensure a depth of understanding of how this unique process operates, specific women's rights issues have been selected as a focus for this study. Further, in addressing this question, and to inform critical analysis of this work, the investigation has employed the most pertinent challenge to any universal claim of human rights: the theory of cultural relativism. At the risk of oversimplification, the theory of cultural relativism challenges the universal claim of human rights by arguing that moral value and judgements, such as the interpretation and implementation of human rights, are relative to different cultural contexts from which such moral judgements arise. At the heart of the theory is an emphasis on the significance of *culture* in influencing and shaping human behaviour and perceptions in society.[91] It is argued that the influence of culture is so fundamental to all aspects of society, that an individual's perception of the world is unconsciously conditioned by the standards and beliefs of a particular culture.[92] On this basis, the cultural relativist critique challenges the international normative universalist claim of human rights by arguing that moral value judgements, such as interpretations of what constitutes human rights, are relative to different cultural contexts from which such moral judgements arise.[93]

The traditionally understood polarised debates between universalism and cultural relativism have been the focus of a substantial and sophisticated line of scholarly works. However, despite far from being resolved, the discussion has now evolved towards the suggestion that a synthesis is emerging which draws on both strands of the debate. These works will be utilised as a framework to both aid understanding and analyses of the nature of human rights discussions held in the UPR process, and assess the wider implications of the findings of this project. For this reason, an in-depth discussion of the most contentious, invigorating, and pertinent discourses on human rights between universalism and cultural relativism will be the focus of the next chapter.

Conclusion

The first part of this chapter provided a historical context to facilitate a fuller understanding as to why the UPR process was established in the first place. In addition, the section aims to shed new light on the incommensurable amount of literature which seeks to explain why the Human Rights Council's predecessor, the Commission on Human Rights was abolished. The explanations provided on the reasons behind the demise of the Commission are challenged, and a new question embedded within the notion of cultural politics was presented as an underappreciated avenue of exploration in the existing literature on the failings of the Commission. The second part of this chapter provided an outline of the mechanics and modalities of the review process, and discussed the practical and normative value that the process provided. The section highlighted the significance of the interactive dialogue element of the review process, and illustrated the opportunities that are envisaged in this format of review in improving the human rights records of states and have an impact in the domestic context. The third and final section unpacked the claimed 'universality' of process, and discussed how the promises of 'universality' of the UPR process lay beyond the mere modalities and applicability of the process to all states. Rather, on a deeper level which is more ambitious in nature, the aim is to give effect to the principle of universality in the operation and work of the review process. Focussing on this, the section discussed the focus of this investigation on this normative claim of universality embedded in work and operation of this process. Any discussion on the claims of universality is left inconclusive without the required theoretical discussion on the cultural relativism, which is the focus of the next chapter.

Notes

1 It is important here to distinguish between Charter-based machinery monitoring human rights, and treaty-based human rights monitoring mechanism. Due to the nature of analysis, the former will be the focus of discussion in this section. The treaty-based human rights monitoring mechanism countries are under an obligation to submit reports on their efforts to implement their obligations under

the treaty. The treaty monitoring bodies, composed of independent experts, undertake a review of the state based on a collection of reports and issue general and country-specific comments on the implementation of the treaties. Some treaties also provide for individual petition procedures. Due to the differing nature, work, and mandate of the treaty body system, its method of monitoring compliance of human rights norms will not be discussed here.

2 Charter of the United Nations, opened for signature 26 June 1945, 1 UNTS XVI (entered into force 24 October 1945) Arts 1(3), 55 and 56.

3 Universal Declaration of Human Rights, GA Res 217A (III), UN Doc A/810 (1948).

4 International Covenant on Civil and Political Rights (adopted 16 December 1966, entered into force 23 March 1976) 999 UNTS 171; International Covenant on Economic, Social and Cultural Rights (adopted 16 December 1966, entered into force 3 January 1976) 993 UNTS 220A (ICESCR).

5 Marc Bossuyt, *International Human Rights Protection* (Intersentia 2016) 59; J Humphrey, 'The Universal Declaration of Human Rights: its history, impact and juridical character' in B Ramcharan (ed), *Human Rights: Thirty Years After the Universal Declaration* (Brill Academic Pub 1979) 439.

6 The case that best encapsulates this criticism is the Commission's failure to respond to the 1994 genocide of Rwanda.

7 UNECOSOC 'Commission on Human Rights' (16 February 1946) ECOSOC resolution 5(I), para 9(ii).

8 UNECOSOC 'Report of the Subcommittee on the Handling of Communication' (6 February 1947) E/CN.4/14/Rev.2 para 3).

9 UNECOSOC 'Report of the Ninth Session of the Commission on Human Rights' (30 May 1953) E/CN.4/689, para 293.

10 Economic and Social Council Resolution 1102 (XL) of 4 March 1966. See also, General Assembly Resolution 2144 (XXI) of 26 October 1966.

11 Alston P, H Steiner and R Goodman, *International Human Rights in Context: Law, Politics and Morals* (Oxford University Press 2009) 754

12 UNECOSOC 'ECOSOC resolution of 1967' ECOSOC Resolution 1235 (XLII).

13 Alston P, H Steiner and R Goodman, *International Human Rights in Context: Law, Politics and Morals* (Oxford University Press 2009) 758. See also, Iain Guest, *Behind the Disappearance: Argentina's Dirt War against Human Rights and the United Nations* (University of Pennsylvania Press 1990) 441. For further criticism of the procedure, see TJM Zuijdwijk, *Petitioning in the United Nations: A Study in Human Rights* (Palgrave Macmillan 1982) 377; William Shawcross, *The Quality of Mercy: Cambodia, Holocaust and Modern Conscience* (Simon & Schuster 1984) 66–67.

14 J Donnelly, 'Human Rights at the United Nations 1955–85: The Question of Bias' (1988) 32 *International Studies Quarterly* 278, 294.

15 P Alston, H Steiner and R Goodman, *International Human Rights in Context: Law, Politics and Morals* (Oxford University Press 2009) 760.

16 Ron Wheeler, 'The United Nations Commission on Human Rights, 1982-1997: A Study of "Targeted" Resolutions' (1999) 32 *Canadian Journal of Political Science* 75, 86. See also, Paul Gordon Lauren, '"To Preserve and Build on Its Achievements and to Redress Its Shortcomings": The Journey from the Commission on Human Rights to the Human Rights Council' (2007) 29 *Human Rights Quarterly* 330.

17 PG Lauren, 'To Preserve and Build on Its Achievements and to Redress Its Shortcomings': The Journey from the Commission on Human Rights to the Human Rights Council' (2007) 29 *Human Rights Quarterly* 307, 330. See also Ron Wheeler, 'The United Nations Commission on Human Rights, 1982–1997:

A Study of "Targeted" Resolutions' (1999) 32 *Canadian Journal of Political Science* 75.

18 Human Rights Watch Russian Federation/Chechnya: Briefing to the 60th Session of the UN Commission on Human Rights (NGO)(2004) www.hrw.or g/legacy/english/docs/2004/01/29/russia7248_txt.htm, accessed 28 August 2019; Reporters Without Border, UN Commission On Human Rights Loses all Creditability www.rsf.org/IMG/pdf/Report_ONU_gb.pdf, July 2003, accessed 28 August 2019; Thomas Franck, *Nation against Nation: What happened to the U.N dream and what the U.S can do about it* (Oxford University Press 1985) 244; Jean-Claude Buhrer, 'UN Commission on Human Rights Loses all Credibility Wheeling and Dealing, Incompetence and "Non-Action"' www.Rsf.Org/Img/ Pdf/Report_Onu_Gb.Pdf, July 2003 7, accessed 28 August 2019 2.

19 Mike Lempinen, *The United Nations Commissions on Human Rights and the Different Treatment of Government; An inseparable part of Promoting and Encouraging Respect for Human Rights?* (Abo Akademi University Press 2005) 231.

20 Ibid.

21 Ibid. 172.

22 See the letter from US ambassador to the United Nations, John Bolton, to all UN member states dated 30 August 2005, stating, inter alia, 'States have sought membership of the Commission not to strengthen human rights, but to protect themselves against criticism or to criticize others. As a result, a credibility deficit has developed, which casts a shadow on the reputation of the United Nations system as a whole'.

23 See UN Information Service, 'Commission on Human Rights Opens Sixty First Session, UN Doc. HR/CN/1107 speech by the Cuban Representative' (14 March 2005).

24 See Richard H. Ullman, 'Human Rights and Economic Power' (1978) 56 *Foreign Affairs* 530; Jean-Claude Buhrer, 'UN Commission on Human Rights Loses all Credibility Wheeling and Dealing, Incompetence and "Non-Action"' www.Rsf.Org/Img/Pdf/Report_Onu_Gb.Pdf, July 2003 7, accessed 28 August 2019; 'U.N. Human Rights Bodies Admits Abusive Members' (May 2003), http://hrw.org/english/docs/2001/05/03/sudan135.htm, accessed 28 August 2019; 'Despots Preventing to Sport and Shame Despots', www.h rw.org/en/news/2001/04/17/despots-pretending-spot-and-shame-despots, accessed 28 August 2019; 'Ending the "Human Rights" Farce, National Rev. Online 13 February 2006', www.nationalreview.com/editorial/editor200602 131102.asp, accessed 28 August 2019; Paul Gordon Lauren, '"To Preserve and Build on Its Achievements and to Redress Its Shortcomings": The Journey from the Commission on Human Rights to the Human Rights Council' (2007) 29 *Human Rights Quarterly* 328.

25 Jean-Claude Buhrer, 'UN Commission on Human Rights Loses All Credibility: Wheeling and Dealing, Incompetence and "Non-Action: Reporters Without Borders Calls for Drastic Overhaul of how He Commission Works"' (Reporters Without Borders, July 2003), www.rsf.org/IMG/pdf/Report_ONU_gb.pdf, accessed 28 August 2019; 'A more Secure World: Our Shared Responsibility' Report of the High-level Panel on Threats, Challenges and Change' (United Nations Foundations 2004), www.un.org/secureworld/report2.pdf, accessed 28 August 2019; Report of the Secretary-General United Nations, General Assembly, A/59/2005, accessed 21 March 2005.

26 Ron Wheeler, 'The United Nations Commission on Human Rights, 1982–1997: A Study of "Targeted" Resolutions' (1999) 32 *Canadian Journal of Political Science* 75; Jean-Claude Buhrer, 'UN Commission on Human Rights Loses all

Credibility: Wheeling and Dealing, Incompetence and "Non-Action: Reporters Without Borders Calls for Drastic Overhaul of How The Commission Works"' (Reporters Without Borders, July 2003), www.rsf.org/IMG/pdf/Report_ONU_gb.pdf, accessed 28 August 2019.

27 See, for example, UN Commission on Human Rights, 'Report on Violence against Women, Its Causes and Consequences, Addendum, Mission to Afghanistan' (15 February 2006) E/CN.4/2006/61/Add.5 para, 22 and 23. See also UN Commission on Human Rights, 'Human Rights Resolution 2005/41: Elimination of Violence against Women' (19 April 2005) E/CN.4/RES/2005/41 para, 17d.

28 UN Commission on Human Rights, 'Question of Integrating the Rights of Women into the Human Rights Mechanisms of the United Nations and the Elimination of Violence against Women' (4 March 1994), E/CN.4/RES/1994/45. See also, UN Commission on Human Rights, 'Report of the Special Rapporteur on Violence against Women, Its Causes and Consequences, Ms. Radhika Coomaraswamy, Submitted in Accordance with Commission on Human Rights Resolution 2001/49: Cultural Practices in the Family That Are Violent towards Women' (31 January 2002), E/CN.4/2002/83. See also, UN Commission on Human Rights, 'Human Rights Resolution 2005/41: Elimination of Violence against Women' (19 April 2005), E/CN.4/RES/2005/41 paragraph 5. UN Commission on Human Rights, 'Commission on Human Rights Resolution 2004/46: Elimination of Violence against Women' (20 April 2004), E/CN.4/RES/2004/46 paragraph 5. UN Commission on Human Rights, 'Human Rights Resolution 2005/25: Women's Equal Ownership, Access to and Control over Land and the Equal Rights to Own Property and to Adequate Housing' (15 April 2005), E/CN.4/RES/2005/25; UN Commission on Human Rights, 'Report of the Special Rapporteur on the Human Rights Aspects of the Victims of Trafficking in Persons, Especially Women and Children, Sigma Huda' (20 February 2006), E/CN.4/2006/62 paragraph 74.

29 UN Commission on Human Rights, 'Report on Violence against Women, Its Causes and Consequences, Addendum, Mission to Afghanistan (9 to 19 July 2005)' (15 February 2006), E/CN.4/2006/61/Add.5 paragraph 22 and 23.

30 Ibid. para 8 and 9.

31 UN Commission on Human Rights, 'Report on the Human Rights Aspects of the Victims of Trafficking in Persons, Especially Women and Children, Addendum, Mission to Lebanon (7 to 16 February 2005)' (20 February 2006), E/CN.4/2006/62/Add.3, paragraph 65.

32 UN Commission on Human Rights, 'Report on Violence against Women, Its Causes and Consequences, Addendum, Mission to the Russian Federation' (26 January 2006), E/CN.4/2006/61/Add.2 para 52.

33 For a discussion on the significance of culture, see Chapter 2.

34 UN Commission on Human Rights, 'The Report of the Commission on Human Rights on Its Fifty-sixth Session' (27 April 2000) E/CN.4/2000/167 para, 10.

35 A Panyarachun, 'A more Secure World: Our Shared Responsibility: Report of the High-level Panel on Threats, Challenges and Change' (United Nations Department of Public Information 2004).

36 K Annan, 'In Larger Freedom: Development, Security and Human Rights for All' (United Nations Department of Public Information 2005).

37 A/RES/60/251.

38 UN General Assembly, 'Addendum to In Larger Freedom, Human Rights Council: Explanatory Note by the Secretary General' (23 May 2005) A/59/2005/Add.1 para, 6.

39 A/RES/60/251 para 5 (e).

40 UNHRC 'Implementation of General Assembly Resolution 60/251 of 15 March 2006 Entitled "Human Rights Council"' (29 June 2006) A/HRC/1/L.12.
41 A/HRC/RES/5/1, Annex 1.
42 Citations of the resolutions adopted for the second cycle of review.
43 A/HRC/RES/5/1, Annex 1 para 4.
44 A/HRC/RES/5/1, Annex 1 paragraph 38.
45 A/HRC/RES/5/1 Annex 1 section I. B (2) (4) (d) (e).
46 E Domínguez-Redondo, 'The Universal Periodic Review - Is There Life beyond Naming and Shaming in Human Rights Implementation' (2012) 4 *New Zealand Law Review* 673, 685.
47 Ibid. 714.
48 R Chauville, 'The Universal Periodic Review's first cycle: successes and failures' in Hilary Charlesworth and Emma Larking (eds), *Human Rights and the Universal Periodic Review: Rituals and Ritualism* (Cambridge University Press 2014) 89; Valentina Carraro 'The United Nations Treaty Bodies and Universal Periodic Review: Advancing Human Rights by Preventing Politicisation' (2017) 39 *Human Rights Quarterly* 943, 967.
49 Ibid.
50 Jane Cowan, 'The Universal Periodic Review as a public audit ritual: anthropological perspective on emerging practices in the global governance of human rights' in Hilary Charlesworth and Emma Larking (eds), *Human Rights and the Universal Periodic Review: Rituals and Ritualism* (Cambridge University Press 2014), 49; Constance de la V and Tamara L N, 'Peer review in the mix: how the UPR transforms human rights discourse' in M Cherif Bassiouni and W A Schabas (eds), *New Challenges for the UN Human Rights Machinery What Future for the UN Treaty Body System and the Human Rights Council Procedures?* (Intersentia 2011).
51 X Li, *Ethics, Human Rights and Culture: Beyond Relativism and Culture* (Palgrave Macmillan 2006).
52 UNHRC 'Implementation of General Assembly Resolution 60/251 of 15 March 2006 Entitled "Human Rights Council"' (29 June 2006) A/HRC/1/L.12.
53 A/HRC/RES/5/1, Annex 1 section I8 (a).
54 A/HRC/RES/5/1, Annex 1 section 21.
55 A/HRC/RES/5/1, Annex 1 section IA (1) (a)–(d).
56 A/HRC/RES/5/1, Annex 1 section IC (8) (9).
57 A/HRC/RES/5/1, Annex 1 section 15 (a).
58 A/HRC/RES/5/1, Annex 1 section 15 (b).
59 A/HRC/RES/5/1, Annex 1 section 15 (C).
60 Vega Constance de la and Lewis N Tamara, 'Peer review in the mix: how the UPR transforms human rights discourse' in M Cherif Bassiouni and WA Schabas (eds), *New Challenges for the UN Human Rights Machinery What Future for the UN Treaty Body System and the Human Rights Council Procedures?* (Intersentia 2011) 568.
61 Ibid.
62 Björn Arp, 'Lessons Learned from Spain's Practice before the United Nations Human Rights Reporting Mechanisms: Treaty Bodies and Universal Periodic Review' (2011) 15 *Spanish Yearbook of International Law* 1, 13.
63 UNHRC (United Nations Human Rights Council), 'Follow-up to the Human Rights Council Resolution 16/121 with regard to the Universal Periodic Review'(19 July 2011b) A/HRC/DEC/17/119. Paragraphs 5–7.
64 Amendment made to the modalities as part of the 2011 Review. See UNHRC, 'Review of the Work and Functioning of the Human Rights Council' (12 April 2011) A/HRC/RES/16/21 (A/HRC/RES/16/21) para 16; A/HRC/RES/5/1, Annex 1 section 18 (b) (c).

65 A/HRC/RES/5/1, Annex 1 section 22. Changes made by UNHRC, 'Follow-up to the Human Rights Council resolution 16/21 with regard to the universal periodic review' (July 2011) A/HRC/DEC/17/119 (A/HRC/DEC/17/119) Resolution Part III;

66 Ibid.

67 Rhona KM Smith, 'Equality of "Nations Large and Small": Testing the Theory of the Universal Periodic Review in the Asia-Pacific' (2011) 2 *Asia-Pacific Journal on Human Rights and the Law* 36, 41.

68 Frederick Cowell and Angelina Milon, 'Decriminalisation of Sexual Orientation through the Universal Periodic Review' (2012) 12 *Human Rights Law Review* 341, 346.

69 A/HRC/RES/5/1, Annex 1 section 26. See also A/HRC/RES/16/21.

70 A/HRC/RES/5/1, Annex 1 section 31.

71 A/HRC/RES/5/1, Annex 1 section 27.

72 A/HRC/DEC/17/119, Annex para 15 and 16.

73 A/HRC/RES/5/1, para 32. On the implications using such 'blunt' tools in the form of categories for the responses of recommendations, and the implications it has on the follow-up and monitoring of compliance, see analysis by Rachel Murray and Debra Long, *The Implementation of the Findings of the African Commission on Human and Peoples' Rights* (Cambridge University Press 2015) 38.

74 E Domínguez-Redondo, 'The Universal Periodic Review – Is There Life beyond Naming and Shaming in Human Rights Implementation' (2012) 4 *New Zealand Law Review* 703–705.

75 A/HRC/RES/5/1, para 34.

76 A/RES/60/251.

77 A/HRC/DEC/17/119, paragraph 6.

78 A/HRC/DEC/17/119, Part II.

79 A/HRC/RES/5/1, Annex section 33–38.

80 A/HRC/RES/16/21, para 17.

81 A/HRC/RES/5/1, para 34.

82 Office of the High Commissioner for Human Rights, 'Universal Periodic Review', www.ohchr.org/en/hrbodies/upr/pages/uprmain.aspx, accessed 28 August 2019.

83 See J Carey, 'The UN Human Rights Council: What Would Eleanor Roosevelt Say?" (2009) 15 *ILSA Journal of International and Comparative Law* 460.

84 KP Sharma Oli, 'Statement by Honourable KP Sharma Oli to the 1st Session of the Human Rights Council' (Geneva, 19 June 2006), www.ohchr.org/Documents/HRBodies/HRCouncil/RegularSession/Session1/HLS/nepal.pdf, accessed 28 August 2019.

85 Peter Mackay, 'Statement by Honourable Peter MacKay to the 1st Session of the Human Rights Council' (Geneva, 19 June 2006), www.ohchr.org/Documents/HRBodies/HRCouncil/RegularSession/Session1/HLS/canada.pdf, accessed 28 August 2019. See also, KP Sharma Oli, 'Statement by Honourable KP Sharma Oli to the 1st Session of the Human Rights Council' (Geneva, 19 June 2006), www.ohchr.org/Documents/HRBodies/HRCouncil/RegularSession/Session1/HLS/nepal.pdf, accessed 28 August 2019.

86 Frank-Walter Steinmeier, 'Speech by Frank-Walkter Steinmeier to the 1st Session of the Human Rights Council' (Geneva, 19 June 2006), www.ohchr.org/Documents/HRBodies/HRCouncil/RegularSession/Session1/HLS/germany.pdf, accessed 28 August 2019.

87 UNGA 'Human Rights Council' (15 March 2006) A/RES/60/251 para, 5 (e).

88 A/HRC/RES/5/1. These principles were reaffirmed in UNHRC, 'Review of the Work and Functioning of the Human Rights Council' (12 April 2011) A/HRC/RES/16/21 (A/HRC/RES/16/21).

89 A/HRC/RES/5/1 para, 3 (a).
90 Hilary Charlesworth and Emma Larking E, 'Introduction: the regulatory power of the Universal Periodic Review' in Hilary Charlesworth and Emma Larking (eds), *Human Rights and the Universal Periodic Review: Rituals and Ritualism* (Cambridge University Press 2014) 13.
91 See C Geertz, *Interpretations of Cultures* (Basic Books 1973) 49; A An-Na'im, 'Problems and prospects of universal cultural legitimacy for human rights' in An- Na'im and Deng (eds), *Human Rights in Africa: Cross Cultural Perspectives* (Brookings Institution 1990) 333.
92 Alison Dundes Renteln, *International Human Rights: Universalism versus Cultural Relativism* (Quid Pro Book 2013) 59; A An-Na'im, 'Problems and prospects of universal cultural legitimacy for human rights' in An- Na'im and Deng (eds), *Human Rights in Africa: Cross Cultural Perspectives* (Brookings Institution 1990) 339.
93 E Hatch, *Cultural and Morality: The Relativity of values in Anthropology* (Columbia University Press 1983). See also, C Joyner and J Dettling, 'Bridging the Cultural Chasm: Cultural Relativism and the Future of International Law (1990) 20 *California Western International Law Journal* 275; Guyora Binder, 'Cultural Relativism and Cultural Imperialism in Human Rights Law (1999) 5 *Buffalo Human Rights Law Review* 211, 214.

Bibliography

'A More Secure World: Our Shared Responsibility' Report of the High-level Panel on Threats, Challenges and Change (United Nations Foundations 2004), http://www.un.org/secureworld/report2.pdf, accessed 28 August 2019.

Alston P, Steiner H and Goodman R, *International Human Rights in Context: Law, Politics and Morals* (Oxford University Press 2009).

Annan K, *In Larger Freedom: Development, Security and Human Rights for All* (United Nations Department of Public Information 2005).

An-Na'im A, 'Problems and Prospects of Universal Cultural Legitimacy for Human Rights' in An- Na'im and Deng (eds), *Human Rights in Africa: Cross Cultural Perspectives* (Brookings Institution 1990).

Arp B, 'Lessons Learned from Spain's Practice before the United Nations Human Rights Reporting Mechanisms: Treaty Bodies and Universal Periodic Review' (2011) 15 Spanish Yearbook of International Law 1.

Binder G, 'Cultural Relativism and Cultural Imperialism in Human Rights Law' (1999) 5 Buffalo Human Rights Law Review 211.

Buhrer, 'UN Commission on Human Rights Loses All Credibility: Wheeling and Dealing, Incompetence and "Non-Action: Reporters without Borders Calls for drastic overhaul of how he Commission Works"' (*Reporters Without Borders*, July 2003), http://www.rsf.org/IMG/pdf/Report_ONU_gb.pdf, accessed 28 August 2019.

Bossuyt Marc, *International Human Rights Protection* (Intersentia, 2016)

Carey J, 'The UN Human Rights Council: What would Eleanor Roosevelt say?' (2009) 15 ILSA Journal of International and Comparative Law 460.

Charlesworth H and Larking E, 'Introduction: The Regulatory Power of the Universal Periodic Review' in Hilary Charlesworth and Emma Larking (eds), *Human Rights and the Universal Periodic Review: Rituals and Ritualism* (Cambridge University Press, 2014).

Charter of the United Nations, opened for signature 26 June 1945, 1 UNTS XVI (entered into force 24 October 1945). Universal Declaration of Human Rights, GA Res 217A (III), UN Doc A/810 (1948).

Constance de la V and Tamara L, 'Peer Review in the Mix: How the UPR Transforms Human Rights Discourse' in M Cherif Bassiouni and W A Schabas (eds), *New Challenges for the UN Human Rights Machinery What Future for the UN Treaty Body System and the Human Rights Council Procedures?* (Intersentia 2011).

Cowan J, 'The Universal Periodic Review as a Public Audit Ritual: Anthropological Perspective on Emerging Practices in the Global Governance of Human Rights' in Hilary Charlesworth and Emma Larking (eds), *Human Rights and the Universal Periodic Review: Rituals and Ritualism* (Cambridge University Press 2014).

Cowell F and Milon A, 'Decriminalisation of Sexual Orientation through the Universal Periodic Review' (2012) 12 Human Rights Law Review 341.

Domínguez-Redondo E, 'The Universal Periodic Review - Is There Life beyond Naming and Shaming in Human Rights Implementation' (2012) 4 New Zealand Law Review 673.

Donnelly J, 'Human Rights at the United Nations 1955–85: The Question of Bias' (1988) 32 International Studies Quarterly 279.

Economic and Social Council Resolution 1102 (XL) of 4th March 1966.

'Ending the 'Human Rights' Farce, National Rev.' Online 13th February 2006., www.nationalreview.com/editorial/editor200602131102.asp, accessed 28 August 2019.

Franck T, *Nation Against Nation:What Happened to the U.N Dream and What the U.S Can Do About It* (Oxford University Press 1985).

Geertz C, *Interpretations of Cultures* (Basic Books 1973).

General Assembly Resolution 2144 (XXI) of 26th of October 1966.

Guest I, *Behind the Disappearance: Argentina's Dirt War Against Human Rights and the United Nations* (University of Pennsylvania Press 1990).

Hatch E, *Cultural and Morality: The Relativity of values in Anthropology* (Columbia University Press, 1983).

Human Rights Watch Russian Federation/Chechnya: Briefing to the 60th Session of the UN Commission on Human Rights (NGO) (2004), http://www.hrw.org/legacy/english/docs/2004/01/29/russia7248_txt.htm, accessed 28 August 2019.

Humphrey J, 'The Universal Declaration of Human Rights: Its History, Impact and Juridical Character' in B Ramcharan (ed), *Human Rights: Thirty Years After the Universal Declaration* (Brill Academic Pub 1979) 439.

International Covenant on Civil and Political Rights (adopted 16 December 1966, entered into force 23 March 1976) 999 UNTS 171.

International Covenant on Economic, Social and Cultural Rights (adopted 16 December 1966, entered into force 3 January 1976) 993 UNTS 220A (ICESCR).

Joyner C and Dettling J, 'Bridging the Cultural Chasm: Cultural Relativism and the Future of International Law (1990) 20 California Western International Law Journal 275.

Lauren G P, '"To Preserve and Build on its Achievements and to Redress its Shortcomings": The Journey from the Commission on Human Rights to the Human Rights Council' (2007) 29 Human Rights Quarterly 328.

Lempinen M, *The United Nations Commissions on Human Rights and the Different Treatment of Government; An Inseparable Part of Promoting and Encouraging Respect for Human Rights?* (Abo Akademi University Press 2005).

Li X, *Ethics, Human Rights and Culture: Beyond Relativism and Culture* (Palgrave Macmillan 2006).

Mackay P, 'Statement by Honourable Peter MacKay to the 1st Session of the Human Rights Council' (Geneva, 19 June 2006), http://www.ohchr.org/Documents/HRBodies/HRCouncil/RegularSession/Session1/HLS/canada.pdf, accessed 28 August 2019.

Murray R and Long D, *The Implementation of the Findings of the African Commission on Human and Peoples' Rights* (Cambridge University Press, 2015).

Office of the High Commissioner for Human Rights, 'Universal Periodic Review', www.ohchr.org/en/hrbodies/upr/pages/uprmain.aspx, accessed 28 August 2019.

Panyarachun A, *A More Secure World: Our Shared Responsibility: Report of the High-level Panel on Threats, Challenges and Change* (United Nations Department of Public Information 2004).

Renteln D A, *International Human Rights: Universalism versus Cultural Relativism* (Quid Pro Book 2013).

'Report of the Secretary-General United Nations, General Assembly, A/59/2005' (21 March 2005).

'Reporters Without Border, UN Commission On Human Rights loses all Creditability' (July 2003), http://www.rsf.org/IMG/pdf/Report_ONU_gb.pdf, accessed 28 August 2019.

Sharma Oli KP, 'Statement by Honourable KP Sharma Oli to the 1st Session of the Human Rights Council' (Geneva, 19 June 2006), http://www.ohchr.org/Documents/HRBodies/HRCouncil/RegularSession/Session1/HLS/nepal.pdf, accessed 28 August 2019.

Shawcross W, *The Quality of Mercy: Cambodia, Holocaust and Modern Conscience* (Simon & Schuster 1984).

Smith K M R, 'Equality of 'Nations Large and Small': Testing the Theory of the Universal Periodic Review in the Asia-Pacific' (2011) 2 Asia-Pacific Journal on Human Rights and the Law 36.

Steinmeier Frank-Walter, 'Speech by Frank-Walkter Steinmeier to the 1st Session of the Human Rights Council' (Geneva, 19 June 2006), http://www.ohchr.org/Documents/HRBodies/HRCouncil/RegularSession/Session1/HLS/germany.pdf, accessed 28 August 2019.

Ullman H R, 'Human Rights and Economic Power' (1978) 56 *Foreign Affairs* 53.

UNECOSOC, 'Commission on Human Rights' (16 February 1946) ECOSOC Resolution 5(I), para 9(ii).

UNECOSOC, 'Report of the Subcommittee on the Handling of Communication' (6 February 1947) E/CN.4/14/Rev.2.

UNECOSOC, 'Report of the Ninth Session of the Commission on Human Rights' (30 May 1953) E/CN.4/689.

UNHRC, 'Res 5/1 Institution-building of the United Nations Human Rights Council' (18 June 2007) Annex A/HRC/RES/5/1.

UN Commission on Human Rights, 'Question of Integrating the Rights of Women into the Human Rights Mechanisms of the United Nations and the Elimination of Violence Against Women' (4 March 1994) E/CN.4/RES/1994/45.

UN Commission on Human Rights, 'The Report of the Commission on Human Rights on its Fifty-sixth Session' (27 April 2000) E/CN.4/2000/167.

UN Commission on Human Rights, 'Report of the Special Rapporteur on Violence Against Women, Its Causes and Consequences, Ms. Radhika Coomaraswamy, Submitted in Accordance with Commission on Human Rights Resolution 2001/49: Cultural Practices in the Family That Are Violent Towards Women' (31 January 2002) E/CN.4/2002/83.

UN Commission on Human Rights, 'Commission on Human Rights Resolution 2004/46: Elimination of Violence against Women' (20 April 2004) E/CN.4/RES/2004/46.

UN Commission on Human Rights, 'Commission on Human Rights Opens Sixty First Session, speech by the Cuban Representative' (14 March 2005).

UN Commission on Human Rights, 'Human Rights Resolution 2005/25: Women's Equal Ownership, Access to and Control over Land and the Equal Rights to Own Property and to Adequate Housing' (15 April 2005) E/CN.4/RES/2005/25.

UN Commission on Human Rights, 'Human Rights Resolution 2005/41: Elimination of Violence Against Women' (19 April 2005) E/CN.4/RES/2005/41.

UN Commission on Human Rights, 'Report on Violence Against Women, Its Causes and Consequences, Addendum, Mission to the Russian Federation' (26 January 2006) E/CN.4/2006/61/Add.2.

UN Commission on Human Rights, 'Report on Violence Against Women, Its Causes and Consequences, Addendum, Mission to Afghanistan (9 to 19 July 2005)' (15 February 2006) E/CN.4/2006/61/Add.5.

UN Commission on Human Rights, 'Report on Violence against Women, Its Causes and Consequences, Addendum, Mission to Afghanistan' (15 February 2006) E/CN.4/2006/61/Add.5 para, 22 and 23.

UN Commission on Human Rights, 'Report of the Special Rapporteur on the Human Rights Aspects of the Victims of Trafficking in Persons, Especially Women and Children, Sigma Huda' (20 February 2006) E/CN.4/2006/62.

UN Commission on Human Rights, 'Report on the Human Rights Aspects of the Victims of Trafficking In Persons, Especially Women and Children, Addendum, Mission to Lebanon (7 to 16 February 2005)' (20 February 2006) E/CN.4/2006/62/Add.3.

UN General Assembly, 'Addendum to In Larger Freedom, Human Rights Council: Explanatory note by the Secretary General' (23 May 2005) A/59/2005/Add.1 para, 6.

UN Information Service, *Commission on Human Rights Opens Sixty First Session,* UN Doc.HR/CN/1107 speech by the Cuban Representative (14 March 2005).

'U.N Human Rights Bodies Admits Abusive Members' (May, 2003), http://hrw.org/english/docs/2001/05/03/sudan135.htm, accessed 28 August 2019; Despots Preventing to Sport and Shame Despots, http://www.hrw.org/en/news/2001/04/17/despots-pretending-spot-and-shame-despots, accessed 28 August 2019.

UNHRC, 'Implementation of General Assembly Resolution 60/251 of 15 March 2006 Entitled "Human Rights Council"' (29 June 2006) A/HRC/1/L.12.

UNHRC (United Nations Human Rights Council), 2011b. 'Follow-up to the Human Rights Council Resolution 16/121 with regard to the Universal Periodic Review' A/HRC/DEC/17/119 (July 19).

Wheeler R, 'The United Nations Commission on Human Rights, 1982–1997: A Study of "Targeted" Resolutions' (1999) 32 Canadian Journal of Political Science 75.

Zuijdwijk J M T, *Petitioning in the United Nations: A Study in Human Rights* (Palgrave Macmillan 1982).

2 Mediating between the Debate on Universalism and Cultural Relativism: A Practical Application at the UPR

Introduction

As observed in the previous chapter, the notion of culture being incorporated into the dialogue of human rights monitoring is not a new phenomenon at the United Nations. More broadly, amongst the general conversations on the promotion and protection of rights, the most replete and enduring debates have been between universalism and cultural relativism. Discourses on international human rights laws from its very conception during the drafting of the Universal Declaration of Human Rights; to the various conventions and treaties; through to the aims of the Universal Periodic Review process of implementing the principles of universality have all contributed, and invited responses, to the general conversation between universalism and cultural relativism. Although the current debates are less polarised than they have been, with a more synthesised and sophisticated middle ground emerging between the two traditionally perceived polarised positions, the debate between universalism and cultural relativism is far from being harmonised. To varying degrees, both in amongst the scholarly debates and in practice, the merits of universalism are strongly advocated, whilst the need to protect cultural diversity continues to be prominent. Whilst a number of different human rights issues and concerns can form the focus in the universalism and cultural relativism debates, no issue is more perpetually and prominently at the heart of such discussions than the issue surrounding women's rights. There is an inherent relationship between women and culture, primarily due to the traditional understanding of the role of women in the private sphere, which is perpetuated by the 'public' and 'private' divide that exists in the mainstream international human rights law. For this reason, the use of culture and positions that affiliate with the cultural relativist positions on the international human rights discourses, whether conceptually or in practice, are more likely to have an impact on women.

The debates between universalism and cultural relativism have generated a number of different key concepts to the discourse, which include definitions of culture, cultural legitimacy and, naturally, universalism and various forms of cultural relativism themselves. An understanding of these concepts will provide an accurate understanding of the two paradigms, but also avert the risk of discussions becoming polarised and thus enable an appreciation of analysis of the nuanced and more sophisticated middle ground between universalism and cultural relativism. More fundamentally, an analysis of these concepts will help provide tools of analysis to understand the international human rights law framework and its application through the intricate workings of the human rights monitoring mechanism of the Universal Periodic Review (UPR) process. In light of the fundamental aim of the UPR process to give effect to the principles of universality, this chapter will contextualise this monitoring mechanism within the debates between universality and cultural relativism and discuss its possible contribution to the general conversation on promoting and protecting international human rights law. This discussion will help to locate the aims of the UPR process within this crucial debate, as well as provide the tools of analysis for the biggest challenges to the claims of universality of human rights, the critique of cultural relativism. Such a discussion will help us to understand the role of this debate in a practical sense amongst the discussion held in relation to the application of women's rights on an international forum of the UPR process.

This chapter begins by defining universalism and contextualising it within the fundamental aim of implementing the principles of universality of the UPR process. The second section of this chapter discusses the key concepts that have materialised from the universalist and relativist debates, which will help to provide an accurate overview of the discussions as well as the nuanced and more sophisticated middle ground. In keeping with the aims of this chapter, the second section will also contextualise the UPR process within these discussions by providing practical examples of how universalism and cultural relativism materialises in practice during the discussions amongst state reviews in the UPR process. The final section of this chapter will present and analyse the inherent relationship between women and culture, and why the issues surrounding women's rights are more susceptible to the challenge of cultural relativism, and thus an ideal selection as a focus for this investigation.

Universalism and the UPR Process

As Meyer aptly notes, there are 'few scholarly debates more readily engender controversies than the question of the universality of human rights norms'.[1] The renowned optimism that engulfed the UPR process is primarily based on its universal nature, which is exercised through giving effect to the principle of universality. Indeed the aim of promoting, protecting, and indeed giving effect to the principle of universality is not a novel claim at the United Nations, as it is has been proclaimed, reaffirmed, and emphasised in a profound number of international human rights documents. Indeed, despite the existence of several strands of philosophical universalism,[2] the contemporary doctrine of human rights and its proclamation of universality has drawn upon most of the different forms of universalisms for its justification. This is primarily because the history and origins of the doctrine of human rights are founded on the philosophical claim that there exists an identifiable moral order, that is not contingent on social and historical conditions, that applies to all human beings, everywhere and at all times.[3] In fact, the very notion of universalism is often intertwined with the conceptualisation of human rights. For instance, Maurice Cranston conceptualises human rights to mean 'by definition universal moral rights, something which all men, everywhere, at all times ought to have'.[4] Going further, Richard Wasserston's widely cited definition conceives the notions of universality and human rights synonymously, as he suggests that any right, to qualify as a human right, is contingent on the requirement of it being universal.[5] The emphasis on the inalienability of human rights was discussed by the renowned scholar on the issue, Jack Donnelly, who argues that as humanity or human nature is universal, logically, human rights should also be universal, and as such, since being a human cannot be relinquished in any way, human rights are not only egalitarian in their entitlement, but are also inalienable.[6] As such, the broader assertions of universality of human rights are not that they deny that cultures are 'different', but that the individual sameness or similarities amongst humans mean that, in relation to human rights, the implementation of the norms should transcend any cultural boundaries and particularities.[7]

Despite the contemporary conceptualisations of international human rights and the notion of universalism being used largely interchangeably, a more modern form of universalism: international legal universalism can be distinguished as its two core beliefs neatly affiliate with the aims and objectives of the UPR process. First, at the heart of international legal universalism bases its claim of universality is grounded on the expansive standardisation and wide ranging acceptance of a number of long-established human rights treaties and conventions.[8] Indeed, the principle of universality at the UPR process is given effect primarily through holding states accountable to obligations under numerous international human rights laws. Second, the claim of universality is based on the premise that member states, at a number of different forums, have participated in engaging in an international human rights discourse in relation to the adoption, interpretation, and implementation of international human rights norms.[9] Pieter van Dijk states that the declaration of this form of universality encompasses the work of international supervisory institutions that monitor the implementation of human rights norms with the aim of promoting the universality of international human rights laws.[10] Thus, the universalist claim is made on the basis that not only are the obligations embedded in international human rights instruments accepted by the majority of states, but also, states globally participate in the interpretation and implementation of these rights at a number of international forums. Closely aligned with this is the UPR process' key aim of giving the effect to the principle of universality through the promotion of universality through monitoring of state human rights obligations. In particular, the global participation of representatives of all UN member states in the interactive dialogue session provides a forum to discuss the interpretation, and the manner in which the human rights norms are implemented in practice.

Despite the attractive simplicity of both the embedded claims of universalism, as well as core beliefs of international legal universality, it veils the multifaceted issues and concerns that are embedded and continued to be voiced in the interpretation and implementation of international human rights norms on many fronts. Undeniably, the challenge of universality of human rights was most prominently contested by the American Anthropological Association following the adoption of the Universal Declaration of Human Rights in 1948. The Association issued a widely circulated statement rejecting the possibility of the universal implementation of international human rights norms.[11] This statement is rooted in the most profound challenges to the claims of universality: the theory of cultural relativism. Those that adopt the cultural relativist position question the notions of universality of human rights from a range of perspectives from being simply naïve, culturally imperialistic, lacking in empirical validity, to being ahistorical. In this way, at the risk of oversimplification, cultural relativism holds the belief that values and beliefs embedded in culture should be a – or indeed, *the* – legitimating factor in assessing the validity of international human rights law. At the heart of the theory is an emphasis on the significance of *culture* in influencing and shaping human behaviour and perceptions in society.[12] It is argued that the influence of culture is so fundamental to all aspects of society that an individual's perception of the world is unconsciously conditioned by the standards and beliefs of a particular culture.[13] On this basis, the cultural relativist critique challenges the international normative universalist claim of human rights by arguing that moral value judgements, such as interpretations of what constitutes human rights, are relative to different cultural contexts from which such moral judgements arise.[14] Thus, although the universal nature of human rights is often presumed and taken for granted, the influence of cultural relativism and in the interpretation and implementation of rights is undeniable. Presenting the two diverging opinions of universalism and cultural relativism as polarised and irreconcilable extremes is now a distant past, and instead the two schools are now the focus of substantial and sophisticated scholarly works. As the following analysis will demonstrate, there is a shift towards a broad consensus in accepting the merits of the universal project on international human rights law, whilst recognising the importance of culture in supporting its conceptualisation and implementation in the domestic contexts.[15] The nuanced nature of the scholarly discussions have given birth to a range of concepts which can be used to help fully comprehend the interrelatedness of the two previously conceived as polarised extremes, and why it is now nearly impossible to consider either position in isolation of the other.

A Contemporary Perspective: A Middle Ground between the Polarised Debate

One of the fundamental reasons why the cultural relativist critique of the universality of rights has acquired its distinguished status in the discourse of human rights norms is primarily because of their shared foundations upon which the beliefs are based. Universalists draw upon humanity and human nature to claim the inherent value of human rights simply because one is human.[16] Similarly, cultural relativists draw upon the very concept of human nature and humanity by emphasising the significance of 'culture' in shaping and moulding the beliefs, practices, and perceptions of human nature itself. In fact, the scholars Pearce and Kang go to the extent of arguing that 'to be human is to have been encultured to some specific culture whose characteristics have been internalised'.[17] The influence of culture in all aspects of society is so fundamental that an individual's perception of the world is unconsciously conditioned by pre-existing categories and standards of a particular culture.[18] In this way, both the universalist and cultural relativist positions draw upon the inherent nature of human beings in substantiating their respective claims. Going further, it is difficult to dispel the belief that a form of cultural relativism is necessary, if not essential, to provide an appropriate check and balance to the claims of universality of human rights, which often accused of possessing ethnocentric tendencies. Sonia Haris Short strongly condemns the ethnocentric nature of the 'presumed universality of human rights', which asserts that human rights are determined as the 'absolute truth' and thus are by definition universal.[19] Such a pure universalist position not only is impossible to be objectively verified, but also can be rightfully dismissed as being morally imperialistic.[20] Appreciating the merits of a degree of cultural relativism into the discourse of international human rights law, An-Na'im argues that in order to establish genuine universal human rights, there is a need to be aware of the limitations of our own ethnocentricity and appreciate cultural differences.[21] In this way, the challenge of cultural relativism is significant as it helps to enlighten and question one's own ethnocentricity and helps to rebut the accusations of moral imperialism that are often associated with the universalist claims of human rights.

Just as the philosophy of universalism has its justifications based on a variety of theoretical foundations, there are, similarly, various different formulations of the theory of cultural relativism. In fact, it is almost habitual for the most ardent critiques of cultural relativism to presume a uniform construct of the theory, resulting in their censure often only being applicable to the most radical variation.[22] A careful consideration to understand the nuanced differences between the different variations of cultural relativism is significant in not only recognising its invaluable contribution to a form of relativism in the discourse of international human rights, but also providing aid in being able to distinguish and identify the more radical forms of cultural relativism. This will ensure that a radical form of relativism can be appropriately challenged if adopted in the discourse of international human rights law. This task will begin with the following analysis of some of the key concepts that have emerged from universalism and cultural relativism debates, which will provide the foundations to help distinguish between the various formulations of cultural relativism.

Conceptualising 'Culture' within the Context of Cultural Relativism

Anthropological and sociological literature has provided a number of different definitions of culture.[23] Whilst this book of literature carries great significance, a more focused and detailed analysis of the boundaries of culture can provide a tool to understand the refined positions held by scholars along the spectrum of cultural relativist critiques. The most criticised and often dismissed definition of culture is that conceptualised by Franz Boas.[24] Known as the Boasian view of culture, he understood culture to be a bounded, static, and homogenous entity that was distinct and resistant to change.[25] Xiarong Li describes this as the 'classic school vision of culture' which perceives culture as 'time insensitive' and thus determines 'the destiny of the population and the ways in which they think, feel, judge and behave'.[26] One of the most profound criticisms of this narrow interpretation of culture is that not only does it play pretence to being able to maintain boundaries around any human group, but, more importantly, it fails to take into account historical and social changes that occur within cultures over a period of time.[27] This narrow conceptualisation of culture is often aggressively used by repressive regimes who exploit the bounded and static interpretations of culture to justify intolerable practices.[28] This reluctance to accept that cultural norms can be reformed is at the heart of the most radical form of cultural relativism, named for the present analysis as the strictest form of cultural relativism, which will be discussed at length in the next section. For the present purposes, this narrow conceptualisation of culture is often aggressively used by repressive regimes who exploit the bounded and static interpretations of culture to justify intolerable practices.[29] Primarily for this reason, a number of alternative definitions of culture have been proposed.

A modern conceptualisation of culture recognises it as a dynamic process. This position perceives culture as 'unbounded, contested, and connected to the relations of power'.[30] This is a more 'fluid' interpretation of culture, whereby practices and values of a particular culture are subject to 'internal inconsistencies, conflicts and contradictions'.[31] Advocating this view, Sally Engle Merry clarifies the traditional misconceptions of the anthropological definition of culture by arguing that contemporary anthropologists understand cultural 'boundaries as fluid', and thus culture is 'marked by hybridity and creolization rather than uniformity or consistency'.[32] In this way, scholars that adopt this interpretation recognise that cultures are often subject to 'internal inconsistencies, conflicts and contradictions'.[33] In other words, recognising that norms internal to cultures are subject to contestations means that there is a possibility that cultural norms and beliefs are changes and reforms to accommodate and respond to norms that are significant to a particular society.[34] This modern conceptualisation of culture is encapsulated at the heart of the works of a number of scholars that can be broadly defined as moderate cultural relativism. Whilst there are nuanced differences between the suggestions advocated by the scholars, this modern conceptualisation of culture is adopted to advocate the utilisation of the porous definition of culture to gain cultural support of international human rights norms, with the ultimate aim to further enhance implementation of international human rights law in the domestic context.[35] An elaboration of this variation of cultural relativism and how it is positioned within the broader spectrum of universalism and cultural relativism will be the focus of the next section.

Mediating between Universalism and Cultural Relativism

Marie-Benedicte Dembour convincingly insists that it is impossible to consider universalism and cultural relativism in isolation of each other. At the one end of the spectrum of the debate is universalism, which is often perceived as having an interrelated relationship with human rights, whereby the proclaimed universal rights are an inherited entitlement to all human beings simply for being human, which should transcend all cultural boundaries. At the other end of the polarised spectrum, is the most radical variation form of relativism; strict cultural relativism. This form of cultural relativism holds the belief that all values and moral belief systems are culturally specific;[36] consequently, 'what is morally right in relation to one moral framework can be morally wrong in relation to a different moral framework'. Following from this, it is claimed that there are such wide variations between the beliefs of cultures that cultural values are incomprehensible to one another, with no possibility of constructive dialogue between them.[37] Within the context of international human rights law, it means that:

> local cultural traditions ... properly determine the existence and scope of [human] rights enjoyed by individuals in a given society [and] no transboundary legal or moral standards exist against which human rights practices may be judged acceptable or unacceptable.[38]

Consequently, strict cultural relativists use cultural norms as the sole legitimating factor in assessing the acceptability of international human rights law. As such, adherence to such local cultural norms is prioritised over compliance with international human rights law. Despite the repeated reassertion of the universality of human rights norms on numerous international platforms, the critique of strict cultural relativism is not restricted to the theoretical discussion of rights. Despite the political and diplomatic nature of the UPR process, the member states were not coy in adopting a position during their review that strongly affiliated with the beliefs of strict cultural relativism. For example, on the issue of polygamy, the delegate of Ghana was issued with a recommendation to ensure that domestic legislation in relation to polygamy was in compliance with international human rights law. In response, the delegate refused to accept the recommendation on the basis that that marriages that were customary or faith-based 'were in conformity with the customs and traditions of Ghana'.[39] In this way, the delegate of Ghana used cultural norms as a basis for justifying the rejection of reforms to domestic law to provide women's rights protection on the regulation of polygamy in compliance with international human rights law. This form of strict cultural relativism has been the centre of a volume of vehement criticism. The most prevailing criticisms of strict cultural relativism stem from its presumed traditional conceptualisation of culture that falsely presumes that cultural beliefs and values and can be determined by clear boundaries. Such a rigid definition of cultural boundaries is the foundation of an exaggerated claim on the impossibility of cross-cultural dialogue or criticisms of specific cultural norms or practices. The scholar I.C. Jarvie, assessing the implications of rejecting cross-cultural criticism and dialogue, suggests that:

> By limiting critical assessment of human works it disarms us, dehumanizes us, leaves us unable to enter into communicative interaction; that is to say, unable to criticise cross culturally cross sub-culturally; ultimately, relativism leaves no room for criticism at all.[40]

This rejection of cross-cultural criticisms from those external from the culture is often used as a defence to justify intolerable practices,[41] and risks promoting indifference to immoral situations.[42] Leading from this, the static interpretation of cultural norms also presumes that the norms within a culture are not open to adaptability, change, and reform. Further, this closed construction of 'culture' not only ignores internal inconsistencies but is not a representation of the entire society[43] and is often 'misemployed' to veil non-cultural politics within a state.[44] Rein Mullerson gives examples of political leaders, such as Milošević of Serbia and Tudjman of Croatia, who have used cultural and religious particularities as a method to suppress the basic human rights of individuals to meet political aims.[45] For these reasons, this radical form of cultural relativism presents a serious risk of it being open to abuse, and as Alison Dundes Renteln aptly asserts, it is precisely these views which are responsible for the 'scorn of cultural relativism by philosophers'.[46]

So far, the discussion has revolved around the two polarised positions of universalism on the one end, and strict cultural relativism at the other. However, in scholarly terms, the debate has largely moved away from the two extremes, to a more nuanced middle ground. The emergence of this middle ground can be merited to the widely adopted modern conceptualisation of culture by those scholars that engage in the discussions of universalism and cultural relativism within the context of international human rights law. Culture is recognised to have fluid boundaries, that are marked by internal inconsistencies and norms that are open to changes and reforms.[47] In fact, An-Na'im has suggested that the permeability of cultural norms can be utilised to support and ultimately enhance the implementation of human rights protection.[48] The scholars that have adopted this interpretation of culture recognise the merits of cultural support in furthering the acceptability and implementation of the universality of international human rights law in the local context.[49] Whilst there are nuanced variations between the individual suggestions that have been advocated by the scholars, their contributions have formed the fundamental discourse in mediating between universalism and cultural relativism, and will be for the present analysis referred to as moderate cultural relativism.

At the heart of the suggestions posited by scholars that can be categorised as moderate cultural relativist is the ultimate goal of achieving 'cultural legitimacy' of rights. This belief is based on the premise that despite the existence of diversity of cultural values and norms, an agreement on some shared universal principles on human rights is attainable.[50] The leading scholar of this school of thought is An-Na'im who states that:[51]

> Despite their apparent peculiarities and diversity, human beings and societies share certain fundamental interests, concerns, qualities, traits and values that can be identified and articulated as the framework for a "common" culture of universal human rights.[52]

Building on this central belief, the aim of cultural legitimacy of international human rights law is:

> [to] adopt an approach that realistically identifies the lack of cultural support for some human rights and then seeks ways to support and legitimise the particular human rights in terms of the values, norms, and processes of change belonging to the relevant cultural traditions.[53]

Similarly, Federico Lenzerini adheres to the goal of achieving cultural legitimacy of human rights and emphasises the advantages of this approach when he writes that:

> [w]hen human rights are rationalised according to the terms of reference proper of a given culture – i.e. are attributed a meaning which is culturally intelligible in light of the intellectual patterns of the community ... their goal, content, and role are better understood by the members of the society.[54]

In this way, if international human rights norms are incorporated within the 'cultural substate', and are integrated by the community as 'natural components of everyday life', such human rights norms are more likely to be accepted and implemented.[55] The cultural legitimacy of human rights ensures that the support for a particular value is no longer external and as such, those in authority cannot deny its implementation based on 'national sovereignty'.[56] In terms of the practicalities of achieving cultural legitimacy, An-Na'im's contribution forms the most prolific and comprehensive. At the centre of his scholarly works that span over many decades, An-Na'im has developed a two stage approach in achieving cultural legitimacy of international human rights norms. The first is to engage in an 'internal discourse' to reform certain values and beliefs that exist in a culture, that are inconsistent with human rights law, and to bring them in line with current international human rights standards.[57] With the aim to avoid 'dictation by outsiders', individual actors within the culture itself are encouraged to undertake reforms based on cultural principles, norms, and texts.[58] Suggestions of a similar nature have been put forward by Ibhawoh, who argues for a 'sensitive approach that seeks to understand the social basis of cultural traditions and how cultural attitudes may be changed and adapted to complement human rights'.[59] Any changes undertaken must require local involvement, whilst being sensitive to cultural integrity as ultimately, the local people 'must feel a sense of ownership of the process of change and adaptation for it to succeed'.[60] Further, Zwart makes an attempt to reconcile international human rights and local culture as he suggests a 'receptor approach'. He asserts that if social institutions in a particular society fall short of compliance with international human rights law, then changes to the social arrangements need to be 'home grown' remedies, rather than replacing them altogether.[61] Once an adequate level of legitimacy is assumed through an internal discourse, An'Naim suggests that the next stage is to engage in a cross-cultural dialogue.[62] This involves the participation by people of diverse cultures in agreeing upon the meaning, scope, and implementation of human rights.[63] Such a cross-cultural dialogue is to be undertaken between different member states on international human rights norms on an international forum. Similarly, Richard Falk's contribution seeks to mediate between international human rights norms and the various cultural traditions of the world with the aim of alleviating human rights violations.[64] In relation to harmful cultural practices, Richard Falk insists that they are not fixed concepts, and as such, can evolve and develop over time as a result of social interactions and engaging with other cultures.[65] In this way, this approach utilises the fluctuating nature of culture by proposing some recommendations from outside the culture to influence the direction of change.[66] Part of the role of the external actors is to support and encourage those within the culture to legitimatise human rights norms by implementing appropriate internal cultural dialogue and policy implementation. Such a cross-cultural dialogue is to be undertaken between different member's states on an international forum. For the purposes of international human rights law, the aims of moderate cultural relativists are to make the current formulation of rights more acceptable and better implemented in the various cultures, rather than to outrightly reject the current international human rights instruments.[67]

Recognising the merits of achieving cultural legitimacy to further the goal of universality of international human rights norms is not restricted to the scholarly domain. In fact, positions have been adopted at the UPR process, which show strong affiliation with this process. For example, on the issue of FGM, during the review of Cameroon in its second cycle, the recommendation was made to review and implement domestic laws to ensure the prohibition on the practice of FGM. In response, the delegate stated that 'female genital mutilation was an unacceptable human tragedy arising from both cultural and economic factors, that awareness-raising was necessary to end such practices and that excisers should be given the opportunity to retrain'.[68] In this way, whilst the relationship between culture and the practice of FGM is recognised, in line with the central premise of moderate cultural relativism, the intent to undertake incremental changes to end such practices through a dialogue with the appropriate stakeholders to drive towards eliminating the practice.

The move away from demonising culture towards a dialogue with cultural norms is the reason why the moderate cultural relativist position largely avoids many of the well-founded criticisms that are often depicted against the strict form of cultural relativism. One of the main attractive elements of the moderate cultural relativists' position is that the manner in which the fluid nature of which boundaries of cultures are conceptualised, which allows the possibility to not only hold some obscure cultural values to account, but also, to undertake reforms of such values to prevent culture being used as a veil for practices amounting to human rights violations. An-Na'im emphasises the importance of this process to be undertaken in a sensitive manner as each culture to be prepared to suggest criticism in a sensitive manner, whilst at the same time accepting that the values of their own cultures can be open to criticism.[69] This will help to reduce the risk of culture being abused to defend human rights violations, as all beliefs will be subject to scrutiny, either externally or internally, against international human rights standards. Going further, the cross-cultural dialogue on complying with international human rights law permits the possibility the values and beliefs from different cultural perspectives be incorporated into the discourse of international human rights law, or more optimistically, inform the interpretation of human rights norms.

Supporting this optimism, An-Na'im emphasises that the interpretation given to human rights norms should be perceived as a 'project to be constructed through a global dialogue and collaboration, not as a predetermined concept of accomplished fact'.[70] Therefore, the interpretation of human rights norms is perceived as a continuing, flexible, and inclusive project, which welcomes a contribution from different member states' cultural perspectives.[71] In this way, different cultures and member states are encouraged to see themselves, and be seen by others, as proactively contributing to the protection and promotion of universal human rights norms.[72] Such contributions from different cultural perspectives will, in turn, provide the opportunity to raise 'new areas of concern', 'add more rights', and generally provide an 'informed interpretation and application of accepted norms'.[73] In addition, this approach is likely to increase compliance with the human rights laws if cultures themselves have contributed to the definition of human rights norms. Describing it as the 'process of retroactive legitimation' of existing international standards, An-Na'im asserts that the current interpretation of human rights norms must itself be 'open and responsive to the changing priorities and concerns of the various peoples of the world'.[74] Similarly, Lenzerini explains that if culture is considered as a living organism that is subject to constant change, and the terms of human rights adjudication are to be determined to a certain extent by cultural needs, then the terms of human rights norms will need to be modified to reflect the development of cultural patterns.[75] The moderate cultural relativist core belief is that the international standing of human rights laws both influences and is influenced by the universal acceptability at local level, recognising the importance of universality of human rights and cultural diversity in pursuing the ultimate goal of universal international human rights protection.[76] Appreciating international human rights norms and cultural particularities are accepted, to some extent, to influence and validate each other will help ensure that international human rights laws are appropriately adopted and protected, with gravity and conviction, by the authorities in the domestic context. This dialectical relationship should be emphasised during the discourse and monitoring of human rights norms, as it is one of the fundamental ways of incorporating various cultural value perspectives into the discourse of human rights to further the goal of making human rights culturally legitimate.

The above analysis illustrates that the contemporary discourse on international human rights law has moved away from the polarised debates between universalism and cultural relativism, towards a more moderate middle ground, which recognises the merits of the universal project of human rights, as well as the significance of culture in ensuring a successful implementation of international human rights law. Marie-Benedicte Dembour has dedicated a significant amount of her scholarly works in mediating between universalism and relativism. She criticises the sole reliance on universalism as breeding moral arrogance, as 'it excludes the experience of the other'.[77] However, warning against the strict adherence to relativism, she highlights the risks of abuse of culture and moral indifference to immoral situations that result from a radical form of cultural relativist positions. As a solution, she calls for a conceptualisation of human rights that 'allows local circumstances to be taken in to account, to be part of the equation' in the discourse of human rights.[78] Similarly, Alison Dundes Rentlen has attempted to rectify the misconceptions of cultural relativism that have contributed to the polarised debate by highlighting that there is 'nothing in the theory if relativism that prevent relativists from criticising activities and beliefs in other cultures', and rather advocating to establish 'cross cultural universal' values on human rights.[79] In order to extract the positives from both positions of universalism and cultural relativism, to ensure ultimately the success of promoting and protecting international human rights norms, it is essential to formulate a balance between the advocating of universal rights, the entitlement of which is justified by virtue of humanity, with recognition that as such the conceptualisation and implementation of such rights may be contested due to cultural diversity. In this way, the modern mediation between universalism and cultural relativism has refined the contemporary discourse on international human rights laws.

However, the analysis above of mediating between universalism and cultural relativism is not without its flaws. One of the biggest challenges that the moderate cultural relativist position is faced with is the representation of culture. For instance, whose voices and concerns are represented as the 'culture' with which an internal discourse held amongst those of shared cultural values, or a cross-cultural dialogue on an international platform? Which standards of cultural legitimacy should apply? What about alternative or competing standards of cultural legitimacy? Who selects which views and positions are to be represented as culture? Scholars of this position have addressed the challenge directly. An'Naim calls this internal struggle and problems posed by the contestability of cultural norms as 'politics of culture', between those who challenge the status quo against those who wish to legitimise their power and privilege.[80] Within this political struggle, An-Na'im writes that human rights advocates need to recognise their role in the constantly changing cultural makeup and utilise this process effectively to enhance the recognition and implementation of human rights.[81] Therefore, the goal of achieving internal cultural legitimacy will facilitate the political struggles within a particular society and mobilise those oppressed individuals or groups to challenge the status quo of those in power.[82] Even though outsiders may offer sympathy to the less dominant groups or classes within society, those external of the culture cannot legitimately claim a valid view of internal cultural norms.[83] In this way, the mechanics of the internal discourse within a particular culture will facilitate the political struggle of those oppressed groups and individuals that are within the culture itself.

Women are an obvious example of those who may have their voices silenced within a particular culture and who may be actively engaged in an internal political struggle within a society for their rights to be respected. It is undeniable that in some societies, the notion of culture has been interpreted in a way to maintain the privileged status of the dominant group in society, usually men, whilst simultaneously oppressing the rights of women. Thus, it is due to this inherent relationship between women and culture that women's rights are more susceptible to the challenge of universality from a cultural relativism position. For this reason, the next section will elaborate the theoretical reasons why the selection of women's rights is selected for the purposes of this investigation.

The Relationship between Women and Culture

Since the very inception of the Universal Declaration of Human Rights (UDHR), it has long been argued that the interests and concerns of women and their rights have, until recently, been marginalised from the mainstream human rights discourse.[84] This is primarily because dominant interpretations given to international human rights law have been defined to primarily address the types of violations that men are subject to, which excludes the specific violations that women experience.[85] This marginalisation of women from the mainstream human rights discourse was the fundamental reason behind the development of the women's human rights movement between the years 1976 and 1985, which has been described as the UN Decade for Women.[86] In 1979, the General Assembly adopted the Convention on the Elimination of all Forms of Discrimination Against Women (CEDAW), which has been described as the most significant emergence in the evolution of women's rights.[87] This Convention focused on gender issues and brought the interests and concerns of women to the centre stage of the discourse of international human rights by specifically addressing violations carried out against women.[88]

The division between the 'public' and 'private' spheres that exist in the mainstream international human rights instruments and discourse has been one of the prominent issues raised during the women's rights movement.[89] For instance, Berta Esperanza Hernandez-Truyol argues that the public and private dichotomy is one of the fundamental reasons underlying the subordination and marginalisation of women and their rights from the mainstream international human rights discourse.[90]

The public sphere is considered to include 'government, political, and commercial activities', which are often dominated by men and from which women are largely excluded.[91] In contrast, the private realm is the family and domestic life, which is primarily dominated by women,[92] and where governments should not intrude.[93] Donna Sullivan criticises the gendered nature of the public and private divide as where the 'economic, social and political power adheres in the public realm to which women have limited access' and control over.[94] In this way, the actions of individuals in the public realm are subject to government regulation and scrutiny, whilst the actions undertaken in the private realm, largely affecting women, avoids such regulation.[95]

A convincing explanation of the reasons underlying the very existence of the public and private divide in international human rights law is provided by the legal scholar Donna Sullivan.[96] She writes that the 'state centred nature of international law, the dominance of civil and political discourse all account for the emphasis placed on the violations undertaken by the state and the neglect of the gender specific violations that occur in the private sphere'.[97] Similarly, Charlotte Bunch explains that the public and private divide was first initiated by the 'western-educated propertied' men who first advanced the cause of human rights and feared violations of civil and political rights in the public sphere. In contrast, 'they did not fear, however, the violations in the private sphere of the home because they were the masters of that territory'.[98]

With the backdrop of the public and private discussion, the relationship between women and culture becomes more conspicuous. The issues and concerns that largely affect women are often relegated to the private sphere.[99] For instance, the private sphere deals with issues such as sexual and reproductive health, marriage, polygamy, divorce, and inheritance.[100] However, where the issues that arise in the public sphere are subject to scrutiny and regulation by the government and public bodies, the issues that fall within the remit of the private sphere are more inclined to be informed and governed by cultural norms.[101] Following on from this, women's roles have traditionally been dominated in the private sphere, and issues and concerns of women have been seen as intertwined with the symbolisation and continuance of the culture itself.[102] For instance, women are considered as the 'repositories, guardians and transmitters of culture',[103] as they often considered to represent the 'reproduction of the community' as well as being the primary caregivers in the family and domestic life.[104] In this way, a woman's mannerisms, characteristics, and clothing have sometimes become the visible symbolisation of a particular culture.[105] Thus, some societies have continued to defend unequal treatment of women, and their roles in the private sphere, to preserve cultural particularities.[106] Indeed, the sustenance of group boundaries is often considered as the responsibility of women.[107] For this reason, primarily because women's role is predominantly in the private sphere which is regulated and informed by cultural norms, the issues and concerns of women are more susceptible and 'fragile to the claims of culture'.[108] For instance, practices that are often justified and defended in the name of culture often impede human rights that are gender specific.[109] To name some specific examples, FGM, son preference, forced and early marriages, the implications of the dowry system, male control over land and finances, marital rape, family honour killings, and witch hunting all preserve patriarchy at the expense of violating women's rights.[110] In this way, a challenge to the universality of human rights from a cultural relativist perspective is more likely to have direct, or indirect, influence on women's rights issues and concerns. It is primarily for this reason that the issue of women's rights was a natural selection for the purposes of this investigation.

An Analysis of the Relationship between Women and Culture from a Moderate Cultural Relativist Perspective

It is common for human rights scholars to depict the relationship between women and culture in a negative light, with the notion of culture often presumed to be detrimental to women and their rights. The central argument of this school of thought is that culture, and its values, are often used as a justification for carrying out harmful practices against women.[111] For example, Cerna and Wallace argue that despite a number of international human rights conventions to eliminate discrimination against women, 'most cultures continue practices that are detrimental to the wellbeing of girls and women'.[112] Arati Rao on this point argues:

> No social group has suffered greater violation of its human rights in the name of culture than women. Regardless of the particular forms it takes in different societies, the concept of culture in the modern state circumscribes women's lives in deeply symbolic as well as in immediately real ways.[113]

Similarly, Susan Moller Okin strongly emphasises the detrimental impact of culture for women as she argues that the principal aim of most cultures is control of women by men, and to endorse the suppression of women.[114] This position is similarly reflected in an ever increasing number of human rights documents, which perceive culture as an obstacle to the protection of women's rights.[115] For instance, the Committee on the Elimination of Discrimination against Women has often criticised cultural values in relation to women in a number of Concluding Observations and General Comments.[116] One such example is in a General Comment whereby the Committee stated that 'the most significant factors inhibiting women's ability to participate in public life has been the cultural framework of values and religious beliefs'.[117]

Whilst it is recognised that the rich nature of culture means that aspects of its beliefs can be interpreted to veil human rights violations against women, perceiving the relationship between women and culture from a solely negative perspective can be criticised. For example, Sally Goldfarb argues that currently when culture is considered in discussions of domestic violence, it is done so in a negative manner, which considers culture as being harmful to women and which is used as a defence to excuse perpetrators of such violence.[118] However, she argues this position overlooks the support of women's rights that can be offered by some cultures.[119] Moreover, Goldfarb argues that by considering cultural influences on issues such as domestic violence, it can help to gain a better insight into the underlying reasons behind domestic violence and how best to devise suitable legal responses.[120] Similarly, Rupa Reddy asserts that dismissing cultural issues in relation to violence can lead to the lack of contextualisation of important issues.[121] She argues that with respect to violence against women, taking into account the cultural context can benefit women as it provides a better understanding of the difficulties that they face.[122] Therefore, by incorporating cultural values into the discourse of women and their rights, it may help to better understand the violations suffered by women and help direct the correct manner of response that is required. Such reforms can be carried out using the methodologies suggested by moderate cultural relativists, to ensure that the reforms that are suggested are culturally legitimate, and thus stand the best chance of being accepted and implemented.[123] An-Nai'm, who advocates this position, argues that the changes to cultural practices that violate women's human rights need to be proposed by the individuals within the cultures to be effective.[124] Moreover, such changes need to be based on cultural sources and methodologies.[125] A successful practical example of the implementation of this approach can be given in relation to women's rights in Egypt. The representative of Egypt in 2000 presented a report to CEDAW in which she announced that women were now given the right to unilaterally divorce their husbands. The representative stated that the passage of this law was only made possible because the new laws could be justified in line with their own cultural and religious texts.[126] In this way, by adopting the moderate cultural relativist methods, there is a greater chance of the reforms being carried out in a culturally legitimate manner, being thus more likely to be accepted and implemented in the societies and cultures in question.

Conclusion

Meyer's observation that 'few scholarly topics more readily engender controversies than the question of the universality of human rights norms'[127] aptly describes the debates between universalism and cultural relativism. This chapter contextualised the principles of universality underpinning the UPR process within the contextualisation of the debates of universalism and cultural relativism. The key concepts of universalism, defining culture and cultural legitimacy were introduced and analysed to provide an accurate snapshot of the contemporary more nuanced mediation between the traditionally polarised extremes of the discussions. These theoretical concepts were then brought to life through examples that affiliated with these positions on the interactive dialogue sessions at the UPR process. The final discussions in the chapter provided theoretical justifications for the selection of women's rights through the explanation of the inherent relationship between women and culture, which was then contextualised and analysed on the nuanced middle ground of moderate cultural relativism. However, the selection of women's rights for the purposes of this investigation goes much further than the theoretical discussions analysed above. Instead, there are other methodological and pragmatic reasons for the selection of women's rights as the focus for this investigation of the UPR process. The justification for this choice, together with an explanation for the other selections made during this investigation, will be the focus of discussions in the next chapter of this book.

Notes

1 AE Meyer, 'Book Review' (1992) 14 *Human Rights Quarterly* 527.
2 See M Cranston, *What Are Human Rights* (2nd edn, Taplinger 1973); C Bay, 'Self Respect as a Human Rights: Thoughts on the Dialects of Wants and Needs (1982) 4 *Human Rights Quarterly* 53, 55–60; Alan Gewirth, *Human Rights: Essays on Justification and Application* (University of Chicago Press 1982); MK Addo, 'Practice of United Nations Human Rights Treaty Bodies in the Reconciliation of Cultural Diversity with Universal Respect for Human Rights' (2010) 32 *Human Rights Quarterly* 601, 661.
3 See Jack Donnelly, 'Cultural relativism and universal human rights' in J Donnelly (ed), *Universal Human Rights in Theory and Practice* (Cornell University Press 1989) 109.
4 MW Cranston, *What Are Human Rights* (2nd edn, Taplinger 1973) 1. See also R Wasserston, 'Rights, Human Rights and Racial Discrimination' (1964) 61 *Journal of Philosophy* 628; N Ashford, *Human Rights: What They Are and What They Are Not* (Libertarian Alliance 1995) 2.
5 R Wasserston, 'Rights, Human Rights and Racial Discrimination' (1964) 61 *Journal of Philosophy* 628.
6 Jack Donnelly, 'Human Rights: A New Standard of Civilization?' (1998) *International Affairs* 1.
7 R Sloane, 'Outrelativising Relativism: A Liberal Defence of the Universality of International Human Rights' (2001) 34 *Vanderbilt Journal of Transnational Law* 527, 541–542. See also Vitit Muntarbhorn, 'The Universality of Standards', lecture at the René Cassin International Institute of Human Rights, July 1993 cited in Civic M, 'A Comparative Analysis of International and Chinese Human Rights Law – Universality Versus Cultural Relativism' (1995–1996) 2 *Buffalo Journal of International Law* 285, 317. See also, See also Jack Donnelly, 'Human Rights as Natural Rights' (1982) 4 *Human Rights Quarterly* 391.
8 Jack Donnelly, *Universal Human Rights: In Theory and Practice* (3rd edn, Cornell University Press 2013) 94. See also Lone Lindholt, 'The African charter: contextual universality' in Kirsten Hastrup (ed), *Human Rights on Common Grounds: The Quest for Universality* (Kluwer Law International 2001) 125.
9 MK Addo, 'Practice of United Nations Human Rights Treaty Bodies in the Reconciliation of Cultural Diversity with Universal Respect for Human Rights' (2010) 32 *Human Rights Quarterly* 601, 660.
10 Pieter Van Dijk, 'The Law of Human Rights in Europe: instruments and procedures for a uniform implementation' in Academy of European Law (eds), *Collected Courses of the Academy of European Law* (Volume VI Book 2, Kluwer Law International 1997) 1, 29.
11 The Executive Board, American Anthropological Association, 'Statement on Human Rights' (1947) 49 *American Anthropologist* 539; MJ Herskovitz, *Cultural Dynamics* (Knopf 1964) 542.

12 See C Geertz, *Interpretations of Cultures* (Basic Books 1973) 49; A An-Na'im, 'Problems and prospects of universal cultural legitimacy for human rights' in An- Na'im and Deng (eds), *Human Rights in Africa: Cross Cultural Perspectives* (Brookings Institution 1990) 333.

13 Alison Dundes Renteln, *International Human Rights: Universalism versus Cultural Relativism* (Quid Pro Book 2013) 59; A An-Na'im, 'Problems and prospects of universal cultural legitimacy for human rights' in An- Na'im and Deng (eds), *Human Rights in Africa: Cross Cultural Perspectives* (Brookings Institution 1990) 339.

14 E Hatch, *Cultural and Morality: The Relativity of Values in Anthropology* (Columbia University Press 1983). See also Alison Dundes Renteln, *International Human Rights: Universalism versus Relativism* (Quidpro Books 2013) 58; C Joyner and J Dettling, 'Bridging the Cultural Chasm: Cultural Relativism and the Future of International Law (1990) 20 *California Western International Law Journal* 275; Guyora Binder, 'Cultural Relativism and Cultural Imperialism in Human Rights Law' (1999) 5 *Buffalo Human Rights Law Review* 211, 214.

15 Marie-Benedicte Dembour 'Following the movement of a pendulum: between universalism and relativism' in Jane Cowan, Marie-Benedicte Dembour and Richard Wilson (eds), *Culture and Rights: Anthropological Perspectives* (Cambridge University Press 2001); Alison Renteln, 'The Unanswered Challenge of Relativism and the Consequences for Human Rights' (1985) 7 *Human Rights Quarterly* 514; An-Na'im A, '*Toward an Islamic Reformation: Civil Liberties, Human Rights, and International Law* (Syracuse University Press 1990); F Lenzerini, *The Culturalization of Human Rights Law* (Oxford University Press 2014); S Merry, 'Constructing a Global Law—Violence against Women and the Human Rights System' (2003) *Law and Social Enquiry* 941; T Zwart, 'Using Local Culture to Further the Implementation of International Human Rights: The Receptor Approach' (2012) 32 *Human Rights Quarterly* 546; CM Obermeyer, 'A Cross-Cultural Perspective on Reproductive Rights' (1995) 17 *Human Rights Quarterly* 366; Richard Falk, 'Cultural foundations for the International Protection of Human Rights' in A An-Na'im (ed), *Human Rights in Cross Cultural Perspectives* (University of Pennsylvania Press 1995).

16 J Donnelly, *International Human Rights* (4th edn, Westview Press 2013) 37–38. See also R Wasserstrom, 'Rights, Human Rights and Racial Discrimination' (1964) 61 *Journal of Philosophy* 628; MW Cranston, *What Are Human Rights* (2nd edn, Taplinger 1973).

17 WB Pearce and K Kang, 'Conceptual migrations: understanding travellers' tales for cross culture adaptation' in YY Kim and WB Gudykunst (eds), *Cross Cultural Adaptation: Current Approaches* (Sage Publications 1988) 29.

18 A Renteln, *International Human Rights: Universalism versus Cultural Relativism* (Quid Pro Book 2013) 59.

19 Sonia Harris Short, 'Listening to "the other?" The Convention on the Rights of the Child' (2011) 2 *Melbourne General of International Law* 305, 308.

20 Ibid.

21 A An-Na'im, 'Toward a cross culture approach to defining international standards of human right: the meaning of cruel, inhuman or degrading treatment' in Abdullahi An-Naim (ed), *Human Rights in Cross Cultural Perspectives: A Quest for Consensus* (University of Pennsylvania Press 1995) 25.

22 Michel Perry, *The Idea of Human Rights: Four Inquires* (Oxford University Press 1998).

23 See Albert Carl Cafagna, 'A formal analysis of definitions of culture' in Gertrude E Dole and Robert L Carneiro (eds), *Essays in the Science of Culture: In Honor of Leslie A White* (Thomas Y Cromwell 1960) 111–132. See also TS Eliot, *Notes toward the Definition of Culture* (Faber and Faber 1948); Raymond Williams,

Keywords: A Vocabulary of Culture and Society (Oxford University Press 1976) 76–82. C Geertz, *Interpretations of Cultures* (Basic Books 1973); WB Pearce and K Kang, 'Conceptual migrations: understanding travellers' tales for cross culture adaptation' in YY Kim and WB Gudykunst (eds), *Cross Cultural Adaptation: Current Approaches* (Sage Publications 1988); A An-Na'im and J Hammond 'Cultural transformation and human rights in African societies' in A An-Na'im and J Hammond (eds), *Cultural Transformation in African Societies* (London 2000); T Lindholm, 'Coming to terms with traditions' in H Hoibraden and I Gullvag (eds), *Essays in Pragmatic Philosophy* (Norwegian University Press 1985).

24 See Ann-Belinda Preis, 'Human Rights as a Cultural Practice: An Anthropological Critique' (1996) 18 *Human Rights Quarterly* 286, 295.

25 Franz Boas, *The Mind of Primitive Man* (Forgotten Books 2012) 149. See also Ruth Benedict, *Patterns of Culture* (Routledge & K. Paul 1961).

26 X Li, *Ethics, Human Rights and Culture: Beyond Relativism and Culture* (Palgrave Macmillan 2006) 9–10. See also, Lynda Bell, 'Who produces Asian identity? discourse, discrimination, and Chinese Peasant women in the quest for human rights' in L Bell, A Nathan and I Peleg (eds), *Negotiating Culture and Human Rights* (Colombia University Press 2001) 27.

27 A Preis, 'Human Rights as a Cultural Practice: An Anthropological Critique' (1996) 18 *Human Rights Quarterly* 286; M Perry, *The Idea of Human Rights: Four Inquires* (Oxford University Press 1998).

28 See M Iovane, 'The Universality of Human Rights and the International Protection of Cultural Diversity: Some Theoretical and Practical Considerations' (2007) 14 *International Journal on Minority and Group Rights* 231, 24. See also, L Donoho, 'Relativism versus Universality in Human Rights: The Search for Meaningful Standards' (1990–1991) 27 *Stanford Journal of International Law* 345, 380.

29 Ibid.

30 Sally Engle Merry, 'Human Rights Law and the Demonization of Culture (and Anthropology along the way)' (2003) 26 *PoLAR* 55, 67.

31 Ibid.

32 Ibid. 55, 64.

33 Sally Engle Merry, 'Constructing a Global Law-Violence against Women and the Human Rights System' (2003) *Law and Social Enquiry* 941.

34 B Ibhawoh, 'Between Culture and Constitution: Evaluating the Cultural Legitimacy of Human Rights in the African State' (2000) 22 *Human Rights Quarterly* 838, 841.

35 A An-Na'im, 'Toward a cross culture approach to defining international standards of human right: the meaning of cruel, inhuman or degrading treatment' in A An-Na'im (ed), *Human Rights in Cross Cultural Perspectives: A Quest for Consensus* (University of Pennsylvania Press 1995); Sally Engle Merry, *Human Rights and Gender Violence: Translating International Law Into Local Justice* (The University of Chicago Press 2006).

36 W Meyer, 'Toward a Global Culture: Human Rights, Group Rights and Cultural Relativism' 3 (1996) *International Journal on Group Rights* 169, 175.

37 See T Spaak, 'Moral Relativism and Human Rights' (2007) 13 *Buffalo Human Rights Law Review* 73, 75; Thomas Khun, *The Essential Tension: Selected Studies in Scientific Tradition and Change* (University of Chicago Press 1979) 290.

38 FR Tesón, 'International Human Rights and Cultural Relativism' (1984–1985) 25 *Virginia Journal of International Law* 869, 870–871.

39 UNHRC 'Report of the Human Rights Council on Its Eighth Session' (1 September 2008) A/HRC/8/52, para 663.

40 IC Jarvie, 'Rationalism and Relativism' (1983) 34 *The British Journal of Sociology* 45.

41 M Iovane, 'The Universality of Human Rights and the International Protection of Cultural Diversity: Some Theoretical and Practical Considerations' (2007) 14 *International Journal on Minority and Group Rights* 231; L Donoho, 'Relativism versus Universality in Human Rights: The Search for Meaningful Standards' (1990–1991) 27 *Stanford Journal of International Law* 345, 380).

42 Ibid. 58. See also A Renteln, *International Human Rights: Universalism versus Cultural Relativism* (Quid Pro Book 2013).

43 Catherine Powell, 'Introduction: Locating Culture, Identity, and Human Rights' (1999) 30 *Columbia Human Rights Law Review* 201, 211.

44 R Mushkat, 'Culture and International Law: Universalism and Relativism' (2002) 6 *Singapore Journal of International and Comparative Law* 1028, 1032.

45 Rein Mullerson, *Human Rights Diplomacy* (Routledge 1997) 98–100.

46 A Renteln, *International Human Rights: Universalism versus Cultural Relativism* (Quid Pro Book 2013) 51.

47 T Lindholm, 'Coming to terms with traditions' in H Hoibraden and I Gullvag (eds), *Essays in Pragmatic Philosophy* (Norwegian University Press 1985).

48 A An-Na'im, 'Toward a cross culture approach to defining international standards of human right: the meaning of cruel, inhuman or degrading treatment' in A An-Na'im (ed), *Human Rights in Cross Cultural Perspectives: A Quest for Consensus* (University of Pennsylvania Press 1995).

49 Ibid.

50 Charles Taylor, 'Conditions of an unenforced consensus on human rights' in Joanne A Bauer and Daniel A Bell (eds), *The East Asian Challenge for Human Rights* (Cambridge University Press 1999) 124–146.

51 K Schooley, 'Cultural Sovereignty, Islam, and Human Rights – Toward a Communitarian Revision' (1994–1995) 25 *Cumberland Law Review* 651, 682.

52 An-Na'im A, 'Problems and prospects of universal cultural legitimacy for human rights' in An-Na'im and Deng (eds) *Human Rights in Africa: Cross Cultural Perspectives* (Brookings Institution 1990) 78.

53 Ibid. 339.

54 LA Obiora, 'Feminism, Globalization, and Culture: After Beijing' (1997) 4 *Indian Journal of Global Legal Studies* 355, 377.

55 F Lenzerini, *The Culturalization of Human Rights Law* (Oxford University Press 2014) 218. LA Obiora, 'Feminism, Globalization, and Culture: After Beijing' (1997) 4 *Indian Journal of Global Legal Studies* 355, 377.

56 Ibid. 332.

57 A An-Na'im, 'Islam, Islamic Law and the dilemma of cultural legitimacy for universal human rights' in Claude E Welch, Jr. and Virginia A. Leary (eds), *Asian Perspectives on Human Rights* (Westview Press 1990) 46–48.

58 An-Na'im A, 'State responsibility under International Human Rights Law to change Religious and Customary Law' in Rebecca Cook (ed), *Human Rights of Women: National and International Perspectives* (University of Pennsylvania Press 1994).

59 B Ibhawoh, 'Between Culture and Constitution: Evaluating the Cultural Legitimacy of Human Rights in the African State' (2000) 22 *Human Rights Quarterly* 838, 856.

60 Ibid.

61 Tom Zwart, 'Using Local Culture to Further the Implementation of International Human Rights: The Receptor Approach' (2012) 32 *Human Rights Quarterly* 546, 560. See also KL Zaunbrecher, 'When Culture Hurts: Dispelling the Myth of Cultural Justification for Gender Based Human Rights Violation' (2011) 33 *Houston Journal of International Law* 679, 688.

62 A An-Na'im, 'Toward a cross culture approach to defining international standards of human right: the meaning of cruel, inhuman or degrading treatment'

in A An-Na'im (ed), *Human Rights in Cross Cultural Perspectives: A Quest for Consensus* (University of Pennsylvania Press 1995) 27–28.

63 Ibid.

64 R Falk, 'Cultural foundations for the International Protection of Human Rights' in A. An-Na'im (ed) *Human Rights in Cross Cultural Perspectives* (University of Pennsylvania Press 1995) 46.

65 Ibid. 51, 59.

66 A An-Na'im, 'Introduction' in A An-Na'im (ed), *Human Rights in Cross Cultural Perspectives: A Quest for Consensus* (University of Pennsylvania Press 1995) 4.

67 A An-Na'im, 'The cultural mediation of human rights: the Al-Arqam case in Malaysia' in Joanne R. Bauer and Daniel A. Bell (eds), *The East Asian Challenge for Human Rights* (Cambridge University Press 1999) 153.

68 UNHRC 'Report of the Working Group on the Universal Periodic Review: Cameroon' (5 July 2013) A/HRC/24/15 paragraph 89.

69 A An- Na'im, 'Cultural Transformation and Normative Consensus on the Best Interests of the Child' (1994) 8 *International Journal of Law and the Family* 62, 68. See also Boaventura De Sousa Santos 'Toward a multicultural conception of human rights' in Bertea Esperanza Hermansex-Truyol (ed), *A Critical Moral Imperialism Anthology* (New York University Press 2002) 47.

70 A An-Na'im, 'The Contingent Universality of Human Rights: The Case of Freedom of Expression in African and Islamic Context' (1997) 11 *Emory International Law Review* 29, 36.

71 A An-Na'im, 'Religious Minorities under Islamic Law and the Limits of Cultural Relativism' (1987) 9 *Human Rights Quarterly* 1, 5.

72 A An-Na'im, 'The Contingent Universality of Human Rights: The Case of Freedom of Expression in African and Islamic Context' (1997) 11 *Emory International Law Review* 29, 36.

73 A An-Na'im, 'Religious Minorities under Islamic Law and the Limits of Cultural Relativism' (1987) 9 *Human Rights Quarterly* 1, 4.

74 Ibid.

75 F Lenzerini, *The Culturalization of Human Rights Law* (Oxford University Press 2014) 118.

76 A An-Na'im, 'State responsibility under International Human Rights Law to change Religious and Customary Law' in Rebecca Cook (ed), *Human Rights of Women: National and International Perspectives* (University of Pennsylvania Press 1994) 173.

77 M Dembour, 'Following the movement of a pendulum: between universalism and relativism' in Jane Cowan, Marie-Benedicte Dembour and Richard Wilson (eds), *Culture and Rights: Anthropological Perspectives* (Cambridge University Press 2001) 58.

78 Ibid. 92.

79 Alison Renteln 'Relativism and the Search for Human Rights' (1988) 90 *American Anthropologist* 56, 78.

80 A An-Na'im, 'State responsibility under International Human Rights Law to change Religious and Customary Law' in Rebecca Cook (ed), *Human Rights of Women: National and International Perspectives* (University of Pennsylvania Press 1994) 173.

81 Ibid.

82 A An-Na'im, 'Toward an Islamic hermeneutics for human rights' in A An-Na'im, Jernald D Gort, Henry Jansen and Hendrik M Vroom (eds), *Human Rights and Religious Values: An Uneasy Relationship?* (William B. Eerdmans Publishing Company Grand Rapids 1995) 332.

83 A An-Na'im, 'Introduction' in A An-Na'im (ed), *Human Rights in Cross Cultural Perspectives: A Quest for Consensus* (University of Pennsylvania Press 1995) 20.

84 Hilary Charlesworth, Christine Chinkin and Shelley Wright, 'Feminist Approaches to International Law' (1991) 85 *American Journal of International Law* 613, 621–634.

85 Charlotte Bunch, 'Transforming human rights from a feminist perspective' in Julie Peters and Andrea Wolper (eds), *Women's Rights, Human Rights: International Feminist Perspective* (Routledge 1995) 13.

86 Hilkka Pietilä and Jeanne Vickers, *Making Women Matter: The Role of the United Nations* (Zed Books Limited 1990) 75–83.

87 Berta Esperanza Hernandez-Truyol, 'Human rights through a gendered lens: emergence, evolution, revolution' in Kelly D Askin and Dorean M Koenig (eds), *Women and International Human Rights Law* (Volume 1, Transnational Publishers Inc 1999) 4.

88 Berta Esperanza Hernandez-Truyol, 'Women's Rights and Human Rights – Rule, Realities and the Role of Culture: A formula for reform' (1995–1996) 21 *Brooklyn Journal of International Law* 605, 630–631.

89 Hilary Charlesworth, 'Human rights as men's rights' in Julie Peters and Andrea Wolper (eds), *Women's Rights, Human Rights: International Feminist Perspective* (Routledge 1995) 106–110.

90 Berta Esperanza Hernandez-Truyol, 'Human rights through a gendered lens: emergence, evolution, revolution' in Kelly D Askin and Dorean M Koenig (eds), *Women and International Human Rights Law* (Volume 1, Transnational Publishers Inc 1999) 32.

91 Lucinda Joy Peach, 'Are women human? The promise and perils of "women's rights as human rights"' in Lynda Bell, Andrew Nathan and Ilan Peieg (eds), *Negotiating Culture and Human Rights* (Columbia University Press 2001) 159.

92 Ibid.

93 Berta Esperanza Hernandez-Truyol, 'Human rights through a gendered lens: emergence, evolution, revolution' in Kelly D Askin and Dorean M Koenig (eds), *Women and International Human Rights Law* (Volume 1, Transnational Publishers Inc 1999) 32.

94 Donna Sullivan, 'The public/private distinction in International Human Rights Law' in Julie Peters and Andrea Wolper (eds), *Women's Rights, Human Rights: International Feminist Perspective* (Routledge 1995) 128.

95 Charlotte Bunch and Samantha Frost, 'Women's human rights: an introduction' in Cheris Kramarae and Dale Spender (eds), *Routledge International Encyclopedia of Women: Global Women's Issues and Knowledge* (Routledge 2000).

96 Donna Sullivan, 'The public/private distinction in international human rights law' in Julie Peters and Andrea Wolper (eds), *Women's Rights, Human Rights: International Feminist Perspective* (Routledge 1995) 127.

97 Ibid.

98 Charlotte Bunch, 'Transforming human rights from a feminist perspective' in Julie Peters and Andrea Wolper (eds), *Women's Rights, Human Rights: International Feminist Perspective* (Routledge 1995) 13.

99 C Cerna, 'Universality of Human Rights and Cultural Diversity: Implementation of Human Rights in Different Socio–Cultural Contexts' (1994) 16 *Human Rights Quarterly* 740, 746.

100 Ibid.

101 C Cerna and Jennifer Wallace, 'Women and culture' in Kelly D Askin and Dorean M Koenig (eds), *Women and International Human Rights Law* (Volume 1, Transnational Publishers Inc 1999) 629. Julie Mertus, 'State discrimina-

tory family law and customary values' in Julie Peters and Andrea Wolper (eds), *Women's Rights, Human Rights: International Feminist Perspective* (Routledge 1995) 135.

102 Ibid.

103 Arati Rao, 'The politics of gender and culture in International Human Rights discourse' in Dorothy Hodgson (ed), *Gender and Culture at the Limits of Rights* (University of Pennsylvania Press 2011) 169.

104 Ibid.

105 Ibid.

106 Salma Maoulidi, 'Between law and culture: contemplating rights for women in Zanzibar' in Dorothy Hodgson (ed), *Gender and Culture at the Limits of Rights* (University of Pennsylvania Press 2011) 32.

107 Yakin Ertürk, 'Report of the Special Rapporteur on Violence against Women, Its Causes and Consequences: Intersections between Culture and Violence against Women' (United Nations General Assembly 17 January 2007) A/HRC/4/34 para, 63.

108 Hernandez- Truyol B, 'Human rights through a gendered lens: emergence, evolution, revolution' in Kelly D Askin and Dorean M Koenig (eds), *Women and International Human Rights Law* (Volume 1, Transnational Publishers Inc 1999) 32.

109 Frances Raday, 'Culture, Religion, and Gender' (2003) 1 *International Journal of Constitutional Law* 663, 670.

110 Ibid.

111 Rhoda Howard. 'Women's rights in english-speaking Sub-Saharan Africa' in Claude E., Jr. Welch (ed), *Human Rights and Development in Africa* (State University of New York Printers 1984) 46.

112 Christina Cerna and Jennifer Wallace, 'Women and culture' in Kelly D Askin and Dorean M Koenig (eds), *Women and International Human Rights Law* (Volume 1, Transnational Publishers Inc 1999) 624.

113 Arati Rao, 'The politics of gender and culture in International Human Rights discourse' in Dorothy Hodgson (ed), *Gender and Culture at the Limits of Rights* (University of Pennsylvania Press 2011) 169.

114 Susan Moller Okin, 'Is multiculturalism bad for women?' in Susan Okin (eds), *Is Multiculturalism Bad for Women?* (Princeton University Press 1999) 13. Rhoda Howard, 'Women's rights in English-Speaking Sub-Saharan Africa' in Claude E., Jr. Welch (ed), *Human Rights and Development in Africa* (State University of New York Printers 1984) 46.

115 Sally Engle Merry, 'Human Rights Law and the Demonization of Culture (and Anthropology Along the Way)' (2003) 26 *PoLar* 55, 60.

116 See UN Committee on the Elimination of Discrimination Against Women, 'UN Committee on the Elimination of Discrimination against Women' (10 August 2007) CEDAW/C/COK/CO/1, para 28; UNGA 'Resolution Adopted by the General Assembly' (7 January 1997), para 45; UNCEDAW, 'Concluding Observations on Sixth Report' (10 August 2007) CEDAW/C/NZL/CO/6.

117 UNCEDAW, 'CEDAW General Recommendation No. 23: Political and Public Life' (1997) A/52/38, para 10. See also UNCEDAW, 'CEDAW General Recommendation No. 21: Equality in Marriage and Family Relations' (1994) para 41.

118 Sally F Goldfarb, 'A clash of cultures: women, domestic violence, and the law in the United States' in Dorothy Hodgson (ed), *Gender and Culture at the Limits of Rights* (University of Pennsylvania Press 2011) 69.

119 Ibid.

120 Ibid.

121 Rupa Reddy, 'Gender, Culture and the Law: Approaches to "Honor" Crimes in the UK' (2008) 16 *Feminist Legal Studies* 305.
122 Ibid.
123 Ibid.
124 A An-Na'im, 'State responsibility under International Human Rights Law to change Religious and Customary Law' in Rebecca Cook (ed), *Human Rights of Women: National and International Perspectives* (University of Pennsylvania Press 1994) 167. See also A An-Na'im, 'The Rights of Women in International Law in the Muslim Context' (1987) 9 *Whitter Law Review* 491.
125 Ibid.
126 United Nations, 'Report of the Committee on the Elimination of Discrimination against Women' (17 January 2000) A/55/38, para 6–7.
127 AE Meyer, 'Book Review' (1992) 14 *Human Rights Quarterly* 527.

Bibliography

Addo MK, 'Practice of United Nations Human Rights Treaty Bodies in the Reconciliation of Cultural Diversity with Universal Respect for Human Rights' (2010) 32 *Human Rights Quarterly* 601.

An-Na'im A, 'Religious Minorities under Islamic Law and the Limits of Cultural Relativism' (1987) 9 *Human Rights Quarterly* 1.

An-Na'im A, 'The Rights of Women in International Law in the Muslim Context' (1987) 9 *Whitter Law Review* 491.

An-Na'im A, 'Islam, Islamic Law and the Dilemma of Cultural Legitimacy for Universal Human Rights' in Claude E Welch, Jr. and Virginia A Leary (eds), *Asian Perspectives on Human Rights* (Westview Press, 1990).

An-Na'im A, 'Problems and Prospects of Universal Cultural Legitimacy for Human Rights' in A An-Na'im and FM Deng (eds), *Human Rights in Africa: Cross Cultural Perspectives* (Brookings Institution, 1990).

An-Na'im A, *Toward an Islamic Reformation: Civil Liberties, Human Rights, and International Law* (Syracuse University Press, 1990).

An- Na'im A, 'Cultural Transformation and Normative Consensus on the Best Interests of the Child' (1994) 8 *International Journal of Law and the Family* 62, 68.

An-Na'im A, 'State Responsibility Under International Human Rights Law to Change Religious and Customary Law' in Rebecca Cooks (ed), *Human Rights of Women: National and International Perspectives* (University of Pennsylvania Press, 1994).

An-Na'im A, 'Introduction' in A An-Na'im (ed), *Human Rights in Cross Cultural Perspectives: A Quest for Consensus* (University of Pennsylvania Press, 1995).

An-Na'im A, 'Toward a Cross Culture Approach to Defining International Standards of Human Right: The Meaning of Cruel, Inhuman or Degrading Treatment' in Abdullahi An-Naim (ed), *Human Rights in Cross Cultural Perspectives: A Quest for Consensus* (University of Pennsylvania Press, 1995).

An-Na'im A, 'Toward an Islamic Hermeneutics for Human Rights' in A An-Na'im, Jernald D Gort, Henry Jansen and Hendrik M Vroom (eds), *Human Rights and Religious Values: An Uneasy Relationship?* (William B. Eerdmans Publishing Company, 1995).

An-Na'im A, 'The Contingent Universality of Human Rights: The Case of Freedom of Expression in African and Islamic Context' (1997) 11 *Emory International Law Review* 29.

An-Na'im A, 'The Cultural Mediation of Human Rights: The Al-Arqam Case in Malaysia' in Joanne R. Bauer and Daniel A. Bell (eds), *The East Asian Challenge for Human Rights* (Cambridge University Press, 1999).

An-Na'im A and Hammond J, 'Cultural Transformation and Human Rights in African Societies' in A An-Na'im and J Hammond (eds), *Cultural Transformation in African Societies* (Zed Books, 2000).

Ashford N, *Human Rights: What They Are and What They Are Not* (Libertarian Alliance, 1995).

Bay C, 'Self Respect as a Human Rights: Thoughts on the Dialects of Wants and Needs' (1982) 4 *Human Rights Quarterly* 53.

Bell L, 'Who Produces Asian Identity? Discourse, Discrimination, and Chinese Peasant Women in the Quest for Human Rights' in L Bell, A Nathan and I Peleg (eds), *Negotiating Culture and Human Rights* (Colombia University Press, 2001).

Benedict R, *Patterns of Culture* (Routledge & K. Paul, 1961).

Binder G, 'Cultural Relativism and Cultural Imperialism in Human Rights Law' (1999) 5 *Buffalo Human Rights Law Review* 211.

Boas F, *The Mind of Primitive Man* (Forgotten Books, 2012) 149.

Bunch C, 'Transforming Human Rights from a Feminist Perspective' in Julie Peters and Andrea Wolper (eds), *Women's Rights, Human Rights: International Feminist Perspective* (Routledge, 1995) 13.

Bunch C and Frost S, 'Women's Human Rights: An Introduction' in Cheris Kramarae and Dale Spender (eds), *Routledge International Encyclopedia of Women: Global Women's Issues and Knowledge* (Routledge, 2000).

Cafagna A, 'A Formal Analysis of Definitions of Culture' in Gertrude E Dole and Robert L Carneiro (eds), *Essays in the Science of Culture: In Honor of Leslie A White* (Thomas Y Cromwell, 1960).

Cerna C, 'Universality of Human Rights and Cultural Diversity: Implementation of Human Rights in Different Socio – Cultural Contexts' (1994) 16 *Human Rights Quarterly* 740.

Cerna C and Wallace J, 'Women and Culture' in Kelly D Askin and Dorean M Koenig (eds), *Women and International Human Rights Law* (Volume 1, Transnational Publishers Inc, 1999).

Charlesworth H, 'Human Rights as Men's Rights' in Julie Peters and Andrea Wolper (eds), *Women's Rights, Human Rights: International Feminist Perspective* (Routledge, 1995).

Charlesworth H, Chinkin C and Wright S, 'Feminist Approaches to International Law' (1991) 85 *American Journal of International Law* 613.

Cranston M, *What are Human Rights* (2nd edn, Taplinger, 1973).

De Sousa Santos B, 'Toward a Multicultural Conception of Human Rights' in Bertea Esperanza Hermansex-Truyol (ed), *A Critical Moral Imperialism Anthology* (New York University Press, 2002).

Dembour M, 'Following the Movement of a Pendulum: Between Universalism and Relativism' in Jane Cowan, Marie-Benedicte Dembour and Richard Wilson (eds), *Culture and Rights: Anthropological Perspectives* (Cambridge University Press, 2001).

Dijk VP, 'The Law of Human Rights in Europe: Instruments and Procedures for a Uniform Implementation' in Academy of European Law (eds), *Collected Courses of the Academy of European Law* (Volume VI Book 2, Kluwer Law International, 1997) 1.

Donnelly J, 'Human Rights as Natural Rights' (1982) 4 *Human Rights Quarterly* 391.

Donnelly J, 'Cultural Relativism and Universal Human Rights' in J Donnelly (ed), *Universal Human Rights in Theory and Practice* (Cornell University Press, 1989).

Donnelly J, 'Human Rights: A New Standard of Civilization? (1998) 74 *International Affairs* 1.

Donnelly J, *Universal Human Rights: in Theory and Practice* (3rd edn, Cornell University Press, 2013).

Donoho L, 'Relativism versus Universality in Human Rights: The Search for Meaningful Standards' (1990–1991) 27 *Stanford Journal of International Law* 345.

Eliot TS, *Notes Toward the Definition of Culture* (Faber and Faber, 1948).

Ertürk Y, 'Report of the Special Rapporteur on Violence Against Women, Its Causes and Consequences: Intersections Between Culture and Violence Against Women' (United Nations General Assembly 17 January 2007) A/HRC/4/34.

Falk R, 'Cultural Foundations for the International Protection of Human Rights' in AA An-Na'im (ed), *Human Rights in Cross Cultural Perspectives* (University of Pennsylvania, Press 1995).

Geertz C, *Interpretations of Cultures* (Basic Books, 1973).

Gewirth A, *Human Rights: Essays on Justification and Application* (University of Chicago Press, 1982).

Goldfarb SF, 'A Clash of Cultures: Women, Domestic Violence, and the Law in the United States' in Dorothy Hodgson (ed), *Gender and Culture at the Limits of Rights* (University of Pennsylvania Press, 2011).

Griffiths A, 'Gendering Culture: Towards a Plural Perspective on Kwena Women's Rights' in Jane Cowan, Marie-Benedicte Dembour and Richard Wilson (eds), *Culture and Rights: Anthropological Perspectives* (Cambridge University Press, 2001).

Hatch E, *Cultural and Morality: The Relativity of Values in Anthropology* (Columbia University Press, 1983).

Hernandez-Truyol B, 'Women's Rights and Human Rights- Rule, Realities and the Role of Culture: A Formula for Reform' (1995–1996) 21 *Brooklyn Journal of International Law* 605, 630–631

Hernandez-Truyol B, 'Human Rights through a Gendered Lens: Emergence, Evolution, Revolution' in Kelly D Askin and Dorean M Koenig (eds), *Women and International Human Rights Law* (Volume 1, Transnational Publishers Inc, 1999).

Herskovitz MJ, *Cultural Dynamics* (Knopf, 1964).

Howard R. 'Women's Rights in English- Speaking Sub-Saharan Africa' in Claude E. Jr. Welch (ed), *Human Rights and Development in Africa* (State University of New York Printers, 1984).

Ibhawoh B, 'Between Culture and Constitution: Evaluating the Cultural Legitimacy of Human Rights in the African State' (2000) 22 *Human Rights Quarterly* 838.

Iovane M, 'The Universality of Human Rights and the International Protection of Cultural Diversity: Some Theoretical and Practical Considerations' (2007) 14 *International Journal on Minority and Group Rights* 231.

Jarvie IC, 'Rationalism and Relativism' (1983) 34 *The British Journal of Sociology* 45.

Joyner C and Dettling J, 'Bridging the Cultural Chasm: Cultural Relativism and the Future of International Law' (1990) 20 *California Western International Law Journal* 275.

Khun T, *The Essential Tension: Selected Studies in Scientific Tradition and Change* (University of Chicago Press, 1979).

Lenzerini F, *The Culturalization of Human Rights Law* (Oxford University Press, 2014).

Li X, *Ethics, Human Rights and Culture: Beyond Relativism and Culture* (Palgrave Macmillan, 2006).

Lindholm T, 'Coming to Terms with Traditions' in H Hoibraden and I Gullvag (eds), *Essays in Pragmatic Philosophy* (Norwegian University Press, 1985).

Lindholt L, 'The African Charter: Contextual Universality' in Kirsten Hastrup (ed), *Human Rights on Common Grounds: The Quest for Universality* (Kluwer Law International, 2001).

Maoulidi S, 'Between Law and Culture: Contemplating Rights for Women in Zanzibar' in Dorothy Hodgson (ed), *Gender and Culture at the Limits of Rights* (University of Pennsylvania Press, 2011).

Merry S, 'Constructing a Global Law-Violence against Women and the Human Rights System' (2003) *Law and Social Enquiry* 28: 941.

Merry S, *Human Rights and Gender Violence: Translating International Law Into Local Justice* (The University of Chicago Press, 2006) 90.

Merry S, 'Human Rights Law and the Demonization of Culture (And Anthropology Along the Way)' (2003) 26 *PoLAR* 55.

Mertus J, 'State Discriminatory Family Law and Customary Values' in Julie Peters and Andrea Wolper (eds), *Women's Rights, Human Rights: International Feminist Perspective* (Routledge, 1995).

Meyer AE, 'Book Review' (1992) 14 *Human Rights Quarterly* 527.

Meyer W, 'Toward a Global Culture: Human Rights, Group Rights and Cultural Relativism' (1996) 3 *International Journal on Group Rights* 169.

Mullerson R, *Human Rights Diplomacy* (Routledge, 1997).

Muntarbhorn V, 'The Universality of Standards', lecture at the René Cassin International Institute of Human Rights, July 1993 cited in Civic M, 'A Comparative Analysis of International and Chinese Human Rights Law – Universality Versus Cultural Relativism' (1995–1996) 2 *Buffalo Journal of International Law* 285.

Mushkat R, 'Culture and International Law: Universalism and Relativism' (2002) 6 *Singapore Journal of International and Comparative Law* 1028.

Obermeyer CM, 'A Cross-Cultural Perspective on Reproductive Rights' (1995) 17 *Human Rights Quarterly* 366.

Obiora LA, 'Feminism, Globalization, and Culture: After Beijing' (1997) 4 *Indian Journal of Global Legal Studies* 355.

Okin SM, 'Is Multiculturalism Bad for Women?' in Susan Okin (eds), *Is Multiculturalism Bad for Women?* (Princeton University Press, 1999).

Peach LJ, 'Are Women Human? The Promise and Perils of "Women's Rights as Human Rights"' in Lynda Bell, Andrew Nathan and Ilan Peieg (eds), *Negotiating Culture and Human Rights* (Columbia University Press, 2001).

Pearce WB and Kang K, 'Conceptual Migrations: Understanding Travellers' Tales for Cross Culture adaptation' in YY Kim and WB Gudykunst (eds), *Cross Cultural Adaptation: Current Approaches* (Sage Publications, 1988).

Perry M, *The Idea of Human Rights: Four Inquires* (Oxford University Press, 1998).

Pietilä H and Vickers J, *Making Women Matter: The Role of the United Nations* (Zed Books Limited, 1990).

Powell C, 'Introduction: Locating Culture, Identity, and Human Rights' (1999) 30 *Columbia Human Rights Law Review* 201.

Preis A, 'Human Rights as a Cultural Practice: An Anthropological Critique' (1996) 18 *Human Rights Quarterly* 286.

Raday F, 'Culture, Religion, and Gender' (2003) 1 *International Journal of Constitutional Law* 663.

Rao A , 'The Politics of Gender and Culture in International Human Rights Discourse' in Dorothy Hodgson (ed), *Gender and Culture at the Limits of Rights* (University of Pennsylvania Press, 2011).

Reddy R, 'Gender, Culture and the Law: Approaches to "honor" crimes in the UK' (2008) 16 *Feminist Legal Studies* 305.

Renteln A, 'The Unanswered Challenge of Relativism and the Consequences for Human Rights' (1985) 7 *Human Rights Quarterly* 514.

Renteln A, 'Relativism and the Search for Human Rights' (1988) 90 *American Anthropologist* 56, 78.

Renteln A, *International Human Rights: Universalism versus Cultural Relativism* (Quid Pro Book, 2013).

Schooley K, 'Cultural Sovereignty, Islam, and Human Rights-Toward a Communitarian Revision' (1994–1995) 25 *Cumberland Law Review* 651.

Short S, 'Listening to "the other"? The Convention on the Rights of the Child' (2011) 2 *Melbourne General of International Law* 305.

Sloane R, 'Outrelativising Relativism: A Liberal Defence of the Universality of International Human Rights' (2001) 34 *Vanderbilt Journal of Transnational Law* 527.

Spaak T, 'Moral Relativism and Human Rights' (2007) 13 *Buffalo Human Rights Law Review* 73.

Sullivan D, 'The Public/Private Distinction in International Human Rights Law' in Julie Peters and Andrea Wolper (eds), *Women's Rights, Human Rights: International Feminist Perspective* (Routledge, 1995).

Taylor C, 'Conditions of an Unenforced Consensus on Human Rights' in Joanne A Bauer and Daniel A Bell (eds), *The East Asian Challenge for Human Rights* (Cambridge University Press, 1999).

Tesón RF, 'International Human Rights and Cultural Relativism' (1984–1985) 25 *Virginia Journal of International Law* 869.

The Executive Board, American Anthropological Association, 'Statement on Human Rights' (1947) 49 *American Anthropologist* 539.

UN Committee on the Elimination of Discrimination against Women, 'UN Committee on the Elimination of Discrimination Against Women' (10 August 2007) CEDAW/C/COK/CO/1.

UNCEDAW, 'CEDAW General Recommendation No. 21: Equality in Marriage and Family Relations' (1994).

UNCEDAW, 'CEDAW General Recommendation No. 23: Political and Public Life' (1997) A/52/38.

UNGA, 'Resolution Adopted by the General Assembly' (7 January 1997), para 45; UNCEDAW, 'Concluding Observations on sixth report' (10 August 2007) CEDAW/C/NZL/CO/6.

UNHRC, 'Report of the Human Rights Council on Its Eighth Session' (1 September 2008) A/HRC/8/52.

UNHRC, 'Report of the Working Group on the Universal Periodic Review: Cameroon' (5 July 2013) A/HRC/24/15.

United Nations, 'Report of the Committee on the Elimination of Discrimination against Women' (17 January 2000) A/55/38.

Wasserston R, 'Rights, Human Rights and Racial Discrimination' (1964) 61 *Journal of Philosophy* 628.

Williams R, *Keywords: A Vocabulary of Culture and Society* (Oxford University Press, 1976).

Zaunbrecher LK, 'When Culture Hurts: Dispelling the Myth of Cultural Justification for Gender based Human Rights Violation' (2011) 33 *Houston Journal of International Law* 679.

Zwart T, 'Using Local Culture to Further the Implementation of International Human Rights: The Receptor Approach' (2012) 32 *Human Rights Quarterly* 546.

3 Description of the Research Method and Methodology

Introduction

The previous chapter contextualised the inherent relationship between women's rights and culture within the debate of universalism and cultural relativism. It discussed that as the issues and concerns of women's rights are more susceptible to the challenges of the various different formulations of cultural relativism, and as such, there were strong theoretical justifications for the selection of women's rights issues for the purposes of this investigation. Following from this, the aim of this chapter is to provide a reasoned account of the research methods employed for this research project. This chapter will show how the choices and methodological approaches adopted throughout this investigation were carefully and consciously selected with the ultimate aim of addressing the research aims and objectives of this study. The chapter is divided into three main sections. The first section will explain why analysis was the most suitable method to answer the research question of this study. The second section will provide a detailed description of the research design that is adopted for this investigation. The final section will explain the method of interpretation of the data, as well as illustrate how the findings of this research project will be presented in the next three chapters of this book.

Research Method: A Documentary Analysis

Authors of social research methods, such as Judy Payne and Geoff Payne, describe documentary research as investigating, categorising, and interpreting written documents that are in the public domain.[1] The significance of using documents in a research project is emphasised by Lindsay Prior, who writes that 'a document, especially a document in use, can be considered as a site or field of research in itself'.[2] When undertaking documentary research, Jennifer Platt writes that the focus is first, to describe how the documents were examined to answer the research question and second, to assess the quality of the documents used for the study.[3] For the first requirement, for the purposes of this investigation, there are a total of three reports produced at the conclusion of each state reviewed in the Universal Periodic Review (UPR) process. These are the Final Outcome Report, an addendum (if any), and any statements made at the HRC plenary hearing, a record of which is provided in an HRC Session Report. The Final Outcome Reports, together with the supplementary documents, are the primary source of data to analyse as the reports provide a written account of arguably the 'core element' of the entire process, the interactive dialogue session.[4] Therefore, all three reports, for each of the 193 member states reviewed under the process were examined for two full cycles of review. In other words, all the documentation produced as part of the review was examined for both complete cycles at the time of writing. In terms of accessing these reports, there are a number of different databases available, which store all the documents that are used and produced as part of the UPR process. These include United Nations UPR Home,[5] UPR Info,[6] UPR Watch,[7] and the UPR process pages on the International Service Human Rights Website.[8] The official United Nations UPR home website, which was found to be the most informative and accessible, was the primary source from which the data for this study has been gathered.

Lindsay Prior writes that an evaluation of the quality of the documents examined is an important part of any social scientific research project.[9] John Scott provides authoritative criteria to assess the quality of documents to be analysed.[10] For the purposes of this investigation, the most relevant aspects of Scott's criteria for assessing the quality of the documents are the *creditability* and *meaning* of the Final Outcome Reports, and other supplementary material, that were to be examined for this investigation.[11]

The criterion of credibility is concerned with the accuracy of the content of the Final Outcome Reports and the other supplementary reports. There are two main concerns that need to be discussed in relation to the accuracy of the documents. The first is that the Final Outcome Reports are a summary of the interactive dialogue session.[12] As a result, some omissions and the risk of inaccuracies are inevitable. It was therefore significant to assess the extent to which the reports were summarised, and whether the reports continued to provide a true reflection of the nature of the discussions held amongst states in the interactive dialogue session. To this end, a small investigatory project was undertaken to observe the oral reviews of ten selected member states through the video archives obtained from the UPR Info's website.[13] To ensure that the ten selected states represented a wide geographical spread, two states were selected from each of the five UN regional groups.[14] This method was the only way of ensuring that a fair and achievable sample of states was observed for the purposes of this task. The states selected for review were: Burkina Faso, Gambia, Bahrain, India, Slovakia, Poland, the United Kingdom, France, Dominican Republic, and Costa Rica.[15] The sessions were observed with the aim of comparing the dialogue exchanged between states during the interactive session with the written record, which is summarised in the Final Outcome Reports. Any omissions and inaccuracies that were recorded in the report when compared to the video recording were noted down. From these observations, it was revealed that the recommendations that were issued to the state under review by observer states were all recorded with word-for-word accuracy in the Final Outcome Reports. However, the other statements made by states during the interactive dialogue session were not recorded with such accuracy. Nevertheless, the key words mentioned in the oral review by the states were recorded, which meant that the overall gist of the message recorded in the report was clear and accurate. It is also to be noted that the reports are adopted with consensus from all the parties involved during the Working Group sessions and in the HRC sessions. Thus, the state under review and the observer states are given an opportunity to voice any concerns in relation to possible inaccuracies of the statements recorded in the reports.[16] Overall, the Final Outcome Reports represented an accurate summary of the oral review undertaken of states in the interactive dialogue session, and thus met the criterion of creditability.[17]

The second issue of concern in relation to creditability was the implications of the translation of the UPR process documents. The state representatives in the interactive dialogue session often speak in their native languages. A live translating service is available to listen to for the other state representatives present during the review. These discussions, and other supplementary documents, are then translated into the six official languages of the United Nations: Arabic, Chinese, English, French, Russian, and Spanish. The process of translating oral discussions into the six official languages means that an element of inaccuracy will arise in the Final Outcome Reports.[18] However, the implications for such potential inaccuracies are minimal for the purposes of this investigation for two main reasons.

First, as noted above, one of the most fundamental aspects of the discussions is the recommendations issued, and these were noted with total accuracy. In addition, due to the participatory nature of the UPR process, the states approve the accuracy of the recommendations and responses are noted in the reports at the HRC plenary session.[19] Therefore this restricts the implications of potential inaccuracies that may arise during the translation process to a minimum. Second, the fundamental aim of this investigation is not to undertake a purely semantic analysis of the documents. In contrast, the aim of this investigation is to undertake an analysis of the nature of discussions held between states at the interactive dialogue session. This will be undertaken by analysing the nature of the recommendations issued, and the corresponding responses made by the participating states. In this way, the statements will be examined in a holistic manner, in order to understand the nature of positions adopted by states during the review process. From this, an accurate picture will be able to be formed of how the UPR process operates through the positions adopted by the states, rather than undertaking a purely semantic analysis of the statements.

The second relevant criterion to assess the quality of the documents for the purposes of this investigation is 'meaning', which required an assessment to ensure the documents that are to be examined are clear and comprehensible.[20] The HRC Resolution 5/1 provides that the documents prepared in advance of a state review must be made available in one of the six official languages.[21] Despite this, the Final Outcome Reports for some states consisted of segments which were in French, despite the report itself being categorised as being in English on the UN website or on the UPR Info website. This was the case for Senegal, Central African Republic, Chad, Comoros, and the addendum report for Niger. Whilst these segments formed a small part of the overall reports, the responses by the states under review in the interactive dialogue were essential parts for this research project and, as such, these segments were translated to ensure all the reports were analysed in their entirety.

The Research Design

For the purposes of this project, the Qualitative Content Analysis (QCA) approach in interpreting and analysing the Final Outcome Reports was used. In the most general terms, QCA is a method used to describe and analyse the meaning of the qualitative material in a systematic way to address the aims and objectives of a study.[22] Holsti describes content analysis as:

> Any technique for making inferences by objectively and systematically identifying specified characteristics of messages. Content analysis must be objective and systematic, and, if it is to be distinguished from information retrieval, indexing or similar enterprises, it must be undertaken for some theoretical reason.[23]

In this way, to avoid simple data indexing or retrieval, the research question of this investigation provides a theoretical angle from which the data was collected, interpreted, and analysed. The QCA strategy was used to systematically confine the material available on the UPR process to focus on the specific data which was relevant to the theoretical framework of this study.[24] The following section will provide an explanation of this process in more detail.

Confining the Data to Be Analysed Using Qualitative Content Analysis

This investigation focuses on the first two cycles of review of the UPR process. The first cycle of reviews was undertaken between 2008 and 2011, and the second cycle between 2012 and 2016. An analysis of the first two cycles of review is beneficial not only to gauge an accurate picture of two complete cycles of review, but also to draw comparisons of how the issues are different over the two cycles of review. At the time of writing, member states are being reviewed under the third cycle of review being undertaken between 2017 and 2021.

During the review of member states in the first cycle of the UPR process, a vast number of human rights issues and concerns were raised. Naturally, an examination of all the reports in relation to all of the human rights issues was unfeasible, as the final analysis would lack both focus and depth. In light of this, a reasoned and theoretically informed selection was made from the range of human rights issues that were raised in the UPR process. A total of 55 different human rights issues were raised over the two cycles of reviews. The next task was to establish which of these human rights issues were most commonly raised in the reviews of member states in the UPR process over the two cycles. In order to quantify this, the database and search mechanism tools provided on the UPR Info website were used.[25] On the website, under the database tab, each human rights issue was selected in the search tool, and then the recommendations filter was selected.[26] This generated details of the recommendations made on a particular human rights issue in the UPR system, together with the name of the state receiving it. The number of recommendations made for each human rights issue, over the two cycles, is presented in Figures 3.1 and 3.2.

A total of 32,964 recommendations were issued in the first cycle, and a significantly greater number of 58,364 recommendations were issued in the second cycle. Of these, recommendations in relation to women's rights amounted to a total of 3712 recommendations in the first cycle, and a total of 7006 in the

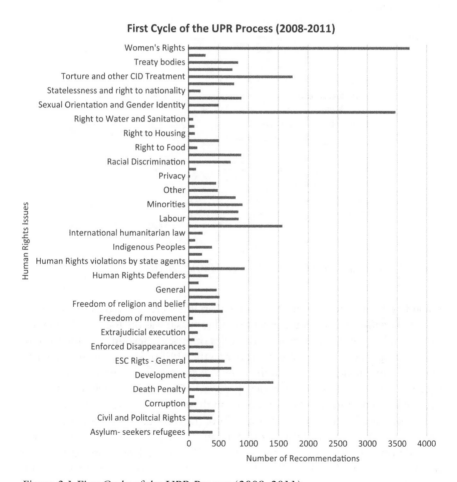

Figure 3.1 First Cycle of the UPR Process (2008–2011).

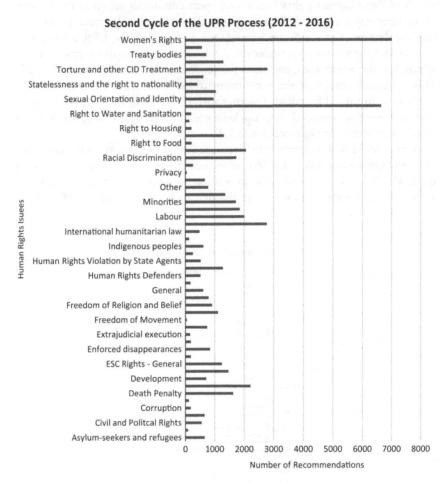

Figure 3.2 Second Cycle of the UPR Process (2012–2016).

second cycle of review. From this, women's rights were selected as the focus for this investigation as it was numerically significant as it was the focus of the highest number of recommendations in both cycles of review. Beyond this, the issue of women's rights was clearly of significance to the UPR process as in the establishing resolution; it clearly specified that a review must 'fully integrate a gender perspective' into all aspects of the review process.[27] The importance attached to the issue of women's rights is clearly reflected in the two cycles of reviews as women's rights amounted to a total of just over 17% of the recommendations issued in the first cycle, and over 12% of the recommendations for the second cycle of reviews. In addition, all 193 member states of the UN received recommendations on the issue of women's rights when their human rights records were reviewed. Of the recommendations that were issued, a total of 9136 recommendations were accepted, which means over 85% of the recommendations on women's rights were accepted by the states under review. These statistics indicate, that at least formally, there are grounds to presume that there is a wider-ranging consensus amongst states on the implementation of women's rights as guaranteed under numerous international human rights instruments.[28]

Overall, the number of recommendations issued to states on women's rights, together with the nature of responses made by the states under review, demonstrates that the issue of women's rights was a widespread concern amongst states during the discussions held in the two cycles of state reviews. In this way, the selection of women's rights as the focus of this investigation ensured it was not confined to the examination of reviews of particular member states or regional groups. Beyond the numerical justifications for the selection of women's rights for the purposes of this investigation, as discussed in the previous chapter, there are theoretical reasons for the selection of women's rights. The critique of cultural relativism to the proclamation of universal human rights on the discourse of international human rights is the theoretical framework for analysis for this investigation. In light of this, issues and concerns that relate to women are more susceptible to the claims of culture.[29] The reasons behind this phenomenon can be explained through the existence of the public and private divide that is present in a number of human rights documents.[30] Women's primary role has traditionally been to preserve and maintain family and domestic life, and therefore, their issues and concerns are often relegated to the private sphere.[31] However, whereas the public sphere is often considered to be subject to regulation and scrutiny by the states, the issues that fall within the private sphere are often informed and governed by cultural values and traditions.[32] Women are sometimes considered to represent 'the reproduction of the community' and pass on the beliefs of culture to the next generation.[33] In this way, a woman's behaviour has often become a visible symbolisation of the beliefs of any particular culture.[34] Consequently as the sustenance of cultural boundaries is sometimes considered to be solely the responsibility of women, the rights of women are most susceptible and fragile to the claims of culture and cultural relativism.[35] Following from this, any defence of

> cultural practices is likely to have much greater impact on the lives of women and girls than on those of men and boys, since far more women's time and energy goes into preserving and maintaining the personal, familial and reproductive side of life.[36]

Arati Rao argues that 'no social group has suffered greater violation of its human rights in the name of culture than women'.[37] In this way, a challenge to the universality of human rights from a cultural relativist perspective is often made in relation to issues that most commonly form part of the private sphere.[38]

It is primarily due to this increased susceptibility of the challenge to the universality of women's rights from a cultural relativist perspective that the issue of women' rights has been selected as the focus for this investigation. Therefore, in answering the research question of this thesis, the selection of women's rights is important, as any arguments from a cultural relativist position are more likely to be introduced, explicitly or implicitly, in areas concerning women's rights.

The Method of Selecting Specific Women's Rights Issues

So far, this investigation has been narrowed down by selecting women's rights as the focus for this study. Despite this selection, it was clear that the category of women's rights itself covered a number of specific issues. Thus, the next stage of the research process was to identify emerging women's rights issues that commonly formed the focus of discussions in the UPR process. For the purposes of this task, all the recommendations over both cycles were examined with the aim of uncovering detailed and specific issues raised in relation to women's rights. The final recommendations were examined because they are issued after a statement or discussion was undertaken on any particular human rights issue. In this way, the recommendations gave an accurate reflection of the issues that were discussed during interactive dialogue in the UPR process. As the recommendations were examined, specific women's rights issues that were raised in each recommendation were noted down. A total of 30 women's rights issues were identified that were the focus of recommendations over the two cycles of review, as depicted in Figure 3.3.

An examination, presentation, and analysis of all 30 women's rights issues was not plausible for the purposes of this book. Therefore, the strategy of *reductive coding* was employed to further narrow down the focus of this study within the remit of women's rights. Reductive coding is a form of indexing, whereby pieces of data are categorised under labels or codes.[39] The aim of reductive coding is to group together data that addresses the same theme, or where there is a link between the data.[40] This form of coding is carried out purely to reduce large amounts of data to a few general categories.[41]

Using the method of reductive coding, the 30 women's rights issues were grouped into categories, under a common theme. If a particular women's rights issue could not be grouped with another, it became a category in its own right, which may be grouped with another category examined later. Using the reductive coding strategy, the women's rights issues were grouped together into a total of six women's rights categories. There were: (1) women's rights to health, (2) private family law, (3) violence against women, (4) equality, (5) rights of minorities, and (6) international human rights instruments/general category of rights. From the six categories, three were selected as the focus for investigating the UPR process. The three women's rights categories that were selected each included a total of three women's rights issues. Therefore, in total I examined nine women's rights issues as the focus for this investigation.

The first category selected as the focus for this research was women's rights to health, which was the subject of 868 recommendations over the two cycles. This category consisted of three issues: (i) Female Genital Mutilation (FGM), which was the subject of 503 recommendations; (ii) abortion, which had 140 recommendations made in relation to it; and (iii) access to health care services, which

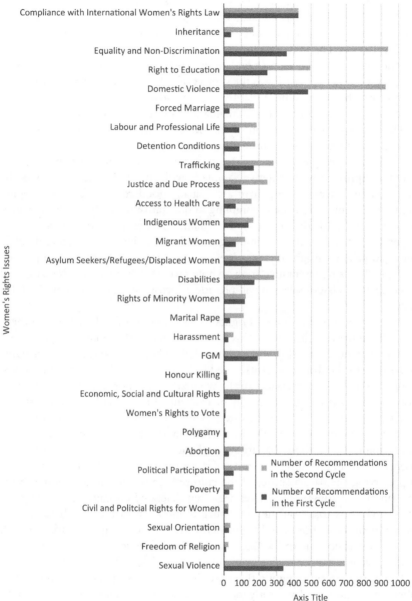

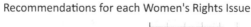

Figure 3.3 Recommendations for each Women's Rights Issue.

was the subject of 225 recommendations. The second category selected as a focus for this investigation was women's rights under private family law, which was the subject of 434 recommendations. This category consisted of three issues. The first was polygamy, which was the subject of 22 recommendations; the second was the issue of inheritance which was associated with 208 recommendations; and finally, the issue of forced and early marriage, which was the focus of 204 recommendations. The third category selected was violence against women, which was the subject of 1585 recommendations. This category consists of three issues: (i) domestic violence, which was the subject of 1407 recommendations; (ii) marital rape, which was the subject of 146 recommendations; and (iii) honour killing, which was the subject of 32 recommendations in the UPR process.

The reasons for the selection of the three women's rights categories as the focus of this investigation is primarily because unlike in a quantitative research study, there is heavy emphasis on the importance of ensuring that the data collected comprises a representative sample,[42] with qualitative research, as is the nature of this investigation, there are 'usually good reasons for side-stepping this requirement'.[43] The use of sampling in qualitative research is to 'refine ideas rather than to satisfy the demands of calculation'.[44] For qualitative research studies, pragmatic and purposive sampling is used, which involves selecting the data purely to gain an insight into a process or organisation, rather than to provide a sample that is representative of the whole process.[45] In this way, the sample of women's rights issues selected will provide a focused insight into how the UPR operates.

The selection of the women's rights issues is also justified based on the theoretical framework of this study. This is because each of the women's rights issues has an inherent relationship with culture. This is because the violations of rights under each of the women's rights issued have been justified on cultural grounds. In other words, the universality of the women's rights norms in relation to each women's rights issue can potentially be challenged from a cultural relativist perspective. For example, under the category of women's rights to health there are three women's rights issues: FGM, abortion, and access to health care services. In relation to FGM, those that are sympathetic to the practice argue that FGM is inseparable from the cultural identity of the groups, and is defended on the basis of preserving the particularities of the culture.[46] In relation to abortion, a blanket ban on accessing such services are often defended on cultural and religious norms, which is based on the belief that all life is inviolable, which extends to the rights of the unborn child.[47] Further, often women's rights to access health care services is not due to the lack of availability of services, but the existence of cultural barriers which prevent women from accessing such services.[48]

Under the second category, there are three women's rights issues: polygamy, inheritance, and forced and early marriage. Each of these issues is open to claims based on cultural grounds. For example, those that are sympathetic to polygamous marriages often argue such marriages are mandated on cultural or religious grounds.[49] In addition, the exclusion of women's rights to acquire land

and property through inheritance is justified on the culturally held belief that women are expected to subsume to their male counterparts, and therefore should not have legal identity on title deeds.[50] Finally, those sympathetic to forced and early marriages of girls and women often justify such marriages on the culturally conceptualised notion to prevent 'shame' on the family. [51]

The third category of violence against women consists of three issues: honour killing, marital rape, and domestic violence. For instance, the perpetrators of honour killing are motivated by a culturally conceptualised notion of honour, which the female victim has apparently defied.[52] The issue of marital rape is often tolerated on the presumption of women's consent to sexual activity in relation to marriage, which is influenced by cultural attitudes towards the subordinate role of women, which mould the acceptability of sexual violence within a marriage.[53] Finally, domestic violence is often perpetuated and tolerated through deeply held cultural norms that treat women as 'wayward creatures who require chastisement for their own or society's good'. [54]

From this, it can be seen that each of the women's rights issues selected have an inherent relationship with culture. Therefore, there is a possibility that observer states will draw on references to culture when making criticisms on issues that fall within the three women's rights categories in the review process. In light of this, it is likely that the states under review, when responding to criticisms on these issues, will introduce arguments from a cultural relativist position. Thus, the hypothesis is that cultural relativist positions will be exercised, either implicitly or explicitly and to varying degrees, by some states when the selected women's rights categories form the focus of discussions in the UPR process.

It is important at this stage to make some remarks on the selection of women's rights issues as the focus of this study. The central aim of this book is to undertake an exploratory investigation of the UPR process. Therefore, the women's rights issues in this investigation are used as a mechanism for exploring the extent to which cultural relativism is raised in the reviews of member states in the UPR process. As such, the aim of this investigation is not to explore or undertake substantive analysis of the individual women's rights issues in themselves. Moreover, it is important to clarify that the aim of this thesis is not to defend or criticise a cultural relativist position for any of the selected women's rights issues.[55] Rather, the focus is on the significance of cultural relativism in the UPR process, and the implications such positions may have in understanding the operation of the review process.

Using the Data and Presenting the Findings

As noted above, for the purposes of this investigation the documents to be examined were the Final Outcome Reports, any addendum and supplementary materials, and the reports of the HRC sessions for all 193 member states over the two cycles. This meant that nearly 1000 reports were analysed for the purposes of this investigation. Therefore, for practical purposes, the Computer Assisted

Qualitative Data Analysis (CAQDAS) software was used to aid this investigation.[56] Alan Bryman writes that 'one of the most notable developments in qualitative research in recent years has been the arrival of computer software that facilitates the analysis of qualitative data'.[57] Such computer programmes allow the researcher to upload reports on the programme, analyse the data by highlighting relevant parts, and then to retrieve the data for further analysis and conclusions. There is a variety of different software available to assist qualitative research; in light of the research aims and objectives for this study, NVivo version 10 was selected to facilitate this research project.[58] This software was particularly suited to the nature of this investigation as it permitted the upload of all of the reports to be examined onto the programme, allowing notes and annotations to be made on the reports themselves.

Methods of Interpretation and Analysis

Once all the reports had been uploaded to the NVivo programme, it was possible to start the process of interpretation and analysis. There are two points that need to be clarified and explained in relation to analysis and interpretation for the purposes of this investigation.

Taking the point of analysis, first: when undertaking documentary analysis, there are two main methods of content analysis: manifest and latent content analysis. Bruce Berg states that manifest content analysis focuses on those elements that are present in the text of the documents.[59] This form of analysis focuses entirely on the 'surface meaning of the text',[60] and therefore focuses on those elements that are physically present in the content of the data.[61] In contrast, latent content analysis is extended to an interpretative reading of the text and focuses 'on the deep structural meaning conveyed by the message'.[62] This method is used to 'analyze the deeper layers of meaning embedded in the document'.[63] The latent content analysis is therefore 'extended to an interpretative reading of the symbolism underlying the physical data'.[64] This form of analysis is comparable to semiotic analysis, founded by Ferdinand de Saussure and Charles Peirce, which is an in-depth method of analysis whereby the researcher goes beyond the literal and face value to 'uncover underlying hidden meaning that is carried in the text'.[65]

As the UPR process in an intergovernmental mechanism, whereby the reviews were undertaken by state representatives, it was highly likely that certain statements or recommendations could be made due to political and diplomatic pressures. More specifically to the research question of the book, states may not openly adopt cultural relativist positions in justifying practices that fell under the women's rights issues selected. Similarly, observer states may not unambiguously criticise a practice that is justified or defended on cultural grounds by the state under review. As a result, states were likely to make statements which implicitly carry assumptions made by the state or implicitly carry a different message. For this reason, for the purposes of this investigation, the latent content method of analysis was adopted to ensure that the final analysis of this project drew out the implicit assumptions and messages in the statements issued by the states in the review process. In this way, a holistic analysis was undertaken of the statements and comments made by the states to understand the nature of the positions adopted by the participating states in the discussion held on the women's rights issues. This form of analysis enabled a fuller understanding of how the UPR process operates through the nature of positions adopted by states during the discussions.

When undertaking latent content analysis in a research project, Berelson stated that whilst it is acceptable to directly *infer* latent meaning in the documents being analysed, the researcher must be aware of the obvious dangers in inferring an interpretation in latent content analysis.[66] To minimise the dangers of inferring a meaning from the document being analysed, he suggests that researchers should adopt 'independent corroborative techniques' to justify this form of 'deciphering' latent content analysis.[67] Suggestions often include agreement from independent coders on the latent interpretation of the text that is coded.[68] However, the aims of this project are restricted to exploring the extent to which cultural relativist positions are raised in the dialogue exchanged between states in the first cycle of review in relation to specific women's rights issues. The aim of this project is not to generalise the findings of this investigation or to predict the mannerisms of review for the second cycle.

With this in mind, the independent corroboration of the latent content meaning will be justified and substantiated using the theoretical framework adopted for this investigation. The positions undertaken by the states in the review process will be verified and confirmed using the different forms of cultural relativism as discussed in the theory chapter. The theoretical framework will also aid in the conclusions derived from the latent content analysis of the data, which will ultimately help answer the research question of this study. In this way, the meanings and interpretations deciphered from the Final Outcome Reports will be justified as the theoretical framework is used to verify any interpretations. In line with the suggestions offered to researchers that undertake latent content analysis detailed excerpts will be provided from the Final Outcome Reports to support the interpretations and analysis in the three findings chapters of this book.[69] In assessing the degree to which cultural relativity is exercised in the UPR process, the Final Outcome Reports were examined using the latent content method of analysis to give the statements a figurative meaning.[70] Such meaning may not necessarily be extracted from the literal meaning of the text, and therefore may be required to be inferred.[71]

In contrast, the manifest content analysis would mean that the focus would be solely on the literal text of the reports. For the purposes of this investigation, this would largely entail a semantic form of analysis, whereby the focus would entirely be on the nature of the words used during the discussions, rather than holistic analysis where the aim is to understand the nature of the positions adopted by the states. The obvious problem with adopting a manifest content analysis for this investigation is due to the construction of the Final Outcome Reports, which means that the accuracy of certain words inevitably suffers from the process of translation of the documents.[72] For this reason, adopting a manifest content analysis of the reports would mean the investigation would lack accuracy and, possibly, creditability. The other problem is that the inherently political nature of the UPR process would mean that manifest content analysis would only lead to a surface-level examination of the UPR process in answering the research question. Therefore, the findings and conclusions of this study would suffer the serious limitation of merely touching the surface of how the UPR operates in practice. In contrast, adopting the latent content analysis means that the final analysis is likely not only to be more insightful, but also to provide a more accurate depiction of the significance of cultural relativism when the focus of discussions was the three selected women's rights categories.

The second point that needs to be clarified is the interpretation of 'culture' when examining the reports. As noted above, it was clear that the states were not likely to explicitly adopt a cultural relativist perspective during the discussions held in the UPR process. Therefore, whilst the method of latent content analysis meant that the analysis undertaken went beyond the mere content of the reports, the precise meaning of 'culture' was important to define to provide a guided focus during the examinations of the reports. As noted in Chapter 2, for the purposes of this book a modern interpretation of culture is adopted. As a brief reminder, culture is interpreted to include a 'totality of values, institutions and forms of behaviour transmitted within a society … this wide conception of culture covers Weltanschauung [world view] ideologies and cognitive behaviour.'[73] In light of this definition, when examining the reports, a careful consideration was made of statements made in relation to key words such as cultural, traditions, customary, patriarchal attitudes, custom, cultural stereotypes, religion, prejudices, and beliefs that are associated with culture.[74] This was a non-exclusive list; however, it helped to focus the analysis during the examination of the reports.

At this point it is important to clarify that a macro definition of culture will be adopted for this project, which subsumes religion and religious values as aspects of culture.[75] Therefore, for the purposes of this investigation, religious norms and arguments will be considered as falling within the definition of culture. However, where states in their discussions expressly isolate religious norms and values in their discussions, then their positions will be analysed and discussed separately in the findings of the investigation to ensure there is no misrepresentation.

Presentation of the Findings of the Investigation

Each of the three women's rights issues will be presented in three separate chapters. Chapter 4 is dedicated to presenting and discussing women's rights to health; Chapter 5 will present the findings of women's rights under private and family law, and Chapter 6 is dedicated to discussing violence against women. The three women's rights issues that fall within each of the women's rights categories will be discussed under three separate sections.

The presentation of the findings of each of the nine women's rights issues follows the same structure. Each section begins with contextualising the specific women's rights issue by discussing the international human rights norms in relation to each issue. This is followed by the findings section, which is divided into two main parts. The first part will present an overview of the findings by providing details of the number of recommendations issued, the regional states that participated in the discussions, and the number of recommendations that were accepted and noted.

This is followed by the second, more significant, and part of the findings section. This section presents the nature of the recommendations that were made in relation to each women's rights issue, which will be encapsulated in a table. As an example, a template is provided in Table 3.1.

The statements made during the interactive dialogue sessions will be divided into two categories: first, the recommendations issued by the observer states and second, the responses provided by the states under review when accepting or noting the recommendations. In the case of both recommendations and responses, the title given to each category summarises the essence of the statement issued, and a number for identification purposes. In this way, a summary of the nature of the recommendations issued by the state under review are listed on the left side of the table, and a summary of the nature of the response is provided across the tables. For example, a recommendation was made that polygamy was a harmful traditional practice that was required to be abolished will be: 'Recommendation 1: Polygamy declared as a Harmful Traditional Practice'. The nature of the responses will be similarly categorised with a title and number. For example, a recommendation accepted by the state under review with no further comments will be labelled 'A1: Accepted with no further comments'. If the recommendation was not accepted, it will be labelled with an 'N', a number, and a summary of the response. The name of the state under review will then be provided within each box according to the recommendation received and the response issued. Naturally, the title of the recommendations and responses will alter depending on the issue being discussed at the interactive dialogue stage. A detailed discussion of the findings will follow the table for each women's rights issue, with excerpts from the interactive dialogue provided for illustrative purposes. The final section is dedicated to discussing and analysing the findings of the research.

Conclusion

This chapter began by explaining why the method of documentary analysis was best suited to answer the research question for this study. This was followed by assessing the quality of the documents that were used for the purposes of this investigation using authoritative criteria provided by John Scott. In the second part of this chapter, details of the research design of this investigation were provided. An explanation was given on the reasons behind the selection of women's rights as the focus for this investigation. A simple numerical analysis of the human rights issues raised in the state reviews of the first cycle of the UPR process, which revealed the significance of women's rights in the review of states in the process.

Table 3.1 Sample Table to Present Findings

Universal Periodic Review Cycle 1	Responses by States under Review					
	A1 *(Title summarising the nature of the response)*	A2 *(Title summarising the nature of the response)*	N1 *(Title summarising the nature of the response)*	N2 *(Title summarising the nature of the response)*	N3 *(Title summarising the nature of the response)*	N4 *(Title summarising the nature of the response)*
Nature of recommendations issued to states under review	**Recommendation 1** (Title summarising the nature of the recommendations) **Recommendation 2** (Title summarising the nature of the recommendations) **Recommendation 3** (Title summarising the nature of the recommendations) **Recommendation 4** (Title summarising the nature of the recommendations)					

Universal Periodic Review Cycle 2	Responses by States under Review					
	A1 (Title summarising the nature of the response)	*A2* (Title summarising the nature of the response)	*N1* (Title summarising the nature of the response)	*N2* (Title summarising the nature of the response)	*N3* (Title summarising the nature of the response)	*N4* (Title summarising the nature of the response)
Nature of recommendations issued to states under review	**Recommendation 1** (Title summarising the nature of the recommendations) **Recommendation 2** (Title summarising the nature of the recommendations) **Recommendation 3** (Title summarising the nature of the recommendations) **Recommendation 4** (Title summarising the nature of the recommendations)					

Following this, a theoretical justification was provided for selecting women's rights as the focus for this investigation by drawing upon the strong association between women and culture, which explained the reasons why the issue of women's rights was significant for this study. The final section of the chapter provided an outline of how the investigation was conducted. The section began by explaining how the data was examined from the Final Outcome Reports with the aid of the NVivo software. The methods of interpretation and analysis adopted for examining the reports was provided, before an overview of how the findings will be presented in the next three chapters of this book.

In conclusion, this chapter provided the details of the research methods employed for the purposes of this investigation, the methodological choices made during the research process of this project were informed and guided by the theoretical framework adopted for this study, with the ultimate aim of answering the research question of this book. Chapters 4, 5, and 6 will present the findings and analysis of this investigation.

Notes

1 Geoff Payne and Judy Payne, *Key Concepts in Social Research* (Sage Publications 2004).
2 Lindsay Prior, 'Using documents in social research' in David Silverman (ed), *Qualitative Research* (3rd edn, Sage Publications 2011) 93.
3 Jennifer Platt, 'Evidence and proof in documentary research: 1 some specific problems of documentary research' (1981) 29 *Sociological Review* 31. See also John Scott, *A Matter of Record: Documentary Sources and Social Research* (Polity Press 1990); Paul Atkinson and Amanda Coffey, 'Analyzing documentary realities' in David Silverman (ed), *Qualitative Research: Theory, Method and Practice* (3rd edn, Sage Publications 2011) 79.
4 Björn Arp, 'Lessons Learned from Spain's Practice before the United Nations Human Rights reporting mechanisms: treaty bodies and universal periodic review' (2011) 15 *Spanish Yearbook of International Law* 1, 13.
5 www.ohchr.org/en/hrbodies/upr/Pages/UPRMain.aspx, accessed 28 August 2019.
6 www.upr-info.org/, 28 August 2019.
7 http://upr-epu.com/ENG/upr.php?act=2&lang=2, accessed 28 August 2019.
8 www.ishr.ch/upr-monitor?task=view, accessed 28 August 2019.
9 Lindsay Prior, 'Using documents in social research' in David Silverman (ed), *Qualitative Research* (3rd edn, Sage Publications 2011) 26. See also John Scott, *A Matter of Record: Documentary Sources and Social Research* (Polity Press 1990).
10 Ibid. 6.
11 Ibid.
12 UNHRC 'Res 5/1 Institution-building of the United Nations Human Rights Council' (18 June 2007) Annex. A/HRC/RES/5/1 para, 26.
13 www.upr-info.org/en/webcast, accessed 28 August 2019.
14 These Are: African Group, Asia-pacific Group, Eastern European Group, Latin American and Caribbean Group and the Western European and Others Group, www.un.org/depts/DGACM/RegionalGroups.shtml, accessed 28 August 2019.
15 I observed the interactive dialogue sessions of the states being reviewed using the webcast records of all states available on both the United Nations website and the

UPR Info Website, http://webtv.un.org/; http://www.upr-info.org/, accessed 28 August 2019.
16 A/HRC/RES/5/1, para 3 (e).
17 To ensure I was working with the most accurate reports available, I contacted the UN Secretariat enquiring whether a database was available with the full written transcripts of the review, before it was summarised as a report. The response was that no such database existed. However, the representative did provide me with a username and password to access the fuller transcript of the statements made by the observer states in the UPR process. I was optimistic at first with the possibility that these fuller statements could provide a richer and a more accurate source of documents to be analysed. However, when I accessed the written statements, I was found that they were produced in the domestic language of the member state, with no English translation available. Moreover, it was stated by the representative of the UN Secretariat that 'those written statement can differ from what was orally said'. Email from Jean-Claude UPR Info to Gayatri Patel (29 July 2013). In light of this, it was decided that seeking translation of such a substantial amount of documents was on balance not practicable, particularly as there was no guarantee that the statements would reflect what was orally stated.
18 See, for example, Christiane Nord, *Text Analysis in Translation: Theory, Methodology, and Didactic Application of a Model for Translation Orientated Text Analysis* (Rodopi 2005), Chapters 1–3.
19 A/HRC/RES/5/1, para 3 (e).
20 John Scott, *A Matter of Record: Documentary Sources and Social Research* (Polity Press 1990); Monageng Mogalake, 'The Use of Documentary Research Methods in Social Research' (2006) 10 *African Sociological Review* 221.
21 UNGA, 'Institution-building of the United Nations Human Rights Council' (18 June 2007) A/HRC/RES/5/1, Section D para 17 (A/HRC/RES/5/1). See also UNGA, 'Review of the Work and Functioning of the Human Rights Council' (12 April 2011) A/HRC/RES/16/21, section E para 51 (A/HRC/RES/16/21).
22 Margrit Schreier, *Qualitative Content Analysis in Practice* (Sage Publications 2012) 1.
23 OR Holsti, *Content Analysis for the Social Sciences and Humanities* (Addison-Wesley 1969).
24 Ibid. 1–7.
25 All the statistical data and information was gathered from the UPR info database as of January 2013, www.upr-info.org/database/, accessed 28 August 2019.
26 I focused on quantifying the recommendations as they gave a good indication of the issues that formed the focus of discussions at the interactive dialogue stage in the UPR process.
27 A/HRC/RES/5/1.
28 See UN Committee on the Elimination of Discrimination against Women, 'UN Committee on the Elimination of Discrimination against Women' (10 August 2007) CEDAW/C/COK/CO/1, para 28.
    UNGA 'Resolution Adopted by the General Assembly' (7 January 1997), para 45; UNCEDAW, 'Concluding Observations on Sixth Report' (10 August 2007) CEDAW/C/NZL/CO/6.
29 See discussion in Chapter 2.
30 Lucinda Joy Peach, 'Are women human? The promise and perils of "Women's Rights as Human Rights"' in Lynda Bell, Andrew Nathan and Ilan Peieg (eds), *Negotiating Culture and Human Rights* (Columbia University Press 2001) 159.
31 Ibid.

32 Christina Cerna and Jennifer Wallace, 'Women and culture' in Kelly D Askin and Dorean M Koenig (eds), *Women and International Human Rights Law* (Volume 1, Transnational Publishers Inc 1999) 629.

33 A Rao, 'The politics of gender and culture in International Human Rights discourse' in Dorothy Hodgson (ed), *Gender and Culture at the Limits of Rights* (University of Pennsylvania Press 2011) 169.

34 Ibid.

35 Berta Esperanza Hernandez-Truyol, 'Human rights through a gendered lens: emergence, evolution, revolution' in Kelly D Askin and Dorean M Koenig (eds), *Women and International Human Rights Law* (Volume 1, Transnational Publishers Inc 1999).

36 Susan Moller, 'Is multiculturalism bad for women?' in Susan Okin (eds), *Is Multiculturalism Bad for Women?* (Princeton University Press 1999) 13.

37 A Rao, 'The politics of gender and culture in international human rights discourse' in Dorothy Hodgson (ed), *Gender and Culture at the Limits of Rights* (University of Pennsylvania Press 2011).

38 Christina Cerna and Jennifer Wallace, 'Women and Culture' in Kelly D Askin and Dorean M Koenig (eds), *Women and International Human Rights Law* (Volume 1, Transnational Publishers Inc 1999) 629. Elisabeth Friedman, 'Women's Human Rights: The Emergence of a Movement' in Julie Peter and Andrea Wolper (eds), *Women's Rights Human Rights: International Feminist Perspective* (Routledge 1995) 38.

39 Margrit Schreier, *Qualitative Content Analysis in Practice* (Sage Publications 2012) 38.

40 Ibid. See also Matt Henn, Mark Weinstein and Nick Ford, *A Short Introduction to Social Research* (Sage Publications 2006).

41 Margrit Schreier, *Qualitative Content Analysis in Practice* (Sage Publications 2012) 38.

42 Lindsay Prior, 'Using documents in social research' in David Sliverman (ed), *Qualitative Research* (3rd edn, Sage Publications 2011) 153.

43 Ibid.

44 Ibid.

45 Ibid.

46 Isabelle Gunning, 'Arrogant Perception, World Travelling and Multicultural Feminism: The Case of Female Genital Surgeries' (1991–1992) 23 *Columbia Human Rights Law Review* 238; *Female Genital Mutilation/Cutting: A Statistical Exploration* (UNICEF 2005) 17–19, www.unicef.org/publications/files/FGM-C_final_10_October.pdf, accessed 28 August 2019. Further elaboration, see Chapter 4.

47 Michel Perry, *The Idea of Human Rights: Four Inquiries* (Oxford University Press 1998) 9–10. For an overview on the different religious positions for and against abortion, see www.bbc.co.uk/ethics/abortion/religion/religion.shtml, accessed 28 August 2019. For further elaboration, see Chapter 5.

48 UN Commission on Human Rights, 'Report of the Special Rapporteur on Violence against Women, Its Causes and Consequences, Ms. Radhika Coomaraswamy, Submitted in Accordance with Commission on Human Rights Resolution 2001/49: Cultural Practices in the Family That Are Violent Towards Women' (31 January 2002) E/CN.4/2002/83 para 94. For further elaboration, see Chapter 4.

49 Javaid Rehman, 'The Sharia, Islamic Family Laws and International Human Rights Law: Examining the Theory and Practice of Polygamy and Talaq' (2007) 21 *International Journal of Law, Policy and the Family* 108, 115.

50 Ibid.

51 Anne Bunting, 'Theorizing Women's Cultural Diversity in Feminist International Human Rights Strategies' (1993) 20 *Journal of Law and Society* 6, 26. For further elaboration, see Chapter 5.
52 See GM Kressel, 'Sororicide/Filiacide: Homicide for Family Honour' (1981) 22 *Current Anthropology* 141–158; M Kurkiala, 'Interpreting Honour Killings: The Story of Fadime Sahindal (1975–2002)' (2003) in the Swedish Press. *Anthropology Today*, 19, 6–7.
53 Owen D. Jones, Sex, 'Culture, and the Biology of Rape: Toward Explanation and Prevention' (1999) 87 *Cal. L.R.* 827, 840. See also, Peggy Reeves Sanday, 'The Socio-Cultural Context of Rape: A Cross-Cultural Study' (1981) 37 *Journal of Social Issues* 5; World Health Organization, 'First World Report on Violence and Health' (2002) 161.
54 Joan Fitzpatrick, 'The use of International Human Rights norms to combat violence against women' in Rebecca Cook (ed) *Human Rights of Women: National and International Perspectives* (University of Pennsylvania Press 1994) 562.
55 For cultural relativism being used as a method rather than a substantive theory, see Melville Herskovits, *Cultural Relativism: Perspectives in Cultural Pluralism* (Vintage Books 1973) 32; Ben White, 'Defining the Intolerable: Child work, Global Standards and Cultural Relativism' (1999) 6 *Childhood* 133, 136.
56 The term was first coined in Nigel Fielding and Raymond Lee, 'Computing for Qualitative Research: Options, Problems and Potential' in Nigel Fielding and Raymond Lee (eds), *Using Computers in Qualitative Research* (Sage Publications 1991) 1–13.
57 Alan Bryman, *Social Research Methods* (4th edn, OUP 2012) 591.
58 http://www.surrey.ac.uk/sociology/research/researchcentres/caqdas/supp ort/choosing/, accessed 28 August 2019. See also Pat Bazeley and Kristi Jackson, *Qualitative Data Analysis with NVivo* (2nd edn, Sage Publications 2013).
59 Bruce Berg, *Qualitative Research Methods for Social Sciences* (7th edn, Allyn & Bacon 2007) 342.
60 RO Holsti, *Content Analysis for the Social Sciences and Humanities* (Addison-Wesley 1969) 12.
61 Bruce Berg, *Qualitative Research Methods for Social Sciences* (7th edn, Allyn & Bacon 2007) 34.
62 Ibid.
63 RO Holsti, *Content Analysis for the Social Sciences and Humanities* (Addison-Wesley 1969) 12.
64 Bruce Berg, *Qualitative Research Methods for Social Sciences* (7th edn, Allyn & Bacon 2007) 342.
65 John Scott, *A Matter of Record: Documentary Sources and Social Research* (Polity Press 1990) 32. See also, Margrit Schreier, *Qualitative Content Analysis in Practice* (Sage Publications 2012) 53.
66 B Berelson, *Content Analysis in Communications Research* (Free Press, 1952) 488. See also, RK Merton, *Social Theory and Social Structure* (Free Press, 1968) 366–370. See also, RO Holsti, *Content Analysis for the Social Sciences and Humanities* (Addison-Wesley 1969) 598; B Berelson, *Content Analysis in Communications Research* (Free Press 1952) 488. See also, RK Merton, *Social Theory and Social Structure* (Free Press 1968) 366–370.
67 S Hielman, *Synagogue for Life: A Study in Symbolic Interaction* (Prentice Hall 1976); RO Holsti, *Content Analysis for the Social Sciences and Humanities* (Addison-Wesley 1969) 12.
68 Bruce Berg, *Qualitative Research Methods for Social Sciences* (7th edn, Allyn & Bacon 2007) 343.
69 Ibid.

70 Margrit Schreier, *Qualitative Content Analysis in Practice* (Sage Publications 2012) 52. See also, John Scott, *A Matter of Record: Documentary Sources and Social Research* (Polity Press 1990) 31.
71 Ibid.
72 Christiane Nord, *Text Analysis in Translation: Theory, Methodology, and Didactic Application of a Model for Translation Orientated Text Analysis* (Rodopi 2005) Chapters 1–3.
73 A An-Naim, 'Introduction' in Abdullahi Ahmed An-Naim (eds), *Human Rights in Cross Cultural Perspectives: A Quest for Consensus* (University of Pennsylvania Press 1995) 3.
74 This list of key words was derived through a data-driven strategy. See further Norman Denzin, *The Research Act* (McGraw-Hill 1978); Barney Glaser and Anselm Strauss, *The Discovery of Grounded Theory: Strategies for Qualitative Research* (Transaction Publishers 1967). See also Philip Mayring, *Qualitative Inhaltsanalyse. Grundlagen und Techniken* [Qualitative Content Analysis. Basics and Techniques] (11 edn, Weinham Beltz 2010) cited in Margrit Schreier, *Qualitative Content Analysis in Practice* (Sage Publications 2012) 115.
75 Frances Raday, 'Culture, Religion, and Gender' (2003) 1 *International Journal of Constitutional Law* 663, 665. See also, An-Na'im and J Hammon 'Cultural Transformation and Human Rights in African Societies' in An-Na'im and Hammond (eds) *Cultural Transformation in African Societies* (London, 2000) 21.

Bibliography

An-Naim A, 'Introduction' in Abdullahi Ahmed An-Naim (eds), *Human Rights in Cross Cultural Perspectives: A Quest for Consensus* (University of Pennsylvania Press, 1995).

An-Na'im A and Hammond J, 'Cultural Transformation and Human Rights in African Societies' in A An-Na'im and J Hammond (eds), *Cultural Transformation in African Societies* (Zed Books, 2000).

Arp B, 'Lessons Learned from Spain's Practice before the United Nations Human Rights Reporting Mechanisms: Treaty Bodies and Universal Periodic Review' (2011) 15 *Spanish Yearbook of International Law* 1.

Atkinson P and Coffey A, 'Analyzing Documentary Realities' in David Silverman (ed), *Qualitative Research: Theory, Method and Practice* (3rd edn, Sage Publications, 2011).

Bazeley P and Jackson K, *Qualitative Data Analysis with NVivo* (2nd edn, Sage Publications, 2013).

Berelson B, *Content Analysis in Communications Research* (Free Press, 1952).

Berg B, *Qualitative Research Methods for Social Sciences* (7th edn, Allyn & Bacon, 2007).

Bryman A, *Social Research Methods* (4th edn, Oxford University Press, 2012) 591.

Bunting A, 'Theorizing Women's Cultural Diversity in Feminist International Human Rights Strategies' (1993) 20 *Journal of Law and Society* 6.

Cerna C and Wallace J, 'Women and Culture' in Kelly D Askin and Dorean M Koenig (eds), *Women and International Human Rights Law* (Volume 1, Transnational Publishers Inc, 1999).

Denzin N, *The Research Act* (McGraw-Hill, 1978).

Fielding N and Lee R, 'Computing for Qualitative Research: Options, Problems and Potential' in Nigel Fielding and Raymond Lee (eds), *Using Computers in Qualitative Research* (Sage Publications, 1991).

Fitzpatrick J, 'The Use of International Human Rights Norms to Combat Violence Against Women' in Rebecca Cook (eds), *Human Rights of Women: National and International Perspectives* (University of Pennsylvania Press, 1994).

Friedman E, 'Women's Human Rights: The Emergence of a Movement' in Julie Peter and Andrea Wolper (eds), *Women's Rights Human Rights: International Feminist Perspective* (Routledge, 1995).

Glaser B and Strauss A, *The Discovery of Grounded Theory: Strategies for Qualitative Research* (Transaction Publishers, 1967).

Gunning I, 'Arrogant Perception, World Travelling and Multicultural Feminism: The Case of Female Genital Surgeries' (1991–1992) 23 *Columbia Human Rights Law Review* 238.

Henn M, Weinstein M and Ford N, *A Short Introduction to Social Research* (Sage Publications, 2006).

Hernandez-Truyol EB, 'Human Rights through a Gendered Lens: Emergence, Evolution, Revolution' in Kelly D Askin and Dorean M Koenig (eds), *Women and International Human Rights Law* (Volume 1, Transnational Publishers Inc, 1999).

Herskovits M, *Cultural Relativism: Perspectives in Cultural Pluralism* (Vintage Books, 1973) 32.

Hielman S, *Synagogue for Life: A Study in Symbolic Interaction* (Prentice Hall, 1976).

Holsti RO, *Content Analysis for the Social Sciences and Humanities* (Addison-Wesley, 1969).

Jones DO, 'Sex, Culture, and the Biology of Rape: Toward Explanation and Prevention' (1999) 87 *California Law Review* 827.

Kressel MG, 'Sororicide/Filiacide: Homicide for Family Honour' (1981) 22 *Current Anthropology* 141.

Kurkiala M, 'Interpreting Honour Killings: The Story of Fadime Sahindal (1975–2002) in the Swedish Press' (2003) 19 *Anthropology Today* 6.

Mayring P, *Qualitative Inhaltsanalyse. Grundlagen und Techniken* [Qualitative Content Analysis. Basics and Techniques] (11th edn, Weinham Beltz, 2010).

Merton KR, *Social Theory and Social Structure* (Free Press, 1968).

Mogalake M, 'The Use of Documentary Research Methods in Social Research' (2006) 10 *African Sociological Review* 221.

Moller S, 'Is Multiculturalism Bad for Women?' in Susan Okin (eds), *Is Multiculturalism Bad for Women?* (Princeton University Press, 1999).

Nord C, *Text Analysis in Translation: Theory, Methodology, and Didactic Application of a Model for Translation Orientated Text Analysis* (Rodopi, 2005).

Payne G and Payne J, *Key Concepts in Social Research* (Sage Publications, 2004).

Peach JL, 'Are Women Human? The Promise and Perils of "Women's Rights as Human Rights"' in Lynda Bell, Andrew Nathan and Ilan Peieg (eds), *Negotiating Culture and Human Rights* (Columbia University Press, 2001).

Perry M, *The Idea of Human Rights: Four Inquires* (Oxford University Press, 1998).

Platt J, 'Evidence and Proof in Documentary Research: 1 Some Specific Problems of Documentary Research' (1981) 29 *Sociological Review* 31.

Prior L, 'Using Documents in Social Research' in David Silverman (ed), *Qualitative Research* (3rd edn, Sage Publications, 2011).

Raday F, 'Culture, Religion, and Gender' (2003) 1 *International Journal of Constitutional Law* 663.

Rao A, 'The Politics of Gender and Culture in International Human Rights Discourse' in Dorothy Hodgson (ed), *Gender and Culture at the Limits of Rights* (University of Pennsylvania Press, 2011).

Rehman J, 'The Sharia, Islamic Family Laws and International Human Rights Law: Examining the Theory and Practice of Polygamy and Talaq' (2007) 21 *International Journal of Law, Policy and the Family* 108.

Sanday RP, 'The Socio-Cultural Context of Rape: A Cross-Cultural Study' (1981) 37 *Journal of Social Issues* 5.

Schreier M, *Qualitative Content Analysis in Practice* (Sage Publications, 2012).

Scott J, *A Matter of Record: Documentary Sources and Social Research* (Polity Press, 1990).

UN Commission on Human Rights, *Report of the Special Rapporteur on Violence against Women, Its Causes and Consequences, Ms. Radhika Coomaraswamy, Submitted in Accordance with Commission on Human Rights Resolution 2001/49: Cultural Practices in the Family that are Violent towards Women* (31 January 2002) E/CN.4/2002/83.

UN Committee on the Elimination of Discrimination Against Women, 'UN Committee on the Elimination of Discrimination Against Women' (10 August 2007) CEDAW/C/COK/CO/1.

UNCEDAW, 'Concluding Observations on Sixth Report' (10 August 2007) CEDAW/C/NZL/CO/6.

UNGA, 'Resolution adopted by the General Assembly' (7 January 1997).

UNGA, 'Institution-Building of the United Nations Human Rights Council' (18 June 2007) A/HRC/RES/5/1.

UNGA, 'Review of the Work and Functioning of the Human Rights Council' (12 April 2011) A/HRC/RES/16/21.

UNHRC, 'Res 5/1 Institution-building of the United Nations Human Rights Council' (18 June 2007) Annex. A/HRC/RES/5/1.

White B, 'Defining the Intolerable: Child Work, Global Standards and Cultural Relativism' (1999) 6 *Childhood* 133.

World Health Organization, *First World Report on Violence and Health* (2002) 161.

4 Women's Right to Health

Introduction

Despite the fact that women's right to health has been recognised under international human rights law since the 1950s, the issue has not received consistent and effective consideration, and therefore, actions to bring any substantial changes have been described as slow and often superficial.[1] One of the most prevalent reasons for the persistent violation of women's right to health is primarily due to the failure of relevant national and international organisations to fully comprehend and understand the pain, suffering, and sometimes death that is inflicted on women due to restricted access to sufficient health care services.[2] This ignorance, or unawareness of issues in relation to women's right to health, is often perpetuated through the artificial divide between the public and private sphere that has traditionally existed in the context of international human rights protection.[3] Within this divide, women's rights, issues, and concerns are often relegated to the private sphere primarily because women are often considered the main caregivers in the family and domestic life.[4] In this way, issues and concerns about women's health, such as those affecting woman's sexuality and reproductive health, have traditionally been perceived as falling within the private sphere.[5] One of the most significant implications of the artificial divide is that the public realm is largely considered to be subject to government regulation and scrutiny. In contrast, the private sphere is traditionally considered to avoid such regulation, and is therefore more prone to be governed by values and norms embedded in culture.[6] It is primarily due to this increased susceptibility of women's rights to health to claims of culture that it has been selected as a focus of investigation.[7]

With this in mind, the purpose of this chapter is to explore, present, and analyse the dialogues that were undertaken by member states during their reviews in relation to three issues in relation to women's right to health: female genital mutilation (FGM), abortion, and access to health. A total of 868 recommendations were made on the three issues in relation to women's right to health. Looking beyond the numbers, this investigation uniquely considered the substance and nature of the interactive dialogue at the Universal Periodic Review

(UPR) process. Using these issues as a focus for this investigation first and fore mostly help assess whether the central aims of the UPR process of promoting and protecting the universality of human rights has been met or challenged during the state reviews in the first two cycles. Going further, considering the controversial nature of the issues under examination, the aim is to understand the role and significance of culture and cultural relativism in the modern-day discussions of controversial international human rights norms during the UPR process.

This chapter is divided into three main sections: FGM, abortion, and women's rights to access health care services, which will all follow the same structure. Each of the three main sections will begin by contextualising the issue by providing a brief introduction to the international human rights law on each issue. The second sections are dedicated to presenting the findings of these explorations, with the third and final sections dedicated to discussing the findings of each of these issues.

Female Genital Mutilation at the UPR Process

Contextualising Women's Rights in Relation to Female Genital Mutilation

Amongst the various different forms of definitions for FGM, for the present purposes, the following is adopted: 'all procedures involving partial or total removal of the external female genitalia ... whether for cultural or other non-therapeutic reasons'. The jurisprudence has emanated from various international human rights law treaties that persistently declared FGM as a violation of women's (and girls') rights under a range of international human rights instruments.[8] More significantly, the Committee on the Elimination of Discrimination against Women (Committee on the Women's Convention) has clarified that FGM, together with any underlying cultural justifications that endorse the practice, should be eliminated.[9] With the practice still being continued, despite repeated declarations of the practice of FGM being a violation of women's rights,[10] there is clearly a discrepancy between human rights norms and the obligations of the state in relation to the implementation and practice.[11] Those that are sympathetic to the practice argue that it is inseparable from the religious and cultural identity of some groups[12] and, therefore, its continuance is often defended as an expression of the traditional and cultural values of a particular society.[13] Justifications for the practice are sometimes based on preserving women and girls' virginity,[14] birth control,[15] or to protect the family honour by preventing immorality and preserving group identity.[16] This inherent relationship between the practice of FGM and cultural norms was reflected in the discussions held on the issue in the UPR process. Over the two cycles, 36 member states, explicitly or implicitly, recognised the inherent association between FGM and culture during the interactive dialogue.

Findings on FGM in the UPR Process

First Cycle of Review

During the first cycle of review, a total of 192 recommendations were issued on the issue of FGM. A total of five different types of recommendations were issued. In response, the states under review responded with a total of 12 different types of responses, 6 for those states that accepted the recommendation and 6 for those that noted the recommendations.

RECOMMENDATION 1

Under this category of recommendation, observer states expressly recognised FGM to be a harmful traditional/cultural practice, before suggesting that the state under review should take action to eliminate it. A typical example of this recommendation was issued during the review of Cameroon when Chile 'flagged the persistence of deep rooted cultural practice affecting women such as FGM ... [and] inquired about steps to ... eradicate FGM'.[17] In another example, Mexico issued a recommendation to Ethiopia 'to eliminate harmful traditional practices such as female genital mutilations'.[18] A total of 16 states were issued with this recommendation in the first cycle, of these 15 states accepted the recommendation. The majority of those that accepted provided an A4 response. For example, the delegate of Mali stated that that FGM is a 'cultural practice deeply rooted in Malian society' and that 'it had given priority to public education and awareness-raising campaigns rather than the adoption of repressive measures whose application in the field cannot be guaranteed'.[19] The only state that noted a recommendation under this category, over both cycles, was Malawi, who provided an N6 response, as the delegate explained that it could not accept the recommendation because 'female genital mutilation ... had never been practiced here'.[20]

RECOMMENDATION 2

Under the second category of recommendation observer states recognised the inherent association between culture and FGM, and then suggested that the state under review should implement incremental policies, such as engaging in a constructive dialogue with relevant stakeholders, with the aim to reform any sympathetic attitudes in favour of FGM. A typical example of recommendation under this category was when Slovenia suggested that Niger implement 'sensitization activities for practitioners, families, traditional or religious leaders and the general public in order to encourage change in traditional attitudes'.[21] This form of recommendation was the most popular in the first cycle with a total of 26 states being issued with this recommendation, of which 24 states accepted it. Of these, the overwhelming majority of the states provided an A4 response. A typical example is when the delegate of Somalia stated that it recognised the importance of 'dialogue

Table 4.1 Nature of Discussions on the issue of FGM in the First Cycle

	Universal Periodic Review Cycle 1 Accepted Recommendations	Responses by States under Review					
Nature of recommendations issued to states under review		A1 Accepted recommendations with no further comments	A2 Domestic law already in place against FGM	A3 Domestic laws under review on FGM	A4 Incremental reforms in place to help eliminate FGM	A5 Cultural justifications for FGM make its elimination challenging	A6 FGM is not embedded in culture
	Recommendation 1 FGM Is a harmful cultural practice that is required to be eliminated	Ghana Djibouti Tanzania	Botswana	Guinea Bissau Cameroon	Mali Mauritania Niger Nigeria Senegal Sierra Leone Togo Somalia Ethiopia		
	Recommendation 2 To implement incremental reforms to address the practice	Chad Cote d'Ivoire Ethiopia Oman Tanzania Uganda	Iraq	Cameroon Guinea Bissau	Benin Djibouti Guinea · Liberia Mali Kenya Mauritania Nigeria Niger Senegal Sierra Leone Somalia Yemen	Central African Republic Eritrea · Gambia	Republic of Congo
	Recommendation 3 Implement laws to prohibit FGM	Chad Tanzania Uganda	Egypt Iraq Sudan	Cameroon Guinea Bissau Somalia	Benin Guinea Kenya Mauritania Niger Nigeria Senegal Sierra Leone · Togo	Eritrea · Republic of Congo	
	Recommendation 4 Comply with international obligations on FGM	Oman		Cameroon Guinea Bissau Somalia	Mauritania Niger Nigeria Sierra Leone		

Noted Recommendations

Nature of recommendations issued to states under review	Responses by states under review					
	N1 Noted recommendation with no further comments	N2 Laws already in place or under review against FGM	N3 Legislation is not the answer to FGM	N4 Incremental reforms in place to address FGM	N5 Cultural justifications hinder the elimination of FGM	N6 FGM does not exist in the state
Recommendation 1 FGM Is a harmful cultural practice that is required to be eliminated						Malawi
Recommendation 2 To implement incremental reforms to address the practice						Lesotho Malawi
Recommendation 3 Implement laws to prohibit FGM				Djibouti Gambia	Liberia Mali	Lesotho
Recommendation 4 Comply with international obligations on FGM				Liberia Mali	Central African Republic Gambia	

Table 4.2 Nature of Discussions on the issue of FGM in the Second Cycle

Universal Periodic Review Cycle 2 Accepted Recommendations	Responses by States under Review					
Nature of recommendations issued to states under review	A1 Accepted recommendations with no further comments	A2 Domestic law already in place against FGM	A3 Domestic laws under review on FGM	A4 Incremental reforms in place to help eliminate FGM	A5 Cultural justifications for FGM make its elimination challenging but incremental reforms in place	A6 Incidence of FGM has dropped
Recommendation 1 FGM Is a harmful cultural practice that is required to be eliminated	Burkina Faso Central African Republic Ghana	Kenya	Liberia Sudan Uganda	Ethiopia Mali Niger Sudan Tanzania Yemen	Gambia Guinea	
Recommendation 2 To implement incremental reforms to address the practice	Burkina Faso Cote d'Ivoire Senegal Oman	Kenya Uganda	Chad Liberia	Benin Djibouti Eritrea Ethiopia Indonesia Mali Mauritania · Somalia Republic of Congo Sierra Leone Yemen	Cameroon Gambia Guinea Guinea Bissau Nigeria	Togo
Recommendation 3 Implement laws to prohibit FGM	Austria Cote d'Ivoire Ghana Malawi Maldives Oman	Belgium Kenya Sudan Uganda	Chad Liberia	Benin Djibouti Ethiopia Mali Mauritania Niger Sudan Republic of Congo Tanzania	Cameroon Guinea Guinea Bissau Nigeria	Togo
Recommendation 4 Comply with international obligations on FGM	Cote d'Ivoire Oman			Mali Sierra Leone Tanzania		
Recommendation 5 Implement measures to eradicate FGM	Burkina Faso DR Congo Ghana Senegal	Egypt Iraq Kenya New Zealand	Chad Liberia Sudan	Benin Djibouti Ethiopia Niger Somalia · Sudan · Republic of Congo Tanzania	Cameroon Gambia Guinea	
Recommendation 6 Learn/Share best practices with other countries and continue efforts to eradicate FGM	Burkina Faso Cote d'Ivoire					

Universal Periodic Review Cycle 2
Noted Recommendations

Responses by States under Review

Nature of recommendations issued to states under review	N1 Noted recommendation with no further comments	N2 Laws already in place or under review against FGM	N3 Legislation is not the answer to FGM	N4 Incremental reforms in place to address FGM	N5 Engaging with cultural/religious leaders with the aim of eliminating the practice	N6 FGM does not exist in the state
Recommendation 1 FGM Is a harmful cultural practice that is required to be eliminated					Indonesia	
Recommendation 2 To implement incremental reforms to address the practice						
Recommendation 3 Implement laws to prohibit FGM	Malawi				Gambia Somalia Sierra Leone	
Recommendation 4 Comply with international obligations on FGM		Sudan				
Recommendation 5 Implement measures to eradicate FGM	Malawi			Sierra Leone		
Recommendation 6 Learn/Share best practices with other countries and continue efforts to eradicate FGM						

with traditional and religious leaders, women's groups and practitioners of FGM to eliminate the practice of FGM'.[22] Aside from the instances where states remained silent whilst accepting this form of recommendation, the other form of response that was often cited was an A5 response, which was utilised by Central African Republic, Eritrea, and Gambia. For example, Eritrea's delegation referred to

> the extensive campaign by the government to educate the public about this issue. The delegate explained that whilst the practice was rooted in very traditional culture, which will take time to wipe out, the government is committed to addressing the issue.[23]

On the other hand, in the first cycle when Congo was issued with a recommendation under this category, the delegate provided an A6 response insisting that the 'the practices of genital mutilation that had been referred to were not rooted in Congolese culture'.[24] In terms of those that did not accept the recommendation, only Lesotho and Malawi both provided an N6 response as they noted the recommendations in the first cycle, with both denying the practice of FGM in their states.[25]

RECOMMENDATION 3

The third category of recommendations suggested that states under review should enact legislation against the practice of FGM. A typical example of this recommendation is when the Czech Republic 'recommended the adoption and implementation of legislation prohibiting and criminalizing FGM' during the review of Mali.[26] Again, this form of recommendation was amongst the most popular in the first cycle with a total of 25 states being issued with it, of which 20 states accepted the recommendation. Whilst the responses were varied, the most popular form of response was the A4 response. A total of six states responded by either insisting that domestic laws were already in place to address the practice (A2), or that the laws were under review (A3). For example, Iraq responded by pointing to existing legislation that addressed the practice. For instance, Iraq stated that 'the crime of female genital mutilation was dealt with under the Penal Code'.[27] On the other hand, Cameroon provided an A3 stating that 'on eliminating practices concerning, inter alia … FGM … the reform of the criminal code is underway'.[28]

This form of recommendation received the highest number of noted responses over both cycles. A total of five states noted the recommendation in the first cycle. Of these, the delegate of Lesotho provided an N6 response as it was insisted that 'Lesotho did not practice female genital mutilation'.[29] Gambia provided an N4 response, stating that 'continued public education on the dangers of the practice were under way'.[30] The states of Mali[31] and Liberia both noted the recommendation issued under this category and provided an N5 response. For example, Liberia at the interactive dialogue stage began by stating that it 'was engaging all segments of society in inclusive and constructive nationwide dialogues to determine the extent and the forms of harmful traditional practices, and those dialogues would form the basis for programme planning in the eradication of female genital mutilation'.[32] Liberia stated that it 'continued to take measures to eliminate the practice of female genital mutilation, while respecting the cultural rights of citizens to engage in non-harmful, human rights-conscious traditional and cultural practices'.[33]At the HRC plenary session, the delegate of Liberia explained that FGM is a

> deep-rooted traditional practice [and] still shrouded in myth and secrecy. Often, discussions of both are strongly resisted and perceived as attempts to destroy the cultural and traditional heritage of the country ... it is currently unable to take a position on recommendation relating to female genital mutilation.[34]

This statement indicates that whilst the delegate of Liberia was committed to taking measures to eliminate FGM, such action was contingent to respecting the cultural rights to engage in 'non harmful' cultural/traditional practices. This point of discussion then turns on the definition of 'harm' as interpreted by Liberia. Indeed, if Liberia considered some forms of FGM to be 'non harmful', then the statement indicates that the state will consider it to fall within the cultural right of the citizens, which ought to be respected.

RECOMMENDATION 4

Under this category of recommendations states under review were recommended to take measures against FGM to ensure compliance with the state's international obligations in relation to the practice. A typical example is when Mali was issued with a recommendation by Canada to 'take the necessary measures to implement the recommendations of CEDAW and the Human Rights Committee concerning ... FGM'.[35] A total of 12 states under review were issued with a recommendation under this category, of which eight states accepted the recommendations with the majority of them issuing a response which is pointing to the existing laws that were in place to address the practice, or to that the practice required incremental reforms to be implemented. For example, Cameroon, Guinea Bissau, and Somalia provided an A3 response as they accepted the recommendation whilst stating that domestic laws on the issue were under review. The remaining five states all provided an A4 response. Sierra Leone issued an A4 response and stated that whilst 'the Government accepted in principle that the practice ought to be abolished, but recalled that some traditions were deeply rooted and pleaded for implementation on a progressive basis'.[36] In other instances, Liberia, Mali, Central African Republic, and Gambia all noted the recommendation. Liberia and Mali provided an N4 response, as it stated whilst awareness-raising campaigns against FGM were in place, the cultural nature of the practice was the reason why it continued to exist in the state.[37]

Second Cycle of Review

In the second cycle of review, there were a significantly greater number of recommendations issued, with a total of 311. Aside from one recommendation, all
remained the same form as in the previous cycle. The new form of recommendation introduced in the second cycle has been labelled as Recommendation 6. No
new forms of responses were issued by the states under review from the previous
cycle, but for the sake of clarity in relation to the presentation, the table in relation to the responses has largely been the same, with two exceptions, which will
be noted below.

RECOMMENDATION 1

A total of 15 states were issued with a recommendation under this cycle, which
was only one less to the number of states that were issued with it in the first
cycle. However, unlike the first cycle, no state in the second cycle noted the
recommendation. The states of Ghana, Tanzania, Mali, and Niger were issued
with this form of recommendation under both cycles. Of these, only Tanzania
provided a different response. Ghana maintained its position in the second cycle
as it accepted the recommendation and made no further comments. Whereas
Mali and Niger both accepted the recommendations both issued an A4 response
under both cycles. Tanzania moved from an A1 response in the first cycle, to an
A4 type of response in the second cycle. In fact, as with the first cycle, this was
the most popular form of response by states when issued with this recommendation. For example, Somalia noted that it had implemented 'educational awareness campaigns, and a dialogue with traditional and religious leaders, women's
groups and practitioners to eliminate the practice of FGM'.[38] Finally, Gambia and
Guinea both issued an A5 response; both outlined that given the strong cultural
background of the practices, the elimination has been proven challenging, despite
this information on incremental reforms in place was provided.[39]

RECOMMENDATION 2

This form of recommendation which encouraged states to undertake incremental reforms was issued to 26 states in the second cycle, with only one state who
refused to accept the recommendation. In response, the most popular response
was the A4 response, shortly followed by an A5 response. An example of the latter is Cameroon in the second cycle who stated that 'the delegation recognized
that female genital mutilation was an unacceptable human tragedy arising from
both cultural and economic factors, that awareness-raising was necessary to end
such practices and that excisers should be given the opportunity to retrain'.[40]
On the other hand, Indonesia in the second cycle noted the recommendation
and provided an N5 response by stating there is a dialogue with 'religious and
community leaders on the issue of female circumcision with the view to eliminating the practice'.[41] This statement coupled with the state not accepting the

recommendation implies that there are cultural and religious values that hinder the eradication of the practice.

RECOMMENDATION 3

The category of recommendations suggested that the states under review implement domestic laws to prohibit the practice of FGM. This form was issued to a total of 30 states under review, which is a slight increase to the states that were issued with this recommendation in the previous cycle and also the most popular form of recommendation in the second cycle. Of these a total of 26 states accepted the recommendation, and four states noted the recommendation, making it the form of recommendation that was the most highly noted in the second cycle of review. Those states that accepted the recommendation provided a range of response, with an A4 response being the highest cited response, shortly followed by an A1 response. There were a number of instances where states under review have altered their positions in the second cycle from when the same form of recommendation was issued as the first cycle.

There was a total of six states that provided the same response as they had under the previous cycle. The states of Oman and Cote d'Ivoire remained with its position of accepting the recommendation without any further comments, whilst Sudan maintained its position that domestic laws were already in place. Elsewhere, Benin, Mauritania, and Niger all reiterated the incremental reforms that were in place to address the practice, thereby providing an A4 response. On the one hand, Chad, Ethiopia, Tanzania, and Uganda, all submitted an A1 response in the first cycle, but under the second cycle chose to provide additional statements whilst accepting the recommendation. Uganda and Chad made reference to laws that were in place or under review in their dialogue, respectively. On the other hand, Ethiopia and Tanzania provided an A4 response by referring to incremental reforms that were being implemented to help eradicate the practice; both states did not make reference to the issue in relation to laws being implemented on FGM. Guinea, Nigeria, and Togo were also issued with a recommendation of this nature under both cycles. Guinea and Nigeria both changed their positions from submitting that incremental reforms were already in place, towards adding that cultural justifications for the practice of FGM make its elimination challenging in the second cycle. In other instances, Togo, whilst accepting the recommendation formally, insisted that the instances in which FGM had been carried out had dropped. Kenya changed its position from describing incremental reforms in place, to insisting that domestic laws already were in place to address the practice of FGM. Republic of Congo moved from explaining that cultural justifications made the elimination of the practice difficult in the first cycle, to an A4 response of outlining the incremental reforms already in place. Some notable changes are that of Cameroon and Guinea Bissau, who responded with an A3 response in the first cycle as the delegate stated that domestic laws were under review, whilst in the second cycle they drew upon the cultural barriers that existed in preventing the implementation of the practice, thereby provided an A5 response. For instance, the delegate of Cameroon stated that 'female genital mutilation was an unacceptable human tragedy arising from both cultural and economic factors, that awareness-raising was necessary to end such practices and that excisers should be given the opportunity to retrain'.[42]

There were more significant movements when issued with recommendations in relation to three states, who drastically altered their positions. Liberia changed its position on FGM from noting the recommendation by issuing an N5 using cultural justification a hindrance to its elimination to changing its position to accept the recommendation. When issued with the same recommendation, Liberia accepted the recommendation and provided an A3 response, stating that 'Liberia was going through a constitutional review process ... and the law should protect women from all forms of violence including female genital mutilation'. In addition, Somalia and Sierra Leone when issued with this recommendation under the previous cycle accepted, issuing an A3 response by Somalia, and an A4 response by Sierra Leone. In the second cycle, both states changed their position to note the recommendation and provide an N5 response. For example, the delegate of Sierra Leone stated 'we will however continue to maintain a ban on the initiation of under-18 girls while engaging our public on the future of cultural practices such as female genital mutilation'.[43] In this way, whilst the nature of the statements was not dramatically different to the previous cycle, the official position on the recommendation was changed to not being accepted. Finally, the state of Gambia under the previous cycle issued an N4 response; however, under the current cycle, whilst still noting the recommendation the tone of the response was more subtle and instead of justifying the continuance of the practice of FGM on cultural grounds, the state stated that it was engaging with cultural leaders with the aim of eliminating the practice.

RECOMMENDATION 4

Under this recommendation states under review were directed to comply with their international human rights obligations in relation to FGM. There was a drastic reduction in the number of states that were issued with this resolution in the second cycle in comparison to the first. In the second cycle, only Sudan noted the recommendation, and stated that laws in relation to FGM were already in place. Of those that accepted the recommendations, the states' responses were spilt between an A1 response and an A4 response. Oman and Cote d'Ivoire both provided an A1 response; for Oman this was the same response as the previous cycle. Sierra Leone also provided the same responses as the last cycle; an A4 response. The most significant movement was the by the state of Mali, who under the previous cycle refused to accept the recommendation and provided an N4 response. In the second cycle, the state changed its position and accepted the recommendation and issued and stated that it had implemented incremental reforms to address the practice. In this way, whilst the state moved to accepting the recommendation, the nature of the response remained the same.

RECOMMENDATION 5

This form of recommendation was vague in nature. It instructed the states under review to simply implement measures to eradicate the practices of FGM, without providing any specific details as to the nature of the measures. An example of this form of recommendation is when the delegate of the Netherlands issued a recommendation to Chad to 'Continue the eradication of the practice of female genital mutilation'. This form of recommendation was not issued during the discussion on FGM in the first cycle of review. A total of 24 states were issued with this type of recommendation, of which only two states did not accept the recommendation. The states that accepted the recommendations provided a response that was distributed across the different categories. The majority of the states provided an A4 response, with the responses of A1 and referring to existing laws on the practice, an A2 response being equally used. This shows that the majority of the states under review made references to legislation, suggesting that the eradication through implementing laws was a method used to eliminate the practice. Malawi was one of the two states that did not accept the recommendation and did not provide any further comments. Under the previous cycle, when issued with a different form of recommendation, Malawi denied the existence of the practice in the domestic context.

RECOMMENDATION 6

This form of a recommendation was the only that instructed states to share their existing practices. For instance, South Sudan issued a recommendation to Cote d'Ivoire to 'share experience with states within the region and benefit from their experiences in combating female genital mutilation'. The states of Burkina Faso and Cote d'Ivoire were the only states that were issued with this recommendation, and they accepted the recommendation without any further comment.

Discussion and Analysis

Whilst a total of 85% acceptance rate of recommendation may indicate a certain level of consensus on the issue of FGM amongst states, an analysis of the nature of the positions adopted by states during the discussions reveals how some states grappled with the complex relationship between FGM and culture during the discussions held over both cycles. In particular, it was interesting to observe that the vast majority of states in responding to recommendations provided implicit or explicit reference to the association between FGM and cultures in their responses, particularly when the recommendation was being noted. From the findings there are four main patterns that have emerged.

First, observer states that issued recommendations under the first category in both cycles expressly declared FGM to be a harmful cultural practice that was required to be eliminated. From the nature of the recommendations under this category there are two implicit suggestions made by the observer states.

The statements indicate, first, that the observer states believed that FGM continued to be practised due to justifications that were embedded in some aspects of cultural belief systems; second, that the observer states are at the outset making clear that the continuance of the practice, despite being condoned by some cultural values and traditions, is in violation of international norms and thus should be eliminated. Observer states that adopted this position over the two cycles strongly resonate with the strict universalist position, which recognises that whilst cultural differences exist, it insists that universal human rights norms should transcend cultural idiosyncrasies.[44] The implications of the strict universalist position adopted by some observer states during the discussions of FGM becomes apparent when one analyses the underlying presumptions of the states adopting this position. To begin with, the essence of the recommendations issued under the first category is that whilst observer states recognised the cultural nature of FGM, suggestions were made to eliminate the practice. This recognition that FGM is embedded in some aspects of culture means that the observer states hold the presumption that such beliefs are formulated over a period of time. On the nature of culture, Clifford Geertz argues that cultural values are a synthesis of moral belief systems that are formulated, developed, and reaffirmed over a period of time.[45] In this way the standards, values, and categories of culture are acquired unconsciously by individuals through a process of 'enculturation'.[46] Following this logic, any reforms to values and beliefs embedded in culture must be undertaken gradually over a period of time to ensure that such reforms are accepted.[47] Therefore, reforms undertaken to discourage attitudes in favour of the practice cannot be undertaken in a precipitous manner, and rather require long-term reform policies, and a constructive dialogue with relevant stakeholders in a community.[48] In light of this, suggestions made by observer states under the first category to precipitously eliminate the cultural practice of FGM indicates that the observer states have not fully appreciated the nature of culture and process of enculturation, which deeply embeds the sympathetic attitudes held by individuals towards FGM.[49] In fact, the observer states' lack of appreciation of the nature of culture and the enculturation process, in relation to sympathetic attitudes towards FGM, confirms some of the theatrical critiques of the strict universalist position.[50] Consequently, whilst the overwhelming acceptance of the recommendations from a strict universalist position may indicate a universal consensus on the issue, the underlying assumptions held by the states give reason to question whether recommendations issued by observer states under the first category are realistically attainable in the manner suggested.

The second significant aspect of discussions on FGM also emanated from states recognising the association between culture and FGM. However, in contrast to those observer states that used the link between FGM and culture to adopt a strict universalist position, Liberia, Mali, Central African Republic, and Gambia in the first cycle used the same association as a basis to challenge and refuse to accept the reforms suggested. In this way, whilst the states did not use culture to explicitly *justify* the practice, they used the association between FGM and culture to *explain* why the practice continued to exist in the respective states under review. This with the fact that the recommendations were noted, gives reason to suggest the states implicitly challenged the suggested reforms to enact laws against the practice on the basis that the cultural nature of the practice hindered the implementation and acceptance of such laws. Whilst it is clear that neither of the states have directly and expressively adopted a strict cultural relativist position to justify FGM, the implications of the nature of the responses mean that the positions adopted by the states are open to the same profound criticism that are often subject to the strict cultural relativist position. One of the most profound criticisms of strict cultural relativism is the possibility of the notion of culture being invoked by, sometimes oppressive, states to justify 'cruel and degrading practices' and to deflect international scrutiny.[51] The states noted above in their responses have used the cultural association of FGM as a basis to not accept the suggested reforms during their state reviews. In the second cycle, a slightly more nuanced form of response was provided by Indonesia, Sierra Leone, Somalia, and Gambia who refused to accept the recommendations, however, it was emphasised that the states were engaging in dialogue with the religious and cultural leaders with the view to eliminating the practice. There is arguably some merit in this response when compared to those states that noted the response in the previous cycle. Here, whilst the states have still noted the recommendations, the nature of the response is more subtle, and the language suggests there is clear intent in moving towards eliminating the practice. Indeed, it can be argued that engaging in a dialogue with the relevant stake holders, religious, and cultural leaders can be more of a productive method to help address the practice. Despite this reason for optimism, ultimately, the state has noted the recommendation and thereby has refused to undertake any suggestions for reforms from peers in relation to FGM. In this way, the extent of the reforms that will be implemented are restricted to the discretion of the state under review, and are not influenced by external sources. Thus, whilst the tone of the responses under the second cycle is slightly more subtle than those positions that are advocated by the states providing a similar response in the first cycle, ultimately, the association of FGM and culture is, albeit, more implicitly being used as a justification to not accept the recommendation.

The third position adopted by states can be described as being a more nuanced approach when discussing the issue of FGM and its association with culture. By far the most prevalent position adopted, by both states under review and observer states, during the discussions on FGM in both cycles is the recognition that the practice can be effectively eliminated through incremental reforms. recognised the significance of implementing incremental methods of reform to help modify cultural norms and attitudes that condone the practice. For instance, some states insisted that changes in the attitudes towards FGM needed to be instigated from within the culture itself. This was to be carried out by incorporating relevant stakeholders such as tribal chiefs, religious leaders, and FGM practitioners in a national dialogue as part of the reform process. More specifically, this means to undertake a dialogue with relevant stakeholders, including religious and cultural leaders, as well as public education and awareness-raising campaigns. This incremental nature of reforms was amongst the most popular forms of recommendations, categorised as number 2 for both cycles. Similarly, an A4 response whereby the states under review provided information as to the different policies, strategies, and dialogues that were being undertaken with the relevant stakeholders was similarly the most popular form of response over both cycles. In fact, even in the A5 response in the first cycle where the states directly acknowledged that the strong affiliation with the practice and cultural norm was making addressing the practice difficult, policies and strategies were in place to eliminate the practice. Going further, even when the states noted the recommendation, the most popular form of response provided was that incremental reforms were in place. In this way, it is clear that the most prevalent response over both cycles, regardless of whether the state is being reviewed or is a reviewer, or whether the recommendation is accepted or noted, recognised the significance of implementing incremental methods of reform to help modify cultural norms and attitudes that condone the practice.

The nature of this discussion held amongst states affiliates with the moderate cultural relativist position, which aims to implement reforms in a culturally legitimate manner.[52] This is because one of the central premises of moderate cultural relativism is the belief that the only way of furthering universal human rights is to ground international human rights norms in cultural values and beliefs.[53] One method of doing this is to undertake an internal discourse within the culture itself with the aim of reinterpreting certain values and beliefs, which are inconsistent with human rights law, to bring them in line with current international human rights standards.[54] The fundamental aspect of such a discourse is that any reforms of cultural beliefs need to be undertaken from within the culture itself, by 'internal actors', to avoid the appearance of 'dictation by others'.[55] Evidence of suggestions that affiliate with this internal discourse was recognised by some states during discussions on FGM, who encouraged a constructive dialogue between relevant stakeholders with the aim of changing sympathetic attitudes towards the practice.

The implications of states adopting a position that is comparable with the moderate cultural relativist position is that they indicate that some states in the UPR process recognise that international norms on FGM are more likely to be observed if such norms are rationalised at local level, so that the content and the goals of the norms are better understood by members of local societies.[56] In this way, by encouraging the involvement of local leaders in the reform process, any suggested reinterpretations of cultural values and beliefs are more likely to be observed by individuals practising FGM.[57] Further, evidence of states recognising the significance of an internal discourse on FGM indicates a substantial commitment by the states involved in ending the practice. This is because implementing policies and strategies with the aim of encouraging an internal dialogue to discourage FGM requires demanding levels of political, social, and economic commitment, through initiatives such as public awareness campaigns and engaging in a dialogue with relevant stakeholders. By comparison, acceptance of recommendations by states to enact laws arguably requires less commitment than those committing to reforms based on moderate cultural relativism.

Abortion at the UPR Process

Contextualising Women's Rights in Relation to Abortion

Women's rights in relation to abortion have been described as 'the most controversial of all rights'.[58] This is because there is a passionate debate between those that defend women's rights to decide whether and when to bear children, and the defenders of the foetal rights who contend that the right to life is extended to the foetus.[59] The controversy of the issue was recently hailed back into the spotlight with President Trump's repeated pledges to severely limit women's access to abortion, as well as a referendum on the issue more closer to home in the Republic of Ireland which resulted in a landslide win in favour of repealing the ban on termination of pregnancies in very limited circumstances. The controversial nature of abortion was reflected in the UPR process, as over half of all the recommendations issued on abortion were not accepted by states under review under both cycles of review. Of course, there are a number of positions in between these two extremes, however, for the purposes of this study, the focus will be on states imposing a blanket ban on women's access to procedures for terminating an unwanted pregnancy, which is often accompanied with laws criminalising all forms of abortion.[60]

Given the controversial nature of abortion, it is not surprising that there is no international human rights norm that directly resolves the conflict of rights in relation to abortion. Nevertheless, the jurisprudence of the treaty monitoring bodies has played a significant role in advancing women's reproductive rights.[61] For instance, the Committee on the Women's Convention in its General Recommendation 24 on 'women and health' provides that state 'legislation criminalising abortion should be amended, in order to withdraw punitive measures imposed on women who undergo abortion'. Further, in 2002, a UN Special Rapporteur reaffirmed that hindrances on women's own sexual and reproductive lives, which are based on cultural and traditional norms, were a violation of a woman's human right to health.[62] Despite the advancement of women's reproductive rights, women are often denied control over their ability to bear children due to a blanket ban on abortion services. The pressure in some societies to produce a child within a reasonable time often means that women do not have access to abortion facilities due to cultural barriers in societies.[63] In other instances, a ban on the availability of abortion services is based on the religious belief that all human life is inviolable, which is argued to extend to human foetuses.[64] It is primarily due to this association between culture/religious norms and abortion services, whereby restrictions on abortion services are sometimes justified on such cultural/religious grounds, that the issue has been selected for the purposes of this investigation.

Findings on Abortion in the UPR Process

A total of 140 recommendations were issued to 54 different states over the two cycles of review. Of the recommendations issued, in the first cycle over 50% were not accepted, which increased to over 70% of the recommendations being noted in the second cycle. This is a strong indicator of how controversial the issue of abortion is to the extent there is even a lack of formal acceptance on the regulation of the issue despite the platform of the UPR process being heavily reliant on diplomacy. This shows that states were not coy in expressly expressing their views on abortion, despite being in contrast to international human rights law, on an international platform such as the UPR process.

First Cycle of Review

In the first cycle, 29 states were issued recommendations on abortion during state reviews, of four different types. In response, a total of 12 recommendations were accepted, whilst a total of 17 recommendations were noted. The states accompanied their responses with statements of six different categories; four for those that were noted, and two forms of statements issued with those that were accepted.

RECOMMENDATION 1

Under the first category of recommendations, the observer states were issued recommendations to amend, repeal, or review domestic legislation in order to decriminalise abortion so that it was permitted under certain circumstances. A typical example of a recommendation issued under this category was when the delegate of Sweden suggested Nicaragua 'consider reviewing laws regarding abortion, removing punitive provisions against women who have had abortion'.[65] A total of nine states received recommendations of this nature.

Strikingly, all recommendations issued under this category were noted. The delegates of Hungary,[66] Malawi,[67] and El Salvador[68] provided an N1 response, as the states noted the recommendation without providing any other comments. The delegate of Costa Rica[69] provided an N2 response as it stated that action was undertaken even before the UPR process.[70] The states of Andorra, Nicaragua, Papua New Guinea, and Ireland all provided an N3 response, as the states insisted that the domestic law and constitution extended the protection of rights to the unborn child, and on this basis, the states could not accept the recommendation to lift the legal ban on abortion. A typical response is when Nicaragua stated that it did not accept the recommendation 'for the amendment of the law prohibiting therapeutic abortion'.[71] The delegate added that 'this was clearly an issue of sovereignty, not a religious one. The majority of Nicaraguans believed that the right to life of the unborn was important'.[72] Similarly, the delegate of Papua New Guinea in its response stated that 'accepting this recommendation will go against the spirit of our Constitution, which is founded on Christian principles'.[73] This response is noteworthy because it is the only instance when a state, either observer or state under review, introduced religious values in their explanation for the position that was adopted in relation to abortion.

The delegate of the Dominican Republic provided a slightly different explanation for noting the recommendation, as it provided an N4 general response that provided no reference to the issue of abortion, and instead provided a very general response in the area of women's rights. Overall, when states under review were issued with a recommendation to lift a blanket ban on abortion, no state accepted the recommendation.

RECOMMENDATION 2

Observer states issuing recommendations under this category sought to encourage the states under review to lift the blanket ban on abortion by drawing upon the state's international human rights obligations. A typical example of a recommendation under this category was issued by Norway to Ireland 'to bring its abortion laws in line with ICCPR'.[74] A total of four states under review were issued with a recommendation of this nature. In response, only the state of Paraguay accepted a recommendation under this category and provided an A2 response. The state explained that the process of reforms on the ban on abortion was being implemented even before the UPR process.[75] The other three states noted the recommendation issued under this category and provided explanations for their positions which were very similar in nature. The states of Ireland,[76] Nicaragua,[77] and Chile provided an N3 response, explaining that to accept the recommendation would mean that it was contrary to the domestic laws and the constitutional regulation of abortion. For example, the delegate of Chile explained that 'induced abortion is forbidden in Chilean legislation'.[78] From the analysis above, it can be seen that even when states are issued with recommendations that draw upon their international obligations to encourage states to lift the ban on abortion, the states under review challenged such suggestions on the basis of exercising state sovereignty. From this it can be observed that the states under review are directly challenging the universality of international human rights standards, which have interpreted a blanket ban on abortion as a violation of women's rights to health.

RECOMMENDATION 3

The nature of the recommendations issued under this category were generic in nature as observer states made no specific references to the domestic criminalisation or blanket ban on abortion. Rather, the observer states focused their recommendations on encouraging the state under review to enact measures to prevent any form of unsafe abortion. A typical example of a recommendation under this category was issued by Sweden, who suggested that Sierra Leone 'address other causes of maternal mortality and other related issues ... such as ... unsafe abortion'. [79]

A total of three states were issued with a recommendation under this category. In response, the delegate of El Salvador accepted the recommendation and provided an A1 response as no further comments were made. It is notable that this

Table 4.3 Nature of Discussions on the issue of Abortion in the First Cycle

Universal Periodic Review Cycle 1		Responses by States under Review						
		A1 Accepted recommendations with no further comments	A2 Domestic laws/ policies already in place on abortion	N1 Noted recommendation/ further comments	N2 Laws already in place/ Abortion law under review	N3 Domestic laws used to challenge the reforms to blanket ban on abortion	N4 Generic response to recommendation	No response
Nature of Recommendations issued to states under review	**Recommendation 1** Decriminalise abortion under certain circumstances			Hungary Malawi El Salvador	Costa Rica	Andorra Nicaragua Papua New Guinea Ireland	Dominican Republic	
	Recommendation 2 Comply with international human rights obligations against a blanket ban on abortion		Paraguay			Ireland Nicaragua Chile		
	Recommendation 3 Generic suggestions in relation to abortion	El Salvador	Sierra Leone		Costa Rica	Ireland		
	Recommendation 4 To defend the right to life of the unborn child							Netherlands Timor-Leste San Marino

was El Salvador's only acceptance of a recommendation on abortion; other more specific recommendations issued to El Salvador were noted. On the one hand, when Sierra Leone was issued with a recommendation under this category, it accepted the recommendation but, at the HRC plenary session, it stated that it only accepted the recommendation 'subject to constitutional review', and therefore provided an A2 response.[80] On the other hand, the delegate of Ireland noted the recommendation and provided an N3 response as it drew upon its domestic constitution to justify not accepting the reforms on abortion.

The findings of the nature of discussions under this category lend further support to the suggestion that the issue of abortion was contentious in nature. This is because even the recommendations that were generic in nature, and therefore arguably less demanding, were not received well by the states under review. For instance, one state remained silent in their response, and the other two states suggested that the domestic law in the area held priority over any suggestions of reforms on abortion.

RECOMMENDATION 4

All the recommendations made under this category were issued by the Holy See, who holds a Permanent Observer State status at the United Nations. For the purposes of the UPR process, this means that a representative from the Holy See is permitted to participate in the discussions held at the interactive stage of the review process.[81] When abortion was discussed at the interactive dialogue stage, the Holy See issued recommendations during the reviews of three states. First, during the review of the Netherlands, the Holy See stated that 'the best way to respect the human rights of the child starts with the rejection of any forcible termination of his/her life, and with the recognition that the right to life is inviolable'.[82] Second, during the review of Timor-Leste, the delegate suggested that it should 'persevere in its efforts to protect human life from conception until natural demise'.[83] Third, at the review of San Marino, the 'Holy See highlighted the efforts ... to protect the rights of unborn children'. As the three recommendations were not classified as official recommendations, no states under review provided specific responses to the suggestions made by the Holy See.

From these recommendations, it can be observed that the representative of the Holy See adopted a position to actively encourage the state under review to protect the rights of the unborn child, and therefore, to restrict women's rights to access abortion services. The striking fact is that the delegate of Holy See was the *only* state that issued the recommendations on abortion to the three states under review in question. In addition, it is notable that the position adopted by the Holy See to expressly suggest that the state under review defend the rights of the unborn child was not adopted by any other observer state. For instance, the states of Andorra, Nicaragua, Papa New Guinea, Ireland, and Chile expressly challenged recommendations issued to them to lift the blanket ban on abortion based on the protection of rights of the unborn child. However, in their capacity as observer states, none of the five states listed above issued recommendations to states under review to ban abortion services based on protecting the rights of the foetus. This shows that whilst the five states justified their challenge to lift the ban on abortion based on the protection of the rights of the unborn child, none of the states themselves attempted to use this justification as a basis to issue recommendation to ban abortion services during the review of other states. The Holy See's recommendations to protect the rights of the unborn child are therefore unique in nature.

Second Cycle of Review

When the issue of abortion was raised in the second cycle, there was a drastic increase in the number of recommendations issued from 29 in the first cycle, to a 111 in the second cycle. However, it is notable the proportion of recommendations that were noted already increased to over 70% of the recommendations being noted. The biggest difference between the two cycles is the range of different types of recommendations that were issued, with a total of five different forms of recommendations in the second cycle. Similarly, the types of statements issued with the responses were also different, with ten different forms of response. This indicates that the nature of discussions on the issue of abortion varied considerably, in comparison to the first cycle, where there was a more restricted nature of discussion. However, despite such variation, it cannot be unnoticed that the number of recommendations issued in the second cycle were still overwhelming not accepted.

RECOMMENDATION 1

This form of recommendation was one of only two types of recommendations that were issued both in the first and the second cycle, which was to decriminalise abortion. Unlike the first cycle, where all recommendations of this nature were rejected by the states under review, a total of four were accepted, whilst 16 were noted. Columbia and Malawi accepted the recommendation without any further comments, the latter of which had under the previous cycle noted the recommendation without any further comments. In this way, for Malawi, whilst the delegate did not provide any further statement, it formally altered its response and accepted the recommendation. Whereas Bolivia provided an A2 response as it stated that 'it had recently adopted a constitutional decision permitting a procedure in cases of permitted legal abortion, based on the right of women and mothers to decide'.[84] Chile provided an A3 response, and insisted that abortion was permitted in certain circumstances. What is notable here is that whilst some states have accepted recommendations of this type in the second cycle, the substance of the statements that accompanied the response do not indicate any further commitments of forms of actions has been agreed by the states under review. States have simply remained silent on the issue or have referred to existing laws and permitted instances where abortion is permitted in their responses.

Of the states that noted the recommendation, Antiqua and Barbuda, DPR Korea, and Grenada all provided an N1 response as they noted the recommendation without any further response; this was the second most popular form of response. In line with the reviews in the first cycle, the most prevalent response to this form of recommendation was an N2 response, whereby states used national sovereignty as a justification for not reforming laws on abortion. In the second cycle, a total of eight states responded in this manner. Interestingly, Andorra and Ireland both provided the same response in both cycles, thereby not changing their position on the issue. The Dominican Republic maintained its formal position of noting the recommendation, however, the delegation changed its very generic statements issued in the first cycle, to an N2 response in the second cycle stating that the recommendation on abortion was 'inconsistent with the constitutional principles and domestic law and do not enjoy the support of the government'.[85] Costa Rica when issued with this recommendation in the first cycle, insisted that laws were under review and action was being undertaken in relation. Strikingly, in the second cycle of review the delegate of Costa Rica used national sovereignty as a justification of not decriminalising the laws on abortion. However, the states of Jamaica, Nicaragua, Paraguay, and Philippines also issued an N2 response. The state of Argentina provided an N3 response stating that 'the technical guide on nonpunishable abortion … had been revised and updated in order to explain in which cases a court order to perform abortion was not necessary'.[86] However, here, the delegate has not directly addressed the recommendation that has been issued, as Argentina has very restrictive abortion laws, and even when the criteria are met, doctors are not readily willing to undertake the termination with fears of prosecution. Here, the response provided by Argentina is clearly a strategy for deflection as whilst an update to policy may be undertaken, the crux of the recommendation to decriminalise abortion laws is not addressed. In this way, whilst the delegate has participated in the dialogue on abortion, it is clearly not fruitful and is used merely as a deflection tactic from the recommendation of decriminalising abortion.

The states of El Salvador and Honduras note the recommendation and provide an N4 response on the basis that such changes in the law would require a national dialogue. Whilst under the previous cycle, the state of El Salvador noted this recommendation without any further response, in this cycle the delegate began the response by insisting that 'the right to life [was recognised] at the moment of conception. It takes note of the recommendations since it believes that any legislative changes at this level would depend on a … comprehensive and participatory national dialogue'.[87] Unfortunately, in neither instance the states failed to make a commitment to commence steps to engage in this national dialogue.

The delegate of Malta was the only state that provided an N5 response. Whilst noting the recommendation, the delegate insisted that 'Malta had made declaration under article 16 of CEDAW and, thus, it was not bound by an obligation to legalize abortion'.[88] In this way, the delegate of Malta expressly used its reservation to the treaty as a justification for not accepting the recommendations on decriminalising abortion. Similarly, the state of Myanmar, provided a unique response by explaining that 'abortion is prohibited by law as it is not socially and culturally acceptable in its society'.[89] This response is unique in nature as it was the only instance, over the two cycles of review, where a state under review made references to cultural norms of society as a justification for not accepting the recommendation to decriminalise abortion.

Overall, unlike under the previous cycle, there were some states that accepted the recommendation under this cycle. However, on closer examination, the states that accepted the recommendations either remained silent, or made references to laws that permitted abortion, albeit in very restrictive circumstances. In this way, it can be observed that issuing such an arguably extreme form and demanding form of recommendation to decriminalise abortion has led to no commitments of actions being accepted by the states under review over either cycle.

RECOMMENDATION 2

The second form of recommendation was unique to the second cycle, and was issued to only two states, who were recommended to issue gradual changes to legislation on abortion. For example, Uruguay issued a recommendation to Nicaragua to 'consider the possibility of contemplating exceptions to the general prohibition of abortion, especially in cases of therapeutic abortion when the mother's life is in danger as well as in cases of pregnancies resulting from rape or incest'. Both Nicaragua and Rwanda noted the recommendation. Nicaragua issued an N2 response and insisted that 'legislation on the matter had been adopted by a majority vote in the National Assembly and was supported by the public opinion'.[90] In another instance, Rwanda provided an N3 response and stated the recommendation requested 'legal protection and guarantees are already in place and actively implemented'.[91] In this way, despite the recommendations themselves being incremental suggestions in nature, both states justified not accepting the recommendation by referring to existing laws on the issue in the domestic context. This, of course, does not demonstrate that the laws adequately permit abortion and are in compliance with the international norms on the issues in relation to women's rights, but in fact simply state that the issue is being regulated by law in the domestic context.

RECOMMENDATION 3

The third recommendation was again unique to the second cycle of review. The recommendations suggested that the states under review should initiate a public dialogue and education awareness campaign as steps towards introducing laws in relation to permitting abortion. A typical example of this is when the delegate of Czechia issued a recommendation to Malta to 'incite open, cognizant, public and expert discussions in Malta on introducing abortion legislation'. In response, all states noted the recommendation. Malta provided an N5 response pointing out to its reservation on CEDAW. On the other hand, the delegate of Myanmar

Table 4.4 Nature of Discussions on the issue of Abortion in the Second Cycle

Universal Periodic Review Cycle 2	Responses by States under Review									
	A1 Accepted recommendations with no further comments	A2 Laws have been revised	A3 In some circumstances abortion is permitted	A4 Deny the existence of sanctions of women undergoing abortion	N1 No comments	N2 National sovereignty on laws	N3 Laws have been revised	N4 Changes would require a national dialogue on the issue	N5 Exemption already made to International obligations and against national law	N6 Abortion is not culturally acceptable
Nature of recommendations issued to states under review										
Recommendation 1 Decriminalise abortion under certain circumstances	Colombia Malawi	Bolivia	Chile		Antiqua and Barbuda DPR Korea Grenada	Andorra Costa Rica Dominican Republic Ireland Jamaica Nicaragua Paraguay Philippines	Argentina	El Salvador Honduras	Malta	Myanmar
Recommendation 2 Gradually implement changes to the legislation on abortion						Nicaragua	Rwanda			
Recommendation 3 Initiate and promote public debate/education on abortion								El Salvador		Myanmar
Recommendation 4 Brings laws in line with international human rights obligations.	Malawi	Peru	Chile			Ireland			Malta	
Recommendation 5 Ensure abortion services are available and accessible to all	Georgia India Mexico Mozambique	Peru		Poland	Lebanon	Ireland Lesotho		Kenya	Malta	

Table 4.5 Nature of Discussions on Access to Health Care in the First Cycle

Universal Periodic Review Cycle 1		Responses by States under Review					
Nature of recommendations issued to states under review		A1 Accepted recommendation with no further comments	A2 Domestic laws already implemented/under review	A3 Information on measures and policies that are already in place	A4 Recognition of cultural barriers	N1 Noted recommendations with no further comments	N2 Policies already in place
	Recommendation 1 Generic recommendations on access to health care services	Bangladesh Benin Canada Costa Rica Cuba Democratic Republic of Congo Dominican Republic Equatorial Guinea Iran Laos Libya Malawi Niger Sao Tome and Principe Senegal Sierra Leone Syria Tanzania Thailand Togo Turkey Venezuela Viet Nam Yemen	Afghanistan	Afghanistan Bolivia El Salvador Romania Armenia Laos Macedonia Namibia Sao Tome Seychelles Sierra Leone Thailand		Suriname Malta Mexico	Bosnia and Herzegovina
	Recommendation 2 Amend/Reform/Implement law to protect women's rights to access health care services	Angola Nicaragua Timor-Leste		El Salvador	Paraguay		
	Recommendation 3 References to states' international obligations	Belize Spain Burkina Faso Guinea Gambia Guatemala Saudi Arabia				Israel	

Table 4.6 Nature of Discussions on Access to Health Care in the Second Cycle

Universal Periodic Review Cycle 2		Responses by the States under Review				
		A1 Accepted recommendation with no further comments	A2 Information on measures and policies that are already in place	N1 Noted recommendations with no further comments	N2 Policies already in place	N3 Denial of any discrimination on grounds of gender
Nature of recommendations issued to states under review	*Recommendation 1* Generic recommendations on access to health care services	Afghanistan Albania Andorra Croatia Cyprus DPR Korea Democratic Republic of Congo Ecuador El Salvador Ethiopia Guinea Iran Kyrgyzstan Malawi Malaysia Nepal Niger Republic of Congo Romania Saudi Arabia Somalia St Vincent and the Grenadines Yemen	Benin Central African Republic Chile Comoros Gambia Georgia Hungary Lesotho Macedonia Madagascar Maldives Micronesia Morocco Namibia Peru Philippines Senegal Sierra Leone Singapore Tajikistan Thailand Uzbekistan	Lebanon	Antigua and Barbuda Papua New Guinea	Kuwait
	Recommendation 2 Amend/Reform Implement law to protect women's rights to access health care services		Bangladesh		Nicaragua	Myanmar

provided cultural norms of society will not permit the acceptance of recommendation. Considering the recommendation is to consult a public dialogue on the
issue, it is clear here that Myanmar is presuming and presenting that the values
and norms of society in the domestic context are both unanimous and not subject to change. Finally, the state of El Salvador insisted that such changes would
require a public dialogue on the issue. This response is unusual, particularly as the
recommendation is to initiate such dialogues in the domestic context.

RECOMMENDATION 4

This form of recommendation is the same as recommendation 2 in the first cycle,
as it suggests that the state under review brings its domestic laws on abortion in
line with its international human rights obligations. A total of five states were
issued with this recommendation, of which three states accepted the recommendation, and two noted it. Malawi accepted the recommendation and provided no
further statements. Peru accepted the recommendations but insisted that therapeutic abortion was not illegal and permitted whereby there is a risk to permanent
harm to the female. In addition, it insisted that 'a draft technical guide regarding
its application had been developed and was under consultation'.[92] The state of
Ireland maintained its position from the previous cycle and claimed national sovereignty on the issue. On the other hand, Chile under the previous cycle noted
the recommendation and used the domestic laws to challenge the reforms that
were suggested. Under the second cycle, Chile changed its position to formally
accept the recommendation but insisted that abortion was permitted in some
circumstances. Whilst Malta expressly made references to its reservation on the
issue to the women's rights treaty, and thereby insisted that it was not subject to
any international human rights obligations on this matter.

RECOMMENDATION 5

The fifth recommendation was unique to the second cycle of reviews on abortion. This form of recommendation asked the states under review to ensure that
abortion services were available and accessible to all. For example, the delegate
of Finland issued a recommendation to Peru to 'adopt and implement a national
protocol to guarantee equal access to therapeutic abortion for women and girls as
part of sexual and reproductive health services'. Whilst in essence this form of recommendation was similar to recommendation 1, this form is more diplomatic in
nature, less confrontational, and more consensual in nature, which is in keeping
with the character of the review process. A total of nine states were issued with
this recommendation. In response, a total of six states accepted this type of recommendation making it the most accepted recommendation over the two cycles.
Georgia, India, Mexico, and Mozambique all provided an A1 response. Peru,
providing an A2 response, stated that domestic laws in relation to abortion have
been revised. On the other hand, Poland responded with an A4 response and

stated that 'the penal code did not envisage any sanctions for women that had undergone an illegal abortion'.[93] Despite the state accepting the recommendation, the statement accompanied does not correspond with the suggestions that were made by the state under review. The statement does not address the issue of accessibility of abortion, and rather clarifies that there are no sanctions on illegal abortions, rather than addressing the issues of the laws surrounding the issue of abortion, itself. As with many other responses by other states, the response provided by Poland indicates an attempted deflection away from discussing and addressing the laws of abortion itself, and instead generically talking about the subject and an issue that has not been raised.

On the other hand, a total of five states noted this recommendation. Lebanon was the only state that provided an N1 response. Ireland and Lesotho claimed sovereignty of national laws on the issue and therefore provided an N2 response. The delegates of Kenya and Malta noted the recommendation and provided an N3 and N4 response, respectively.

Discussion and Analysis

The issue of abortion is clearly contentious, and this has been reflected in the discussions held on the issue during states reviews over both cycles. Aside from the high number of recommendations that were noted over the two cycles, what is striking are the three key themes that have emerged in the nature of discussions that were held on the issue. First, the most prevalent recommendation issued under both cycles was to decriminalise abortion. In fact, in the first cycle no states accepted this recommendation, and most of the states under review provided an explanation for their position. This indicates that states not only directly challenged the reforms suggested on abortion but were also willing to explain the reasons why women's rights to abortion services were restricted in the domestic context. It is notable that the most common response issued by states for this recommendation and overall in both cycles was that national laws were sovereign on the issue of abortion. In this way, despite international human rights jurisprudence expressly providing that such legislation is contrary to women's right to health, an overwhelming number of states refused to accept this recommendation. In fact, a more direct challenge to the universality of women's right to access to abortion services was made when states, again in both cycles, were recommended to observe their international human rights law obligations in relation to abortion. These recommendations were more directly referring to the jurisprudence on women's rights to access abortion facilities. In this case too, the majority of the states under review noted the recommendations providing justifications of national sovereignty of laws as a reason for noting the recommendation. In fact, Malta in the second cycle when issued with a recommendation to comply with its international human rights obligations made reference to the reservations that were made to the treaty in relation to abortion. The overwhelming refusal to accept the recommendation to decriminalise abortion and to comply with international human rights obligations on the issue of abortion indicates a strong challenge to the universality of the women's rights universality of the international treaty jurisprudence that guarantees women's rights to abortion services. The overwhelming majority of the states responded using national sovereignty as a reason for not accepting the recommendation.

The implication of states adopting a position, whereby a challenge to the universality of women's rights to abortion is based on national sovereignty is, arguably, a more confrontational challenge to international norms than those that are justified on cultural grounds. This is because a justification of the non-acceptance of recommendations based on state sovereignty can be considered as being more definitive in nature, and arguably indicates a non-negotiable position on abortion adopted by the state in question. In contrast, when states adopted positions that resembled the cultural relativist perspective during the discussions of FGM, the nature of the statements indicated that their positions were not as definitive as projected by the states during the discussions on abortion. For instance, when states adopted positions that resembled the strict cultural relativist position on FGM, the states did make clear that it perceived the practice was against its international obligations and did not categorically deny the implementation of all aspects of the suggested reforms in the recommendation. By contrast, in the context of abortion, states using national sovereignty and the provisions in the domestic constitution as the basis for the categorical defence to accepting the suggested reforms aimed at lifting the ban on abortion. In this way, the states challenged the universality of women's rights to abortion services on the basis of national sovereignty, which clearly cannot be altered without state authorities initiating the reforms on the issue.

The second significant pattern that emerged was in the second cycle of review. The state of Myanmar when issued with Recommendations 1 and 3, responded by stating that abortion was prohibited by the state as it was not socially or culturally acceptable in society. This justification for not accepting reforms based on cultural norms was unique, as no other state over both cycles issued a response of this nature. This response is unique in nature as it was the only instance, over the two cycles of review, where a state under review made references to cultural norms of society as a justification for not accepting the recommendation to decriminalise abortion. This position adopted by Myanmar strongly affiliates with the strict cultural relativist perspective, as the state through its response has implicitly shared two of its core values. First, Myanmar adopts the traditional and closed definition of culture, and then portrays it as the claimed position on the international platform. This is because the delegate presumes that the proclaimed cultural norms that do not allegedly accept the decriminalisation of abortion are not only shared by all, but also that these views are to be held perpetually. The delegate does not provide any indication in the response that recognises the possible diversity in the values held within the cultural norms of society or of the possibility of them being subject to change or reform. A similar position was taken, albeit in a more implicit manner, by Nicaragua when it was issued with a recommendation to implement gradual changes to the law on abortion. In response, the state noted the recommendation, and stated the legislation adopted was voted for by a majority in the national assembly and supported by public opinion. In the cases of Myanmar explicitly, and Nicaragua more implicitly, the states held a static interpretation of public opinions on the issue of abortion, and presumed this not to be open to changes and reform. In addition, both states based their justifications for not accepting reforms on the presenting of, and very likely falsely, uncontentious public opinions on the issue. Second, the response of Myanmar uses the cultural norms of society as a justification for not accepting changes and reforms. This, again, is at the heart of the strict cultural relativist position whereby there is a strongly held rejection of any form of transcultural dialogue, and thereby refusing to accept the reforms suggested by those living outside the cultural boundaries. Myanmar used the cultural values and norms of society as a justification for not accepting any reforms from others that were beyond its perceived cultural boundaries.

The final pattern to emerge is that, over the two cycles of discussion on abortion no state under review committed itself to taking any particular action regarding their existing regulation of abortion. Now, at the outset, it is clear that the UPR process is a mechanism whereby changes and reforms are likely to be slow and evolutionary in nature. However, over the two cycles of discussions an overwhelming number of states noted that recommendation, and whilst the number of states accepting a recommendation in the second cycle had risen, an analysis of the nature of responses provided indicates a rather superficial nature of discussion. In all of the responses that were accepted over the two cycles, states either accepted the recommendation and did not provide any further comments, or simply referred to existing law. In relation to the latter, states either referred to domestic laws that regulated abortion, implying that laws were already in place or the states under review responded by stating that policies were currently being drafted to make the existing laws clearer. In this way, in the few recommendations that were accepted, the states under review failed to commit to any substantial actions that were to be taken as to reform the existing practices in relation to the issue of abortion.

Women's Right to Access to Health Care Services in the UPR Process at the UPR Process

Contextualising Women's Rights in Relation to Access to Health Care Services

For the purposes of this section, women's right to access health care services includes information and services made available by health authorities such as preventative medical care, reproductive choices, screening procedures, dietary factors, and other information on facilities to maintain health.[94] Access to such information is guaranteed under article 12 of the International Covenant on Economic, Social and Cultural Rights (ICESCR), which contains four interrelated elements, which include the accessibility of health care facilities.[95] On women's rights more specifically, the CEDAW places an obligation on states to take appropriate measures to enable women to 'access health care services, including those related to family planning ... and pregnancy'.[96] In fact, the Committee on the Women's Convention has recommended that states should remove 'all barriers to women's access to health services, education and information, including in the area of sexual and reproductive health'.[97]

Despite this apparent consensus amongst states in the review process and the numerous declarations of women's rights to access health services under international law, women continue to face restrictions when accessing health care services. These restrictions on women's access to health care are not always necessarily due to the lack of existence of such services. On the contrary, often the traditionally perceived role of women in the private sphere means that a woman's right to access health care services is more susceptible to restrictions from cultural barriers.[98] For instance, women are sometimes prevented from controlling their own fertility, subject to nutritional taboos, and traditional birth practices,[99] and prevented from accessing scientific medicine in favour of traditional remedies during pregnancy; all of which sometimes result in long-term harm or fatality.[100] On this issue, Radhika Coomaraswamy explains that it is often considered that women's primary duty is to reproduce, and, therefore, any health consequences from the process of childbirth are often explained by fate, destiny, and social and cultural practices, rather than a violation of women's rights to health services.[101] It is primarily this relationship between culture and women's rights to access health care services, whereby cultural barriers can impede women's right to access health care, which will be the focus of analysis.

Findings on Women's Right to Access Health Care Services

Over the two cycles of the UPR process, a total of 225 recommendations were issued to states on women's right to access health care services over the two cycles of review, with the majority of the recommendations being accepted. This suggests, at least formally, there is a consensus amongst the majority of states that were reviewed in the UPR process on the universal nature of women's rights to access health care services.

First Cycle of Review

In the first cycle of review a total of 67 recommendations were issued in the first cycle, of which over 92% were accepted. In terms of the dialogue, there were three different forms of recommendations issued by the observer states, and the states under review provided five different forms of responses.

RECOMMENDATION 1

Under this category of recommendation, observer states instructed states under review to ensure that women were provided with adequate access to health care services. The nature of the recommendations can be described as being generic in nature, as observer states did not make any references to the state's international obligations in the suggestions made, or provide any specific guidance as to the laws or polices that should be implemented. Instead, the observer states simply raised concerns, or made suggestions, that women should be provided with access to health services. Encapsulating the essence of this recommendation, during the review of Andorra, the Chinese delegate recommended to 'improve policy on healthcare and provide affordable health care services to women'. In the first cycle, this was the most prevalent form of recommendation. A total of 41 states were issued with a recommendation under this category, of which, only four noted the recommendation. The other 13 states that accepted the recommendation drew references to existing laws (A2) or policies (A3) that were already in place to ensure women have access to health care services. A typical example is the response of Bolivia who provided an A3 response and stated that 'the Plan of Sexual and Reproductive Health ... is being implemented to respond to the needs of the population, especially women ... Bolivia has strengthened its integral healthcare'.[102] The delegate of Afghanistan was the only state that provided a combined A2 and A3 response as it was stated that the right to health was enshrined in the constitution, and that polices were already in place to expand the public health service and improve maternal health.[103] The most popular form of response to this category of recommendation was an A1 response, whereby the states accepted the recommendation without any further comments.

On the other hand, a total of four states noted the recommendation, of which Suriname, Malta, and Mexico noted the recommendation without any further comments. The delegate of Bosnia and Herzegovina provided an explanation with its refusal to accept the recommendations by stating that 'gynaecological services at the primary, second and tertiary levels of health care during pregnancy, child birth and after childbirth and other health services are available to meet the needs of women'.[104]

RECOMMENDATION 2

Under this category of recommendations, the observer states instructed the states under review to reform domestic legislation to guarantee women's rights to access health care services. The nature of these recommendations is captured during the review of Myanmar, when the delegate of Canada issued a recommendation to 'repeal and mend Bill on Population Control and Health Care Bill ... and ensure respect for the human rights of women'.[105] A total of five states were issued with a recommendation of this nature; all of the states in question accepted this recommendation. The states of Angola, Nicaragua, and Timor-Leste accepted the recommendation without any further comments, and thereby provided an A1 response. The delegate of El Salvador issued and made reference to existing polices and measures that were already in place.[106]

On the other hand, the delegate of Paraguay adopted a distinguished position. The delegate began by stating that the government had taken initiatives focusing on the implementation of women's right to health; it then went on to add that Paraguay 'expects to achieve a significant reduction in the existing cultural, geographic and economic barriers that hinder access to health services' (UNHRC 'Paraguay, Addendum' 2011, A/HRC/17/18/Add.1 para 13). The nature of this response is significant as it is the first, and only time, in the two cycles of reviews where a state has recognised the significance of cultural barriers that can potentially impede women's rights to access health care services. Despite being the most demanding form of recommendation issued, which required the most action by the states under review, it was interesting to note that no state noted this recommendation.

RECOMMENDATION 3

Observer states that issued recommendations under this category drew upon the international human rights obligation of the state under review when making suggestion to ensure that women's rights to access health care services were protected. A typical example is when the delegate of the Netherlands issued a recommendation to Belize to 'take further concrete measures to enhance women's access to health care ... as recommended by the Committee on the Elimination of Discrimination against Women'.[107] This type of recommendation was only issued in the first cycle of review, and was issued to a total of eight states. In response, seven states accepted the recommendation without any further comments. The only state that noted the recommendation was Israel, who provided no further explanation.

Second Cycle of Review

In the second cycle, 158 recommendations were issued with states accepting a total of 87% being accepted. In terms of the nature of the discussions held, the scope was much narrower, with states only issuing two forms of recommendations, both of which were the same from the first cycle. There were five different forms of responses, largely the same as the previous cycle, with an additional form of explanation for not accepting a recommendation in the form of an N3 response.

RECOMMENDATION 1

As with the first cycle, in the second cycle of reviews, recommendations under the first category were most frequently issued, with a total of 49 states being issued with this type of recommendation. Similar to the first cycle, the most prominent response was the A1 response, to accept the recommendation without any comments with a total of 23 states opting to provide this response. A total of 22 states provided an A2 response, whereby states made references to existing policies that are in place to ensure women have appropriate access to health care services. An example is when the delegate of Comoros responded by referring to the government's existing health policies and stated that 'huge priorities had been made in ensuring vulnerable persons have access to health care'.[108]

On the other hand, a total of four states under review noted the recommendation, of these Lebanon noted the recommendation without any further comments. The states of Antiqua and Barbuda Papua New Guinea, whilst noting the recommendations, made references to existing health policies in place; the delegate of Papua New Guinea explained that 'health for women is supported and promoted at all levels in the country'.[109] Providing a more defensive response, Kuwait noted the recommendation and explained that 'all persons, without distinction on the basis of gender, enjoy equality in relation to healthcare'.[110]

RECOMMENDATION 2

In the second cycle, this recommendation was only issued during the reviews of three states. Bangladesh was the only state that accepted the recommendation, and provided information on existing policy measures that were in place to address the issue.[111] In contrast, Nicaragua noted the recommendation stating that 'the national strategy on sexual and reproductive health established strategic objectives' in relation to women's health.[112] The state of Myanmar also noted the recommendation, and explained that 'the objective of the law on health protection and coordination regarding population increase was to reduce poverty and promote maternal and child health'.[113]

Discussion and Analysis

Over the two cycles of review, just over 90% of all recommendations issued in relation to women's rights to access health care services were accepted. Based on the large numbers of acceptances of the recommendations on the issue, in the first instance, one may conclude that, at least formally, states share a consensus on the importance of protection of women's rights to access health care services, and to taking appropriate action in the domestic context to ensure that this right is guaranteed. However, on closer examination the nature of discussions held on the issue indicate that the apparent consensus veils the unfruitful dialogue that is held on the issue during state reviews. In light of this, it is argued that complex and multifaceted issues, particularly in relation to cultural barriers that women face in accessing health care services, were largely absent during the discussions amongst states in the two cycles of review. There are three main themes that have emerged from the nature of discussions that have been held on women's rights to access health care services over the two cycles of review. Each theme will be discussed separately, with a final section analysing the implications of these findings for the UPR process, and the protection of rights in the domestic context.

In the two cycles of review, the majority of the observer states when discussing women's rights to access health care services adopted positions by issuing recommendations that were generic in nature. Despite the apparent positive outcome with the majority of these recommendations being accepted, on closer examination, the recommendations lacked rigour and potency in suggesting significant reforms to be implemented to ensure that women were guaranteed to have sufficient access to health care services. In fact, the nature of the recommendations was so generic, that the suggestions made to implement rights were almost trivial. The issuance of these recommendations is problematic as its generic nature means that the states under review are not directed to implement any specific and significant policies in the domestic context to ensure that women are provided adequate protection of their right to access health care. Going further, the lack of a clear and detailed set of actions in these recommendations means that despite the wide-ranging acceptance, it is difficult to measure the extent to which the recommendations have been implemented both in the national and international context, and in particular, the future cycles of the review process. Consequently, this lack of clarity in the recommendations and commitment by states on actions to be taken to better protect women's access to health care in the most frequently cited recommendations gives reason to call into question one of the fundamental aims of the UPR process, which is to improve human rights issues and concerns in the domestic context.

When the issue of women's right to health was the focus of discussions during state reviews, the most frequent position adopted by states under review in response to recommendations was to accept the recommendation. However, a more detailed examination of the positions adopted by states indicates a less positive outcome. For instance, the majority of the states accepted the recommendation without any further explanations. The absence of any further comments by the states in the overwhelming number of instances on the issue firstly indicates unfruitful discussions between the states on further guaranteeing access to health care services for women, which is the sole purpose of the interactive dialogue. Further, the failure to provide a clear response by the states under review means that whilst the recommendations are accepted, it is not clear how it will be implemented in practice in the domestic context. As a result, any progression on the implementation of recommendations will be difficult to monitor, but in addition, it gives reason to doubt whether any substantial or comprehensive reforms will be implemented to better guarantee the right for women.

The second most frequent position provided by states under review in response to recommendations on women's right to access health care services was that whilst accepting the recommendation, information was provided on measures and polices on the issue that were already in place. This response was frequently issued in relation to the generic recommendations and El Salvador and Bangladesh adopted this response when suggested to reform domestic law to ensure better protection of the right. However, it can be noted that far more states responded in the second cycle by providing information on measures that were already in place. In this way, it can be argued that when generic recommendations were made in the second cycle, states were far more defensive in comparison to the first cycle as rather than remain quiet on the issue they chose to provide information on the policies in place to provide the protection. These positions adopted by states under review results in an unfortunate outcome. Whilst it is clear that the issue of women's right to health is clearly, to some extent, an issue of concern, the states under review have failed to adopt any new commitments or policy initiatives to ensure better protection of women's rights to access health care. In fact, the reference to existing policies would suggest that there is a fair possibility of the lack of *any* further initiatives being taken in the domestic context to provide better protection of the right. In this way, unfortunately, there is little in terms of substantial outcome from the UPR process, whereby the states have expressed commitments to reforms or implemented new practice to better guarantee the protection.

The subdued nature of responses continued even when the states under review noted the recommendations issued to them. In fact, in all instances when states noted recommendations on the issue, the responses have been one of the following three; to not provide any further explanation, to refer to existing practices or to deny the existence of any form of discrimination on gender. The ramifications of the subdued and defensive positions have resulted in these states not accepting any concrete commitments to improve the guarantee of this right for women as an outcome of being reviewed in the UPR process. For this reason, it can be argued that the promise of improving human rights on the ground through encouraging further promotion and protection of rights of the UPR process can be called into question.

The state of Paraguay provided a distinguished response when issued with recommendations to amend existing laws and policies to ensure the guarantee of women's right to access health care services. It is the only state in over nearly a decade of discussions on women's right to access health care in the UPR process, who recognised the significance of cultural barriers in women's rights to access health care and endeavoured to remove them. No other states, whether in their capacity as an observer state or state under review, recognised the possibility of cultural barriers potentially hindering women's rights to access health care services. This shows that despite the concerns raised in the academic literature of the culturally influenced barriers that women may face in accessing health care services, states when undertaking reviews or being reviewed in the UPR process largely failed to recognise the cultural norms and values that may impede women's right to access health care services.

The implications of states failing to recognise the association between culture and women's rights to access health care services are that there are only superficial, surface-level reviews of states on the issue. This is because some of the underlying and significant reasons as to why women are restricted from accessing health care services were not even raised during the discussions, not to mind being addressed. This absence by states in exploring the complex cultural barriers that often impede women's access to health care services is disappointing, particularly as it was expected that the dialogical and peer review nature of the review process was an apt platform to raise and discuss controversial and complex issues.[114]

Conclusion

This chapter presented the findings of the discussions held amongst states during state reviews on three issues under the broad category of women's rights to health: FGM, abortion, and women's access to health care services. Through an analysis of the positions and attitudes adopted by states during these discussions, the aim of this investigation was to gain a better understanding of the nature of the UPR process and how it operates. The findings of this investigation revealed that the nature of the discussions held amongst states differed significantly across the three women's rights issues. For the purposes of answering the research question, there were three significant positions adopted by states during the discussions of all three issues.

First, the findings of this study revealed that observer states adopted varied forms of the universalist positions during the discussions of all three issues selected for this project. For example, during the discussions of FGM, states that issued recommendations under the first category adopted positions that resonated with the strict universalist position. Further, in response to recommendations from a strict universalist position, it was found that states under review were overtly defensive in their responses as they either referred to existing laws and policies that were already in place or justified the continuance of the practice on cultural grounds. By comparison, during the discussions of abortion and access to health care services, the observer states adopted a less strict form of universalism. For instance, observer states during the discussions of abortion and access to health services simply made references to the states under review's international obligations in relation to the issue and encouraged the state to adopt measures to ensure compliance. Therefore, observer states during the states' reviews on abortion and health care services did not adopt positions which expressly indicate that international human rights norms on the two issues should be implemented, and that they should transcend cultural and religious norms. Further, the findings revealed that when observer states issued recommendations that were of a less strict form of universalism, the states under review provided different responses in relation to the issue of abortion and access to health care services. For example, in relation to abortion, states challenged the universality of the norms on national sovereignty. On the other hand, in relation to access to health care services, the states under review accepted the recommendations, but provided no further comments. The findings show that the nature of the universalist position adopted by some observer states in relation to the three issues does not instigate a certain form of response by the states under review. In this way, it can be observed that states under review were not coy to either expressly challenge, or to remain silent, on proclaimed norms of universality in relation to women's rights to which the states did not entirely concur.

The second significant difference that emerged between the discussions of the three issues was the significance of the strict form of cultural relativism. For example, this investigation found that states under review used the platform of the UPR process to challenge the universality of international norms in relation to abortion and FGM, albeit to varying extents and on different grounds. For example, in relation to FGM, whilst the states did not expressly challenge the universality of international norms on FGM from a strict cultural relativist perspective, the implications of the positions adopted by Mali and Liberia were similar to that of the strict cultural relativist position. In contrast, the states under review in relation to abortion expressly challenged the universality of women's rights to access abortion services largely on grounds of national sovereignty, with the state of Myanmar, in the second cycle, justifying the rejection of reforms on the grounds that it was not compatible with cultural norms. By comparison, it is interesting to note here that the responses by states in relation to access to health care services differed. No states expressly challenged the universality of human rights either from a national sovereignty or on cultural grounds. This may be because the nature of the discussions as a whole was largely generic, which may possibly explain the wide-ranging silence on the issue of access to health services.

The third significant difference between the discussions held amongst states on the three issues is the extent to which states adopted positions that affiliated with the moderate cultural relativist perspective during the review cycles. This position was the most prevalent position during the discussions held in relation to FGM, whereby the predominate nature of discussion was based around the implementation of gradual reforms to attitudes sympathetic to the practice, including through a form of internal discourse on FGM. The nature of this discussion can be contrasted with the overall discussions held amongst states in relation to abortion and access to health care services, where there was no evidence of states adopting a position that indicated a sympathetic attitude towards the moderate cultural relativist position. Instead the focus was entirely on eliminating laws against the practice, international obligations, or generic suggestions.

The implications of the lack of appreciation of the moderate cultural relativist position by the states can be seen when the nature and outcome of the discussions between the three issues are compared. For instance, where states adopted positions resonating with the moderate cultural relativist position during state reviews on FGM, states not only recognised the association between FGM and culture, but also suggested reforms to engage in an internal discourse on the issue, as well as implementing awareness-raising programmes, to help discourage the sympathetic attitudes in relation to the practices that are deeply embedded in cultural and traditional norms. In this way, not only have the states acknowledged the relationship between culture and FGM but have recognised the significance of suggesting reforms that are culturally legitimate to ensure compliance with international human rights norms.[115]

In contrast to the discussions on FGM, there was no evidence of the moderate cultural relativist position during the discussions on abortion and access to health care services. Instead, both observer states and states under review focused entirely on implementing or reforming domestic laws in relation to the issue, ensuring compliance with international human rights obligations or the implementation of generic actions in relation to abortion and access to health care services. There was a minimal level of discussion on the potential religious influences on the blanket ban on abortion laws or the potential cultural barriers that may be in place in relation to women's access to health care services. For this reason, there are grounds to suggest that the findings of these investigations show that lack of appreciation and understanding of the significance of culture in the discussion of international human rights in relation to abortion and access to health care services has led to arguably less productive discussions. This is because the possible cultural and religious barriers that may impede women from accessing abortion and health care services were not brought to the centre of discussions. In contrast, in relation to FGM, where there was evidence of some states adopting a moderate cultural relativist position, these lines of discussions were more fruitful as states recognised the need to engage in an internal discourse with those that sympathise with the practice to help eliminate it.

In conclusion, the findings of this study reveal that whilst aspects of the universalistic positions are evident through the positions adopted by observer states in all three issues in the UPR process, similarly a challenge to the universality of rights has also been raised by the states under review. However, it is noted that where states adopted positions of a moderate cultural relativist perspective, the result was that the discussions in relation to reasons why women's rights to health were violated through the practice of FGM were more productive and fruitful. In contrast, during the discussions of abortion and access, where there is an underappreciation of the moderate cultural relativist position, states resorted to more simplistic discussions on the issue, which focused entirely on the laws and compliance with international human rights norms.

Notes

1 UN OHCHR, 'Factsheet No. 23, Harmful Traditional Practices Affecting the Health of Women and Children' (August 1995), www.ohchr.org/Documents/Publications/FactSheet23en.pdf, accessed 31 August 2015.

2 Ibid.

3 Berta Esperanza Hernandez-Truyol, 'Human rights through a gendered lens: emergence, evolution, revolution' in Kelly D Askin and Dorean M Koenig (eds), *Women and International Human Rights Law* (Volume 1, Transnational Publishers Inc 1999) 32.

4 A Rao, 'The politics of gender and culture in International Human Rights discourse' in Dorothy Hodgson (ed), *Gender and Culture at the Limits of Rights* (University of Pennsylvania Press 2011) 169.

5 Ibid.

6 Julie Mertus, 'State discriminatory family law and customary values' in Julie Peters and Andrea Wolper (eds), *Women's Rights, Human Rights: International Feminist Perspective* (Routledge 1995) 135.

7 Berta Esperanza Hernandez-Truyol, 'Human rights through a gendered lens: emergence, evolution, revolution' in Kelly D Askin and Dorean M Koenig (eds), *Women and International Human Rights Law* (Volume 1, Transnational Publishers Inc 1999) 35.

8 See UN Human Rights Committee, 'CCPR General Comment No. 28: Article 3 (The Equality of Rights between Men and Women' (29 March 2000) CCPR/C/21/Rev.1/Add.10; UN Committee Against Torture, 'General

Comment No. 2: Implementation of Article 2 by States Parties' (24 January 2008) CAT/C/GC/2; UNGA, 'Intensifying Global Efforts for the Elimination of Female Genital Mutilations' (20 December 2012) A/RES/67/146; UN Committee on the Rights of the Child, 'CRC General Comment No. 7 (2005): Implementing Child Rights in Early Childhood' (20 September 2006) CRC/C/GC/7/Rev.1.

9 UN Committee on the Elimination of Discrimination against Women, 'CEDAW General Recommendation No. 14: Female Circumcision' (1990) A/45/38 and Corrigendum 1; UN Committee on the Elimination of Discrimination against Women, 'CEDAW General Recommendation No. 24: Article 12 of the Convention (Women and Health)' (1999) A/54/38/Rev.1, Chapter 1.

10 Ibid.

11 Dr Babatunde Osotimehin, 'Let's End Female Genital Mutilation/Cutting in Our Generation' (October 2013) www.unfpa.org/public/home/news/pid/15460, accessed 28 August 2019.

12 UNICEF, 'Female Genital Mutilation/Cutting: A Statistical Exploration' (UNICEF 2005) 17–19, www.unicef.org/publications/files/FGM-C_final_10_October.pdf (accessed 28 August 2019).

13 Isabelle Gunning, 'Arrogant Perception, World Travelling and Multicultural Feminism: The Case of Female Genital Surgeries' (1991–1992) 23 *Columbia Human Rights Law Review* 238.

14 MA Morgan, 'Female Genital Mutilation: An Issue on the Doorstep of the American Medical Community' (1997) 18 *J. Legal. Med.* 93, 95–96.

15 LF Lowenstein, 'Attitudes and Attitude Difference to Female Genital Mutilation in the Sudan: Is There a Change on the Horizon' (1978) 12 *Soc. Sci. & Merd* 417.

16 Layli Miller Bashir, 'Female Genital Mutilation in the United States: An examination of Criminal and Asylum Law' (1996) 4 *Am U J Gender & L* 415, 424.

17 UNHRC 'Cameroon' (3 March 2009) A/HRC/11/21, para 24.

18 UNHRC 'Ethiopia' (4 January 2010) A/HRC/13/17, para 41.

19 UNHRC 'Mali Addendum' (26 June 2018) A/HRC/38/7/Add.1

20 UNHRC 'Malawi' (4 January 2011) A/HRC/16/4, para 77.

21 UNHRC 'Niger' (25 March 2011) A/HRC/17/15, para 29.

22 UNHRC 'Somalia, Addendum' A/HRC/18/6/Add.1, para 98.21.

23 UNHRC 'Eritrea' (4 January 2010) A/HRC/13/2, para 72.

24 UNHRC 'Democratic Republic of the Congo' (4 January 2010) A/HRC/13/8, para 45.

25 UNHRC 'Lesotho' (16 June 2010) A/HRC/15/7, para 62; UNHRC 'Malawi' (4 January 2011) A/HRC/16/4, para 77.

26 UNHRC 'Mali' (13 June 2008) A/HRC/8/50, para 16.

27 UNHRC 'Iraq' (15 March 2010) A/HRC/14/14, para 48.

28 UNHRC 'Cameroon' (3 March 2009) A/HRC?11/21.

29 UNHRC 'Lesotho' (16 June 2010) A/HRC/15/7, para 62.

30 UNHRC 'Report of the Human Rights Council on Its Fourteenth Session' (23 October 2012) A/HRC/14/37, para 542.

31 UNHRC 'Report of the Human Rights Council on Its Eighth Session' (1 September 2008) A/HRC/8/52, para 997.

32 UNHRC 'Liberia' (4 January 2011) A/HRC/16/3, para 50.

33 Ibid.

34 UNHRC 'Liberia Addendum' (2011) A/HRC/16/3 Add.1, para 10.

35 UNHRC 'Mali' (13 June 2008) A/HRC/8/50, para 27.

36 UNHRC 'Sierra Leone' (11 July 2011) A/HRC/18/10, para 26.

37 UNHRC 'Mali' (13 June 2008) A/HRC/8/50, para 27.

38 UNHRC 'Somalia, Addendum' (16 December 2011) A/HRC/18/6/Add.1, para 98.1.
39 UNHRC 'Gambia' (24 March 2010) A/HRC/14/6, para 98.
40 UNHRC 'Cameroon' (5 July 2013) A/HRC/24/15, para 89.
41 UNHRC 'Indonesia, Addendum' (5 September 2012) A/HRC/21/7Add.1.
42 UNHRC 'Cameroon' (5 July 2013) A/HRC/24/15, para 89.
43 UNHRC 'Sierra Leone' (13 September 2011) A/HRC/18/10/Add.1.
44 R Sloane, 'Outrelativising Relativism: A Liberal Defence of the Universality of International Human Rights' (2001) 34 *Vanderbilt Journal of Transnational Law* 527, 541–542.
45 C Geertz, *Interpretations of Cultures* (Basic Books 1973) 49.
46 A Renteln, *International Human Rights: Universalism versus Cultural Relativism* (Quid Pro Book 2013) 58.
47 Ibid 49.
48 See the nature of internal discourse on human rights suggested by A An-Na'im, 'The cultural mediation of human rights: the Al-Arqam Case in Malaysia' in Joanne R. Bauer and Daniel A. Bell (eds), *The East Asian Challenge for Human Rights* (Cambridge University Press 1999) 156.
49 On the process of enculturation, see Alison Dundes Renteln, *International Human Rights: Universalism versus Relativism* (Quid Pro Book 2013) 58.
50 Sonia Harris Short, 'Listening to "the other"? The Convention on the Rights of the Child' (2011) 2 *Melbourne General of International Law* 305, 308; A An-Na'im, 'Toward a cross culture approach to defining international standards of human right: the meaning of cruel, inhuman or degrading treatment' in Abdullahi An-Nai'm (ed), *Human Rights in Cross Cultural Perspectives: A Quest for Consensus* (University of Pennsylvania Press 1995) 25.
51 M Iovane, 'The Universality of Human Rights and the International Protection of Cultural Diversity; Some Theoretical and Practical Considerations' (2007) 14 *International Journal on Minority and Group Rights* 231, 241.
52 A An-Na'im, 'Problems and prospects of Universal Cultural Legitimacy for human rights' in A An-Na'im and Deng (eds), *Human Rights in Africa: Cross Cultural Perspectives* (Brookings Institution 1990) 332.
53 A Renteln, *International Human Rights: Universalism versus Cultural Relativism* (Quid Pro Book 2013) 116.
54 A An-Na'im, 'State responsibility under International Human Rights Law to change Religious and Customary Law' in Rebecca Cook (ed), *Human Rights of Women: National and International Perspectives* (University of Pennsylvania Press 1994) 175.
55 A An-Na'im, 'The Rights of Women in International Law in the Muslim Context' (1987) 9 *Whitter Law Review* 515.
56 LA Obiora, 'Feminism, Globalization, and Culture: After Beijing' (1997) 4 *Indian Journal of Global Legal Studies* 355, 377.
57 See A An-Na'im, 'The Rights of Women in International Law in the Muslim Context' (1987) 9 *Whitter Law Review* 515.
58 Susan Deller Ross, *Women's Human Rights International and Comparative Law Casebook* (University of Pennsylvania Press) 571.
59 Ibid.
60 WHO, 'From Concept to Measurement: Operationalizing WHO's Definition of Unsafe Abortion', www.who.int/bulletin/volumes/92/3/14-136333/en/, accessed 28 August 2019.
    UN Committee on Economic, Social and Cultural Rights (CESCR), 'UN Committee on Economic, Social and Cultural Rights: Concluding Observations: Chile' (1 December 2004) E/C.12/1/Add.105, para 53; UN Committee on

Economic, Social and Cultural Rights (CESCR), 'UN Committee on Economic, Social and Cultural Rights: Concluding Observations, Malta' (14 December 2004) E/C.12/1/Add.101, para 41; UN Committee on Economic, Social and Cultural Rights (CESCR), 'UN Committee on Economic, Social and Cultural Rights: Concluding Observations, Monaco' (13 June 2006) E/C.12/MCO/CO/1, para 23.

61 Ibid.
62 UN Commission on Human Rights, 'Report of the Special Rapporteur on Violence against Women, Its Causes and Consequences, Ms. Radhika Coomaraswamy, Submitted in Accordance with Commission on Human Rights Resolution 2001/49: Cultural Practices in the Family That Are Violent towards Women' (31 January 2002) E/CN.4/2002/83, para 90.
63 Ibid 91.
64 M Perry, 'Religion, Politics and Abortion' (2001–2002) 79 *U. Det. Mercy. L. Rev* 1, 9–10; For an overview on the different religious positions for and against abortion, see www.bbc.co.uk/ethics/abortion/religion/religion.sh tml, accessed 31 August 2015); R Rainey and G Magill, *Abortion and Public Policy: An Interdisciplinary Investigation within the Catholic Tradition* (2nd edn, Fordham University Press 1996).
65 UNHRC 'Sweden' (16 June 2010) A/HRC/15/11, para 23.
66 UNHRC 'Hungary' (11 July 2011) A/HRC/18/17, para 95.15.
67 UNHRC 'Malawi' (4 January 2011) A/HRC/16/4, para 105.32.
68 UNHRC 'El Salvador' (18 March 2010) A/HRC/14/5, para 37.
69 UNHRC 'Costa Rica' (4 January 2010) A/HRC/13/15, para 12.
70 UNHRC 'Costa Rica, Addendum' (17 March 2010) A/HRC/13/15/Add.1, page 6.
71 UNHRC 'Nicaragua' (17 March 2010) A/HRC/14/3, para 31.
72 Ibid.
73 UNHRC 'Papua New Guinea, Addendum' (30 September 2011) A/HRC/18/18/Add, page 6.
74 UNHRC 'Ireland' (21 December 2011) A/HRC/19/9, para 108.3.
75 UNHRC 'Paraguay, Addendum' (31 May 2011) A/HRC/17/18/Add.1, para 10.
76 UNHRC 'Ireland' (21 December 2011) A/HRC/19/9, para 108.9.
77 UNHRC 'Nicaragua' (17 March 2010) A/HRC/14/3, para 31.
78 UNHRC 'Chile' (4 June 2009) A/HRC/12/10, para 54.
79 UNHRC 'Sierra Leone' (11 July 2011) A/HRC/18/10, para 80.21.
80 UNHRC 'Sierra Leone: Addendum' (13 September 2011) A/HRC/18/10/Add.1.3 page 6.
81 UNGA, 'General Assembly Resolution A/58/314 Participation of the Holy See in the work of the United Nations' (14 July 2004) A/58/L.64.
82 UNHRC 'The Netherlands' (13 May 2008) A/HRC/8/31, para 21.
83 UNHRC 'Timor-Leste' (3 January 2012) A/HRC/19/17, para 79.21.
84 UNHRC 'Bolivia' (17 December 2014) A/HRC/28/7, para 8.
85 UNHRC 'Dominican Republic Addendum 1' (11 June 2014) A/HRC/26/15/Add.1 para 98.
86 UNHRC 'Argentina' (12 December 2012) A/HRC/22/4, para 63
87 UNHRC 'El Salvador' (17 December 2014) A/HRC/28/5, para 20.
88 UNHRC 'Malta' (4 December 2013) A/HRC/25/17, para 90.
89 UNHRC 'Myanmar Addendum' (10 March 2016) A/HRC/31/13/Add.1, para 17.
90 UNHRC 'Nicaragua' (1 July 2014) A/HRC/27/16, para 62.
91 UNHRC 'Rwanda Addendum' (10 March 2016) A/HRC/31/8/Add 1, para 12.

92 UNHRC 'Peru' (27 December 2012) A/HRC/22/15, para 111.
93 UNHRC 'Poland' (9 July 2012) A/HRC/21/14, para 31.
94 Rebecca Cook, 'Women's Health and Human Rights in Afghanistan' (1998) 4 *Journal of American Medical Association* 19, 34. See also Mervyn Susser, 'Women's Health, Women's Lives, Women's Rights' (1992) 82 *American Journal of Public Health* 663.
95 UN Committee on Economic, Social and Cultural Rights (CESCR), 'General Comment No. 14: The Right to the Highest Attainable Standard of Health (Art. 12 of the Covenant)' (11 August 2000) E/C.12/2000/4, para 9.
96 UN Committee on the Elimination of Discrimination against Women, 'CEDAW General Recommendation No. 24: Article 12 of the Convention (Women and Health)' (1999) A/54/38/Rev.1, Chapter I, para 29.
97 Ibid. para 31(b) and 13.
98 Frances Raday, 'Culture, Religion, and Gender' (2003) 1 *International Journal of Constitutional Law* 663, 670.
99 UN Commission on Human Rights, 'Cultural practices in the Family That Are Violent towards Women' E/CN.4/2002/83, para 94.
100 UN OHCHR, 'Fact Sheet No. 23, Harmful Traditional Practices Affecting the Health of Women and Children' (August 1995), para 89.
101 Ibid.
102 UNHRC 'Bolivia (Plurinational State of)' (15 March 2010) A/HRC/14/7, para 55.
103 UNHRC 'Afghanistan' (2009) A/HRC/12/9, para 89.
104 UNHRC, 'Bosnia and Herzegovina' (4 December 2014) A/HRC/14/16, para 6.
105 UNHRC 'Myanmar' (24 March 2011) A/HRC/31/13, para 145.19.
106 UNHRC, 'El Salvador' (18 March 2010) A/HRC/14/5.
107 UNHRC, 'Belize' (4 June 2009) A/HRC/12/4, para 35.
108 UNHRC, 'Comoros' (7 April 2014) A/HRC/26/11, para 70.
109 UNHRC, 'Papua New Guinea' (13 July 2016) A/HRC/33/10/Add.1.
110 UNHRC, 'Kuwait' (13 April 2015) A/HRC/29/17/Add.1.
111 UNHRC, 'Bangladesh' (8 July 2013) A/HRC/24/12.
112 UNHRC, 'Nicaragua' (1 July 2014) A/HRC/27/16.
113 UNHRC, 'Myanmar' (23 December 2015) A/HRC/31/13.
114 F Cowell and A Milon, 'Decriminalisation of Sexual Orientation through the Universal Periodic Review' (2012) 12 *Human Rights Law Review* 341.
115 A An-Na'im, 'Problems and prospects of Universal Cultural Legitimacy for human rights' in A An-Na'im and Deng (eds), *Human Rights in Africa: Cross Cultural Perspectives* (Brookings Institution 1990) 332.

Bibliography

An-Na'im A, 'The Rights of Women in International Law in the Muslim Context' (1987) 9 *Whitter Law Review* 515.

An-Na'im A, 'Problems and Prospects of Universal Cultural Legitimacy for Human Rights' in A An-Na'im and FM Deng (eds), *Human Rights in Africa: Cross Cultural Perspectives* (Brookings Institution, 1990).

An-Na'im A, 'State Responsibility Under International Human Rights Law to Change Religious and Customary Law' in Rebecca Cook (ed), *Human Rights of Women: National and International Perspectives* (University of Pennsylvania Press, 1994).

An-Na'im A, 'Toward a Cross Culture Approach to Defining International Standards of Human Right: The Meaning of Cruel, Inhuman or Degrading Treatment' in

Abdullahi An-Naim (ed), *Human Rights in Cross Cultural Perspectives: A Quest for Consensus* (University of Pennsylvania Press, 1995).

An-Na'im A, 'The Cultural Mediation of Human Rights: The Al-Arqam Case in Malaysia' in Joanne R. Bauer and Daniel A. Bell (eds), *The East Asian Challenge for Human Rights* (Cambridge University Press, 1999).

Bashir ML, 'Female Genital Mutilation in the United States: An Examination of Criminal and Asylum Law' (1996) 4 *American University Journal of Gender, Social Policy & the Law* 415.

Cook R, 'Women's Health and Human Rights in Afghanistan' (1998) 4 *Journal of American Medical Association* 19.

Geertz C, *Interpretations of Cultures* (Basic Books, 1973).

Gunning I, 'Arrogant Perception, World Travelling and Multicultural Feminism: The Case of Female Genital Surgeries' (1991–1992) 23 *Columbia Human Rights Law Review* 238.

Hernandez-Truyol EB, 'Human Rights through a Gendered Lens: Emergence, Evolution, Revolution' in Kelly D Askin and Dorean M Koenig (eds), *Women and International Human Rights Law* (Volume 1, Transnational Publishers Inc, 1999).

Iovane M, 'The Universality of Human Rights and the International Protection of Cultural Diversity; Some Theoretical and Practical Considerations' (2007) 14 *International Journal on Minority and Group Rights* 231.

Lowenstein FL, 'Attitudes and Attitude Difference to Female Genital Mutilation in the Sudan: Is there a Change on the Horizon' (1978) 12 *Social Science & Medicine* 417.

Mertus J, 'State Discriminatory Family Law and Customary Values' in Julie Peters and Andrea Wolper (eds), *Women's Rights, Human Rights: International Feminist Perspective* (Routledge, 1995).

Morgan AM, 'Female Genital Mutilation: An Issue on the Doorstep of the American Medical Community' (1997) 18 *Journal of Legal Medicine* 93.

Obiora AL, 'Feminism, Globalization, and Culture: After Beijing' (1997) 4 *Indian Journal of Global Legal Studies* 355.

Osotimehin B, 'Let's End Female Genital Mutilation/Cutting in Our Generation' (October 2013), http://www.unfpa.org/public/home/news/pid/15460, accessed 28 August 2019.

Perry M, 'Religion, Politics and Abortion' (2001–2002) 79 *University of Detroit Mercy Law Review* 1, 9.

Raday F, 'Culture, Religion, and Gender' (2003) 1 *International Journal of Constitutional Law* 663.

Rainey R and Magill G, *Abortion and Public Policy: An Interdisciplinary Investigation within the Catholic Tradition* (2nd edn, Fordham University Press, 1996).

Rao A, 'The Politics of Gender and Culture in International Human Rights Discourse' in Dorothy Hodgson (ed), *Gender and Culture at the Limits of Rights* (University of Pennsylvania Press, 2011).

'Religion and Abortion' http://www.bbc.co.uk/ethics/abortion/religion/religion.shtml, accessed 28 August 2019.

Renteln A, *International Human Rights: Universalism versus Cultural Relativism* (Quid Pro Book, 2013).

Ross DS, *Women's Human Rights International and Comparative Law Casebook* (University of Pennsylvania, press).

Sloane R, 'Outrelativising Relativism: A Liberal Defence of the Universality of International Human Rights' (2001) 34 *Vanderbilt Journal of Transnational Law*, 527.

Short HS, 'Listening to "the other"? The Convention on the Rights of the Child' (2011) 2 *Melbourne General of International Law* 305.

Susser M, 'Women's Health, Women's Lives, Women's Rights' (1992) 82 *American Journal of Public Health* 663.

UN Commission on Human Rights, 'Cultural Practices in the Family That Are Violent Towards Women' E/CN.4/2002/83.

UN Commission on Human Rights, 'Report of the Special Rapporteur on Violence against Women, Its Causes and Consequences, Ms. Radhika Coomaraswamy, Submitted in Accordance with Commission on Human Rights resolution 2001/49: Cultural Practices in the Family That Are Violent Towards Women' (31 January 2002) E/CN.4/2002/83.

UN Committee Against Torture, 'General Comment No. 2: Implementation of Article 2 by States Parties' (24 January 2008) CAT/C/GC/2.

UN Committee on Economic, Social and Cultural Rights (CESCR), 'General Comment No. 14: The Right to the Highest Attainable Standard of Health (Art. 12 of the Covenant)' (11 August 2000) E/C.12/2000/4.

UN Committee on Economic, Social and Cultural Rights (CESCR), 'UN Committee on Economic, Social and Cultural Rights: Concluding Observations: Chile' (1 December 2004) E/C.12/1/Add.105.

UN Committee on Economic, Social and Cultural Rights (CESCR), 'UN Committee on Economic, Social and Cultural Rights: Concluding Observations, Malta' (14 December 2004) E/C.12/1/Add.101.

UN Committee on Economic, Social and Cultural Rights (CESCR), 'UN Committee on Economic, Social and Cultural Rights: Concluding Observations, Monaco' (13 June 2006) E/C.12/MCO/CO/1.

UN Committee on the Elimination of Discrimination Against Women, 'CEDAW General Recommendation No. 14: Female Circumcision' (1990) A/45/38 and Corrigendum 1.

UN Committee on the Elimination of Discrimination Against Women, 'CEDAW General Recommendation No. 24: Article 12 of the Convention (Women and Health)' (1999) A/54/38/Rev.1, chap. I.

UN Committee on the Rights of the Child, 'CRC General Comment No. 7 (2005): Implementing Child Rights in Early Childhood' (20 September 2006) CRC/C/GC/7/Rev.1.

UNGA, 'General Assembly Resolution A/58/314 Participation of the Holy See in the work of the United Nations' (14 July 2004) A/58/L.64.

UNGA, 'Intensifying Global Efforts for the Elimination of Female Genital Mutilations' (20 December 2012) A/RES/67/146.

UN Human Rights Committee, 'CCPR General Comment No. 28: Article 3 (The Equality of Rights Between between Men and Women' (29 March 2000) CCPR/C/21/Rev.1/Add.10.

UNHRC, 'Somalia, Addendum' A/HRC/18/6/Add.1.

UNHRC, 'The Netherlands' (13 May 2008) A/HRC/8/31.

UNHRC, 'Mali' (13 June 2008) A/HRC/8/50.

UNHRC, 'Report of the Human Rights Council on Its Eighth Session' (1 September 2008) A/HRC/8/52.

UNHRC, 'Afghanistan' (2009) A/HRC/12/9.

UNHRC, 'Cameroon' (3 March 2009) A/HRC/11/21.

UNHRC, 'Belize' (4 June 2009) A/HRC/12/4.

UNHRC, 'Chile' (4 June 2009) A/HRC/12/10.
UNHRC, 'Eritrea' (4 January 2010) A/HRC/13/2.
UNHRC, 'Democratic Republic of the Congo' (4 January 2010) A/HRC/13/8.
UNHRC, 'Costa Rica' (4 January 2010) A/HRC/13/15.
UNHRC, 'Ethiopia' (4 January 2010) A/HRC/13/17.
UNHRC, 'Iraq' (15 March 2010) A/HRC/14/14.
UNHRC, 'Bolivia (Plurinational State of)' (15 March 2010) A/HRC/14/7.
UNHRC, 'Costa Rica, Addendum' (17 March 2010) A/HRC/13/15/Add.1.
UNHRC, 'Nicaragua' (17 March 2010) A/HRC/14/3.
UNHRC, 'El Salvador' (18 March 2010) A/HRC/14/5.
UNHRC, 'Gambia' (24 March 2010) A/HRC/14/6.
UNHRC, 'Lesotho' (16 June 2010) A/HRC/15/7.
UNHRC, 'Sweden' (16 June 2010) A/HRC/15/11.
UNHRC, 'Liberia' (4 January 2011) A/HRC/16/3.
UNHRC, 'Liberia Addendum' (2011) A/HRC/16/3 Add.1.
UNHRC, 'Malawi' (4 January 2011) A/HRC/16/4.
UNHRC, 'Myanmar' (24 March 2011) A/HRC/31/13.
UNHRC, 'Niger' (25 March 2011) A/HRC/17/15.
UNHRC, 'Paraguay, Addendum' (31 May 2011) A/HRC/17/18/Add.1.
UNHRC, 'Sierra Leone' (11 July 2011) A/HRC/18/10.
UNHRC, 'Hungary' (11 July 2011) A/HRC/18/17.
UNHRC, 'Sierra Leone' (13 September 2011) A/HRC/18/10/Add.1.
UNHRC, 'Sierra Leone: Addendum' (13 September 2011) A/HRC/18/10/Add.1.3.
UNHRC, 'Papua New Guinea, Addendum' (30 September 2011) A/HRC/18/18/Add.
UNHRC, 'Somalia, Addendum' (16 December 2011) A/HRC/18/6/Add.1.
UNHRC, 'Ireland' (21 December 2011) A/HRC/19/9.
UNHRC, 'Timor-Leste' (3 January 2012) A/HRC/19/17.
UNHRC, 'Poland' (9 July 2012) A/HRC/21/14.
UNHRC, 'Report of the Human Rights Council on its fourteenth session' (23 October 2012) A/HRC/14/37.
UNHRC, 'Argentina' (12 December 2012) A/HRC/22/4.
UNHRC, 'Peru' (27 December 2012) A/HRC/22/15.
UNHRC, 'Cameroon' (5 July 2013) A/HRC/24/15.
UNHRC, 'Bangladesh' (8 July 2013) A/HRC/24/12.
UNHRC, 'Malta' (4 December 2013) A/HRC/25/17.
UNHRC, 'Comoros' (7 April 2014) A/HRC/26/11.
UNHRC, 'Dominican Republic Addendum 1' (11 June 2014) A/HRC/26/15/Add.1.
UNHRC, 'Nicaragua' 2014 (1 July 2014) A/HRC/27/16.
UNHRC, 'Nicaragua' (1 July 2014) A/HRC/27/16.
UNHRC, 'Bosnia and Herzegovina' (4 December 2014) A/HRC/14/16.
UNHRC, 'El Salvador' (17 December 2014) A/HRC/28/5.
UNHRC, 'Bolivia' (17 December 2014) A/HRC/28/7.
UNHRC, 'Kuwait' (13 April 2015) A/HRC/29/17/Add.1.
UNHRC, 'Myanmar' (23 December 2015) A/HRC/31/13.
UNHRC, 'Myanmar Addendum' (10 March 2016) A/HRC/31/13/Add.1.
UNHRC, 'Rwanda Addendum' (10 March 2016) A/HRC/31/8/Add 1.

UNHRC, 'Papua New Guinea' (13 July 2016) A/HRC/33/10/Add.1.

UNHRC, 'Mali Addendum' (26 June 2018) A/HRC/38/7/Add.1.

UNICEF, 'Female Genital Mutilation/Cutting: A Statistical Exploration' (UNICEF 2005) 17–19, http://www.unicef.org/publications/files/FGM-C_final_10 _October.pdf, accessed 28 August 2019.

UN OHCHR, 'Fact Sheet No. 23, Harmful Traditional Practices Affecting the Health of Women and Children' (August 1995).

UN OHCHR, 'Factsheet No.23, Harmful Traditional Practices Affecting the Health of Women and Children' (August 1995), http://www.ohchr.org/Documents/ Publications/FactSheet23en.pdf, accessed 31 August 2015.

WHO, 'From Concept to Measurement: Operationalizing WHO's Definition of Unsafe Abortion', http://www.who.int/bulletin/volumes/92/3/14-136333/ en/, accessed 28 August 2019.

5 Women's Rights under Private and Family Law

Introduction

Up until the recent past, the artificial divide between the public and private sphere in the international human rights framework has resulted in human rights norms being conceptualised in such a way that women's experiences of oppression, violence, and perpetual discrimination that exist in the private sphere, have been largely unappreciated.[1] Since the 1980s, a number of international human rights instruments, together with treaty body jurisprudence, have strongly affirmed that states are considered to be under an obligation to protect women's rights from being violated in the private sphere.[2] More specifically, the incursion of the Convention on the Elimination of Discrimination against Women (CEDAW) into the private sphere is predominately illustrated by Article 16, which obligates states to 'take all appropriate measures to eliminate discrimination against women in all matters relating to marriage and family relations'.[3] Despite the repeated declarations at international level, women continue to face violations of their rights under private and family law. One possible explanation for this is that issues that largely affect women are often relegated to the private sphere, which is significantly more likely to be governed by values and beliefs that are embedded in culture.[4] As a result, the universality of women's rights protection on issues relating to private and family law is more likely to be challenged from a cultural relativist perspective.[5]

This chapter will present and analyse the findings for the three issues that were selected under women's rights under private and family law; inheritance, polygamy, and the issue of forced and early marriage. A total of 434 recommendations were made on the three issues in relation to women's rights in relation to private and family law. Focusing on the nature of the discussions held on the issues over the two cycles, the aim of the examination is to enable the assessment of whether the core aim of the Universal Periodic Review (UPR) process is being met or challenged by the most profound criticism of universality, the cultural relativist critique; this core aim being to give effect to the principle of universality of international human rights norms.. The structure of the chapter will follow that of the previous chapter. The chapter is divided into three main sections, according to the issues that are being examined. Each of the three sections will begin with contextualising the issue, and then will move on to present the findings and analysis of each investigation.

Polygamy at the UPR Process

Contextualising Women's Rights in Relation to Polygamy

Polygamy is a general term used to describe a marriage where a husband has more than one wife.[6] Whilst there are no international human rights norms that expressly prohibit polygamy, treaty jurisprudence has interpreted the practice of such marriages as being incompatible with the principles of equality and non-discrimination in relation to the right to marry, and therefore, recommended polygamy be abolished.[7] The most profound claim is that such marriages are contrary to the protection of the right to non-discrimination and equality before the law, as polygamous marriages permit a man to take an additional spouse, but do not grant a similar right to a woman to take a husband; on this basis, it has been stated that such marriages should be prohibited.[8] Moreover, the Committee on the CEDAW has made it clear that as polygamous marriages are incompatible with a number of women's rights, they should be prohibited regardless of whether such marriages are deeply rooted in cultural and traditional values.[9] Despite the repeated declarations by treaty bodies that polygamous marriages contravene a number of women's rights, such marriages continue to be practised,[10] and are regulated in a variety of different ways. Those that are sympathetic to the practice often justify the continuance of such marriages using religious and/or cultural justifications.[11] For instance, Quranic verses IV: 3–5 is cited by some as legitimising, or even mandating, the practice of polygamy.[12] Others support the existence of polygamous marriages based on cultural values as they insist that this form of marriage institution facilitates sociopolitical alliances, as well as being the source of prestige, power, and influence.[13] In essence, within the traditional public and private divide, the issue of polygamy is considered to fall within the 'private' sphere, whereby issues of family and domestic life are more susceptible to the regulation by cultural norms.[14] It is because of this increased susceptibility to the possible justifications based on cultural norms for the practice of polygamy that it has been selected for the purposes of this investigation.

Findings on Polygamy in the UPR Process

Over the two cycles of review, the issue of polygamy was raised during the reviews of 18 states with a total of 22 recommendations being issued over the two cycles. The discussions on polygamy were predominately held in the first cycle, as the issue was only raised during the review of five states in the second cycle of the UPR process. Over 45% of the recommendations were noted by the states under review, which demonstrates the controversial nature of the issue.

First Cycle of Review

In the first cycle, a total of 14 recommendations were issued to states under review, a majority of which were not accepted. In terms of the nature of discussions, four different types of recommendations were issued, and six different types of responses were provided by the states under review on the issue of polygamy.

RECOMMENDATION 1

Observer states that issued recommendations under the first category expressly declared polygamous marriages to be a harmful traditional practice that was required to be eliminated. Encapsulating the essence of this recommendation, during the review of Equatorial Guinea, the Norwegian delegate recommended to 'combat harmful traditional practices under customary law, such as … polygamy'.[15] A total of four states were issued with recommendations under this category. The state of Madagascar provided an A1 response and accepted the recommendation without any comments, whilst Equatorial Guinea noted the recommendation, without any response providing an N1 response. However, Botswana adopted a different position. The state provided an N2 response, at it noted the recommendations and denied that the 'existence of harmful practices to women, especially those alleging the … existence of polygamy'.[16] The denial of the existence of polygamous marriage is surprising as Botswanaian law operates under a dual system, whereby customary laws are applied alongside common law. Thus, whilst a person may only have one registered spouse under common law, a man can take more than one wife under customary law.[17] This demonstrates an oversight of the de facto existence of such marriages under customary law. One common factor that can be observed from the dialogue above is that when issued with a recommendation under the first category, the responses by the states under review were overwhelming subdued. This is because states under review either accepted or noted the recommendations with no further comments or denied the existence of polygamous marriages. See Tables 5.1 and 5.2.

RECOMMENDATION 2

The second category of recommendations issued by observer states focused on the enactment or amendment of domestic legislative provisions in relation to polygamy. A typical example under this category is Argentina's recommendation to Kyrgyzstan to 'enact laws criminalizing … polygamy'.[18] A total of four states were issued with this form of recommendation. In response, Kyrgyzstan was the only state that accepted a recommendation under this category, and provided an A1 response. The Central African Republic (CAR) issued an N3 response as the delegate stated that the current 'family code was being reviewed to ensure its compliance with international standards with a view to either maintaining or abolishing polygamy'.[19] The refusal to formally accept the recommendation, together with the statement that indicates that CAR is open to the possibility of polygamous marriages, suggests that such marriages continue to exist, or be implicitly condoned, in the domestic context. This gives reason to suggest that the CAR may adopt a position under domestic law which may be contrary to its international human rights position in relation to polygamous marriages.

Table 5.1 Nature of Discussions on the issue of Polygamy in the First Cycle

Universal Periodic Review Cycle 1	Responses by States under Review					
	A1 Accepted with no further comments	*A2 Domestic laws already in place which prohibit polygamy*	*N1 No further comments*	*N2 Denial of the existence of any practices harmful to women*	*N3 Domestic laws on polygamy under review*	*N4 Reforms challenged on cultural and/or religious grounds*
Nature of recommendations issued to states under review						
Recommendation 1 Polygamy declared as a harmful traditional practice	Madagascar	Turkey	Equatorial Guinea	Botswana		
Recommendation 2 Reforms to domestic legislation on polygamy	Kyrgyzstan				CAR	Burkina Faso Tanzania
Recommendation 3 Ensure compliance with international human rights law on polygamy		Israel				Libya Ghana
Recommendation 4 Adopt measures to eliminate polygamy	Kyrgyzstan Mauritania					Senegal

Table 5.2 Nature of Discussions on the issue of Polygamy in the Second Cycle

Universal Periodic Review Cycle 2	Responses by States under Review			
	A1 (Accepted with no further comments)	A2 (Domestic laws already in place which prohibit polygamy)	N1 (No further comments)	N2 (Reforms challenged on cultural and/or religious grounds)
Nature of recommendations issued to states under review				
Recommendation 1 Reforms to domestic legislation on polygamy		Equatorial Guiana		
Recommendation 2 Ensure compliance with international human rights law on polygamy			Morocco	
Recommendation 3 Adopt measures to eliminate polygamy	Democratic Republic of Congo Russia			Burkina Faso

The responses provided by Burkina Faso and Tanzania were bold and distinctive in nature. This is because the states justified the continuance of polygamous marriages on the basis that they were condoned by cultural or religious norms of the state under review. Having noted the recommendation, the delegate of Burkina Faso began by explaining that 'polygamous marriage was optional whereas monogamy was the rule'.[20] Going further, Burkina noted the recommendation and explained that polygamy was 'one of the secular aspects of the culture of Burkina Faso'.[21] Similarly, the delegate of Tanzania explained that the recommendation was noted 'on the basis of the enjoyment of cultural and religious rights'.[22] In this way, both states noted the recommendation and provided an N4 explanation for their responses.

RECOMMENDATION 3

Under the third category the observer states recommended that the state under review should ensure that the domestic legislation was in compliance with the international human rights law in relation to polygamy. A typical example under this category is when Slovenia issued a recommendation under this category to Ghana 'to effectively implement measures aimed at eliminating polygamy and bring the norms in line with the CEDAW in the shortest time possible'.[23] In total, three observer states were each issued with recommendations under this category. Of these, Israel was the only state that accepted the recommendation and provided an A2 response, as it outlined the domestic action that was already being undertaken in relation to polygamy. The delegate stated that it 'agreed to adopt the recommendation … on polygamy, and had recently reinstructed the Qaddi's of the sharia courts to refer every suspected case of polygamy to the police'.[24]

In other instances during the review, the delegates of Ghana and Libya both noted the recommendations and provided explanations that were similar in nature. The delegate of Ghana explained that marriages that were customary or faith-based 'were in conformity with the customs and traditions of Ghana'.[25] Similarly, the Libyan delegate noted the recommendation under this category explaining that the suggested reforms were 'in conflict with the Islamic religion and the customs, cultural specificities and principles of the Libyan people'.[26] It can be observed that in both instances, the delegates of Ghana and Libya justified not accepting reforms to domestic law to comply with international norms on polygamy by drawing upon customs, traditions, and cultural particularities of the states. The two state delegates were not reluctant to expressly prioritise the cultural and traditional particularities of the state above compliance with international human rights norms in relation to polygamy on an international forum such as the UPR.

RECOMMENDATION 4

This category of recommendation can be described as being more generic in nature. Here, observer states suggested that the state under review should adopt measures to eliminate polygamy, without any references to the states' domestic legislation or its international human rights obligations. A typical example is during the review of Kyrgyzstan when Lithuania and Uruguay[27] issued a recommendation to 'take additional actions to eliminate ... polygamy'.[28] There were a total of three states that were issued with recommendations of this nature. In response to recommendations under this fourth category, two states under review accepted the recommendations, whilst one state noted it. The delegates of Kyrgyzstan and Mauritania accepted the recommendations and provided an A1 response.[29] By comparison, the delegate of Senegal noted the recommendations and provided an N4 response as it noted the recommendation and insisted that the observer states 'should take into account the particularities of the Muslim religion which explains the existence of polygamy'.[30] Thus, the delegate of Senegal expressly challenged the suggested reforms in relation to polygamy on the basis of the religious particularities of the states, which justified the existence of polygamous marriages.

Second Cycle of Review

Given the contentious nature of discussions on the issue of polygamy in the first cycle, one may be forgiven for speculating that this issue may have been raised more often during the reviews in the second cycle. To the contrary, the number of recommendations issued to states dramatically dropped in the second cycle, as only five states were issued with this recommendation in the second cycle. This deviates from the pattern set in relation to the other issues that have been examined whereby there is an increase in the number of recommendations issued in the second cycle. Reflecting the reduction in dialogue, there were only three forms of recommendations, and four types of responses issued on polygamy.

RECOMMENDATION 1

In the second cycle of review, a recommendation under this category was only issued once, which was accepted by Equatorial Guinea; the delegate noted that existing laws to prohibit polygamy were already in place.[31] It is noteworthy that in the first cycle, the state of Equatorial Guinea was issued with a recommendation under the first category, where it noted the response with no further comments. In the second cycle, when issued with a different form of recommendation that focused on reforms on domestic legislation on polygamy, as opposed to it being a harmful practice, the state altered its position and accepted the recommendations.

RECOMMENDATION 2

In the second cycle of review, only the delegate of Morocco was issued with a recommendation to comply with its international human rights obligations. In response, the delegate noted the recommendation and provided no further explanation, thereby providing an N1 response.

RECOMMENDATION 3

In the second cycle, a total of three states were issued with a recommendation to adopt measures to eliminate polygamy. In response, the Democratic Republic of Congo and Russia accepted the recommendations without any further comments. In contrast, Burkina Faso noted the recommendation and explained that 'those recommendations which were not accepted did not adapt easily to the present cultural and socio-economic realities of Burkina Faso'.[32] Here, it is important to note that Burkina Faso was one of the two states that were issued with a recommendation on polygamy both in the first and second cycle. In the first cycle, the state was issued with a recommendation category 2, which was more specific in nature as the state was instructed to undertake reforms to domestic legislation on polygamy. In both instances, despite the change in recommendation in the second cycle of being arguably vague and less demanding in nature, the state provided the same response, that the reforms cannot be adopted due to cultural factors. In addition, Burkina Faso was the only state that provided cultural justification as an explanation for rejecting reforms on polygamy.

Discussion and Analysis

As noted above, over 45% of recommendations issued in relation to polygamy over the two cycles have been noted. This demonstrates not only the contentious nature of the issue, but also, that the contentious nature is significant to the extent that there is a lack of formal consensus on the issue on a non-confrontational and diplomatic platform such as the UPR process. There are two prevailing findings in relation to the nature of discussions held on polygamy over the two cycles.

The first finding is that there is a noticeable discrepancy in states being held accountable for the recommendations that were noted in the first cycle. For instance, the states of Tanzania, Libya, Ghana, and Senegal provided unwavering reasons for declining to accept the recommendations on polygamy in the first cycle. None of these states were held accountable for their strong positions on the issue in the second cycle. Some of this blame can be laid in the establishing resolutions of the UPR process, which, unfortunately, provide that the aim of the second cycle is to focus on the implementation of accepted recommendations,[33] and provide no guidance for action on those recommendations that are noted. For instance, not only was Burkina Faso the only state that was held accountable on the issue of polygamy in the second cycle as well as the first but also the delegate provided the same N4 response in the second cycle. For this reason, it is suggested that it is likely that the noted recommendations should be the issue of further concern, and areas in which further discussions should take place on the UPR process. This lack of accountability of states that held a strong position on declined recommendations on polygamy is a cause for concern, as it calls into question the fundamental purpose of the UPR process to improve and address all human rights situations on the ground.[34]

The second finding is largely in relation to the discussions held on polygamy in the first cycle about how some states, either in their capacity as observer states or states under review, expressly recognised the association between polygamous marriages and cultural norms in one of two ways. First, observer states that issued recommendations under the first category used the relationship between polygamy and culture as a foundation to criticise the practice and recommend that it be eradicated. The nature of these statements indicates any deviations from the international human rights jurisprudence, which provided protection to women's rights against polygamous marriages, will not be accepted; despite such marriages being embedded in the traditional values of the state. It is posited that the essence of this position adopted by observer states resonates with the strictest interpretation of universalism. At the heart of this position is that the implementation of human rights norms should transcend any cultural boundaries and particularities.[35] In this regard, it is notable that when statements of the very strong form of universalism were issued, the states under review demonstrated a very subdued and defensive position. For instance, the states under review either accepted or noted the recommendation and remained silent or emphasised that existing laws were already in place. This ultimately resulted in an arguably unfruitful dialogue, as the states under review failed to agree on any commitments on reforms to domestic regulation on polygamy to abide by the international position on such marriages.

The second manner in which the relationship between polygamy and culture was recognised was in the issuance of N4 responses. Here, some states under review used the relationship between culture and polygamy as a foundation to justify the existence of such marriages, and to decline to accept the recommendations on the issue. This position, which was adopted by the vast majority of states under review that did not accept the recommendations on polygamy, affiliates with the strongest form of cultural relativism. At the heart of this belief is the position that legal and moral standards, which are determined by cultural values, trump any universal claims on a particular issue.[36] This belief is reflected in the essence of the position posited by Burkina Faso, Chile, Ghana, Libya, and Senegal, who all expressly challenged the suggested reforms to the regulation of polygamy, and justified their position on the ground that such marriages were embedded in cultural and religious norms. This implies that the legitimisation of polygamy by internal cultural norms of the states takes priority over any external moral or legal standards that may declare polygamous marriages to be contrary to international human rights norms. Despite such an express and obvious challenge to the universality of the international human rights jurisprudence on polygamy, it was notable that no observer states capitalised on the benefits of an instantaneous dialogue at the UPR process to hold the states under review accountable for such a bold rejection of reforms. One of the fundamental criticisms of strict cultural relativism is its exaggerated claim of the impossibility of cross-cultural dialogue, which is used as a basis to provide immunity from criticism to any norms and values that emanate from culture.[37] The failing by observer states to hold states that affiliated with the strictest form of relativism to account lends support to these very criticisms. This is disappointing, particularly as the UPR process is characterised by its constructive and cooperative dialogue, which was envisaged to create an apt international platform to discuss culturally sensitive and controversial issues.[38]

So far it can be observed that whenever the relationship between polygamy and culture has been recognised during state reviews, the positions adopted by states affiliate with the strongest forms of either universalist or relativist positions. This is in sharp contrast to the contemporary scholarly debates on the issue, where the conversation on the conceptualisation and implementation of rights has moved away from such polarised extremes, towards more nuanced alternatives that have focused on reaping the benefits of both positions.[39] Going further, when the polarised extremes are adopted in *practice* on an international discourse on human rights norms, the findings of this investigation reveal that the presumed conceptualisation of culture, and the implications that derive from this interpretation, gives grounds to suggest that there are more similarities with the two positions than is initially apparent.

To begin with, state representatives that have adopted a universalist or relativist approach have, either explicitly or implicitly, adopted a traditional conceptualisation of culture.[40] This is because those states that issued category 1 recommendations, or N4 responses, have presumed the very belief that has subjected this interpretation of culture to wide criticism, which is that norms and values within culture are immune from changes and reforms. For example, states that posited a universalist position under category 1 recommendations not only suggested the prohibition of polygamous marriages, but the references to culture also implied that the cultural values and beliefs, which may condone polygamous marriages should also be eliminated. This shows that the observer states issuing the recommendations failed to consider if, and how, the cultural norms that condone such marriages can be reformed. Similarly, the states that issued N4 responses to defend polygamy, from a position that resonated with cultural relativism, failed to recognise the possibility that cultural and religious particularities that underpin such marriages may be subject to contentions within the proclaimed culture, or even subject to reforms.

The implications of such a polarised debate during state reviews are that the discussions on the relationship between culture and polygamy are oversimplified. Drawing upon the analysis of Ann-Belinda Pries, she explains that in between the strict opposite positions of the relativist and universalist debate, 'it is as if larger, more important questions are lurking under the surface, but they remained unexplored and somewhat blocked precisely because of the rigid "us" and "them" dichotomy inherent in the "culture contact" perspective'.[41] This oversight of larger unexplored issues is evident in the polarised manner in which the discussions of polygamy in the UPR process were held.

This oversimplistic nature of discussions on the relationship between polygamy and culture draws emphasis on the absence of one clear dimension of discussions being held in the UPR process. Both in the first and second cycle of the debate, the discussions held in the interactive dialogue sessions have failed to recognise the merits of cultural support in the conversations of implementing universal human rights. In other words, there is a clear absence of discussions affiliating with the mediated middle ground between universalism and relativism towards achieving culturally legitimate human rights. One aspect of furthering the goal of culturally legitimate human rights is for external actors not only to discuss the scope and implementation of rights, but also to encourage those within the culture to engage in an internal discourse to help legitimise human rights in the domestic context.[42] The unique and innovative character of the interactive dialogue session is one of the most obvious platforms for this cross-cultural dialogue to be undertaken on. Unfortunately, there is no evidence of the discussions in either cycle that even vaguely resonated with this approach.

Women's Rights to Inheritance at the UPR Process

Contextualising Women's Rights in Relation to Inheritance

For the purposes of this investigation, women's rights in relation to inheritance refers to those instances when women are denied, or restricted, the right to own or control the disposition of land through succession laws. Whilst there is no specific human right norm in relation to inheritance, the human rights treaty bodies have interpreted the denial or restriction of women's rights to inheritance as a violation of the principles of equality and non-discrimination, which are embedded in numerous international human rights documents.[43] Providing further clarification in relation to the possible justifications of inequality between men and women, the Committee on the Women's Convention has stated on a number of occasions that 'any law or custom that grants men a right to a greater share of property' is discriminatory and should be eliminated.[44]

Despite the jurisprudence of the human rights treaty bodies, some state laws continue to deny or restrict women from acquiring land through succession.[45] Of the states that were issued with the recommendation, over 46% of the time the recommendation to eliminate inheritance laws that discriminated against women was not accepted. In those states where unequal inheritance laws continue to exist, cultural values and customary law often dictate the access and inheritance of land, which excludes women from property ownership and inheriting land.[46] In some instances, the justification of such inequality is based on the culturally held belief that women are expected to subsume their identity to the husband after marriage, and as a result, only the husband's name is placed on the title deed of the land.[47] In other instances, traditional interpretations of sharia norms are used to justify men receiving a greater proportion of inheritance than their female counterparts.[48] The relationship between inheritance laws and culture, whereby women's rights to inheritance laws may be denied or restricted based on cultural and religious norms is one of the primary reasons why this issue has been selected as a focus for this investigation. Below, the findings of the investigation will be presented as to whether the aim of the UPR process to implement the principle of universality is met, and whether it was challenged over the two cycles of review.

Findings on Women's Right to Inheritance in the UPR Process

First Cycle of Review

In the first cycle of review, a total of 41 recommendations were issued on the issue of inheritance. In terms of the nature of discussions held at the interactive dialogue stage, four different types of recommendations were issued, and a total of six forms of responses were provided by the state under review.

RECOMMENDATION 1

Under this category of recommendations, observer states during the state reviews focused on the barriers women face in acquiring property when certain religious and cultural norms influence the regulation of inheritance law. The observer states suggested that the states under review undertake appropriate actions to combat the impediments that women face in relation to acquiring property through succession law when such religious and cultural norms are applied. Greece and Madagascar were the only two states that were issued with recommendations under this category. First, during the review of Greece, the delegate of the Netherlands issued a recommendation to 'take action with regard to the impediments that Muslim minority women may face … when sharia law is applied on family and inheritance law matters'[49]. Second, Madagascar was issued a recommendation by the Chilean delegate who suggested 'to continue to adopt legislation to eliminate … cultural stereotypes that discriminate against women, especially … in the areas of inheritance'.[50]

In response to the recommendations under this category, both states issued comments that were categorised as A2 responses. The delegate of Greece accepted the recommendation and added that 'sharia law may be applied … for the members of the Muslim minority on certain matters of … inheritance law to the extent that its rules are not in conflict with … the Greek legal and constitutional order'.[51] The delegate of Madagascar accepted the recommendation and stated that it 'welcomes the invitation to adopt specific legislative measures to combat discriminatory acts against women'.[52] The responses by both Greece and Madagascar show that, at least formally, the states accepted that action should be taken to address religious and cultural barriers that impede women's right to inheritance. However, what is striking is that the responses issued by both states have focused entirely on the domestic legislation that is already in place, or will be implemented, to address the religious and cultural barriers in relation to inheritance. See Tables 5.3 to 5.6.

RECOMMENDATION 2

The central focus of the recommendations issued under this category is that the observer states' suggestions were to enact or reform domestic legislation to guarantee women's rights to inheritance. A typical example of a recommendation under this category is the Netherland's recommendation to Algeria to update

Table 5.3 Nature of Discussions on the issue of Inheritance in the First Cycle

Universal Periodic Review Cycle 1	Responses by States under Review					
	A1 No further comments	*A2* Laws to protect women's rights to inheritance already in place/will be implemented/under review	*N1* No further comments	*N2* Suggested reforms contrary to domestic law/constitution on inheritance	*N3* Laws addressing inheritance are already in place	*N4* Reforms challenged on cultural and/or religious grounds
Nature of recommendations issued to states under review						
Recommendation 1 Tackle impediments women face when cultural/religious norms are applied to inheritance laws		Greece Madagascar				
Recommendation 2 Enact/Reform domestic laws to guarantee women's equal rights to inheritance	Guinea Madagascar Maldives Mozambique Palau Republic of Congo	Burundi Liechtenstein	Gambia	Algeria	Chad Kiribati Lebanon Timor-Leste Tonga	Solomon Islands
Recommendation 3 Enact/Reform domestic laws to comply with international norms on inheritance.	Guinea Maldives	Burundi	Gambia Yemen		Lebanon	Libya
Recommendation 4 Generic recommendations to enact measures to ensure equality on inheritance.	GhanaCongo	Lesotho Liechtenstein			UAE Samoa	

Table 5.4 Nature of Discussions on the issue of Inheritance in the Second Cycle

Universal Periodic Review Cycle 2	Responses by States under Review									
	A1 No further comments	A2 Incremental reforms in place to ensure equality in relation to inheritance	A3 Policy and/or legislation under review	A4 Religious laws will not be implemented. If contrary to constitution or International Human Rights Law (IHRL)	N1 No further comments	N2 Incremental reforms in place to ensure equality in relation to inheritance	N4 Under review	N5 Contrary to domestic laws and Islamic values	N6 Percentages are fixed in sharia laws – denial of discrimination	N7 Efforts in place to bring laws in line with sharia and IHRL
Nature of recommendations issued to states under review										
Recommendation 1 Tackle impediments women face when cultural/religious norms are applied to inheritance laws	Burkina Faso	Republic of Congo	Kenya							
Recommendation 2 Enact/Reforms domestic laws to guarantee women's equal rights to inheritance.	Bahrain Togo Mozambique Namibia Tonga	Republic of Congo	Burundi		Equatorial Guinea Iraq Lebanon Morocco Uganda	Botswana	Djibouti	Tunisia UAE	Jordan	
Recommendation 3 Enact/Reform domestic laws to comply with international norms on inheritance	Algeria Cambodia Timor-Leste	Republic of Congo Tanzania			Lebanon Lesotho	Palau				Libya
Recommendation 4 Generic recommendations to enact measures to ensure equality on inheritance	Equatorial Guinea Namibia Republic of Korea South Sudan	Botswana		Greece	Oman			Iran Tunisia UAE		
Recommendation 5 Incremental reforms to be put in place to eliminate discrimination in relation to inheritance			Djibouti		Lebanon			Tunisia UAE		

Table 5.5 Nature of Discussions on Forced and Early Marriages in the First Cycle

Universal Periodic Review Cycle 1	Responses by States under Review								
	A1 Accepted recommendations with no further comments	*A2* Reviewed the state legislation on forced and early marriages	*A3* Domestic laws on forced and early marriages were already in place	*A4* Changes to be brought about through incremental reforms and constructive dialogue	*A5* Shedding light on reasons why forced and early marriages continue to be practised	*N1* Noted recommendations without any further comments	*N2* Laws protecting women from forced and early marriages are already in place	*N3* Incremental reforms to discourage forced and early marriage were already in place	*N4* No harmful practices existed in the state
Nature of recommendations issued to states under review									
Recommendation 1 Forced and early marriages are harmful cultural practices that are required to be eliminated	Mauritania Togo		Sierra Leone Bangladesh	Guinea Bissau				Gambia	Botswana
Recommendation 2 Enact or reform domestic legislation on forced and early marriages	Afghanistan Benin Kyrgyzstan Mauritania Sudan	El Salvador Azerbaijan Yemen Japan	Iran Bangladesh	Guinea Bissau		Trinidad and Tobago	Mali Gabon	Gambia	

(Continued)

Table 5.5 Continued

Universal Periodic Review Cycle 1	Responses by States under Review								
	A1 Accepted recommendations with no further comments	*A2 Reviewed the state legislation on forced and early marriages*	*A3 Domestic laws on forced and early marriages were already in place*	*A4 Changes to be brought about through incremental reforms and constructive dialogue*	*A5 Shedding light on reasons why forced and early marriages continue to be practised*	*N1 Noted recommendations without any further comments*	*N2 Laws protecting women from forced and early marriages are already in place*	*N3 Incremental reforms to discourage forced and early marriage were already in place*	*N4 No harmful practices existed in the state*
Recommendation 3 To engage local/ religious/ community leaders to discourage forced and early marriages	Afghanistan			Timor-Leste	Liberia				
Recommendation 4 Generic suggestions to address forced and early marriages	Bahrain Bangladesh Ethiopia Guinea Kyrgyzstan Oman Pakistan	Niger Yemen	Sierra Leone		Liberia	United Arab Emirates	Chad Oman Bahrain Gambia		

Table 5.6 Nature of Discussions on Forced and Early Marriages in the Second Cycle

Universal Periodic Review Cycle 2	Responses by States under Review				
	A1 Accepted recommendations with no further comments	A2 Reviewed the state legislation on forced and early marriages	A3 Domestic laws/policies on forced and early marriages were already in place	A4 Changes to be brought about through incremental reforms and constructive dialogue	A5 Legalise traditional marriages, so now no discrimination on grounds of sex
Nature of recommendations issued to states under review					
Recommendation 1 Forced and early marriages are harmful cultural practices that are required to be eliminated	Equatorial Guinea Niger		Cote d'Ivoire		Gabon
Recommendation 2 Enact/Reform/Implement domestic legislation on forced and early marriages	Cameroon Congo Gambia Guinea Maldives Niger Pakistan		Djibouti Georgia Guyana Kyrgyzstan Laos Malawi Mauritania Nepal Nigeria Saudi Arabia Swaziland Yemen	Afghanistan Guinea Bissau Mauritania Nigeria Turkey Yemen	Gabon
Recommendation 3 To engage local/religious/ community leaders to discourage forced and early marriages	Bangladesh Burkina Faso Cameroon		Djibouti	Guinea Bissau Mozambique	

(Continued)

Table 5.6 Continued

Universal Periodic Review Cycle 2

	Responses by States under Review				
	A1 Accepted recommendations with no further comments	A2 Reviewed the state legislation on forced and early marriages	A3 Domestic laws/policies on forced and early marriages were already in place	A4 Changes to be brought about through incremental reforms and constructive dialogue	A5 Legalise traditional marriages, so now no discrimination on grounds of sex
Recommendation 4 Generic suggestions to address forced and early marriages	Bangladesh Benin Bosnia and Herzegovina Burkina Faso Cameroon Congo Egypt Equatorial Guinea Guinea Kenya Madagascar Namibia Nauru Niger Pakistan Somalia South Sudan Uganda	Liberia Syria	Cote d'Ivoire Eritrea Ethiopia Georgia Jordan Kazakhstan Kyrgyzstan Mauritania Myanmar New Zealand Nigeria Russian Federation Saudi Arabia Swaziland Turkey Yemen Zimbabwe	Bhutan Guinea Bissau Mauritania Mozambique Nigeria Togo Yemen	
Recommendation 5 Engage in incremental reforms to eliminate the practice	Armenia Indonesia Macedonia Madagascar Niger	Liberia	Kyrgyzstan Malawi Yemen	Afghanistan Guinea Bissau Mozambique Turkey Yemen	

'legislation regarding the situation of women, such as the Family Code in the areas of ... inheritance'.[53] In total 16 states were issued with recommendations of this nature, and therefore this was the most popular form of recommendation issued on inheritance in the first cycle.

In terms of the responses to such recommendations, eight states accepted the recommendations; six of which were accepted without any further response. The two states that did provide additional statements were Burundi[54] and Liechtenstein,[55] who provided A2 responses as they insisted that the current laws in the area of inheritance were being reviewed in the domestic context.

On the other hand, a total of eight states under review noted the recommendations. Gambia was the only state that provided an N1 response, as the delegate did not provide any additional comments.[56] Algeria provided an N2 response, as it justified not accepting the recommendation on the basis that suggested reforms to inheritance laws were contrary to the domestic constitution.[57] Adopting a different position, a total of five states under review justified their non-acceptance of recommendations on the basis that domestic laws in relation to inheritance either did not exist, or that they were under review, and as such, the suggested recommendations under this category were considered as being misguided or redundant. This was categorised as an N3 response which was issued by Chad, Kiribati,[58] Lebanon, Timor-Leste,[59] and Tonga.[60] A typical example of this response was when Chad noted the recommendation as being 'simply redundant, as they referred to matters on which legislative measures had already been taken'.[61] What is notable here is that neither Chad, Tonga, or Timor-Leste expressly denied the fact that discriminatory practices in relation to inheritance existed in the state. Instead, the responses of the three states focused entirely on denying that the domestic laws in relation to inheritance were discriminatory.

The delegate of the Solomon Islands adopted a different position as the state initially accepted the recommendation, without any further explanations. Surprisingly, in direct contradiction to its official position on the recommendation, the state at the Human Rights Committee (HRC) plenary session provided that it was 'not ready to change the property and inheritance law'. The delegate stated that 'most of the perceived inconsistencies with internationally accepted standards of ... inheritance were due to long defined customary norms'.[62] In this way, the delegate provided an N4 response, as it justified the differences between domestic laws and international norms on the basis that the inheritance laws on the land were regulated by long-standing customary norms, which interpret inheritance laws differently.

RECOMMENDATION 3

The third category of recommendations focused on encouraging reforms to domestic laws on inheritance to comply with the international obligations of the state under review. A typical example of a recommendation under this category was issued by Switzerland who suggested that 'Burundi take the necessary steps to amend ... the law governing inheritance, to bring them into conformity with the principles of non-discrimination as set out in the Convention on the Elimination of All Forms of Discrimination against Women'.[63] In total seven states under review were issued with a recommendation of this nature. In response, a total of four states noted the recommendations under this category, and three states accepted them. Of the three states that accepted the recommendation, the states of Guinea[64] and Maldives[65] provided an A1 response as it accepted the recommendation without any further comments. The delegate of Burundi provided an A2 response, as the delegate insisted that reforms to the domestic laws on inheritance were already in place.[66]

The four states that noted the recommendation under this category provided three different responses. The delegates of Gambia[67] and Yemen[68] provided an N1 response, as they did not provide any further explanations for their position. In other instances, the delegate of Lebanon noted the recommendation and provided an N3 response, stating that six draft laws were already in place to eliminate discriminatory provisions from domestic legislation'.[69] The delegate of Libya's response was the most significant for the purposes of this investigation, which was categorised as an N4 response. To provide some background, the domestic codes of Libya are based on a traditional interpretation of sharia, which provides that whilst women may inherit land from family members, their share is generally smaller than that of men.[70] During its review, Libya was issued with a recommendation by Mexico that it should, 'in line with the recommendations of the Committee on the Elimination of Discrimination against Women, adopt a national plan to ... guarantee equality between men and women ... with regard ... [to] inheritance'.[71] In response, the delegate of Libya formally noted the recommendation. Interestingly, later on at the HRC plenary session, the delegate stated that 'Libya accepts this recommendation from the delegation of Mexico but without prejudice to the provisions of the sharia on ... inheritance'.[72] It explained that matters of inheritance 'have been regulated by Islam for 1,400 years. These are matters on which there is complete consensus'.[73] From this response, it can be observed that the delegate of Libya expressly challenged the universality of the equality provisions under CEDAW on inheritance as the delegate only accepted the recommendation subject to the religious norms of Libya, which govern the provisions of inheritance.

RECOMMENDATION 4

Observer states under the fourth category of recommendations suggested that the state under review should implement reforms to ensure that women are guaranteed equality and protected against discrimination in relation to inheritance laws. Observer states did not provide any specific details on how the provisions of equality and non-discrimination should be implemented in practice, nor make any references to the state's international human rights obligations in relation to women's rights to inheritance. For this reason, this category of recommendation is described as being more generic in nature. A typical example of a recommendation under this category is when Hungary issued a recommendation to Ghana to 'take proactive measures to ensure the equality of women in all matters related to property inheritance'.[74]

A total of six states were issued with recommendations under this category. In response, four states accepted, of which the delegates of Ghana and Congo issued an A1 response, as no comments were provided. The delegates of Lesotho[75] and Liechtenstein[76] provided an A2 response, as both delegates insisted that the current laws in the area were being reviewed, and the drafts of amended laws on inheritance were being submitted to the relevant domestic legislative bodies. The states of United Arab Emirates (UAE) and Samoa were the only two states that did not accept recommendations under this category and issued statements that are categorised as an N3 response. The delegates of UAE[77] and Samoa[78] explained that the recommendations were noted because they were misguided as domestic provisions already guaranteed women's rights to equality and non-discrimination in relation to inheritance. Overall, when states were issued with recommendations to guarantee equality and non-discrimination in relation to inheritance laws, there was no commitment that was agreed on by the states under review in response. Instead, the states under review provided that current laws were being reviewed or that such guarantees were already protected in relation to inheritance by the state.

Second Cycle of Review

During the second cycle of review, there was a significant increase in the number of recommendations with a total of 167 issued, which is double the number from the previous cycle. In terms of the dialogue in the second cycle, there was one additional form of recommendation issued in the second cycle, than in the first. In terms of response, there were 11 different types of responses provided by the states under review when accepting or noting a recommendation. This is a dramatic increase from the previous cycle, demonstrating that the states under review provided a more varied response to recommendations on inheritance in the second cycle of review.

RECOMMENDATION 1

Under this category of recommendations, states were instructed to address cultural and religious impediments that women face, in relation to inheritance laws. Three states were issued with this recommendation, all of whom accepted the recommendation, which is similar to the previous cycle whereby two states were issued with this recommendation and both accepted it. In the second cycle, Burkina Faso accepted the recommendation without any further response, thus providing an A1 response. The delegate of the Republic of Congo provided an A2 response by emphasising the need for incremental reforms. For example, the delegate stated that 'numerous awareness-raising activities are undertaken by the Ministry for the Advancement of Women and the Integration of Women in Development with a view to changing attitudes'.[79] Also accepting the recommendation, the delegate of Kenya provided an A3 response, by stating that currently the state was undertaking 'the enactment of legislation to increase women's access to land ownership and use through inheritance and personal acquisition'.[80]

RECOMMENDATION 2

This form of recommendation focuses on the state's domestic legislation and suggests that the state enacts or reforms laws so that women have equal right to inheritance. As with the first cycle of review, this was the most prevailing form of recommendation in the second cycle of review, with a total of 18 states being suggested to undertake this form of reform. In response, seven states accepted the recommendation, and ten states noted the recommendation.

Of the states that have accepted the recommendation, Bahrain, Togo, Mozambique, Namibia, and Tonga all provided no further comments on accepting the recommendation, and therefore provided an A1 response. It is notable that Tonga was issued with the same form of recommendation in the previous cycle, and provided an N3 response as the delegate noted the recommendation and insisted that law in relation to inheritance already existed. The delegate of the Republic of Congo issued an A2 response, stating that incremental reforms in the form of awareness-raising campaigns were being implemented to change attitudes in relation to inheritance laws. It is noteworthy that in the previous cycle the Republic of Congo was issued with the same recommendation and the delegate responded with an A1 response and provided no response. Burundi was another state that was issued with the same recommendation under the first and second cycle of review. In the first cycle, the state provided an A2 response, and provided laws in relation to women's rights to inheritance were being reviewed. In the second cycle, the state provided 'concerning inheritance, a bill had been submitted to parliament, but for the time being the Government had decided to launch a study on the impact and benefits of such a law'.[81] In keeping with the evolutionary nature of the UPR process, the position of the laws being under review, to a bill being submitted to parliament is a positive move. Those that are more pessimistic in nature may point out that ultimately, not only has the bill not been enacted in relation to inheritance, but, moreover, the statement by Burundi in relation to the impact and benefits of the law seems to stall the enactment process. This indeed may be the case; however, the delegate of Burundi is evidently still engaging in a dialogue on the issue on the platform, and to some extent is indicating suggestions of reform, despite them being incremental in nature. Considering the contentious nature of the issue, and the very nature of the review process itself, provided that Burundi is still engaged in this dialogue and progress is made in the next cycle, there is reason to be optimistic about the successes of the review process.

A total of ten states under review noted this form of recommendation, which is two fewer than those noted in the first cycle. The states of Equatorial Guinea,

Iraq, Lebanon, Morocco, and Uganda noted this recommendation but provided no further explanation or comment. The delegate of Botswana issued an N2 response as it said that measures such as public awareness and educational campaigns 'were being implemented to ensure equal rights to inheritance by men and women'.[82] Djibouti issued an N4 response; the issue was under review as it stated that a 'small committee appointed by the Ministry of Justice was studying the current Family Code and was responsible for the necessary reforms'.[83] The states of Tunisia and the UAE both provided an N5 response and rejected the recommendation on the basis that the suggested recommendations were contrary to domestic law and Islamic values. For example, Tunisia stated that 'the Personal Status Code approved in 1956, although bringing about substantial reforms, had not affected existing legal concepts of inheritance, due to religious sensitivities'.[84] Similarly, the UAE stated that

> State is not in a position to comply with at this stage, because their incompatibility with the application of the provisions of the Islamic Sharia or the national constitutional and legal legislation, or their inconsistency with the value and civilisational system of the UAE society are not considered to be within the universally agreed basic principles of human rights.[85]

In both instances the states have used religious norms as a foundation to justify the rejection of reforms in relation to women's rights to inheritance. In fact, the UAE goes further and firmly deny the universality of women's rights in relation to inheritance laws. Finally, Jordan uniquely over the two cycles provided an N6 response,

> the delegation noted that the percentages of inheritance for women are fixed in sharia law. However, for the first time in Jordan, the personal status law clearly defines the rights of women to inheritance with a fixed percentage and shares that cannot be reduced. There are also cases where men inherit less than women.[86]

Despite this statement, it is clear that the Personal Status Law in Jordan is based on Islamic Sharia, which regulates the individuals' rights to inheritance, under which men can inherit twice as much as women in a number of circumstances. In this way, the guarantee of equality between women and men is not equal, despite the declarations made by the delegate.

RECOMMENDATION 3

This form of recommendation can be distinguished from recommendation 2 as the observer states here insisted that the domestic laws were enacted or reformed to ensure conformity with international human rights norms in relation to women's rights to inheritance. A total of nine states were issued with this form of recommendation, which is an increase from the previous cycle. Of these, six states accepted the recommendation, with Algeria, Cambodia, and Timor-Leste accepting the recommendation without any further comments. Tanzania and the Republic of Congo both provided an A2 response, and insisted that incremental reforms were in place to ensure that the issue in relation to inheritance laws and women's rights was addressed. In total, four states noted this recommendation, with the states of Lebanon and Lesotho providing no further comment.

In other instances during the review, the delegate of Palau noted the recommendation and stated that 'we will continue to work with the people of Palau especially the women's group on the awareness of this treaty'.[87] In this way, whilst the delegate did not accept immediately to undertake reforms of the issue, the delegate stated that actions in relation to raising awareness of the treaty provisions will be undertaken. Here, whilst the recommendation has been noted, the state has on an international platform such as the UPR process declared commitment to raise awareness on the treaty obligations in relation to inheritance. This itself can be beneficial, particularly to generate momentum in the dialogues undertaken by human rights activists and relevant stakeholders in the domestic context. The delegate of Libya also noted the recommendation, but provided an N7 response. The delegate began with explaining that the 'The Constitution Drafting Assembly had addressed, in its proposals, all aspects of equality between men and women: divorce, inheritance and passing on nationality to children'. It then continued and stated its intentions that 'efforts were being made to bring national legislation into conformity with international standards and the rules of the sharia law'.[88] Again, similar to Palau, whilst the delegate of Libya did not accept the recommendation, there is commitment expressed to working on conforming to international standards and the rules of sharia law. However, in order to ensure that advantage can be taken of both Libya's commitment to conform to international obligations and Palau's willingness to raise awareness on the issue of inheritance law it is important that this dialogue on inheritance law is continued not only in the domestic context, but also in the next cycle of the review process. The momentum of the discussions in relation to reforms, albeit incremental, can only be truly realised if there are continuous and developing discussions on the issue of inheritance laws on the UPR process.

RECOMMENDATION 4

This form of recommendation was generic in nature and suggested that the state under review implement measures to ensure equality in relation to inheritance laws. A total of ten states under review were issued with a recommendation of this nature, which is more in number than under the first cycle of review. Of these, six states under review accepted the recommendation, whilst four states under review noted it. Of those that accepted the recommendation, the states of Equatorial Guinea, Namibia, Republic of Korea, and South Sudan all accepted the recommendation and provided no further response. The delegate Greece accepted the recommendation and provided an A4 response, and explained that whilst the

Muslim minority in Thrace were free to address either the civil courts or the local muftis concerning sharia law in family and inheritance matters ... the law provided that the courts should not enforce muftis' decisions that were contrary to the Constitution or regional and international human rights treaties.[89]

Therefore, Greece confirmed that the domestic constitution in relation to equality, and the protection of international human rights treaties would have priority, should any inconsistencies arise.

In total four states under review noted this recommendation. Oman provided an N1 response and did not provide any further comments when noting the recommendation. Tunisia, UAE, and Iran all issued an N5 response stating that the reforms were contrary to religious norms in the country.

RECOMMENDATION 5

The fifth recommendation recommended states to undertake incremental reforms that should be implemented to eliminate discrimination in relation to inheritance. A typical example of this form of recommendation was issued to Djibouti when Canada provided that the state should

> develop and implement a comprehensive strategy to eliminate ... unequal access to inheritance, based on the recognition of the equality between men and women, and supported by religious and traditional leaders, civil society, men and boys, as well as other relevant stakeholders.[90]

This form of recommendation was unique to the second cycle, as no states under review issued it in the first cycle of review. Only four states under review were issued with this recommendation, and only one state accepted it. Djibouti accepted the recommendation, and provided an A3 response, insisting that 'a bill had been submitted to parliament, but for the time being the Government had decided to launch a study on the impact and benefits of such a law'.[91] In another instance, the delegate of Lebanon noted the recommendation and provided no further recommendation. The states of Tunisia and the UAE both provided an N5 response.

Discussion and Analysis

Analysing the findings, there are four significant patterns that have emerged over the nature of the discussion that has been held on inheritance in the first cycle. First, it is noticeable that over both cycles, observer states issued two forms of recommendations that, to varying degrees, resonated with the strict universalist position on protecting women's rights to inheritance. One of the two recommendations was more audacious in nature, as it resonated with one of the core values of strict universality of rights transcending any cultural barriers. The states issuing recommendation 1 explicitly highlighted the cultural and religious norms that formed impediments that prevented women's rights to equal inheritance, and suggested that states should remove these norms. This type of recommendation was not widely raised, as it was only issued to five states over the two cycles. The other form of recommendation that resonated with a universalist position, but in a less bold and explicit manner in comparison, states issuing recommendation 3 suggested reform laws to comply with international human rights obligations, and was amongst the most popular recommendations under both cycles. What is noticeable is that when looking beyond the formal response of either accepting or noting these recommendations, the responses by the states under review to these reforms based on a universalist stance were either overwhelming muted, as states did not provide any further comments in addition to accepting or noting the recommendation or they simply referred to laws that were in place or under review in relation to women's rights to inheritance. It is notable that only the Republic of Congo highlighted that incremental reforms were being put in place to ensure that women's rights to equality were being protected in relation to inheritance. This indicates that when states were issued with recommendations that resonated with the Universalist position, states under review responded with either pointing out that policies and laws were under review (the implications of this will be discussed below) or that incremental reforms were being undertaken to address the issue.

The second significant finding that emerged was that states adopted positions, which implicitly or explicitly indicated a challenge to the universality of women's rights to inheritance. For instance, the states of Solomon Islands, Libya, Tunisia, UAE, Iran, and Jordan all noted the recommendation issued to them on women's rights to inheritance. What is common in their responses is that they have used domestic religious customary norms to challenge the suggested recommendation to reform domestic laws on inheritance. Thus, it is clear from the statements issued that both states under review perceive their international human rights obligations in relation to inheritance laws to be contingent to the religious or customary norms of the state under review. The explanations provided by both states indicate they adopted a strict cultural relativist position in the discussions on inheritance, which uses local and cultural traditions to determine the existence and scope of international human rights norms.[92] Amongst the various criticisms that can be raised in relation to the theoretical underpinning of the strict cultural relativist position, one particular criticism is applicable in relation to the positions adopted by the states during the review process. One of the most profound criticisms of using culture as the sole factor for challenging the validity of international human rights norms is that the construction of 'culture' that is often used by some political leaders is not a representation of the entire society[93] and is often 'misemployed' to veil non-cultural politics within a state.[94] On the nature of culture, An-Na'im writes that one defining feature of culture is that it consists of a constantly contested political struggle between those who want to legitimise their power and those that want to challenge the status quo to address grievances.[95] He describes this as the 'politics of culture'.[96] In this way, when culture is used as a sole factor to challenge the universality of human rights, such a position from a strict cultural relativist perspective is open to the critique of over-looking the politics and power imbalances within a culture itself. In the context of the UPR process, the positions of the states of Tunisia, UAE, Iran, and Jordan give reason to question whether the voices of those women that are deprived of equal rights to inheritance are accurately represented by the state representatives who claim an interpretation of sharia and customary norms should limit women's rights to equal inheritance. The implications of states adopting a strict cultural relativist position have been that the discussions on women's rights to inheritance during the reviews of the four states have been brought to a close. This is because observer states have failed to hold the two states to account when the representa-tives introduced arguments from a strict cultural relativist position in relation to inheritance. This is problematic because the central tenet of the UPR process is for it to encourage states to engage in a cooperative dialogue on potentially controversial human rights issues. However, the lack of observer states' responses to hold those states that challenge universal norms on inheritance to account defies one of the fundamental objectives of the UPR process to promote universal human rights norms based on a constructive dialogue on potentially controversial human rights issues.

The third significant finding is that a line of discourse was emerging in the second cycle of review, which was absent in the first cycle on the issue. In the first cycle, there was no recognition, by the states undertaking the review or states under review, that practices and laws in relation to inheritance that dis-criminated against women should be reformed on an incremental basis. In the second cycle of review, a new category of recommendations emerged in the form of Recommendation 5, whereby five states under review were recommended to undertaken incremental reforms in the domestic context to ensure that women's rights to inheritance were being protected. These recommendations included suggestions through awareness-raising campaigns, gradual reforms to the laws, and entering into discussions with relevant stakeholders. This focus on using the method of bringing about reforms in relation to women's inequality on inherit-ance laws affiliates with the moderate cultural relativist position. In line with this position, the states that recognised incremental reforms, whether through recom-mendations or responses, indicated an appreciation that a dialogical approach is to be adopted to advance global implementation of human rights by suggesting reforms to comply with human rights obligations in a manner that is reflected in the cultural and religious norms that are recognisable to the society in question. In addition, it is implicitly recognised that such reforms, particularly those prac-tices that may be embedded in religious and cultural norms cannot be reformed immediately, and rather over an incremental process. In this way, the emergence of discussions in the second cycle of reform indicates that religious and cultural norms, that are ordinarily ostracised and used to justify human rights violations, can be used as a pragmatic tool to culturally legitimise women's rights protection in relation to inheritance.[97] The implications of this form of discussions are that they can be used as advocacy tools by the civil society and stakeholders to inform the reform process to be implemented on the ground. The statements issued on the UPR process in relation to incremental reforms can be used in the national coordination, planning, and monitoring for the promotion and protection of human rights issues in the domestic context.

The final emerging finding was that the discussions were overwhelmingly focused on domestic laws on inheritance leads one to question whether the discussions of more complex issues, which may explain the persistence of unequal treatment of women on the issue, has been restricted from the discussions on the issue of inheritance. For instance, Askin and Koeing argue that the lack of legal protection for women is not always the sole reason why women are denied access to inheritance.[98] The authors use the examples of India, Nigeria, Palestine, and Kenya, where whilst domestic laws guarantee women legal rights to inherit land, the customary, religious, and cultural norms of those societies continue to deny women equal rights to inheriting land.[99] As Abby Morrow Richardson explains, there is often a disconnection between the official domestic policy on the issue of inheritance, and the actual practice.[100] As such, it is argued that simply enacting or reforming statutory legislation on inheritance is unlikely to have any practical effect on the great majority of the population, which is governed by customary law based on culture and traditional values.[101]

Contrary to the analysis in the literature, which raises concerns on the inconsistency between legal protection of women's rights on inheritance and actual practice, the focus of the majority of the discourse undertaken in the UPR process has been on the enactment, reform, or implementation of domestic laws on inheritance. The states in the review process seemed to overlook the potential discrepancy between the protection provided by domestic laws in the state in question, and the reasons why some women continue to be discriminated against in relation to inheritance. For instance, even if laws are in place to ensure the equality of women in relation to inheritance rights, in some cases, women often voluntarily renounce their rights in favour of their male siblings, as demanding or retaining their share would disrupt the kinship, which is likely to leave the woman deprived of support and assistance from siblings.[102] In other instances, where religious norms such as the sharia law have an influence on the regulation of inheritance, women do not voice their concerns at the risk of being labelled as unfaithful to their religion.[103] In this way, cultural and social factors often deter women from exercising their rights to inheritance; therefore, any statutory provisions that govern women's rights to inheritance are frequently unpopular and not complied with.[104]

Protection of Women's Rights against Early and Forced Marriages at the UPR Process

Contextualising the Issue of Early and Forced Marriages

The term forced marriage is defined as 'a marriage that takes place without the free or valid consent of one or both of the partners and involves either physical or emotional duress'.[105] The term 'early marriage' is considered as a specific form of forced marriage as minors are deemed incapable of giving informed consent.[106]

Early and forced marriages of women have been the subject of international human rights regulation since the 1960s. For example, the Convention on Consent to Marriage, Minimum Age for Marriage and Registration of Marriages[107] and CEDAW[108] both state that a marriage must be between 'men and women of full age', 'with the free and full consent of the intending spouses and ensure that both parties receive equal rights and protections'.[109] More recently the HRC, on the 2 July 2015, has adopted its first substantive resolution on child marriage, which recognised such marriages as a violation of human rights.[110] Providing further clarity in response to any possible justifications of such marriages, General Recommendation 29 on Article 16 issued in 2013 by the Committee on the Women's Convention stated that any inequalities between men and women in the marriage institution that are justified on traditional or cultural norms, are contrary to the principles of CEDAW.[111] There is no single reason for the continuance of forced and early marriages, which are often a result of a combination of social, economic, and cultural factors.[112] Gender stereotypes and cultural norms in relation to women's role in society, sexuality, and virginity contribute to forced and early marriages of women in some communities.[113] In places where such marriages are practised, communities talk of a culturally conceptualised notion of 'shame' that will be imposed on the family of the female child or woman should she become pregnant out of wedlock.[114] The 'fear that a daughter who was married late would lose her virginity before marriage, and thus disgrace her family' means some girls are forced into an early marriage.[115] It is because of this inherent relationship between culture and forced and early marriages, whereby the culturally conceptualised notion of 'shame' is often used to justify forced and early marriages, that this issue was selected as a focus for this investigation.

Findings on the Issue of Early and Forced Marriages in the UPR Process

First Cycle of Review

During the first cycle of review, the issue of forced and early marriage was the focus of 32 recommendations during state reviews. There were four different types of recommendations, and a total of nine different types of responses issued by the states under review.

RECOMMENDATION 1

Observer states issuing recommendations under the first category expressly drew a link between the existence of forced and early marriages, and values embedded in the traditions and culture of the state under review, before recommending that actions needed to be implemented to bring such marriages to an end. A typical example of a statement issued under this category was during the review of Gambia when Slovenia, whilst commending the enactment of the Children's Act 2005, 'noted with concern that social and cultural norms hindered its implementation ... as early and forced marriage ... remained widespread'.[116] A total of seven states received recommendations under this category.

In response, five states accepted recommendation under this category, of which Mauritania and Togo provided an A1 response, as both states provided no comments for their position. The states of Sierra Leone[117] and Bangladesh, whilst accepted the recommendations, provided an A3 response as they insisted that domestic laws were in place that prohibited such marriages. For example, Bangladesh responded that 'early marriages ... are prohibited [and] have been made a punishable offence under Child Marriage Restraint Act, 1929'.[118] In another instance, the delegate of Guinea Bissau 'emphasized that the fight against practices, such as early and forced marriage, in a society such as in Guinea Bissau should be conducted gradually, through awareness-raising campaigns, sensitisa-tion, and continuous dialogue with the targeted sectors of the population before legislative measures sanctioning these practices could be taken'.[119] The delegate of Guinea Bissau therefore provided an A4 response as it stated that reforms to attitudes in relation to forced and early marriage required incremental reforms through constructive dialogue with those that sympathise with the practice.

The two states under review that did not accept recommendations under this category both provided explanations for their positions. For example, the del-egate of Gambia, in response to a recommendation by Slovenia, insisted that the 'Children's Act prohibits child marriage. In addition, the Government uses community child protection committees to educate communities about this issue and encourage them to abandon harmful practices such as early and forced mar-riage'.[120] Thus, Gambia provided an N3 response on the basis that incremental reforms to discourage the practice were already in place. The second state that noted a recommendation under this category was Botswana, who provided an N4 response as the delegate insisted that 'there are no traditions harmful to the rights of women'.[121] The response by Botswana centres on the state's interpretation of 'harmful'. One of two interpretations can be given to this response. First, either that forced or early marriages, which were labelled as harmful by Argentina who issued the recommendation, did not exist in the state. Or, second that Botswana did not consider forced and early marriages as harmful in nature.

From the dialogue above, what is notable is that whilst the states under review may differ in their official positions to the recommendation, the content of their explanations was very similar. For instance, whilst Guinea accepted and Gambia noted the recommendation under this category, an examination of their com-ments reveals that both states similarly emphasised the importance of incremental reforms to discourage sympathetic attitudes towards forced and early marriages. Another pattern that was observed was in relation to the noted recommenda-tions; both Gambia and Botswana in their comments implicitly stated that it did not accept the nature of the recommendations that were issued, rather than the content of addressing forced and early marriages per se. For instance, Botswana denied the existence of traditional harmful practices, whilst the delegate of Gambia explained that more incremental methods of reforms were suitable for addressing such marriages.

RECOMMENDATION 2

The recommendations listed under the second category issued by observer states focused on the suggestions to enact or reform domestic legislation to ensure that women and girls were protected from early and forced marriages. A typical example of a recommendation issued under this category was issued to Sudan by Slovenia to 'pass legislation at the federal level to prohibit … early forced marriages, and ensure that such legislation is enforced in practice'.[122]

A total of 16 states received recommendations under this category. Of these, 12 states under review accepted. The states of Afghanistan, Benin, Kyrgyzstan, Mauritania, and Sudan accepted the recommendations without any further response, and therefore provided an A1 response. The delegates of El Salvad or,[123]Azerbaijan,[124] Yemen,[125] and Japan[126] accepted the recommendations and provided an A2 response as the state delegates explained the state will review domestic legislation on forced and early marriages.

A different response was provided by the states of Iran and Bangladesh,[127] who insisted that laws were already in place which prohibited such marriages, and therefore, were categorised as A3 responses. For example, Iran highlighted its 'legislative achievements regarding women's rights and family issues, including laws to combat … forced marriage'.[128] The state of Guinea Bissau provided an A4 response, as it explained that incremental reforms to address such marriages needed to be implemented 'before legislative measures sanctioning these practices could be taken'.[129] Therefore, whilst officially Guinea Bissau accepted the recommendation to implement domestic laws to prevent forced and early marriages, the comments by the delegate clearly indicated that laws will not be implemented in relation to forced marriages.

In other instances of the review, four states under review noted recommendations that were issued under this category. The delegate of Trinidad and Tobago provided an N1 response, as the recommendation was noted without providing any further comments. The delegates of Mali and Gabon,[130] issued an N2 response on the basis that laws protecting women from such marriages were already in place. For instance, Mali stated that 'the current Marriage and Guardianship Code provided that marriage must be based on mutual consent, and set a minimum age of 18 for boys and 15 for girls'.[131] The delegate of Gambia provided an N3 response, as it insisted that existing laws already prohibit early marriages.[132]

Overall, one may be optimistic that the majority of the recommendations under this category were accepted. However, a detailed examination of the statements shows that all the states that were issued with a recommendation under this category either remained silent in response, or resorted to highlighting the laws and policies already put in place in the states under review to protect women against forced and early marriages.

RECOMMENDATION 3

The essence of the recommendations issued under this category was to engage local community and religious leaders in a dialogue to help reform and change attitudes that condone such marriages through public awareness campaigns. The states of Afghanistan, Liberia,[133] and Timor-Leste received recommendations under this category. For example, during the review of Afghanistan, the delegate of the United States suggested to 'launch public information campaigns and work with religious leaders to raise awareness of the legal rights for women … including the legal age of marriage'.[134] In another example, referring to the law protecting women against forced and early marriage, Germany recommended that Timor-Leste continue 'raising awareness of this law to public officials, to local community leaders and by citizenship educations; and additionally to discourage cultural practice and violations to women's rights, such as forced and early marriage'.[135]

In response to the recommendations of this nature, the delegate of Afghanistan provided an A1 response. Liberia accepted the recommendation and stated that 'victims of … forced marriage … had been ostracised by their communities and families, whilst perpetrators had gone unpunished. Fearing such stigmatization, victims have often chosen not to report crimes'.[136] Liberia's response is striking because it was the first time in the investigation under this chapter that a state had attempted to explain the possible reasons why victims of forced and early marriages may not report or implement their right that may well be protected under domestic legislation. Liberia's comments shed light on the complex dilemma that women face when they are subject to forced and early marriages in reporting such marriages. Timor-Leste responded by accepting the recommendation issued by Germany and stated that the 'advancement of economic conditions especially those of women, would soon allow for gradual change in attitudes, resulting in the decrease of early marriages'.[137] Here, Timor-Leste provided an A4 response to the recommendation, as the delegate highlighted that incremental reforms expected to take place to discourage attitudes in favour of early and forced marriages are due to the economic development.

RECOMMENDATION 4

Under this category, observer states issued recommendations that can be described as generic in nature. This is because states simply identified forced and early marriages as an area of concern, before suggesting the issues be addressed by implementing measures. These observer states did not make any direct references to any legislative provisions or any international norms when issuing these recommendations. A typical example of this recommendation was issued to Pakistan where the delegate of Switzerland recommended Pakistan do 'everything possible to prevent early and forced marriage'.[138] A total of 16 states in the first cycle were issued with a recommendation under this category.

In response, 11 states accepted the recommendations issued under this category. A total of seven states provided an A1 response. The states of Niger[139] and Yemen[140] provided an A2 response as they stated that reviews of the domestic laws on forced and early marriages were either already in place, or soon to be undertaken. The delegate of Sierra Leone insisted that 'legislation had been passed to mandate the age of consent at 18 years', which is categorised as an A3 response.[141] The delegate of Liberia's response to the recommendation is categorised as A5.[142]

A total of five states under review refused to accept recommendations under this category. The UAE provided an N1 response. The states of Chad,[143] Oman,[144] Bahrain,[145] and Gambia[146] provided responses in line with an N2 response, as the states noted the recommendations and insisted that domestic laws were already in place to protect women from forced and early marriage.

Second Cycle of Review

In the second cycle of review, there was a dramatic increase in recommendations issued to a total of 172. The nature of discussions was also considerably varied with observer states issuing five different forms of recommendations in the second cycle. In response, the states under review provided an equally varied response with a total of 13 different forms of responses.

RECOMMENDATION 1

A total of four states under review were issued with this recommendation under the second cycle, which is fewer in number than those under the first cycle. In addition, unlike the first cycle, no states under review in the second cycle noted that recommendation, as all four states accepted it. Also, it is notable that no states under review that were issued with this recommendation under the first cycle were repeat issued with it in the second cycle. The states of Equatorial Guinea and Niger both accepted the recommendation with no further comments. In contrast, the state of Cote d'Ivoire accepted the recommendation and referred to the existing legislation on the legal age of marriage and stated that 'any derogation from that was punishable by law'.[147] The state of Gabon, whilst accepting the recommendation, stated that 'regarding forced marriage, Gabon recognised that traditional marriages had no legal value'. The delegate continued that Gabon had launched a project, 'to pass legislation on traditional marriage that would enable women ... to fully enjoy their inherent dignity'.[148] Here, it can be observed that when states accepted this recommendation, the nature of the statements that were issued focused on the legislation that was already in place to protect women's rights in relation to forced and early marriage.

RECOMMENDATION 2

This form of recommendation was amongst the most popular issued in the second cycle. A total of 35 states were issued with this recommendation, of which 26 accepted and nine noted the recommendation.

Of those that accepted the recommendation, seven states accepted it without any further comments. By far the most common response to this form of recommendation was the A3 response, whereby 12 states under review referred to domestic laws and policies in relation to forced and early marriages that were already in place. For example, the state of Nepal stated that 'measures to combat child marriages had been adopted'.[149] In total, six states under review responded to the recommendation by providing evidence of policies that were in place in the country to addressing the practice through a process of dialogue with appropriate stakeholders. For example, the Guinea Bissau stated that forced and early marriage 'was embedded in traditional culture. Eliminating the practice would take a great deal of time and require careful handling'. In addition, the delegate noted progress on the ground in relation to policies in place, and committed to continue to work on the subject.[150] Whereas, the delegate of Gabon accepted the recommendation and stated that traditional marriages were not legalised, so that no discrimination existed on the grounds of sex in relation to marriages. As is obvious, Gabon's response to the recommendation is vague, and simply referred to existing laws to ensure equality in a marriage, but not on the issue of forced and early marriage. This response is disingenuous and ambiguous, as it does not directly address the recommendation issued, yet the recommendation is recorded as accepted.

A total of nine states noted the recommendation in the second cycle of review. Of these, the states of Belize and Sierra Leone noted the recommendation without any further comments. The state of Iraq noted the recommendation and pointed out that sanctions on forced marriage were already in place, whilst the age of marriage of 18 was already in place.[151] The delegates of Chad and Sudan both noted the recommendation, and stated that measures were already being undertaken through 'awareness campaigns ... targeting traditional and religious leaders ... to eradicate these practices'.[152] The states of Rwanda and Somalia refused to accept the recommendations on the basis that the suggestions to enact laws to protect women from forced and early marriages were incompatible with the domestic law and constitutional obligations. In contrast, the delegate of Saudi Arabia noted the recommendation and insisted that 'Islamic Sharia prohibits forced marriage ... and the marriage of minors is an issue that is currently under study ... and therefore inappropriate to specify a minimum age for marriage before learning the outcome of the study'.[153] The delegate of Tanzania noted the recommendation and provided that 'increasing the minimum age of marriage was a sensitive issue, as sentiments, traditions and religion were connected to it. A white paper was being prepared and legislative were being considered to address the issue'. This response is unique in nature, as no state under review, over the two cycles categorically denied a recommendation to address early marriages on the basis of traditional and religious norms. Having said that, the delegate did provide that some steps were being taken in draft legislation to address the issue.

RECOMMENDATION 3

Similar to the first cycle, no state under review refused to accept this recommendation when it was issued. A total of six states were issued with this recommendation in the second cycle. Of which, the states of Bangladesh, Burkina Faso, and Cameroon all accepted the recommendation without any further comments. The state of Djibouti accepted the recommendation, and insisted the domestic laws were already in place to protect women and girls from early and forced marriage. In other instances, the states of Mozambique and Guinea Bissau both accepted the recommendation provided information on strategies that were in place to facilitate a constructive dialogue for reforms. For example, the delegate of Mozambique stated that the 'National Strategy for Preventing and Combating Early Marriages, which aimed to create an enabling environment for the progressive reduction and elimination of such practices'.

RECOMMENDATION 4

As with the first cycle, this category was the most prevailing form of recommendation that was issued in the second cycle of review. A total of 51 states under review were issued with this recommendation. Of these, a total of 44 states accepted the recommendation, and only seven noted the recommendation. Of those that accepted the recommendation, a total of 18 states accepted the recommendation without any further comments. The states of Liberia and Syria accepted the recommendation and stated that the legislation on forced and early marriage was under review. The most dominant response is an A3 response, whereby states insisted that domestic laws and policies were already in place to address the issue, with a total of 17 states providing this form of response. A total of seven states accepted the recommendation, and stated that changes were being brought through implementing national strategies and policies to engage in a dialogue with relevant stakeholders to address the practice.

A total of seven states under review noted this recommendation when issued to them during their review. Of these, the states of Belize, Kuwait, and Sierra Leone all noted the recommendation without any further comments. In other instances, Iran noted the recommendations and stated that the laws regarding early and forced marriage were already in place. The state of Malaysia also noted the recommendation and provided a much broader response and insisted that the state does not discriminate against women. The Solomon Islands insisted that it noted the recommendation as it made a very broad and vague commitment in 'seeking way to better approach this issue'.[154] Finally, the state of Tanzania provided an N8 response, as it stated that on the issue of early marriage, raising the age was a sensitive issue that was related to traditions and religion, nevertheless, legislative measures on it were in preparation.[155]

RECOMMENDATION 5

Observer states issuing a recommendation under this category insisted that states should implement policies and strategies on the ground to help eradicate forced and early marriages. This recommendation can be distinguished from recommendation 3, as the observer states made no references to local religious or cultural leaders, and thereby did not make any implicit references to the relationship between such marriages and the justifications of them based on cultural norms. An example of a recommendation issued under this category is when the United Kingdom recommended that Guinea Bissau 'take practical steps, including through public information campaigns and greater community-level engagement, to accelerate the eradication of ... early and forced marriages'. In response, a total of 15 states were issued with this recommendation, and only one stated noted it without acceptation. Of the 14 states that did accept the recommendation, Armenia, Indonesia, Macedonia, Madagascar, and Niger all accepted the recommendation without any further comments. The delegate of Liberia accepted the recommendation and referred to laws that were under review in relation to the issue. The states of Kyrgyzstan, Malawi, and Yemen all referred to the existing domestic laws and policies that were in place to protect women from forced and early marriages. The states of Afghanistan, Guinea Bissau, Mozambique, Turkey, and Yemen all accepted the recommendation and stated that any reforms to be made to address the practices. For example, the delegate of Turkey provided that National Strategy Document and Action Plan on the Rights of the Child 2013–2017 was focused on keeping girls in the education system with an aim to prevent early marriages'.[156]

Discussion and Analysis

From the findings of the nature of discussions held on forced and early marriages, three main themes have emerged, which help to answer the research question that has guided this investigation. The first is that there is evidence in the discussions whereby the relationship between forced and early marriages and cultural norms have explicitly or implicitly been drawn upon both in the recommendations and the responses, albeit in different formats. For instance, under both cycles of review, observer states issued recommendations that drew association between forced and early marriages and cultural norms, before suggesting eliminating this practice to 12 states under review. This position adopted by observer states when discussing the issue of forced and early marriages resonates with the strict Universalist position. This is because the strict Universalist position advocates for the implementation of universal human rights norms, which are to transcend any cultural boundaries.[157] By referring explicitly to cultural norms in their discussions and recommendations on the issue, the observer states have insisted that the practice of forced and early marriages should be eradicated, despite being embedded in cultural norms. It is important to note that when states under review were issued with this recommendation, only the states of Botswana and Gambia noted the recommendation. In fact, no states under review noted this form of recommendation in the second cycle of review. This gives reason to suggest that, at least formally, states when held accountable to the practices of early and forced marriages during their review, in which the nature of discussions expressly made reference to its cultural associations, only two states under review challenged this form of recommendation. This means that when states under review are held accountable, there is not an express challenge to the suggestion that these practices should be eliminated, despite being embedded in culture. In fact, even in the responses of Gambia and Botswana, who noted the recommendation, they did not expressly challenge the centre premise of the recommendation that this practice, despite being embedded in cultural norms, should be eliminated. For instance, Gambia referenced incremental reforms that were in place, whilst the delegate of Botswana insisted that such harmful practices do not exist. The essence of the nature of these discussions is that in the UPR process, when states were being held accountable for early and forced marriages, which suggested the elimination of the practice, despite being embedded in culture, no states under review directly challenged this practice. Going further, over the two cycles of review, Tanzania, in the second cycle, was the only state that rejected a recommendation on the basis that it was inconsistent with the traditional values of the state. Thus, over the two cycles of review where this issue was discussed, only one state in the second cycle rejected the norms based on cultural norms. This indicates that there is a large degree of consensus amongst states that were held accountable on this issue, forced and early marriages cannot be justified on cultural norms.

Another common theme that emerged in the discussions held is that some observer states, and states under review, took the position that the best method to bring forced and early marriage to an end was by implementing policies and strategies to gradually reform attitudes that were sympathetic to forced and early marriages. For instance, peer states reviewing the state under review adopted a position that reforms should be undertaken in relation to individual attitudes towards forced and early marriages through 'awareness-raising campaigns, sensitization',[158] 'public information campaigns',[159] 'raising awareness with public officials',[160] and 'citizenship education'.[161] The nature of these reforms was also vocalised by states under review that responded with an A4, A5, and N3 response in the first cycle, and A4 and N3 in the second cycle. In these cases, the states under review focused on implementing incremental reforms to attitudes that are sympathetic towards forced and early marriages. This position adopted by the states in the discussions of marriages affiliates with the moderate cultural relativist position. This is because the suggested long-term reforms in relation to such marriages indicate that the states recognise that sympathetic attitudes towards such marriages are deeply engraved in the belief systems of societies, and therefore require long-term reform policies and strategies. In light of this, it is difficult to deny the significant role culture plays in influencing any moral, political, or ideological developments, which occur over a period of time, for the collective and individual human behaviour in any particular society.[162] Therefore, the suggestion to undertake incremental reform to change attitudes towards the practices indicates that the selected states are not only implicitly recognising the inherent association between forced and early marriage and culture, but suggesting culturally legitimate reforms of such attitudes to bring them into compliance with international norms.[163] Culturally legitimate reforms ensure that human rights standards reflect the values emanated from within cultures, and are thereby not perceived to have been imposed by others.[164]

The suggestion that some of these states adopted a position that affiliates with the moderate cultural relativist position can further be supported by the specific reforms suggested by four of the states. In addition to the statements described above, the states of Guinea Bissau, United States, Germany, and Norway all discussed that forced and early marriages should be addressed by engaging in a constructive dialogue with targeted 'sectors of the population'[165] 'involving local level' participation,[166] and to work with 'religious leaders'[167] and 'local community leaders'.[168] In this way, states encouraged a constructive dialogue within the local communities and religious leaders with the aim to discourage sympathetic attitudes to forced and early marriages. This position resonates with An-Na'im's suggestion of engaging an internal cultural discourse as a means of enhancing the legitimacy of international human rights norms.[169] The aim of an internal discourse is to reform certain values and beliefs that exist in a culture that are inconsistent with human rights law and to bring them in line with current international human rights standards.[170] Such reforms of cultural beliefs are undertaken from within the culture itself, according to the beliefs embedded in the cultural and religious texts, to ensure that the international human rights norms in question are accepted as binding.[171] In this way, the aim is to promote cultural legitimacy of international human rights standards, which means that the norms derive their authority from internal validity of the culture itself.[172] These suggestions made by authors to further the cultural legitimacy of rights are present in the essence of the suggestions made by some states in the discussions of forced and early marriages. The nature of this recommendation instigated a more fruitful dialogue on the issue. This is because the states under review in their responses discussed complex issues as to why women do not report such marriages despite laws being enacted against them, whilst other states responded with a form of internal discourse that was being undertaken at national level to help discourage such marriages. Thus, for the first time in this investigation for this chapter, states have adopted a position during discussions which aims to undertake reforms to any potential cultural justifications for forced and early marriages, with the ultimate aim to discourage such marriages. In this way, by introducing a moderate cultural relativist position into the discussions, the states began to engage in a more fruitful dialogue and move away from the surface discussions on the issue, which focus largely on either criticising the cultural nature of the practice or domestic laws enacted to address the issue.

Whilst there are obvious benefits to the moderate cultural relativist position, and its prominence on the UPR process is promising, it cannot be overlooked that discussions of this nature were few and far between. In fact, the most prominent theme that emerged is that the majority of the discussions held on the issue, over both cycles, were in reference to laws and policies that were already in place. There are two main problems with this position. The first is related to the point made previously that the issue of forced and early marriages is complex, and cannot simply be eliminated through the enacting, and even implementing, of legislation. The inherent relationship with the issue and cultural norms means that eradicating the issue is more of a long-term process that requires strategies to put in place for constructive dialogues to be held to discourage the practice. Indeed, the very nature of the UPR process is such to accommodate this type of reforms, and to hold the states accountable to them. The second problem is that the discussions that relate to laws and the implementation of them invite a very limited form of discussion on the issue. It closes the line of dialogue on the issue, and the ability to engage in a meaningful discussion to address the practice. In fact, many states under review have responded with statements in relation to laws already being in place, or under review and reforms. The very nature of the UPR process accommodates a much deeper and constructive level of discussions on this, often, controversial issue. For this reason, the discussions held in relation to legislation on the issue can be considered to some extent unproductive for this platform that is based more on incremental reforms and periodic reviews on the progress of such reforms, rather than holding states formally accountable for enacting and implementing laws; it is arguable, the latter of which the process simply does not possesses the mandate for.

Conclusion

This chapter presented the findings on the nature of the discussions held amongst states on three issues under the category of women's rights under private and family law, with the aim of gaining a better understanding of how the UPR process operates through the positions adopted by states during state reviews over the two cycles of reviews. The study has identified that states adopted the positions that affiliated with strict universalism during the discussions of *all* three issues in the two cycles. In response, the states under review responded in a highly subdued and defensive manner. Further, it is notable that no states under review agreed to any commitments as a result of being suggested recommendations from a strict universalist position on the three issues. This means, when the states adopted a strict universalist position in the discussions of the three issues, the outcome of such discussions has, to a large extent, been unfruitful.

This investigation has also found that when the issues of polygamy and inheritance were being discussed, some states under review adopted a position which resonated with a strict cultural relativist position. This shows that when some states under review did not adhere to the international standards on inheritance and polygamy, the UPR process was used to directly challenge the universality of international human rights norms on the two issues. A significant point to note from the findings was that in *all* the cases that the states adopted a strict cultural relativist position, it was voiced in the HRC plenary session, as opposed to the interactive dialogue session. The implication of this is that due to the heavy time restraints, observer states were not able to hold states fully accountable or scrutinise the strict cultural relativist positions adopted by some states under review.

It was interesting to note that the nature of the discussions held on forced and early marriages differed from the state discussions on inheritance and polygamy. For instance, no states under review challenged the universality of the norms in relation to such marriages from a cultural relativist perspective. In addition, it was only during the discussions on forced and early marriages that there was evidence of states issuing statements which could be interpreted as a moderate cultural relativist position. This is because states issued statements which recognised the significance of incremental reforms and public awareness campaigns to discourage sympathetic attitudes towards such marriages. Further, states adopting aspects of moderate cultural relativist positions also shed light on the complex nature of the issue as states emphasised the importance of engaging in a constructive dialogue with religious and local leaders to help discourage deeply engraved sympathies towards the practice. From this, it can be seen that when states adopted a position that affiliated with the moderate cultural relativist position in the discussions on forced marriages, it resulted in a shift away from a surface-level discussion on the issue during state reviews. Instead the discussions drew the complex nature of the issue to the centre of discussions as states recognised the need to undertake wide ranging reforms to help eliminate forced and early marriages.

In contrast, when the states failed to appreciate the moderate cultural relativist positions in the discussions on polygamy and inheritance, states failed to draw the cultural and religious impediments to the centre of the discussions in the UPR process with the aim of suggesting culturally legitimate reforms. Instead, where there was evidence of a strict universalist or strict cultural relativist position being adopted by states, the discussions focused largely on a superficial level, where it focused on the laws to be implemented in the area and states under review responded by insisting that the laws were already in place. This overwhelming focus on the domestic legislation in relation to inheritance resulted in a lack of fruitful dialogue, and instead acted as a veil from discussing and suggesting reforms in relation to cultural and religious influences on inheritance. Thus, the findings of this chapter confirm the theoretical critique of the polarised debate between strict universalism and strict cultural relativism, and the beneficial outcome of the moderate cultural relativist perspective.

Notes

1   BE Hernandez-Truyol, 'Women's Rights and Human Rights – Rule, Realities and the Role of Culture: A Formula for Reform' (1995–1996) 21 *Brooklyn Journal of International Law* 605, 630–631.
2   Sheila Dauer, "Indivisible or invisible: women's human rights in the public and private sphere", in Marjorie Agosín (ed), *Women, Gender, and Human Rights: A Global Perspective* (Rutgers University Press 2001).
3   Convention on the Elimination of All Forms of Discrimination against Women (adopted 18 December 1979, entry into force 3 September 1981) 1249 UNTS (CEDAW), Article 16.
4   Julie Mertus, 'State discriminatory family law and customary values' in Julie Peters and Andrea Wolper (eds), *Women's Rights, Human Rights: International Feminist Perspective* (Routledge 1995) 135.
5   Ibid.
6   Amira Mashour, 'Islamic Law and Gender Equality – Could There Be a Common Ground? A Study of Divorce and Polygamy in Sharia Law and Contemporary Legislation in Tunisia and Egypt' (2005) 27 *Human Rights Quarterly* 562.

See also Javaid Rehman, 'The Sharia, Islamic Family Laws and International Human Rights Law: Examining the Theory and Practice of Polygamy and Talaq' (2007) 21 *International Journal of Law, Policy and the Family* 108, 115.

7 UN Human Rights Committee, 'CCPR General Comment No. 28: Article 3 (The Equality of Rights between Men and Women' (29 March 2000) CCPR/C/21/Rev.1/Add.10, para 24; UNCEDAW, 'CEDAW General Recommendation No. 21: Equality in Marriage and Family Relations' (1994), para 41.

8 International Covenant on Civil and Political Rights (adopted 16 December 1966, entered into force 23 March 1976) 999 UNTS 171 Article 23(4) 1966.

9 UN Press Release WOM/1452 2004; UN Committee on the Elimination of Discrimination against Women (CEDAW), CEDAW *General Recommendation No. 21: Equality in Marriage and Family Relations*, 1994, www.refworld.org/docid/48abd52c0.html (accessed 1 August 2019) para 41; UN Press Release, 'Customs, Traditions Remain Obstacles to Women's Rights in Equatorial Guinea say Anti-Discrimination Committee Experts' (8 July 2004) WOM/1452, www.un.org/press/en/2004/wom1452.doc.htm, accessed 28 August 2019.

10 Ibid.

11 Amira Mashour, 'Islamic Law and Gender Equality – Could There Be a Common Ground? A Study of Divorce and Polygamy in Sharia Law and Contemporary Legislation in Tunisia and Egypt' (2005) 27 *Human Rights Quarterly* 568.

12 Javaid Rehman, 'The Sharia, Islamic Family Laws and International Human Rights Law: Examining the Theory and Practice of Polygamy and Talaq' (2007) 21 *International Journal of Law, Policy and the Family* 108, 115.

13 Fidelis Nkomazana, 'Polygamy and Women within the Cultural Context in Botswana' (2006) 92 *Scripture* 265, 269.

14 L J Peach, 'Are women human? The promise and perils of "women's rights as human rights"' in Lynda Bell, Andrew Nathan and Ilan Peieg (eds), *Negotiating Culture and Human Rights* (Columbia University Press 2001).

15 UNHRC 'Equatorial Guinea' (4 January 2010) A/HRC/13/16, para 67.4

16 UNHRC 'Report of the Human Rights Council on its tenth session' (9 November 2009) A/HRC/10/29, page 272.

17 UN Human Rights Council, 'Summary prepared by the Office of the High Commissioner for Human' (2008b) A/HRC/WG.6/3/BWA/3).

18 UNHRC, 'Kyrgyzstan' (16 June 2010) A/HRC/15/2, para 76.61.

19 UNHRC, 'Report of the Human Rights Council on Its Twelfth Session' (25 February 2010) A/HRC/12/50, para 221.

20 UNHRC, 'Report of the Human Rights Council on its tenth session' (2009c) A/HRC/10/29, para 577.

21 UNHRC, 'Report of the Human Rights Council on Its Tenth Session' (9 November 2009) A/HRC/10/29, para 577.

22 UNHRC 'Report of the Human Rights Council on Its Nineteenth Session' (24 May 2013) A/HRC/19/2, para 376.

23 UNHRC, 'Ghana' (29 May 2008) A/HRC/8/36, para 50.

24 UNHRC, 'Report of the Human Rights Council on Its Tenth Session' (9 November 2009) A/HRC/10/29, para 460.

25 UNHRC, 'Report of the Human Rights Council on Its Eighth Session' (1 September 2008) A/HRC/8/52, para 663.

26 UNHRC, 'Report of the Human Rights Council on Its Nineteenth Session' (2013b) A/HRC/19/2, para 38.

27 UNHRC, 'Kyrgyzstan' (16 June 2010) A/HRC/15/2, para 76.62.

28 Ibid. para 76.77.

29 UNHRC, 'Mauritania' (4 January 2011) A/HRC/16/17, para 92.

30 UNHRC, 'Senegal' (3 March 2009) A/HRC/11/24, para 54.

31 UNHRC, 'Equatorial Guinea, Addendum' (19 September 2014) A/HRC/27/13/Add.1

32 'Report of the Human Rights Council on Its Twenty-Fourth Session' (27 January 2014) A/HRC/24/2, para 323.

33 UN Human Rights Council, 'Follow-up to the Human Rights Council Resolution 16/21 with Regard to the Universal Periodic Review' (July 2011) A/HRC/DEC/17/119.

34 UNHRC 'Res 5/1 Institution-building of the United Nations Human Rights Council' (18 June 2007) Annex A/HRC/RES/5/1, para 4(a).

35 R Sloane, 'Outrelativising Relativism: A Liberal Defence of the Universality of International Human Rights' (2001) 34 *Vanderbilt Journal of Transnational Law* 527.

36 FR Tesón, 'International Human Rights and Cultural Relativism' (1984–1985) 25 *Virginia Journal of International Law* 869.

37 T Spaak, 'Moral Relativism and Human Rights' (2007) 13 *Buffalo Human Rights Law Review* 73; G Harman and J Thomson, *Moral Relativism and Moral Objectivity* (Wiley-Blackwell 1995); CJ Jarvie, 'Rationalism and Relativism' (1983) 34 *British Journal of Sociology* 45.

38 E Domínguez-Redondo, 'The Universal Periodic Review – Is There Life beyond Naming and Shaming in Human Rights Implementation' (2012) 4 *New Zealand Law Review* 673.

39 Marie-Benedicte Dembour 'Following the movement of a pendulum: between universalism and relativism' in Jane Cowan, Marie-Benedicte Dembour and Richard Wilson (eds), *Culture and Rights: Anthropological Perspectives* (Cambridge University Press 2001) 58; R Falk, 'Cultural foundations for the international protection of human rights' in AA An-Na'im (ed), *Human Rights in Cross Cultural Perspectives* (University of Pennsylvania Press 1995) 46; F Lenzerini, *The Culturalization of Human Rights Law* (Oxford University Press 2014).

40 F Boas, *The Mind of Primitive Man* (Forgotten Books 2012).

41 Ann-Belinda Pries, 'Human Rights as a Cultural Practice: An Anthropological Critique' (1996) 19 *Human Rights Quarterly* 289; Robert Ulin, 'Revisiting Cultural Relativism: Old Prospects for a New Cultural Critique (2007) 80 *Anthropological Quarterly* 803.

42 A An-Na'im, 'Toward a cross culture approach to defining international standards of human right: the meaning of cruel, inhuman or degrading treatment' in Abdullahi An-Na'im (ed), *Human Rights in Cross Cultural Perspectives: A Quest for Consensus* (University of Pennsylvania Press 1995) 23; S Merry, 'Constructing a Global Law-Violence against Women and the Human Rights System' (2003) *Law and Social Enquiry* 941.

43 United Charter of the United Nations (adopted 17 December 1963, entered into force 31 August 1965) UNTS XVI; International Covenant on Civil and Political Rights (adopted 16 December 1966, entered into force 23 March 1976) 999 UNTS 171 article 2(1) and 26; International Covenant on Economic, Social and Cultural Rights (adopted 16 December 1966, entered into force 3 January 1976) 993 UNTS 220A, article 3.

44 UN Committee on the Elimination of Discrimination against Women, 'CEDAW General Recommendation No. 24: Article 12 of the Convention (Women and Health)' (1999) A/54/38/Rev.1, Chapter I, para 28. See also UN Human Rights Committee, 'CCPR General Comment No. 28: Article 3 (The Equality of Rights Between Men and Women' (29 March 2000) CCPR/C/21/Rev.1/Add.10; UN Office of the High Commissioner for Human Rights, 'Report of the Special Rapporteur on Adequate Housing as a

Component of the Right to an Adequate Standard of Living, and on the Right to Non-Discrimination in This Context, Raquel Rolnik' (16 December 2011) A/HRC/19/53, para 55.

45 UN Office of the High Commissioner for Human Rights, 'Report of the Special Rapporteur on Adequate Housing as a Component of the Right to an Adequate Standard of Living, and on the Right to Non-Discrimination in This Context, Raquel Rolnik' (16 December 2011) A/HRC/19/53, para 55.

46 SM Burns, *Women across Cultures* (2nd edn, McGraw Hill 2005); Abby Morrow Richardson, 'Women's Inheritance Rights in Africa: The Need Integrate Cultural Understanding and Legal Reform' (2004) 11 *Human Rights Brief* 19.

47 Ibid.

48 Niaz Shah, 'Women's Human Rights in the Koran: An Interpretative Approach' (2006) 28 *Human Rights Quarterly* 868, 897; UN Committee on the Elimination of Discrimination against Women, 'Concluding observations of the Committee on the Elimination of Discrimination against Women: Libyan Arab Jamahiriya' (6 February 2009) CEDAW/C/LBY/CO/5, para 17.

49 UNHRC, 'Greece' (11 July 2011) A/HRC/18/13, para 83.22.

50 UNHRC, 'Madagascar' (26 March 2010) A/HRC/14/13, para 25.

51 UNHRC, 'Greece' (11 July 2011) A/HRC/18/13, para 15.

52 Ibid. para 15.

53 UNHRC, 'Algeria' (23 May 2008) A/HRC/8/29, para 63.

54 UNHRC, 'Burundi' (8 January 2009) A/HRC/10/71, para 41.

55 UNHRC, 'Liechtenstein' (7 January 2009) A/HRC/10/77, para 34.

56 UNHRC, 'Gambia' (24 March 2010) A/HRC/14/6, para 38.

57 UNHRC, 'Report of the Human Rights Council on Its Eighth Session' (1 September 2008) A/HRC/8/52, para 501.

58 UNHRC, 'Kiribati, Addendum' (30 September 2010) A/HRC/15/3/Add.1, para 18.

59 UNHRC, 'Timor-Leste, Addendum' (15 March 2012) A/HRC/19/17/Add.1, page 3.

60 UNHRC, 'Report of the Human Rights Council on Its Nineteenth Session' (24 May 2013) A/HRC/19/2, para 553.

61 UNHRC, 'Report of the Human Rights Council on Its Twelfth Session' (25 February 2010) A/HRC/12/50, para 444.

62 UNHRC, 'Report of the Human Rights Council on Its Eighteenth Session' (18 November 2011) A/HRC/18/2, para 379.

63 UNHRC, 'Burundi' (8 January 2009) A/HRC/10/71, para 35.

64 UNHRC, 'Equatorial Guinea' (4 January 2010) A/HRC/13/16, para 71.40.

65 UNHRC, 'Maldives' (4 January 2011) A/HRC/16/7, para 100.23.

66 UNHRC, 'Burundi' (8 January 2009) A/HRC/10/71, para 4.

67 UNHRC, 'Gambia' (24 March 2010) A/HRC/14/6, para 100.3.

68 UNHRC, 'Yemen' (5 June 2009) A/HRC/12/13, para 94.2.

69 UNHRC, 'Report of the Human Rights Council on Its Sixteenth Session' (14 November 2011) A/HRC/16/2, para 553.

70 Niaz Shah, 'Women's Human Rights in the Koran: An Interpretative Approach' Women's Human Rights in the Koran: An Interpretative Approach' (2006) 28 *Human Rights Quarterly* 868, 897; UN Committee on the Elimination of Discrimination against Women, 'Concluding observations of the Committee on the Elimination of Discrimination against Women: Libyan Arab Jamahiriya' (6 February 2009) CEDAW/C/LBY/CO/5, para 17.

71 UNHRC, 'Libyan Arab Jamahiriya' (4 January 2011) A/HRC/16/15, para 95.8.

72 Ibid. para 57.

73 UNHRC, 'Libya, Addendum' (22 February 2012) A/HRC/16/15/Add.1, page 3.
74 UNHRC, 'Ghana' (29 May 2008) A/HRC/8/36, para 22.
75 UNHRC, 'Report of the Human Rights Council on Its Fifteenth Session' (31 October 2011) A/HRC/15/60, para 391.
76 UNHRC, 'Liechtenstein' (7 January 2009) A/HRC/10/77, para 36.
77 UNHRC, 'United Arab Emirates' (12 January 2009) A/HRC/10/75, para 89.
78 UNHRC, 'Samoa' (11 July 2011) A/HRC/18/14, para 15.
79 UNHRC, 'Democratic Republic of the Congo' (7 July 2014) A/HRC/27/5.
80 UNHRC, 'Kenya' (26 March 2019) A/HRC/29/10, para 14.
81 UNHRC, 'Burundi' (25 March 2013) A/HRC/23/9, para 62.
82 UNHRC, 'Botswana' (22 March 2013) A/HRC/23/7, para 36.
83 Report of the Human Rights Council on Its Twenty-Fourth Session' (29 January 2014) A/HRC/24/2, para 573.
84 UNHRC, 'Tunisia' (9 July 2012) A/HRC/21/5, para 109
85 UNHRC, 'United Arab Emirates' 4 June 2013 (A/HRC/23/13/Add.1) Add 1 paragraph 1.
86 UNHRC, 'Jordan' 6 January 2014 (A/HRC/25/9), para 70.
87 UNHRC, 'Palau' 13 April 2016 (A/HRC/32/11, Add1 para 5.
88 UNHRC, 'Libya' 22 July 2015 (A/HRC/30/16, para 98.
89 UNHRC, 'Greece' (8 July 2016) A/HRC/33/7, para 80.
90 UNHRC, 'Djibouti' (8 July 2013) A/HRC/24/10.
91 Ibid. 62.
92 FR Tesón, 'International Human Rights and Cultural Relativism' (1984–1985) 25 *Virginia Journal of International Law* 869, 870–871. See also T Higgins, 'Anti-Essentialism, Relativism, and Human Rights' (1996) 19 *Harvard Women's Law Journal* 89, 95.
93 Catherine Powell, 'Introduction: Locating Culture, Identity, and Human Rights' (1999) 30 *Columbia Human Rights Law Review* 211.
94 R Mushkat, 'Culture and International Law: Universalism and Relativism' (2002) 6 *Singapore Journal of International and Comparative Law* 1032.
95 Ibid.
96 A An-Naim, 'State responsibility under International Human Rights Law to change Religious and Customary Law' in Rebecca Cook (ed), *Human Rights of Women: National and International Perspectives* (University of Pennsylvania Press 1994) 173.
97 Ibid.
98 L Farha, 'Women and housing' in Kelly D Askin and Dorean M Koenig (eds), *Women and International Human Rights Law* (Volume 1, Transnational Publishers Inc 1999) 512–513.
99 Ibid.
100 Abby Morrow Richardson, 'Women's Inheritance Rights in Africa: The Need Integrate Cultural Understanding and Legal Reform' (2004) 11 *Human Rights Brief* 19.
101 Ibid.
102 L Farha, 'Women and housing' in Kelly D Askin and Dorean M Koenig (eds), *Women and International Human Rights Law* (Volume 1, Transnational Publishers Inc 1999) 512.
103 Azizah Yahia al-Hibri, 'Islam, Law and Custom: Redefining Muslim Women's Rights (1997) 12 *Am. U. J. Int'l L. & Pol'y* (1997) 1, 3.
104 Abby Morrow Richardson, 'Women's Inheritance Rights in Africa: The Need Integrate Cultural Understanding and Legal Reform' (2004) 11 *Human Rights Brief* 19, 22.

105 Cheryl Thomas, 'Forced and Early Marriage: A Focus on Central and Eastern Europe and Former Soviet Union Countries with Selected Laws from Other Countries' EGM/GPLHP/2009/EP.08 (United Nations Economic Commission for Africa, 2009)

106 UN General Assembly, '*Convention on Consent to Marriage, Minimum Age for Marriage and Registration of Marriages*' (7 November 1962), para 1, Articles 1 and 2.

107 Ibid.

108 Convention on the Elimination of All Forms of Discrimination against Women (adopted 18 December 1979, entry into force 3 September 1981) 1249 UNTS, Article 16 (b) CEDAW.

109 See UN Human Rights Committee (HRC), 'CCPR General Comment No. 19: Article 23 (The Family) Protection of the Family, the Right to Marriage and Equality of the Spouses' (27 July 1990) para 4,6,8.

110 UNHRC, 'Strengthening Efforts to Prevent and Eliminate Child, Early and Forced Marriage: Challenges, Achievements, Best Practices and Implementation Gaps' (25th September 2013) A/HRC/24/L.34/Rev.1.

111 UN Committee on the Elimination of Discrimination against Women, 'General Recommendation on Article 16 of the Convention on the Elimination of all Forms of Discrimination against Women (Economic consequences of marriage, family relations and their dissolution)' (30 October 2013) CEDAW/C/GC/29, para 2.

112 Anne Bunting, 'Theorizing Women's Cultural Diversity in Feminist International Human Rights Strategies' (1993) 20 *Journal of Law and Society* 6, 24.

113 Ibid. 29.

114 Ibid. 26.

115 HG Dagne, 'Early Marriages in Northern Ethiopia' (1994) 4 *Reproductive Health Matters* 35.

116 UNHRC, 'Gambia' (24 March 2010) A/HRC/14/6, para 44.

117 UNHRC, 'Sierra Leone' (11 July 2011) A/HRC/18/10, para 10.

118 UNHRC, 'Sierra Leone Addendum' (13 September 2011) A/HRC/18/10/Add.1, page 3.

119 UNHRC, 'Report of the Human Rights Council on Its Fifteenth Session' (31 October 2011) A/HRC/15/60, para 676.

120 UNHRC, 'Gambia' (24 March 2010) A/HRC/14/6, para 18.

121 UNHRC, 'Report of the Human Rights Council on Its Tenth Session' (9 November 2009) A/HRC/10/29, page 4.

122 UNHRC, 'Sudan' (11 July 2011) A/HRC/18/16, para 83.107.

123 UNHRC, 'El Salvador' (18 March 2010) A/HRC/14/5, para 76.

124 UNHRC, 'Azerbaijan' (6 March 2009) A/HRC/11/20, para 61.

125 UNHRC, 'Yemen: Addendum' (23 September 2009) A/HRC/12/13/Add.1, page 2.

126 UNHRC, 'Japan' (30 May 2008) A/HRC/8/44, para 7.

127 UNHRC, 'Bangladesh: Addendum' (9 June 2009) A/HRC/11/18/Add.1, page 3.

128 UNHRC, 'Iran' (15 March 2010) A/HRC/14/12, para 65.

129 UNHRC, 'Report of the Human Rights Council on Its Fifteenth Session' (31 October 2011) A/HRC/15/60, para 676.

130 UNHRC, 'Report of the Human Rights Council on Its Eighth Session' (1 September 2008) A/HRC/8/52, para 642.

131 UNHRC, 'Mali' (13 June 2008) A/HRC/8/50, para 55.

132 UNHRC, 'Report of the Working Group on the Universal Periodic Review: Gambia' (24 March 2010) A/HRC/14/6, para 18.

133 UNHRC, 'Liberia' (4 January 2011) A/HRC/16/3, para 77.33.
134 UNHRC, 'Afghanistan' (20 July 2009) A/HRC/12/9, para 35.
135 UNHRC, 'Timor-Leste' (3 January 2012) A/HRC/19/17, para 78.15.
136 UNHRC, 'Liberia' (4 January 2011) A/HRC/16/3, para 48.
137 UNHRC, 'Timor-Leste' (3 January 2012) A/HRC/19/17, para 23.
138 UNHRC, 'Pakistan' (4 June 2008) A/HRC/8/42, para 43.
139 UNHRC, 'Niger' (25 March 2011) A/HRC/17/15, para 49.
140 UNHRC, 'Report of the Human Rights Council on Its Twelfth Session' (25 February 2010) A/HRC/12/50, page 2.
141 UNHRC, 'Sierra Leone' (11 July 2011) A/HRC/18/10, para 8.
142 UNHRC, 'Liberia' (4 January 2011) A/HRC/16/3, para 48.
143 UNHRC, 'Report of the Human Rights Council on Its Twelfth Session' (25 February 2010) A/HRC/12/50, para 444.
144 UNHRC, 'Report of the Working Group on the Universal Periodic Review: Chad' (5 October 2009) A/HRC/12/5, para 18.
145 UNHRC, 'Report of the Working Group on the Universal Periodic Review: Bahrain' (22 May 2008) A/HRC/8/19, para 59.
146 UNHRC, 'Report of the Working Group on the Universal Periodic Review: Gambia' (24 March 2010) A/HRC/14/6, para 18.
147 UNHRC, 'Cote d'Ivoire' (7 July 2014) A/HRC/27/6, para 71.
148 UNHRC, 'Gabon' (13 December 2012) A/HRC/22/5, para 52.
149 UNHRC, 'Nepal' (23 December 2015) A/HRC/31/9, para 60.
150 UNHRC, 'Guinea Bissau' (13 April 2015), para 43.
151 UNHRC, 'Iraq' (12 December 2014), para 76.
152 UNHRC, 'Report of the Human Rights Council on Its Thirty-Third Session' (16 December 2016) A/HRC/33/3, para 761.
153 UNHRC, 'Saudi Arabia' (26 December 2013) A/HRC/25/3, para 12.
154 UNHRC, 'Solomon Islands' (22 June 2016) A/HRC/32/14/Add.1.
155 UNHRC, 'Tanzania' (14 July 2016) A/HRC/33/12.
156 UNHRC, 'Turkey' (13 April 2015) A/HRC/29/15, para 145.
157 R Sloane, 'Outrelativising Relativism: A Liberal Defence of the Universality of International Human Rights' (2001) 34 *Vanderbilt Journal of Transnational Law* 527, 541–542.
158 UNHRC, 'Report of the Human Rights Council on Its Fifteenth Session' (31 October 2011) A/HRC/15/60, para 676.
159 UNHRC, 'Afghanistan' (20 July 2009) A/HRC/12/9, para 18.
160 UNHRC, 'Timor-Leste' (3 January 2012) A/HRC/19/17, paragraph 78.15.
161 Ibid.
162 A An-Na'im, 'Problems and prospects of universal cultural legitimacy for human rights' in An- Na'im and Francis Deng (eds), *Human Rights in Africa: Cross Cultural Perspectives* in (Brookings Institution 1990) 333.
163 Clifford Geertz, *The Interpretation of Cultures* (Basic Books 1973) 49.
164 An –Nai'm, 'Conclusion' in Abdullahi Ahmed An-Na'im (eds) *Human Rights in Cross Cultural Perspectives: A Quest for Consensus* (University of Pennsylvania Press, 1995) 431.
165 UNHRC, 'Report of the Human Rights Council on Its Fifteenth Session' (31 October 2011) A/HRC/15/60, para 676.
166 UNHRC, 'Liberia' (4 January 2011) A/HRC/16/3, paragraph 77.33.
167 UNHRC, 'Afghanistan' (20 July 2009) A/HRC/12/9, para 35.
168 UNHRC, 'Timor-Leste' (3 January 2012) A/HRC/19/17, para 78.15.
169 A An-Na'im, 'State responsibility under International Human Rights Law to Change Religious and Customary Law' in Rebecca Cook (ed), *Human Rights of Women: National and International Perspectives* (University of Pennsylvania Press 1994) 174.

170 A An-Na'im, 'Islam, Islamic Law and the dilemma of cultural legitimacy for Universal Human Rights' in Claude E Welch, Jr. and Virginia A. Leary (eds), *Asian Perspectives on Human Rights* (Westview Press 1990) 46–48.
171 A An-Na'im, 'Toward an Islamic hermeneutics for human rights' in Abdullahi Ahmed An-Na'im, Jernald D Gort, Henry Jansen and Hendrik M Vroom (eds), *Human Rights and Religious Values: An Uneasy Relationship?* (William B. Eerdmans Publishing Company 1995).
172 A An-Na'im, 'Problems and prospects of Universal Cultural Legitimacy for human rights' in An- Na'im and Deng (eds), *Human Rights in Africa: Cross Cultural Perspectives* in, (Brookings Institution, 1990) 336.

Bibliography

An-Na'im A, 'Problems and Prospects of Universal Cultural Legitimacy for Human Rights' in A An- Na'im and FM Deng (eds), *Human Rights in Africa: Cross Cultural Perspectives In* (Brookings Institution, 1990).

An-Na'im A, 'Islam, Islamic Law and the Dilemma of Cultural Legitimacy for Universal Human Rights' in Claude E Welch, Jr. and Virginia A. Leary (eds), *Asian Perspectives on Human Rights* (Westview Press, 1990).

An-Na'im A, 'State Responsibility Under International Human Rights Law to Change Religious and Customary Law' in Rebecca Cook (ed), *Human Rights of Women: National and International Perspectives* (University of Pennsylvania Press, 1994).

An-Nai'm A, 'Conclusion' in Abdullahi Ahmed An-Naim (eds), *Human Rights in Cross Cultural Perspectives: A Quest for Consensus* (University of Pennsylvania Press 1995).

An-Na'im A, 'Toward a Cross Culture Approach to Defining International Standards of Human Right: The Meaning of Cruel, Inhuman or Degrading Treatment' in Abdullahi An-Naim (ed), *Human Rights in Cross Cultural Perspectives: A Quest for Consensus* (University of Pennsylvania Press, 1995).

An-Na'im A, 'Toward an Islamic Hermeneutics for Human Rights' in Abdullahi Ahmed An-Na'im, Jernald D Gort, Henry Jansen and Hendrik M Vroom (eds), *Human Rights and Religious Values: An Uneasy Relationship?* (William B. Eerdmans Publishing Company, 1995).

Burns MS, *Women Across Cultures* (2nd edn, McGraw Hill, 2005); Abby Morrow Richardson, 'Women's Inheritance Rights in Africa: The Need Integrate Cultural Understanding and Legal Reform' (2004) 11 *Human Rights Brief* 19.

Bunting A, 'Theorizing Women's Cultural Diversity in Feminist International Human Rights Strategies' (1993) 20 *Journal of Law and Society* 6.

Convention on the Elimination of All Forms of Discrimination against Women (adopted 18 December 1979, entry into force 3 September 1981) 1249 UNTS (CEDAW), Article 16.

Dagne GH 'Early Marriages in Northern Ethiopia' (1994) 4 *Reproductive Health Matters* 35.

Dauer S, 'Indivisible or Invisible: Women's Human Rights in the Public and Private Sphere' in Marjorie Agosín (ed), *Women, Gender, and Human Rights: A Global Perspective* (Rutgers University Press, 2001).

Dembour M 'Following the Movement of a Pendulum: Between Universalism and Relativism' in Jane Cowan, Marie-Benedicte Dembour and Richard Wilson (eds),

Culture and Rights: Anthropological Perspectives (Cambridge University Press, 2001).

Domínguez-Redondo E, 'The Universal Periodic Review – Is There Life beyond Naming and Shaming in Human Rights Implementation' (2012) 4 *New Zealand Law Review* 673.

Falk R, 'Cultural Foundations for the International Protection of Human Rights' in AA An-Na'im (ed), *Human Rights in Cross Cultural Perspectives* (University of Pennsylvania Press, 1995).

Farha L, 'Women and Housing' in Kelly D Askin and Dorean M Koenig (eds), *Women and International Human Rights Law* (Volume 1, Transnational Publishers Inc, 1999).

Geertz C, *The Interpretation of Cultures* (Basic Books, 1973).

Harman G and Thomson J, *Moral Relativism and Moral Objectivity* (Wiley-Blackwell, 1995).

Hernandez-Truyol EB, 'Women's Rights and Human Rights- Rule, Realities and the Role of Culture: A Formula for Reform' (1995–1996) 21 *Brooklyn Journal of International Law* 605.

Higgins T, 'Anti-Essentialism, Relativism, and Human Rights' (1996) 19 *Harvard Women's Law Journal* 89.

International Covenant on Civil and Political Rights (adopted 16 December 1966, entered into force 23 March 1976).

International Covenant on Economic, Social and Cultural Rights (adopted 16 December 1966, entered into force 3 January 1976) 993 UNTS 220A, article 3.

Jarvie JC, 'Rationalism and Relativism' (1983) 34 *British Journal of Sociology* 4.

Lenzerini F, *The Culturalization of Human Rights Law* (Oxford University Press, 2014).

Li X, *Ethics, Human Rights and Culture: Beyond Relativism and Culture* (Palgrave Macmillan 2006).

Nkomazana F, 'Polygamy and Women within the Cultural Context in Botswana' (2006) 92 *Scripture* 265.

Mashour A, 'Islamic Law and Gender Equality – Could There Be a Common Ground?: A study of Divorce and Polygamy in Sharia Law and Contemporary Legislation in Tunisia and Egypt' (2005) 27 *Human Rights Quarterly* 562.

Merry S, 'Constructing a Global Law-Violence against Women and the Human Rights System' (2003) 28 *Law and Social Enquiry* 941.

Mertus J, 'Stat *Women's Rights, Human Rights: International Feminist Perspective* e Discriminatory Family Law and Customary Values' in Julie Peters and Andrea Wolper (eds), (Routledge, 1995) 135.

Mushkat R, 'Culture and International Law: Universalism and Relativism' (2002) 6 *Singapore Journal of International and Comparative Law* 1032.

Powell C, 'Introduction: Locating Culture, Identity, and Human Rights' (1999) 30 *Columbia Human Rights Law Review* 211.

Pries BA, 'Human Rights as a Cultural Practice: An Anthropological Critique' (1996) 19 *Human Rights Quarterly* 289.

Rehman J, 'The Sharia, Islamic Family Laws and International Human Rights Law: Examining the Theory and Practice of Polygamy and Talaq' (2007) 21 *International Journal of Law, Policy and the Family* 108.

'Report of the Human Rights Council on its Twenty-Fourth Session' (29 January 2014) A/HRC/24/2.

Richardson MA, 'Women's Inheritance Rights in Africa: The Need Integrate Cultural Understanding and Legal Reform' (2004) 11 *Human Rights Brief* 19.

Shah N, 'Women's Human Rights in the Koran: An Interpretative Approach' (2006) 28 *Human Rights Quarterly* 868.

Sloane R, 'Outrelativising Relativism: A Liberal Defence of the Universality of International Human Rights' (2001) 34 *Vanderbilt Journal of Transnational Law* 527.

Tesón RF, 'International Human Rights and Cultural Relativism' (1984–1985) 25 *Virginia Journal of International Law* 869.

Thomas C, 'Forced and Early Marriage: A Focus on Central and Eastern Europe and Former Soviet Union Countries with Selected Laws from Other Countries' EGM/GPLHP/2009/EP.08 (United Nations Economic Commission for Africa, 2009).

UNCEDAW, 'CEDAW General Recommendation No. 21: Equality in Marriage and Family Relations' (1994).

UN Committee on the Elimination of Discrimination against Women, 'CEDAW General Recommendation No. 24: Article 12 of the Convention (Women and Health)' (1999) A/54/38/Rev.1, chap. I.

UN Committee on the Elimination of Discrimination against Women, 'Concluding observations of the Committee on the Elimination of Discrimination against Women : Libyan Arab Jamahiriya' (6 February 2009) CEDAW/C/LBY/CO/5.

UN Committee on the Elimination of Discrimination against Women, 'Concluding observations of the Committee on the Elimination of Discrimination against Women: Libyan Arab Jamahiriya' (6 February 2009) CEDAW/C/LBY/CO/5, para 17.

UN Committee on the Elimination of Discrimination against Women (CEDAW), *CEDAW General Recommendation No. 21: Equality in Marriage and Family Relations* (1994), https://www.refworld.org/docid/48abd52c0.html> accessed 1 August 2019.

UN Committee on the Elimination of Discrimination against Women, *'General Recommendation on Article 16 of the Convention on the Elimination of All Forms of Discrimination against Women (Economic Consequences of Marriage, Family Relations and their Dissolution)'* (30 October 2013) CEDAW/C/GC/29.

UN General Assembly, *'Convention on Consent to Marriage, Minimum Age for Marriage and Registration of Marriages'* (7 November 1962), para 1, Articles 1 and 2.

UN Human Rights Committee (HRC), 'CCPR General Comment No. 19: Article 23 (The Family) Protection of the Family, the Right to Marriage and Equality of the Spouses' (27 July 1990).

UN Human Rights Committee, 'CCPR General Comment No. 28: Article 3 (The Equality of Rights Between Men and Women' (29 March 2000) CCPR/C/21/Rev.1/Add.10.

UN Human Rights Council, Summary Prepared by the Office of the High Commissioner for Human (2008b) A/HRC/WG.6/3/BWA/3).

UN Human Rights Council, 'Follow-up to the Human Rights Council Resolution 16/21 with Regard to the Universal Periodic Review' (July 2011) A/HRC/DEC/17/119.

UN Office of the High Commissioner for Human Rights, 'Report of the Special Rapporteur on Adequate Housing as a Component of the Right to an Adequate Standard of Living, and on the Right to Non-Discrimination in this Context, Raquel Rolnik' (16 December 2011) A/HRC/19/53.

UN Press Release, WOM/1452 2004.

UN Press Release, 'Customs, Traditions Remain Obstacles to Women's Rights in Equatorial Guinea say Anti-Discrimination Committee Experts' (8 July 2004) WOM/1452,   http://www.un.org/press/en/2004/wom1452.doc.htm, accessed 28 August 2019.United Charter of the United Nations (adopted 17 December 1963, entered into force 31August 1965) UNTS XVI.

UNHRC, 'Report of the Working Group on the Universal Periodic Review: Bahrain' (22 May 2008) A/HRC/8/19.

UNHRC, 'Algeria' (23 May 2008) A/HRC/8/29.

UNHRC, 'Ghana' (29 May 2008) A/HRC/8/36.

UNHRC, 'Japan' (30 May 2008) A/HRC/8/44.

UNHRC, 'Pakistan' (4 June 2008) A/HRC/8/42.

UNHRC, 'Mali' (13 June 2008) A/HRC/8/50.

UNHRC, 'Report of the Human Rights Council on Its Eighth Session' (1 September 2008) A/HRC/8/52.

UNHRC, 'Report of the Human Rights Council on Its Tenth Session' (2009c) A/HRC/10/29.

UNHRC, 'Liechtenstein' (7 January 2009) A/HRC/10/77.

UNHRC, 'Burundi' (8 January 2009) A/HRC/10/71.

UNHRC, 'Burundi' (8 January 2009) A/HRC/10/71, para 4.

UNHRC, 'Burundi' (8 January 2009) A/HRC/10/71, para 35.

UNHRC, 'United Arab Emirates' (12 January 2009) A/HRC/10/75.

UNHRC, 'Senegal' (3 March 2009) A/HRC/11/24.

UNHRC, 'Azerbaijan' (6 March 2009) A/HRC/11/20.

UNHRC, 'Yemen' (5 June 2009) A/HRC/12/13.

UNHRC, 'Yemen' (5 June 2009) A/HRC/12/13, para 94.2.

UNHRC, 'Bangladesh: Addendum' (9 June 2009) A/HRC/11/18/Add.1.

UNHRC, 'Afghanistan' (20 July 2009) A/HRC/12/9.

UNHRC, 'Yemen: Addendum' (23 September 2009) A/HRC/12/13/Add.1.

UNHRC, 'Report of the Working Group on the Universal Periodic Review: Chad' (5 October 2009) A/HRC/12/5.

UNHRC, 'Report of the Human Rights Council on its tenth session' (9 November 2009) A/HRC/10/29.

UNHRC, 'Equatorial Guinea' (4 January 2010) A/HRC/13/16.

UNHRC, 'Equatorial Guinea' (4 January 2010) A/HRC/13/16, para 67.4.

UNHRC, 'Equatorial Guinea' (4 January 2010) A/HRC/13/16, para 71.40.

UNHRC, 'Report of the Human Rights Council on Its Twelfth Session' (25 February 2010) A/HRC/12/50.

UNHRC, 'Report of the Human Rights Council on Its Twelfth Session' (25 February 2010) A/HRC/12/50, para 444.

UNHRC, 'Iran' (15 March 2010) A/HRC/14/12.

UNHRC, 'El Salvador' (18 March 2010) A/HRC/14/5.

UNHRC, 'Report of the Working Group on the Universal Periodic Review: Gambia' (24 March 2010) A/HRC/14/6.

UNHRC, 'Gambia' (24 March 2010) A/HRC/14/6.

UNHRC, 'Gambia' (24 March 2010) A/HRC/14/6, para 100.3.

UNHRC, 'Report of the Working Group on the Universal Periodic Review: Gambia' (24 March 2010) A/HRC/14/6.

UNHRC, 'Madagascar' (26 March 2010) A/HRC/14/13.
UNHRC, 'Kyrgyzstan' (16 June 2010) A/HRC/15/2.
UNHRC, 'Kyrgyzstan' (16 June 2010) A/HRC/15/2
UNHRC, 'Kiribati, Addendum' (30 September 2010) A/HRC/15/3/Add.1.
UNHRC, 'Mauritania' (4 January 2011) A/HRC/16/17.
UNHRC, 'Maldives' (4 January 2011) A/HRC/16/7.
UNHRC, 'Maldives' (4 January 2011) A/HRC/16/7, para 100.23.
UNHRC, 'Libyan Arab Jamahiriya' (4 January 2011) A/HRC/16/15.
UNHRC, 'Timor-Leste' (3 January 2012) A/HRC/19/17.
UNHRC, 'Liberia' (4 January 2011) A/HRC/16/3.
UNHRC, 'Libyan Arab Jamahiriya' (4 January 2011) A/HRC/16/15.
UNHRC, 'Libya, Addendum' (22 February 2012) A/HRC/16/15/Add.1.
UNHRC, 'Timor-Leste, Addendum' (15 March 2012) A/HRC/19/17/Add.1
UNHRC, 'Tunisia' (9 July 2012) A/HRC/21/5.
UNHRC, 'Niger' (25 March 2011) A/HRC/17/15.
UNHRC, 'Greece' (11 July 2011) A/HRC/18/13.
UNHRC, 'Samoa' (11 July 2011) A/HRC/18/14.
UNHRC, 'Sierra Leone' (11 July 2011) A/HRC/18/10.
UNHRC, 'Sudan' (11 July 2011) A/HRC/18/16.
UNHRC, 'Sierra Leone Addendum' (13 September 2011) A/HRC/18/10/Add.1.
UNHRC, 'Report of the Human Rights Council on Its Fifteenth Session' (31 October 2011) A/HRC/15/60.
UNHRC, 'Report of the Human Rights Council on Its Sixteenth Session' (14 November 2011) A/HRC/16/2.
UNHRC, 'Report of the Human Rights Council on Its Sixteenth Session' (14 November 2011) A/HRC/16/2, para 553.
UNHRC, 'Report of the Human Rights Council on Its Eighteenth Session' (18 November 2011) A/HRC/18/2.
UNHRC, 'Report of the Human Rights Council on Its Eighteenth Session' (18 November 2011) A/HRC/18/2, para 379.
UNHRC, 'Report of the Human Rights Council on Its Nineteenth Session' (2013b) A/HRC/19/2.
UNHRC, 'Botswana' (22 March 2013) A/HRC/23/7.
UNHRC, 'Burundi' (25 March 2013) A/HRC/23/9.
UNHRC, 'Kenya' (26 March 2019) A/HRC/29/10.
UNHRC, 'Report of the Human Rights Council on Its Nineteenth Session' (24 May 2013) A/HRC/19/2.
UNHRC, 'Report of the Human Rights Council on Its Nineteenth Session' (24 May 2013) A/HRC/19/2, para 553.
UNHRC, 'United Arab Emirates' (4 June 2013) (A/HRC/23/13/Add.1).
UNHRC 'Djibouti' (8 July 2013) A/HRC/24/10.
UNHRC, 'Strengthening Efforts to Prevent and Eliminate Child, Early and Forced Marriage: Challenges, Achievements, Best Practices and Implementation Gaps' (25 September 2013) A/HRC/24/L.34/Rev.1.
UNHRC, 'Jordan' (6 January 2014) A/HRC/25/9.
UNHRC, 'Democratic Republic of the Congo' (7 July 2014) A/HRC/27/5.
UNHRC, 'Turkey' (13 April 2015) A/HRC/29/15.
UNHRC, 'Libya' (22 July 2015) (A/HRC/30/16).

UNHRC, 'Palau' (13 April 2016) (A/HRC/32/11 Add1.
UNHRC, 'Solomon Islands' (22 June 2016) A/HRC/32/14/Add.1.
UNHRC, 'Greece' (8 July 2016) A/HRC/33/7.
UNHRC, 'Tanzania' (14 July 2016) A/HRC/33/12.
Yahia al-Hibri A, 'Islam, Law and Custom: Redefining Muslim Women's Rights' (1997) 12 *The American University Journal of International Law and Policy* 16.

6 Women's Rights Protection against Violence

Introduction

Violence against women was a central rallying point in the struggle that waged over two decades for the recognition of women's rights as human rights.[1] In 1993, the General Assembly unanimously passed The Declaration on the Elimination of Violence against Women, which unequivocally articulated standards and principles against violence against women.[2] Despite the repeated declarations at international level,[3] women continue to be subjected to violence.[4] One possible reason for this is that violence against women is often inherent in the patriarchal traditions and culture.[5] Therefore, whilst it cannot be denied that the phenomenon of violence against women is global, its manifestations are often particularised within a community by the values embedded in particularities of culture.[6] For example, wide ranging factors such as son preference, gender differences in nutrition and education, dowry and virginity testing all contribute to the patriarchal culture that perpetuates or contributes to the toleration of violence against women.[7] This inherent relationship between violence against women and culture, forms one of the reasons why it has been selected as the focus for exploring whether, and to what extent, states adopt a cultural relativist position during states' reviews.

This chapter will present the findings and analysis of the discussions held during states reviews in relation to three issues: honour killing, marital rape, and domestic violence. A total of 2472 recommendations were made on the three issues, making it the most frequently cited issue in this investigation. The frequency of the issue being raised during state reviews, together with the large number of acceptances, show that, at least formally, there is largely a consensus that the issues in relation to violence against women are prevailing ones that need to be addressed. Beyond the issuance of recommendations, and acceptance or rejection of them, this investigation will focus on the nature of the discussions held amongst states on the issues itself. The central aim is to examine the extent to which the principle of universality has been met, and the significance of culture in the discourse of women's rights in relation to culture, in light of the inherent relationship between culture and women.

The chapter is divided into three main sections, according to the issues in relation to violence against women: honour killing, marital rape, and domestic violence. Each of these main sections follows the same format as the previous chapters. They begin with contextualising the issue in relation to the international human rights law on the issue, followed by a findings and a discussion section.

Honour Killing at the UPR Process

Contextualising Women's Rights in Relation to Honour Killing

For the purposes of this investigation, the term honour killing is interpreted as the homicide of a woman, by one or more members of her immediate or extended family, usually male, because she is believed to have defiled the honour of the family.[8] Whilst there is no international human rights norm that directly addresses the crime of honour killing, treaty body jurisprudence has made it clear that states should ensure that women are protected against it, and should implement legislation to remove the defence of honour to a murder of a female victim.[9] In 2001, the UN General Assembly issued its first resolution on honour killing, which called upon states to intensify legislative and social efforts to prevent and eliminate honour-based killing.[10] Further clarification has been provided in 2012, when a Special Rapporteur on violence against women stated that customs, traditions, or religious values should not be invoked to avoid member states' obligations to eliminate the crime of honour killings.[11] Despite the overwhelming acceptance of the recommendation issued to states to ensure the protection of women against honour killing, there is evidence to suggest that women continue to be subject to such killings.[12] Honour killings can be distinguished from other forms of homicide as the very act of the homicide, and the motivation of the perpetrators, is often justified using a culturally conceptualised definition of honour.[13] The notion of honour is used to control women's behaviour such as fidelity in a marriage, restrictions on premarital or extramarital relationships with men, and ensuring she meets the maternal and wifely obligations.[14] If a woman fails to comply with the culturally defined rules of women's general or sexual behaviour, then she is perceived to have damaged the honour of the family or the community, and thus, the perceived remedy is for a male relative to kill the female victim to protect the family's honour.[15] This inherent relationship between honour killing and culture, whereby a culturally conceptualised notion of 'honour' is used to justify such killings, is the primary reason why honour killing has been selected as the focus for this study.

Findings on Honour Killing in the UPR Process

First Cycle of Review

During the first cycle of review, a total of 17 recommendations were issued to 13 states under review on the issue of honour killing. These recommendations can be categorised into four different types. In terms of the responses, those states that accepted or noted the recommendations provided three different forms of responses, respectively.

RECOMMENDATION 1

Under this category of recommendations, observer states suggested that states under review should enact or reform domestic legislation to ensure that women are adequately protected against the crime of honour killings. An example of a recommendation issued under this category was when Austria suggested that Afghanistan should 'enact legislation ... to protect and promote women's rights ... especially with regard to ... honour killings'.[16] Some of the recommendations under this category were more detailed in nature, and required the states under review to make more specific reforms in relation to the crime. For example, Syria was issued with a recommendation by Canada to 'remove mitigating factors from the punishment of "honour-crimes" against women'.[17]

A total of six states were issued with recommendations under this category. Of these, the states of Afghanistan, Yemen, and Lebanon accepted the recommendation, but provided no further comments, therefore providing an A1 response.

On the other hand, the delegates of Jordan and Iraq adopted a slightly different position when responding to recommendations under this category. In the case of Iraq, it noted the recommendation by Spain to 'amend the 128 Criminal Code which identifies the commission of an offence with honourable motive as a mitigating excuse'. The delegate of Iraq provided an N2 response, as the state explained that the 'ministry was working towards the abolition of Article 128 of the Penal Code, on mitigating factors for "honour crimes"'.[18] Adopting a slightly different response, Jordan accepted the recommendation issued by Slovenia[19] and provided an A3 response, as it suggested that 'concerning honour crimes, the law has been amended and that there is no such thing as "honour crimes" in Jordanian law'.[20] The delegate continued that 'criminal acts committed in the heat of passion are also declining owing to a collective effort'.[21]

In other instances, the delegate of Syria noted the recommendation issued to it under this category and provided an N3 response. The state explained that 'the [recommendations] were not motivated by cooperation with a view to promoting and protecting human rights but by a desire to accuse and condemn Syria'.[22] In this way, whilst the Syrian delegate did not provide a direct explanation as to why a recommendation under honour killing was rejected, it provided a more general explanation for all the recommendations that were noted and insisted that the suggested reforms were political in nature.

RECOMMENDATION 2

Under this category of recommendation, the observer states insisted that the state under review should implement measures to ensure that perpetrators of honour killings were investigated and prosecuted appropriately. A typical example of a recommendation under this category was issued during the review of Albania, when Austria stated that it should ensure 'effective investigation and prosecution of honour killings'.[23] In total, four states under review were issued with a recommendation of this nature.

Table 6.1 Nature of Discussions on the Issue of Honour Killing in the First Cycle

Universal Periodic Review Cycle 1	Responses by States under Review					
	A1 No further comments	A2 Laws have been amended/currently put in place to prohibit honour killing	A3 Practice of 'honour killing' doesn't exist in the state	N1 No further comments	N2 Laws under review/already have been amended	N3 The recommendations were highly political in nature
Nature of recommendations issued to states under review						
Recommendation 1 Enact or reform laws on honour killing	Afghanistan Yemen Lebanon		Jordan		Iraq	Syria
Recommendation 2 Increase efficiency in the investigation and protection of the crime	Albania		Jordan		Iraq Pakistan	
Recommendation 3 Implement awareness-raising campaigns to eliminate honour killing		Turkey	Jordan	Iraq		
Recommendation 4 Recommendations of a generic nature	Sweden	Pakistan Iraq Turkey			Oman	

Table 6.2 Nature of Discussions on the Issue of Honour Killing in the Second Cycle

Universal Periodic Review Cycle 2	Responses by States under Review					
	A1 No further comments	*A2* Laws have been amended/currently put in place to prohibit honour killing	*A3* Practice of 'honour killing' does not exist in the state	*N1* No further comments	*N2* Laws under review/already have been amended	*N3* The recommendations were highly political in nature
Nature of recommendations issued to states under review **Recommendation 1** Enact or reform laws on honour killing.	Syria	Jordan		Iraq India	Afghanistan	
Recommendation 2 Recommendations of a generic nature		Afghanistan				
Recommendation 3 Eliminate traditional harmful practice of honour killing		Jordan		India		

In response, three states accepted the recommendations. The delegate of Albania provided an A1 response, as it accepted the recommendation without any further response. The delegate of Jordan also accepted the recommendation and provided an A3 response, as it stated that the law has been amended and that 'honour killings' do not exist.[24] When Iraq was issued with a recommendation under this category by Chile,[25] it stated that laws had already been reformed in relation to honour killings.[26]

Pakistan was the only state that noted a recommendation under this category. At the Human Rights Committee (HRC) plenary session, the delegate of Pakistan stated that reforms had been undertaken in relation to the issue as 'the 2004 Criminal Law Act declared honour killings as "murder"'.[27] In this way, the delegate of Pakistan noted the recommendation on the basis that reforms to the domestic law had already been undertaken, and therefore provided an N3 response. The statement issued by Pakistan states that honour killings were classified as 'murder' under domestic laws and therefore followed the same prosecution and investigation methods. It is notable here that Pakistan's statement was strikingly similar to Jordan's response, as both states have detached the 'honour' in the crime of 'honour killing', and instead classified such killings as an alternative form of homicide under domestic laws.

RECOMMENDATION 3

The essence of the recommendations issued under this category focused on implementing awareness-raising campaigns with the aim of eliminating honour killing. A typical example of a recommendation issued under this category was when Spain issued a recommendation to Iraq to 'carry out an awareness raising campaign' against killings 'for reasons of honor'.[28]

A total of three states under review were issued with a recommendation under this category. The delegate of Jordan accepted this recommendation and provided an A3 response, insisting that honour killings did not occur in the state.[29] Adopting a slightly different position, when Turkey was issued with a recommendation under this category, it accepted the recommendation and stated that 'honour killings were punished by aggravated life sentences'.[30] In this way, Turkey highlighted the laws that were already in place to punish the perpetrators of the crime, and thus provided an A2 response. The delegate of Iraq provided an N1 response as it noted the recommendation without any further comments.

RECOMMENDATION 4

Under this category of recommendations, observer states issued recommendations that simply raised the concern of honour killings, and suggested that the states should implement measures to eliminate such killings without providing any details as to the reform process. A typical example of a recommendation under this category is when Canada suggested that Oman should 'put in place appropriate mechanisms to ensure effective protection of women exposed to ...

crimes in the name of honour'.[31] In response, five states under review were issued with a recommendation under this category. A total of four states accepted recommendations under this category. The delegate of Sweden accepted the recommendation and provided no additional explanations, thus providing an A1 response. The states of Pakistan,[32] Iraq,[33] and Turkey[34] all accepted the recommendations under this category and all provided an A2 response as they referred to the legal provisions that were already in place to address the practice. The delegate of Oman was the only state that noted a recommendation, and provided an N2 response, stating that in Omani society 'such acts of violence were punishable under the Criminal Code and that appropriate remedies existed in the courts'.[35]

Second Cycle of Review

In the second cycle of review, a total of 15 recommendations were issued to five states under review. The nature of the recommendations was slightly different from that under the first cycle of review. For example, no suggestions were made in relation to the prosecution of the crime of honour killing; instead states made references to the relationship between honour killings and traditional and customary norms.

RECOMMENDATION 1

This was the most prevalent form of recommendation in the second cycle of review, with a total of five states being issued with this form of recommendation. In response, Syria accepted the recommendation, with no further comments. The delegate of Jordan whilst accepting the recommendations insisted that

> mitigating circumstances for the crime committed based on honour must be proved in accordance with Article 340 of the Penal Code. This imposes an additional burden of proof on the accused. Therefore removing the mitigating circumstances would adversely impact the prosecution of the crimes under the pretext of honour.

In other words, the legal provisions that permit mitigating circumstances for honour killings have not been amended; the argument put forward is that the burden of proof for the mitigating circumstances means that there is not adverse impact on the prosecution of the crime. There are a few points that can be noted with Jordan's positions. First, the response provided by Jordan is directly contrary to the recommendation issued to the state which was to 'to remove the exemption of those accused of honour crimes from prosecution' from the Penal Code. In this way, despite Jordan formally accepting the recommendation, the statement issued by the state clearly shows that the exemptions still exist. Second, the delegate of Jordan has been issued with the same recommendation in the previous cycle, for which it responded that the law has been amended in relation to honour crimes in general, and there is no legal provision of 'honour crimes' under

Jordanian law, and the criminal acts under 'heat of passion' are reducing. In other words, when issued with the same recommendation in the previous cycle, the delegate of Jordan, whilst again accepting the recommendation, insisted that the recognition of the crime did not exist under Jordanian law, despite recommendation for such laws to be amended to recognise honour killing and remove mitigating circumstances. As can be observed, there is no real movement on Jordan's position on the issue. Those that are prosecuted can still potentially be granted mitigating circumstances, thereby failing to provide appropriate protection for women in relation to honour killing.

In total, three states noted the recommendation. Iraq and India both noted the recommendation enact or reform laws on honour killing without any further comments. Strikingly, in the previous cycle, the delegate of Iraq was issued with the same recommendation, to which the Iraq delegate responded with noting the recommendation, however, adding that the ministry was working towards the abolition of the Penal Code which permitted mitigating circumstances for the crime. Disappointingly this was a missed opportunity as in the second cycle, the state noted the recommendation, and provided no explanation, and unfortunately, there is no follow up on the approach adopted by Iraq in the dialogue session. Finally, Afghanistan also noted the recommendation, and provided that the Penal Code does not permit an acquittal of the culprit of an honour killing, rather the mental state of the perpetrator is considered to provide a lower sentence. It also added that the responsible committee was reviewing the Penal Code, to ensure compliance with the international human rights convention to which Afghanistan is a party to.[36] It is notable that Afghanistan was issued with a similar recommendation in the previous cycle, to which the state accepted without any further response. Despite the reiteration of the possible mitigating circumstances of honour killing, there is a clear commitment made here to remove this possibility under the provisions to ensure compliance with the international human rights norms.

RECOMMENDATION 2

Unlike the previous cycle, only the state of Afghanistan was issued with this generic recommendation to address the issue of honour killing in the second cycle. The state responded by accepting the recommendation, whilst making a commitment that laws were currently being amended to ensure compliance with the provisions of the Convention on the Elimination of all Forms of Discrimination Against Women (CEDAW) to which the state was a party to.

RECOMMENDATION 3

This form of recommendation was unique to the second cycle of review. This recommendation explicitly drew references to cultural norms and the crime of honour killings, and suggested that the state take measures to eliminate the practice. For instance, the delegate of Chile issued a recommendation to India to 'further strengthen measures to eliminate traditional harmful practices which are discriminatory to women in particular ... honour killings'. In response the state of India noted the recommendations, and provided no further comments. The delegate of Jordan was also issued with a similar recommendation. Whilst accepting the recommendation, the state of Jordan made reference to the reforms that have been made in relation to honour killing.

Discussion and Analysis

The fundamental finding that emerged from the discussions held in the first cycle was that states adopted a position which indicated a lack of appreciation of the cultural conceptualisation of honour killings. The majority of the discussions on honour killing focused on the domestic legislation that was in place or under review against honour killings. For instance, in the first cycle, over half of the observer states that issued recommendations focused entirely on making suggestions to enact or amend legal provisions against honour killing. In response, over 80% of states under review responded to recommendations on honour killing by providing details of the legislative provisions in place to protect women against honour killing. In the second cycle, five out of the eight observer states issuing recommendations on honour killings focused on laws on the issue, whilst three out of the eight states under review in the second cycle responded with statements focused on the legislation on the issue. This included the largely disingenuous response in relation to reforming laws issued by Jordan. Overall, it can be observed that the majority of the discussions held amongst states focused on the domestic legal provisions in relation to honour killings. The primary focus on enacting legislative provisions against honour killings has been criticised by An-Na'im. He writes that a focus on legislation and prosecution of perpetrators in addressing honour killings is limited to being 'reactive to violations that have already been committed by the action or omission of officials of the state, rather than proactive to pre-empt their happening in the first place'.[37] To the contrary, he suggests that legislative provisions against honour killing should be one amongst many strategies and policies in place to prevent the crime from occurring in the first place.[38] However, contrary to these suggestions in the literature, the findings of the investigation for honour killings show that the majority of the discussions held amongst states have focused entirely on the legislative response to honour killings.

The implications of states' focus on legislative matters in relation to honour killing during reviews are that it tends to restrict discussions on the fundamental reasons why such killings are undertaken in the first place. For instance, it is clear that honour killings can be distinguished from other forms of homicide on the basis that perpetrators' motivation to kill is fundamentally based on the female victim defiling the family honour through her actions.[39] Further, the very notion of honour is culturally conceptualised so as to exercise control over a woman's sexuality and behaviour.[40] However, it is notable that only two states in the second cycle of review draw implicit cultural norms that may underpin the crime of honour killing. The state of Chile issued a recommendation to India, and Sierra Leone to Syria that the traditional and customary practices, such as honour killing, should be eliminated. Despite the benefits of raising the issue of honour killings and its association with cultural norms, which is often used to justify such killings, there are two main issues in the manner in which these two lines of dialogue were made in the review of India and Syria. First, the observer states adopted a position that utilised the notion of culture in a polarised manner in the discussions. Both observer states drew references to cultural norms and the crime, and suggested that the practice should be eliminated. Thus, this position affiliated with the strict universalist positions, as the claimed universalist interpretation of human rights norms should transcend cultural boundaries. Whilst it is most certainly not advocated that cultural justification of honour killing should be accepted, the utilisation of cultural norms in the discourse by observer states hold two underlying presumptions. The first is a traditional conceptualisation of cultural norms. This is because the suggestion by observer states to simply eliminate the practice, despite being embedded in culture presumes that cultural beliefs are static, not subject to reform, and naively presumes that cultural values can be eliminated. Second, on a related point, the position adopted by the observer states fails to see the possibility that cultural norms can be utilised in a way to engage in a deeper and fruitful dialogue, and in fact, be used to bring about changes and reforms to positive progress towards eliminating the practice.

The implications of the position adopted by Chile and Sierra Leone is that important discussions on moving towards eliminating the practice on the reasons why perpetrators undertake killings of female victims have failed to be had. In fact, it is notable that Jordan[41] and Pakistan[42] during their reviews went to the extent of explaining that honour killings were classified as 'murder' or killings 'due to heat of passion' in the domestic legislative provisions. In this way, both states expressly underplayed the gravity of the culturally conceptualised notion of 'honour' in such killings, which often motivates the perpetrators of such crimes. In a more implicit form, the states of Oman and Turkey insisted that existing laws can be used to address the crime of honour killing. In this way, states have, explicitly or implicitly, detached the honour from honour killing during state reviews by explaining that such crimes are addressed using other more generic homicide laws.

The lack of reference to the culturally conceptualised notion of 'honour' is problematic as it indicates that there is little discussion amongst states to implement reforms to discourage attitudes that motivate the perpetrators to undertake the crime in the first place. For instance, An-Na'im explains that no strategy for combating the crime of honour killing can be sustained over a period of time 'without the consent and cooperation of the communities in question', and in fact, purely coercive messages to prevent and punish the crime may be counterproductive and futile.[43] For this reason, An-Na'im suggests a community discourse approach as a method to transform family and community attitudes in relation to the crime of honour killings.[44] This is carried out by engaging in a clear strategic approach to address the difficulties surrounding the issue of honour killing by implementing appropriate local plans and policies amongst various actors of the community to change and to combat this crime.[45] The local individuals already have the necessary access, knowledge, and credibility to engage in an internal discourse about the issue of honour killing.[46]

However, contrary to the suggestions of An-Na'im, the findings of the discussions on honour killing in the Universal Periodic Review (UPR) process reveal that observer states have largely overlooked the significance of implementing reform strategies to change the attitudes that may contribute to the continuance of females being subject to honour killing. In fact, recommendations issued under Category 3 in the first cycle of review were the only form of suggestions that did not centre on the legislations, investigation, and prosecution of honour killing. The delegates of Spain, Mexico, and the Czech Republic issued recommendations that encouraged states to engage in an awareness-raising campaign against killings based on honour. This was the only instance whereby observer states adopted positions during state reviews which indicated a recognition that some values and beliefs adopted by communities contributed to perpetuating the crime of honour killings against women. However, it is notable that the states of Iraq, Jordan, and Turkey, who were issued with recommendations under the third category, all responded by focusing on the legal aspect of honour killings.

Overall, it can be observed that the majority of the discussions held on honour killing focused on the domestic legal provisions in place to ensure perpetrators of the crime were appropriately punished. As discussed above the implication of this has been that states have implicitly, and occasionally explicitly, detached the cultural significance of honour from the crime of honour killing. This lack of appreciation of the cultural significance of the crime has resulted in the underlying motivation of the crime, based on a culturally conceptualised notion of honour, not being addressed during state reviews.[47] In this way, the lack of appreciation of the moderate cultural relativist position amongst states on the issue of honour killing has resulted in the discussions being restricted to providing legislative responses, rather than discouraging and reforming the cultural attitudes that motivate such crimes in the first place.

Women's Rights Protection against Marital Rape

Contextualising Women's Rights Protection against Marital Rape

For the purposes of this investigation, marital rape is defined as any unwanted intercourse or penetration (vaginal, anal, or oral) that is obtained by coercion, threat of force, or when the wife is unable to consent.[48] Whilst there is no international human rights norm that directly addresses marital rape, the issue has been addressed through jurisprudence on sexual violence against women.[49] For instance, the Committee on the Women's Convention in its General Recommendation 12 has confirmed that state parties should take measures to prevent sexual violence against women, which includes marital rape.[50] Providing further clarification, UN treaty bodies and the Committee on the Women's Convention have stated that traditional and cultural attitudes should not be invoked to avoid obligations to eliminate sexual violence against women.[51] Despite the repeated declarations at the international level of state obligations to protect women from marital rape, there was evidence of a disagreement amongst states during reviews on how, and indeed if, protection against marital rape should be provided. For instance, in the first cycle, nearly 40% of the recommendations were noted, whilst in the second cycle nearly 50% of the total recommendations issued were noted. The perception of marital rape being considered as a lesser crime, or in the worst case no crime at all, is often grounded in the notion that the consent of the wife to any sexual contact is presumed.[52] The First World Report on Violence and Health by the World Health Organisation notes that in a number of societies, 'women, as well as men, regard marriage as entailing the obligation on women to be sexually available virtually without limit'.[53] Therefore, the presumption of the wife's consent is often influenced by cultural norms, social conditions, and rules that determine the attitudes in relation to sex in a given society, which ultimately mould the structure of the sexual behaviour of men towards women and the acceptability of sexual violence within a marriage.[54] This inherent association between culture and marital rape, whereby aspects of cultural attitudes and socialisation contribute to the perpetuation and tolerance of marital rape, is one of the primary reasons why the issue of marital rape has been selected as the focus for this investigation.

Findings on Marital Rape in the UPR Process

First Cycle of Review

In the first cycle of review, a total of 34 recommendations were issued to 30 states. Of these, 20 accepted the recommendations, and a total of ten states noted the recommendations. In terms of the discourse, only two different forms of recommendations were issued by the observer states, with a total of eight different types of responses provided by the states under review.

RECOMMENDATION 1

Under the first category of recommendations, observer states suggested that states under review should enact or undertake reforms of domestic laws on marital rape. A typical example of this recommendation was during the review of the United Arab Emirates (UAE) when the delegate of Slovenia issued a recommendation to ensure 'legislative sanctioning of marital rape'.[55] In other cases, observer states suggested reforms to domestic laws so as to ensure that perpetrators of the crime were not granted any form of reduction in penalties. A typical example of this is when the delegate of Belgium issued a recommendation to Denmark 'to remove from the penal code ... any references to marital relations between victims and perpetrators of offences, in order to ensure that there is no impunity in cases of marital rape'.[56]

In total, 25 states under review were issued with recommendations to enact or reform laws so that the crime of marital rape was criminalised or perpetrators punished without immunity. In response, a total of 17 states accepted and eight states noted the recommendations. Of those states that accepted, a total of eight states accepted without any further comments, therefore providing an A1 response. These include Guinea,[57] Laos,[58] Madagascar,[59] Pakistan,[60] Congo,[61] Togo,[62] Tuvalu,[63] Uruguay,[64] and the Solomon Islands.[65] In total, seven states provided an A2 response, whereby the state under review explained that domestic legal provisions criminalising marital rape were already in place. A typical example of this response was provided by Hungary in response to a recommendation by the Netherlands who stated that 'spousal rape is punishable since 1997'.[66]

A total of the eight states that noted the recommendation, the state of Mauritius provided an N1 response. The states of Kuwait,[67] Eritrea, and Malaysia[68] all noted the recommendations issued to them and provided an N2 response, as they explained that domestic laws in relation to rape already existed. A typical example of this response was provided by Eritrea who stated that 'the delegation did not believe that rape was a widespread problem either. Criminal provisions relating to rape and sexual abuse are severe'.[69] What is notable is that all three states under review, in their responses, made references to existing domestic laws on rape, rather than directly address the recommendation to adopt specific legislation to criminalise marital rape. In this way, the three states under review noted the recommendations on the grounds that existing generic laws in relation to rape already existed.

When the delegate of the UAE was issued with a recommendation to criminalise marital rape, it provided a combined N3 response.[70] At the HRC plenary session, it stated that it rejected a number of recommendations, which included marital rape, because it perceived 'the working group report as being in direct contradiction with the Constitution, religious code, traditional values and national interest, and hence did not enjoy the country's support'.[71] In this way, the delegate challenged the reforms to domestic laws to criminalise marital rape as it was contrary to the constitution and the traditional values and religious norms of the country. Similarly, N3 response, the delegate of Brunei Darussalam stated that 'with regard to sexual-related matters … [the state] re-iterated that the core value of Brunei Darussalam society was the family institution. Tradition and cultural factors also played an important role'.[72] From this statement it can be observed that the delegate of Brunei Darussalam emphasised the significant role traditional and cultural factors played in relation to the underlying foundations of the basic unit of society.

Adopting a slightly different position, the states of Singapore and the Bahamas provided an N4 response, as both explicitly or implicitly stated that marital rape was not recognised in the domestic laws of the state, and on this basis, noted the recommendations. For example, the delegate of the Bahamas stated that:

> Bahamian law does not recognize marital rape if a marriage subsists and the couple cohabit in a marital home. Bahamian law recognizes rape as a crime where a married couple are separated but not where the marriage has not been dissolved.[73]

Table 6.3 Nature of Discussions on the Issue of Marital Rape in the First Cycle

Universal Periodic Review Cycle 1		Responses by States under Review						
		A1 No further comments	A2 Domestic laws against marital rape are already in place	A3 Marital rape does not exist	N1 No further comments	N2 Domestic laws already prohibit rape	N3 Prohibiting marital rape is contrary to the culture/traditions of the state	N5 Domestic law does not recognise marital rape
Nature of recommendations issued to states under review	Recommendation 1 Enact/Amend/ Reform legislation so that marital rape is a crime	Guinea Laos Madagascar Pakistan Congo Togo Tuvalu Uruguay Solomon Islands	Hungary Botswana Denmark Latvia Palau Republic of Congo Republic of Korea	Yemen	Mauritius	Kuwait Eritrea Malaysia	United Arab Emirates Brunei Darussalam	Singapore Bahamas
	Recommendation 2 Generic recommendations on marital rape	Somalia	Armenia Hungary			Oman	Tanzania	

Therefore, rather than explain why the Bahamas refused to enact legislation crim-inalizing marital rape, it noted the recommendations and expressly stated that domestic laws do not recognise marital rape. In a more implicit manner, the state of Singapore in its response noted the recommendation to criminalise marital rape and explained that 'changes had recently been made to the Penal Code to protect women whose marriages were on the verge of breakdown or had broken down'.[74] This statement indicates that the state of Singapore provides protection for victims where the marriage has broken down. However, that state continues to deny protection to victims of marital rape where the commitment within a marriage has not been questioned.

RECOMMENDATION 2

The second category of recommendations can be described as more generic in nature. This is because the observer states suggested that the states under review should undertake measures to address marital rape, without any specific details of how this task should be undertaken. In other words, no references were made to international obligations or reforms to domestic laws when issuing suggestions of reforms on marital rape. A typical example of this recommendation was when the United Kingdom issued a recommendation to Armenia 'to step up its efforts to protect women and girls from sexual violence in marriage'.[75] A total of five states were issued with a recommendation of this nature.

In response, four states accepted the recommendation, whilst two states noted them. Of those states that accepted the recommendation, Somalia provided an A1 response, as it did not provide an explanation for the position adopted. The states of Armenia and Hungary[76] provided an A2 response, as they insisted that current laws already prohibited marital rape. For example, the state of Armenia insisted that 'all types of violence … including marital rape… are considered criminal offenses in the Criminal Code of Armenia and are punishable by law'.[77] On the other hand, the states of Tanzania and Oman noted the recommendations under this category. The delegate of Oman issued an N2 response, as it stated that cases of 'sexual violence are prohibited by legislation currently in force in Oman and are classified as criminal offences under the Omani Criminal Code'.[78] In other instances, the delegate of Tanzania, during the interactive dialogue stage, began by providing a similar response as it insisted that 'Penal Code Cap 16 of the laws and the Sexual Offences Special Provisions Act criminalizes … rape'.[79] However, at the HRC plenary session, the delegate provided that:

> Tanzania did not accept any importation of the concept of marital rape embedded therein. Because of the diverse opinions and issues, the question of introducing marital rape for married couples requires a wider and cultur-ally sensitive debate.[80]

Therefore, at the HRC plenary session, the delegate expressly stated that it noted no importation of marital rape in its general laws against rape. Therefore, Tanzania used the notion of culturally embedded values of the state to challenge suggestions to provide protection against marital rape for women. In this way, the delegate provided an N3 response.

Second Cycle of Review

In the second cycle of review, there was a significant increase in the number of recommendations that were issued, which rose from 34 in the first cycle, to 112 in the second cycle. In the dialogue itself, a total of three different types of recommendations were issued, with a staggering seven different types of responses when the issue was raised during state reviews.

RECOMMENDATION 1

Similar to the first cycle of review, this form of recommendation was the most prominent issue in relation to marital rape, with a total of 37 states under review being issued with this recommendation. Of these, an overwhelming majority of the states under review, a total of 16, accepted the recommendation without any further comments. The states of Gabon and Palau, accepted the recommendation and insisted that legal provisions prohibiting marital rape were already in place. The delegate of Botswana provided a unique response as the delegate stated that 'there was no legislation specifically to address marital rape. That was a sensitive matter than hinged on established cultural beliefs'.[81] Thus, whilst the recommendation was formally accepted, the delegate insisted that the regulation of marital rape was embedded on established cultural beliefs.

A total of 19 states refused to accept the recommendation, and noted it. Of these, a total of ten states under review noted the recommendation without any further comments. These included: Antigua and Barbuda, Cameroon, Equatorial Guinea, Ethiopia, Iran, Kuwait, Micronesia, Qatar, Tunisia, and Uganda. The delegate of the Bahamas insisted that a bill was tabled to criminalise marital rape, however, 'consultation with civil society indicated that public opinion was strongly against the bill, and it was subsequently withdrawn'.[82] The delegate of Tanzania noted the recommendation and explained that 'the concept of marital rape was however alien to Tanzanian society and the legal framework was contrary to cultural norms and values. When people get married they become one, so one cannot see how then one spouse could rape the other'.[83] In this way, the delegate was expressly using cultural norms as a justification for not accepting the recommendation to criminalise the marital rape. The delegates of Malaysia and Mauritania provided similar justifications for their non-acceptance of this form of recommendation as they insisted that the domestic legal framework does not recognise marital rape, and to criminalise it would be in direct conflict with the domestic legal provisions. In other words, both states claimed sovereignty of national laws as a reason for not accepting the recommendation. The delegates of Lebanon and Singapore provided an N6 response. Noting the recommendations for the present purposes, the delegates went on to explain that it was taking actions to review and repeal the legislation on marital rape. For instance, the delegate of Singapore stated that it 'would actively review the need to repeal marital rape immunity'.[84] Finally, the delegates of Oman, Sudan, and Zambia all provided similar responses, and insisted the separate legal provisions for marital rape were not required as they fell under the existing legal provisions of violence against women. For example, the delegate of Zambia insisted that the 'Anti Gender Based Violence Act provided comprehensive provisions that criminalised all forms of violence against women. Issues of marital rape will rank within the definition of gender based violence prescribed in the Act'.

RECOMMENDATION 2

A total of four states were issued with a recommendation under this category. The states of Madagascar and Norway accepted the recommendation without any further comments. The delegate of Ghana highlighted that the rape provisions 'in the Criminal Offences Act does not make any distinction among women. It is applicable to all females ... perpetrators of the offence of rape to excluded spouses ... which made marriage a defence to rape has not been expunged from the statute'.[85] The delegate of Bahamas insisted that the public opinion was against taking actions against marital rape.

RECOMMENDATION 3

This form of recommendation was unique to the second cycle of review, and was only issued to one state under review. The delegate of Australia issued a recommendation to Turkmenistan to 'find ways to overcome the culture of silence and impunity around ... marital rape [and] to provide all necessary protection to victims, to enforce applicable legislation against perpetrators'. In this way, the observer states moved beyond the focus of merely focusing on the legal provisions that were in place to address the issue of marital rape, and instead recognise that there was a need to overcome cultural norms that had formed that prevents vocalisation on the issue and may lead to silently condoning the practice. In response, the delegate of Turkmenistan accepted the recommendation without any further comments.

Discussion and Analysis

There are three fundamental themes that emerged from the nature of discussions held on marital rape. The first theme that emerged was that states under review in their statements issued drew upon cultural and traditional factors to challenge the suggested reforms to provide protection against marital rape for women. For instance, in the first cycle of review, the delegate of the UAE stated that the acceptance of the recommendation is in direct contradiction to the cultural values

Universal Periodic Review Cycle 2 — Responses by States under Review

Nature of recommendations issued to states under review		A1 *No further comments*	A2 *Domestic laws against marital rape are already in place*	A3 *Marital rape is established on cultural beliefs*	N1 *No further comments*	N2 *Public opinion against it*	N3 *Prohibiting marital rape is contrary to the culture/ traditions of the state*	N5 *Domestic law/ constitution does not recognise marital rape*	N6 *Laws have already been repealed, and actions underway to criminalise marital rape*	N7 *No need for specific laws on marital rape as covered under violence against women in general*
	Recommendation 1 Enact/Amend/Reform legislation so that marital rape is a crime	Bulgaria, Cote d'Ivoire, Greece, Guinea, Haiti, Latvia, Lithuania, Madagascar, Mongolia, Myanmar, Republic of Korea, Seychelles, Saint Kitts and Nevis, St Lucia Uzbekistan, Yemen	Gabon, Palau	Botswana	Antigua and Barbuda, Cameroon, Equatorial Guinea, Ethiopia, Iran, Kuwait, Micronesia, Qatar, Tunisia, Uganda	Bahamas	Tanzania	Malaysia, Mauritania	Lebanon, Singapore	Oman, Sudan, Zambia
	Recommendation 2 Generic recommendations on marital rape	Madagascar Norway	Ghana			Bahamas				
	Recommendation 3 Legislation to be implemented, and engage with dialogue with stakeholders	Turkmenistan								

of the state and therefore noted the recommendation.[86] Similarly, the delegates of Brunei Darussalam[87] and Tanzania[88] explained that they could not accept the recommendations as cultural and traditional values of the state played an important role in regulating marital rape. In the second cycle, Tanzania repeated the same justifications when issued with a recommendation on marital rape. Whereas Botswana, whilst formally accepting the recommendation insisted that marital rape is established on cultural beliefs, making the essence of the response by Botswana similar to the other states. In this way, the states challenged the international human rights standards on marital rape on the basis that culture and traditional values of the states do not comply with embedding marital rape as a criminal offence. It is argued that the positions adopted by the three states resonate with the strict cultural relativist position, as states have used the cultural norms of the state to assess the validity of international standards on marital rape. Thus, the states challenged the universality of international standards on marital rape by expressly introducing arguments from a strict cultural relativist perspective.

The second form of challenge was based broadly on national sovereignty as some states expressly or implicitly challenged reforms to amend domestic legislative provisions to recognise marital rape on the basis that it was contrary to domestic laws or the constitution. In the first cycle, Yemen, Singapore, and the Bahamas all refused to accept the recommendation to enact legislation to criminalise marital rape because national law does not recognise marital rape. Whilst the official position between the three states differed, the essence of the responses provided was remarkably similar. All three states, implicitly[89] or explicitly,[90] did not recognise marital rape. The responses by the three states make it clear that whilst rape is protected outside the institution of marriage, rape within marriage is not protected. The positions of three states expressed in the UPR process can be explained by using the highly criticised public and private distinction in relation to providing women's rights protection.[91] Traditionally, the public sphere includes those issues and concerns where the government has responsibility to take action; in contrast, the government refrains from interfering with issues in the private sphere.[92] The artificial divide between the public and private sphere has been criticised for denying protection by the state against the violations and oppressions women suffer in the private sphere.[93] In the UPR process, the Bahamas, Singapore, and Yemen have implicitly adopted the public and private framework to deny protection for victims that are subject to marital rape. This is because protection against rape is only provided if it is undertaken outside the marriage institution, but not within it.

The fundamental implication of states challenging reforms to recognise marital rape on the grounds of cultural relativism and national sovereignty was linked to the fact that no observer states held the states under review to account for their positions. Under both cycles of reviews, states under review have expressly challenged implementing reforms to criminalise marital rape during the interactive dialogue sessions, without any ramifications. There were no agreed commitments to improve the rights of women by the states under review in relation to marital rape which emanated from the UPR process. This is problematic because it undermines one of the fundamental objectives of the UPR process, which is to promote universality of international human rights norms by protecting and furthering the international human rights norms through the monitoring of states' human rights records. This gives an indication as to the nature of the UPR process as observer states seem to remain subdued when the universality of norms in relation to marital rape were challenged.

The second significant finding that emerged from the discussions held on marital rape was that the majority of the discussions, both in the first and second cycles of review, held in relation to marital rape focused on the domestic legal provisions in relation to marital rape. When responding to such recommendations, the majority of the states remained silent and provided no additional responses, pointed to existing legal provisions in relation to marital rape or that it falls under provisions on violence against women. The problem with the nature of the positions adopted by states, which focused entirely on the legislative provisions on marital rape, is that states have not agreed any additional policies or programme of action that is to be adopted to prevent the crime of marital rape from occurring in the first place.

It was striking to note, that only the state of Australia in its recommendation to Turkmenistan sought to initiate discussions on reforms to be undertaken to tackle the presumptions of woman's consent to sexuality within a marriage, which is often influenced by deeply embedded cultural and societal norms that determine the sexual behaviour of men towards women within the marriage institution.[94] The delegate of Australia insisted that the 'culture of silence' and impunity around marital rape needs to be addressed. This was the only instance over the two cycles of review and discussions on marital rape where an observer state issued recommendations to undertake actions beyond the legislative provisions to address the crime. Aside from this one instance, no observer states made suggestions to implement policies and strategies through a form of constructive community dialogue within the society to help discourage such attitudes that perpetuate the presumption of consent of women's sexual activity within a marriage.[95] From the nature of discussions on marital rape, it is argued that there was clearly a lack of appreciation of the moderate cultural relativist position by the states.[96] The implication of this is that the cultural norms and attitudes that perpetuate the tolerance of marital rape were not brought to the centre of discussions. This meant that there were no suggestions made to tackle the cultural influences on the tolerance and perpetuation of marital rape during state reviews.

Overall, the discussion reveals that states have expressly or implicitly challenged the international standards on marital rape during their state reviews in the UPR process. The most striking finding of this section was that some states implicitly utilised the relationship between culture and marital rape as a foundation to challenge reforms on marital rape. This very association of the influence of culture on marital rape was not used by the observer states to suggest reforms to discourage attitudes that tolerate and perpetuate marital rape. Instead, the suggestions of reforms issued to states under review largely focused on the legislative reforms in relation to marital rape.

Women's Rights Protection against Domestic Violence

Contextualising Women's Rights Protection against Domestic Violence

For the purposes of this study, domestic violence is defined 'as the use of force or threats of force by a partner for the purpose of coercing and intimidating a woman into submission. The violence can take the form of pushing, hitting, choking, slapping, kicking, burning or stabbing.'[97] Whilst protection against domestic violence is not directly mentioned in a specific international human rights norm, treaty jurisprudence and resolutions issued by bodies at the UN have over the years repeatedly declared domestic violence as a violation of women's rights.[98] For example, the General Assembly adopted its first resolution on domestic violence in 1990, which encourages states to 'develop and implement policies, measures, and strategies, within and outside the criminal justice system, to respond to the problem of domestic violence'.[99] Further clarification was provided under article 4 of the Declaration against Elimination of Violence against Women, which provides that member states 'should condemn violence against women and should not invoke any custom, tradition or religious consideration to avoid their obligations'.[100]

Despite the repeated declarations by bodies at the UN that domestic violence against women was a violation of international human rights standards, women continue to be subject to such violence in the home.[101] The persistence of domestic violence often holds its roots in the artificial divide in the public and private sphere, the latter of which is often considered to be of a private concern of the family, which is more prone to be dictated by social and cultural norms.[102] At its worst, domestic violence is often perpetuated through deeply held cultural norms whereby women are perceived as 'wayward creatures who require chastisement for their own or society's good'.[103] In some instances, the toleration of domestic violence against women in the home stems 'from a dominant focus on male self-identity, using violence against women to define and differentiate men from the inferior "other"… who forgives the man for inflicting violence and terror on his wife'.[104] This relationship between culture and domestic violence, whereby aspects of cultural norms and attitudes contribute to the perpetuation or tolerance of such violence, is one of the primary reasons why it has been selected as the focus for this study.

Findings on Domestic Violence in the UPR Process

First Cycle of Review

In the first cycle of review, the issue of domestic violence was the subject of 481 recommendations. Observer states issued six different types of recommendations, and the states under review issued nine different forms of responses during the interactive dialogue.

RECOMMENDATION 1

Under the first category of recommendations, the observer states suggested that domestic laws should be enacted or reformed to provide legislative protection for women that are subject to domestic violence. A typical example of a recommendation under this category was when Australia issued a recommendation to Micronesia to 'pass laws at the national and state level to address domestic violence'.[105] A total of 51 states were issued with a recommendation under this category.

In response, a total of 41 states accepted the recommendations when issued under this category. Of these, ten states under review accepted the recommendations without any further response, thereby providing an A1 response. A total of 21 states provided an A2 response as they insisted that laws were already in place to protect women from domestic violence. A typical example of a response under this category is when Canada noted that 'domestic violence is not a separate offence in the Criminal Code, but is covered under existing criminal offences'.[106] The states of Albania, Sao Tome Principe,[107] and Kazakhstan[108] insisted that laws were already in place to protect women against domestic violence. In addition, they also highlighted the policies that were in place to support the victims of such violence, and therefore provided an A3 response. For instance, Albania stated that 'the Ministry of Labor, Social Affairs and Equal Opportunities is seeking to build the capacity of local authorities to set up programmes for sheltering victims of domestic violence'.[109]

The delegate of Portugal provided an A4 response, as it stated that as well as 'additional measures to protect women victims of domestic violence', it had implemented 'programmes to avoid repeated offending by aggressors' through 'electronic means of surveillance on perpetrators of domestic violence'.[110] Embracing a different approach, the delegate of Micronesia insisted that 'the government was keen to carry out activities to increase awareness and understanding of the issue'.[111] Adopting a slightly different approach, Saint Kitts and Nevis responded to recommendations under this category by stating that 'there was a need for social transformation on an even deeper level that necessitated not only an examination of the root causes of that evil but also a cultural re-education of built healthy relationships ... between the sexes'.[112] In this way, the delegate provided an A6 response as the state recognised that reforms to cultural norms and deeply embedded attitudes in relation to the two sexes are required to address domestic violence.

A total of ten states noted the recommendations. Of these, the states of Syria, Burkina Faso, Burundi, DPR Korea, and Georgia provided an N1 response, as no further comments were provided. The states of Gambia, Kiribati, Seychelles, and Mali provided an N2 response as they challenged the recommendation on the basis that laws in relation to domestic violence were already in place. The states of Gambia provided an N2 response, as it noted the recommendation on the basis that the 'Women's Bill 2009 ... had an entire section dealing with measures and strategies to eradicate gender based violence'.[113] The state of Kuwait

Table 6.5 Nature of Discussions on the Issue of Domestic Violence in the First Cycle

Universal Periodic Review Cycle 1		Responses by States under Review					
		A1 No further comments	A2 Laws already implemented/ under review to tackle domestic violence	A3 Domestic Violence victim support in place	A4 Policies in place to ensure effective investigation and prosecution of perpetrators	A5 Awareness-raising campaigns	A6 Cultural reforms required
Nature of recommendations issued to states under review	Recommendation 1 Enact/Implement/ Reform laws to protect women from domestic violence	Chile Myanmar Tanzania Togo Spain Slovenia Brazil Liberia Libya Nepal Nicaragua	Fiji Ireland Papa New Guinea Canada Equatorial Guinea Lebanon Madagascar Maldives Solomon Islands Bahamas Bhutan Madagascar Maldives Marshall Islands Moldova Montenegro Oman Samoa St Lucia Suriname Ukraine	Albania Sao Tome Principe Kazakhstan	Portugal	Micronesia Saint Kitts and Nevis	Saint Kitts and Nevis

(Continued)

Table 6.5 Continued

Universal Periodic Review Cycle 1	Responses by States under Review					
	A1 No further comments	A2 Laws already implemented/ under review to tackle domestic violence	A3 Domestic Violence victim support in place	A4 Policies in place to ensure effective investigation and prosecution of perpetrators	A5 Awareness- raising campaigns	A6 Cultural reforms required
Recommendation 2 Ensure compliance with international human rights norms	Canada Guinea Bissau Tanzania Samoa El Salvador Guinea	Hungary Papua New Guinea Kazakhstan Maldives	Tajikistan Nauru	Slovenia	Liechtenstein	
Recommendation 3 Ensure victims are supported	Canada Spain Angola Argentina Belarus Bhutan Comoros Kuwait Panama Rwanda Russia	Equatorial Guinea Moldova Kyrgyzstan Madagascar Palau Switzerland Costa Rica	Russia		Cape Verde Croatia Denmark Iceland Vanuatu Cyprus	
Recommendation 4 Effective investigation and prosecution of domestic violence	Syria Chile Togo Burundi Libya Nicaragua El Salvador Spain Belarus Dominica	Maldives Oman Uganda Austria	Albania Kazakhstan		Mongolia	
Recommendation 5 Effective awareness-raising campaigns	Angola Comoros Liberia Slovenia Tanzania	Iceland Malawi Moldova Timor-Leste	Albania Norway		New Zealand Iraq Vanuatu	

Responses by States under Review

	A1 No further comments	A2 Laws already implemented/ under review to tackle domestic violence	A3 Domestic Violence victim support in place	A4 Policies in place to ensure effective investigation and prosecution of perpetrators	A5 Awareness-raising campaigns	A6 Cultural reforms required
Recommendation 6 Discourage cultural beliefs/norms that may perpetuate domestic violence	Guinea Togo	Madagascar Timor-Leste Maldives Ukraine Malawi				
	N1 No further comments	**N2** Laws to address domestic violence already in place/under review	**N3** Domestic violence victim support in place Kuwait			
Recommendation 1 Enact/Implement/ Reform laws to protect women from domestic violence	Syria Burkina Burkina Faso Burundi DPR Korea Georgia	Gambia Kiribati Seychelles Mali				
Recommendation 2 Ensure compliance with international human rights norms	Burkina Faso	Argentina				
Recommendation 3 Ensure victims are supported	Oman					
Recommendation 5 Effective awareness-raising campaigns	Georgia	Malawi				

Table 6.6 Nature of Discussions on the Issue of Domestic Violence in the Second Cycle

Universal Periodic Review Cycle 2	Responses by States under Review						
	A1 No further comments	A2 Laws already implemented/under review to tackle domestic violence	A3 Domestic Violence victim support in place	A4 Policies in place to ensure effective investigation and prosecution of perpetrators	A5 Awareness-raising campaigns and national policies in place	A6 Cultural reforms required	A7 New provisions in place, but domestic violence will not be considered an offence, the charge would remain an assault
Nature of recommendations issued to states under review	Recommendation 1 Enact/Implement/Reform laws to protect women from domestic violence	Afghanistan Algeria Andorra Antigua and Barbuda Barbados Belarus Benin Burkina Faso Cambodia Cameroon China Comoros Cote d'Ivoire Djibouti Egypt El Salvador Gabon Guinea	Armenia Bangladesh Bhutan Botswana Canada Chile Costa Rica Croatia Dominica Estonia Ethiopia Georgia Ghana Jordan Kazakhstan Kuwait Kyrgyzstan Latvia Luxembourg	Costa Rica Croatia	Angola Georgia Guyana	Costa Rica Estonia Georgia Lesotho		Fiji

	Guinea Bissau Hungary Iraq Ireland Italy Kiribati Liberia Libya Macedonia				
Recommendation 2 Ensure compliance with international human rights norms	Chile Ireland Latvia Lithuania	Croatia Estonia	Croatia Cyprus	Angola	Iceland
Recommendation 3 Ensure victims are supported	Andorra Belarus Bolivia Comoros	Ethiopia	Argentina	Angola	Bulgaria Greece
Recommendation 4 Effective investigation and prosecution of domestic violence	Belarus	Albania Bahamas Barbados Belize Equatorial Guinea Ghana Grenada	Argentina Belize	Barbados	Barbados Belize Greece Grenada Iceland
Recommendation 5 Effective awareness-raising campaigns	Brazil Dominica Dominican republic Germany Greece Indonesia Ireland Japan	Albania Costa Rica	Argentina Costa Rica		Costa Rica Estonia Georgia Iceland

(*Continued*)

Table 6.6 Continued

Universal Periodic Review Cycle 2

	Responses by States under Review						
	A1 *No further comments*	A2 *Laws already implemented/under review to tackle domestic violence*	A3 *Domestic Violence victim support in place*	A4 *Policies in place to ensure effective investigation and prosecution of perpetrators*	A5 *Awareness-raising campaigns and national policies in place*	A6 *Cultural reforms required*	A7 *New provisions in place, but domestic violence will not be considered an offence, the charge would remain an assault*
Recommendation 6 Discourage cultural beliefs/norms that may perpetuate domestic violence	Cote d'Ivoire						
Recommendation 7 Take necessary measures to address domestic violence	Antigua and Barbuda Austria Azerbaijan Belarus Belgium Benin Bolivia Brazil Chile	Bhutan Botswana Jamaica Kazakhstan Kuwait	Cyprus	Guyana	Australia Bulgaria Cape Verde Eritrea Finland Georgia		

	N1 No further comments	N2 Laws to address domestic violence already in place/under review	N3 Domestic violence victim support in place
Recommendation 1 Enact/Implement/Reform laws to protect women from domestic violence	Costa Rica Cyprus Czechia Democratic Republic of Congo Denmark Egypt France Guatemala Haiti Honduras Ireland Madagascar Belgium Chad DPR Korea Egypt Equatorial Guinea Germany Kuwait	Bahamas Bosnia and Herzegovina Gambia Iran Lebanon	
Recommendation 2 Ensure compliance with international human rights norms	Belgium	Bangladesh Bosnia and Herzegovina	
Recommendation 7 Take necessary measures to address domestic violence		Bosnia and Herzegovina	

provided an N3 response as it explained that the issue of domestic violence was being addressed, as actions undertaken by the 'social police authority, the family counselling authority, the domestic violence center and the minors' protection authority' were already in place.[114]

Overall, from the discussions, it became apparent that of the 51 states that were issued with a recommendation under this category, no state under review agreed to implement laws against domestic violence as a form of action emanating from the state being reviewed in the UPR process. Instead, 16 states provided no further comments in response to a recommendation under this category. A total of 22 states suggested that laws against domestic violence already existed, and a further 13 states provided details of other non-legislative measures that were already implemented in the state under review. Therefore, a closer examination of the responses issued by states indicates that there are grounds to question the apparent consensus amongst states who largely accepted recommendations under this category.

RECOMMENDATION 2

Observer states issuing recommendations under the second category centred on the suggestions that the state should ensure that it adequately protected women's rights against domestic violence to ensure compliance with its international human rights obligations. For example, Syria was issued with a recommendation by Canada to 'take necessary measures to end ... domestic violence ... and implement CEDAW and the Human Rights Committee recommendations in this context'.[115] A total of 16 states were issued with a recommendation of this nature.

In response, 14 states accepted the recommendations, and two states noted the recommendations issued under this category. Of those that accepted, the states of Canada, Guinea Bissau, Tanzania, Samoa, El Salvador, and Guinea all accepted the recommendations without any further comments, and therefore provided an A1 response. The states of Hungary,[116] Papua New Guinea,[117] Kazakhstan,[118] and Maldives[119] provided an A2 response, as they insisted that laws in relation to domestic violence already existed in the state under review.

Adopting a slightly different position, the delegates of Tajikistan[120] and Nauru[121] provided an A3 response, as they insisted that support for victims of domestic violence was already established. Further, the state of Slovenia provided an A4 response to the recommendation and explained that 'since such crimes often remained hidden, activities were aimed at better detection, reporting and awareness-raising. The number of detected cases was increasing as the result of efforts to improve detection and prevention'.[122] The delegate of Liechtenstein provided an A5 response, as it highlighted the 'awareness-raising projects on the issue of domestic violence' that were being implemented by the state to 'to break stereotypes'.[123]

There were only two states under review that noted the recommendations issued under this category. The first is the state of Burkina Faso, who provided an N1 response. The delegate of Argentina noted the recommendation and explained that 'in December 2006, the project to create the office of domestic violence within the framework of the judiciary' was begun.[124] Thus, as these plans were in place, the delegate of Argentina noted the recommendation and provided an N2 response.

RECOMMENDATION 3

The focus of the third category of recommendations that were issued by observer states was to ensure that the states under review had implemented measures and policies to provide protection and support to the victims of domestic violence. A typical example of a recommendation under this category was when France issued a recommendation to Cape Verde to 'promote the establishment of places to care for and provide assistance to women victims of domestic violence'.[125] A total of 26 states were issued with a recommendation under this category.

In response, 25 states accepted, whilst only one state noted the recommendations under this category. Of those that accepted, a total of 11 states did not provide any further comments, and therefore issued an A1 response. A total of seven states[126] under review provided an A2 response, insisting that laws were already implemented. Further, the delegate of Russia provided an A3 response as it stated that 'social rehabilitation programmes and services were developed for domestic violence victims'.[127] In other instances, the states of Cape Verde,[128] Croatia,[129] Denmark,[130] Iceland,[131] Vanuatu,[132] and Cyprus provided an A5 response. Here, the states under review provided that awareness campaigns against domestic violence were being implemented. For example, the delegate of Cyprus stated that 'campaigns on violence against women and children were conducted annually by the competent authorities, including to deter and prevent domestic violence and to challenge societal attitudes'.[133] The only state that noted a recommendation under this category was Oman, who provided an N1 response as no further comments were made.

RECOMMENDATION 4

Observer states that issued recommendations under this category suggested that the states should implement laws and policies to ensure effective investigation and/or prosecution of domestic violence. A typical example of a recommendation under this category was when France suggested that the Marshall Islands should 'implement a system to counter domestic violence against women, and ensure that the perpetrators of such violence are prosecuted and appropriately punished'.[134] A total of 21 states were issued with a recommendation under this category.

In response, all 21 states accepted the recommendations; however, the nature of the responses differed. A total of ten states under review provided an A1 response. A total of six states provided an A2 response insisting that laws against the practices were already in place. These were the Maldives, Oman, Uganda, and Austria. Adopting a slightly different approach, the states of Albania[135] and Kazakhstan,[136] provided an A3 response as they provided details of the support that was available to victims of domestic violence.

Only one state under review provided an A5 response. Here, the state made references to the awareness-raising campaigns and public education programmes that were in place to reform such deeply held views that contributed to perpetuating domestic violence. For instance, when issued with a recommendation under this category the delegate of Mongolia stated that 'the Government had continued to work to address those problems, including through the public awareness campaign, to shape a culture of intolerance towards domestic violence'.[137]

RECOMMENDATION 5

The essence of the recommendations issued under this category is that states under review were required to engage in civil society movements, women's groups, and other relevant stakeholder groups to raise public awareness against domestic violence. A typical example of recommendation issued under this category was when Norway issued a recommendation to Georgia to 'give a prominent role to civil society – not least women's organizations – in efforts to address domestic violence ... and place focus on strengthening public awareness'.[138] A total of 17 states were issued with a recommendation under this category.

In response, a total of 14 states accepted, whilst two states noted the recommendations. Of the states that did accept the recommendations, the states of Angola, Comoros, Liberia, Slovenia, and Tanzania all accepted the recommendations without any further response, and therefore provided an A1 response. On the other hand, Iceland, Malawi, Moldova, and Timor-Leste insisted that laws in the states already protected women from domestic violence, therefore providing an A2 response. Adopting a slightly different approach, the delegates of Albania and Norway provided an A3 response; for example, the delegate of Norway provided an A3 response stating that 'legal aid was provided to victims of domestic violence also before any complaint was made to the police'.[139]

New Zealand, Iraq, and Vanuatu provided a different response, and issued an A5 response. The delegate began by stating that it had 'reviewed to strengthen police powers and responses to family violence incidents' and the 'government has recently launched a Campaign for Action on Family Violence, which aims to stimulate change in the way people think and act about domestic violence'.[140] The states of Iraq[141] and Vanuatu[142] provided an A5 response, as they insisted public awareness campaigns against the crime of domestic violence were implemented in the state.

Only two states noted recommendations under this category. First, the delegate of Georgia provided an N1 response, as it failed to provide an explanation for its position. Second, the delegate of Malawi provided an N2 response, as it insisted that laws protecting women from domestic violence were already in place.

RECOMMENDATION 6

The essence of the recommendations that were issued under this category was that states were required to implement policies and practices with the aim of discouraging cultural attitudes and stereotypes that perpetuate domestic violence. The states under review were recommended to implement strategies involving the civil society, and other local stakeholders, to instigate a dialogue with the aim to discourage attitudes that contribute to the tolerance of domestic violence. The nature of these suggestions is usually accompanied with the suggestion to implement and enact laws on domestic violence. A typical example of a recommendation issued under this category was by Germany, who suggested that Timor-Leste should 'effectively implement the Law against Domestic Violence by raising awareness of this law to public officials, to local community leaders and by citizenship education, and additionally discourage cultural practices that violate women's rights'.[143] In another example, Brazil issued a recommendation to Guinea to combat domestic violence against women 'through the prevention of certain abusive socio-cultural practice'.

A total of seven states under review were issued with a recommendation under this category, and all seven accepted the recommendation. Of these, the states of Guinea and Togo accepted the recommendation without any further comments. The states of Madagascar, Timor-Leste, Maldives, Ukraine, and Malawi all provided an A2 response, as they highlighted the state's legal provisions that were in place to protect women from domestic violence. For example, the delegate of Timor-Leste stated that 'it referred to the recent promulgation of the Law on Domestic Violence and mentioned actions taken, including budgetary, to ensure the implementation of the law'.[144]

The states that issued recommendations under this category implicitly recognised that the issue of domestic violence cannot be addressed through legislative provisions alone. Instead, an implementation of strategies was required whereby local and religious leaders are involved to help discourage those attitudes that perpetuate domestic violence against women. In response, all the states accepted these recommendations, however, the comments accompanying the official stance were arguably subdued and defensive. For instance, two states accepted the recommendations without any further comments, whilst the other five states made references to the existing legislative provisions in place to help eradicate domestic violence and offer support to victims. Therefore, whilst the observer states issued recommendations of a preventative nature, the responses by states under this category focused on actions implemented to ensure perpetrators were punished after the violence had been carried out.

Second Cycle of Review

In the second cycle of review a total of 926 recommendations were issued to states under review. In terms of the dialogue, a total of seven different types of recommendations were issued by the observer states. The states under review issued a total of ten different types of responses, making this the most variant of discussions.

RECOMMENDATION 1

Being the most cited form of recommendations in relation to domestic violence in the second cycle of review, observer states under this category of recommendation instructed states under review to implement or reform domestic legislation to increase protection provided for women against domestic violence. Encapsulating the essence of this form of recommendation, the delegate of Romania recommended that Afghanistan 'effectively implement the legislation aimed at ensuring the realisation of rights of women ... especially the legislation on combating domestic violence'. A total of 63 states under review were issued with recommendations under this category.

The most prevalent form of response was for the states under review to accept the recommendation without providing any further comments. A slightly fewer number of 20 states chose to accept the recommendations but insist that laws were already in law or under review to address the issue of domestic violence. The states of Costa Rica and Croatia provided an A3 response as they outlined the domestic violence victim support policies that were already in place. Similarly focusing on existing policies, the states of Angola, Georgia, and Guyana accepted the recommendation and outlined the policies in place to ensure effective investigation and prosecution of perpetrators of domestic violence. A total of four states accepted the recommendation under this category and referred to awareness-raising campaigns that were in place to prevent domestic violence against women. By far the most interesting response was from the state of Fiji. Whilst accepting the recommendation, the delegate of Fiji insisted that the 'domestic violence decree did not establish domestic violence as an offence; the charge would remain one of assault under the Crimes Decree'. In this way, whilst formally accepting the recommendation, in essence, the substance of the response indicates that the recommendation to implement laws to protect against the act of domestic violence will not be implemented, and rather the issue will be addressed under the more generic criminal law offences.

Whilst the majority of the states accepted the recommendation under this category, there were a select few states that refused to accept the suggested action. For instance, a total of seven states noted the recommendation and declined to provide any more comments. In contrast, a total of five states noted the recommendation and insisted that laws to address domestic violence were already in place. For example, the state of Gambia states that 'on the rights of women ... delegation mentioned that a series of laws, such as the Women's Act and the Domestic Violence Act ... had been passed to empower women'.[145] The most notable finding of the dialogue in relation to this form of recommendation is that whilst this is the most common type of recommendation issued, the responding states largely either refrained from commenting any further, simply accepting or noting the recommendation, or simply restricted their response to referring to

generic laws and policies that are in place to address the issue of domestic violence. As a result, many states did not agree to undertake actions to respond to
the recommendation.

RECOMMENDATION 2

The second form of recommendation issued in relation to domestic violence
instructed observer states to ensure compliance with international human rights
law. A typical example of this form of recommendation is illustrated during the
review of Chile, when the delegate of Liechtenstein insisted it to 'step up its efforts
to combat domestic violence in accordance to CEDAW'. A total of 12 states
under review were issued with this form of recommendation. In response, a total
of nine states accepted the recommendation with varying responses. For example,
Chile, Ireland, Latvia, and Lithuania all accepted the recommendation with no
further response. The states of Estonia and Croatia accepted the recommendation and referred to existing laws that were already in place. The states of Cyprus
and Croatia also accepted the recommendation and outlined the policies in relation to victim support that were in place. Similarly, the state of Angola accepted
the recommendation whilst providing alternative references to polices in relation
to effective investigation of crimes in relation to domestic violence that were
already in place. The states of Bulgaria and Greece accepted the recommendation
and referred to awareness-raising campaigns that were in place to help address
the crime of domestic violence. For example, the delegate of Iceland stated that
'regarding gender-based violence, the delegation reported that increased awareness and the resulting change in attitudes had led to an increased number of cases
being reported to the police'.[146]

A total of three states under review noted the recommendations issued under
this category. The state of Belgium noted the recommendation and did not provide any further response. The states of Bangladesh and Bosnia and Herzegovina
noted the recommendation and referred to existing laws that were already in
place to address the issue of domestic violence.

RECOMMENDATION 3

Under the third category, the observer state recommended that the state under
review should ensure that the victims of domestic violence were appropriately
protected. For instance, the delegate of Myanmar stated that Belarus should 'further enhance efforts to address the issue of domestic violence and victim assistance'. A total of nine states were issued with this recommendation; all of which
accepted the recommendation.

The states of Andorra, Belarus, Bolivia, and Comoros all accepted the recommendation, and provided no further comments. The state of Ethiopia accepted
the recommendation but insisted that laws were already in place to tackle the
issue of domestic violence. Argentina and Angola similarly accepted the recommendation and referred to existing policies on domestic violence victim support,

and effective investigative policies, respectively. The states of Bulgaria and Greece referred to the awareness-raising campaigns that were already in place in the states to tackle the issue of domestic violence.

RECOMMENDATION 4

This form of recommendation was issued to a total of 15 states under review. Observer states under this category of recommendation suggested that states under review ensure that there are policies and strategies in place for effective investigation and prosecution of domestic violence. An example of this form of recommendation is when the delegate of Norway issued a recommendation to Ghana during its review to 'ensure that effective and prompt investigations are carried out into all allegations of domestic violence'.

In response, all states under review accepted this category of recommendation. The state of Belarus was the only state that accepted the recommendation without issue of any further comments. A total of seven states under review issued an A2 response and referred to the existing laws in place in relation to domestic violence. The states of Argentina and Belize both referred to the domestic violence victim support that was available, which did not directly respond to the recommendation that was being issued. Barbados accepted the recommendation and referred to the existing policies in relation to effective investigation and prosecution. The states of Barbados, Belize, Greece, Grenada, and Iceland all provided an A5 response, referring to the awareness-raising campaigns that were in place in relation to domestic violence. Similar to the response of Argentina, this response did not directly relate to the recommendation being made, and rather was more of a generic response to the issue of domestic violence.

RECOMMENDATION 5

Under this category of recommendation, the observer states recommended that the states under review implement effective awareness-raising campaigns in relation to domestic violence. A typical example of this form of recommendation was issued to Costa Rica during its review. The delegate of Norway recommended it to 'intensify its efforts in … conducting awareness-raising and public educational campaigns with a view to bring about changes in such attitudes, and underlining that all forms of violence against women should be eliminated.' A total of 12 states under review were issued with this recommendation, all of whom accepted the recommendation. Of these, eight states accepted the recommendation without any further comments. The states of Albania and Costa Rica accepted the recommendation and referred to the existing laws that were in place to address the issue of domestic violence. Similarly, the state of Argentina accepted the recommendation and referred to the policies in place to support the victims of domestic violence. The states of Costa Rica, Estonia, Georgia, and Iceland directly responded to the recommendation and noted that existing awareness-raising campaigns were already in place in relation to the issue.

RECOMMENDATION 6

This category of recommendation was unique in nature as it was the only line of dialogue that made reference to cultural norms and its relationship with domestic violence. The state of Cote d'Ivoire was issued with this recommendation by the state of Ireland. The delegate recommended to 'undertake a comprehensive legal and cultural awareness-raising campaign on ... gender based violence ... including issues such as domestic violence'. In response the state accepted this recommendation with no further comments. It was noteworthy that in the second cycle of review, this was the only instance whereby the relationship between culture and domestic violence was recognised and a line of dialogue was initiated on this basis. In contrast, the nexus between cultural norms and domestic violence was more prominently recognised in the first cycle of review when the issue of domestic violence was discussed.

RECOMMENDATION 7

The final category was more generic in nature and is the second more prevalent form of recommendation issued with a total of 35 states being issued with it during their state reviews. The recommendation focused on directing the state under review to take necessary measures to address domestic violence. The essence of this format of recommendation is illustrated in the review of Finland, when the delegate of Mexico stated that the state should 'give special attention to the prevention of domestic violence against women'. In response, 34 states accepted the recommendation. Of these, the majority of the states, a total of 21, accepted the recommendation without any further comments. A total of six states accepted the recommendation, and referred to laws that were already in place to address the issue of domestic violence. For example, the delegate of Kuwait responded with 'The law criminalizes all acts of violence and aggression against women'.[147] The delegates of Cyprus and Guyana, both referenced victim support and policies in place in relation to effective investigation and prosecution of perpetrators, respectively. The only state to have noted the recommendation was Bosnia and Herzegovina, who referred to the existing laws in place in relation to domestic violence. The delegate stated that 'notably, the criminal code had been amended to treat domestic violence as a crime rather than a misdemeanour'. Therefore, it is notable that the delegate responded with a very direct response to a relatively vague recommendation in relation to domestic violence.

Discussion and Analysis

A total of 1407 recommendations were issued to states on the issue of domestic violence over two UPR cycles, making this issue the subject of the highest number of recommendations considered in this investigation. Of these, a total of 1301 recommendations were accepted by member states, thereby indicating that states, at least formally, are in consensus that the issue should be eradicated, and measures should be put in place to ensure women's rights against such violence are protected. Further, in depth analysis of the discussions held over the two cycles supported the view that there was no state that explicitly challenged the universal protection of rights that should be granted to women in relation to domestic violence. In light of the prominence of the issue of domestic violence being raised in the discussions during state reviews, one may have expected that there would be a variety of different positions adopted by states, resulting in the discussions on domestic violence being relatively varied. However, the findings reveal that the dialogue held amongst states can be divided into two main forms.

First, the most common form of discussions held in relation to domestic violence over the two cycles focused on the legislation to be implemented in relation to domestic violence. For example, it was the most prevalent form of recommendation issued over the two cycles. Moreover, it is notable that the focus of the responses by states under review in relation to domestic violence focused on states referring to existing laws in place to protect women against domestic violence. In fact, one of the most striking findings is that, aside from one, in all of the responses provided by states under review, states simply referred to existing laws and policies that were in place to protect women against domestic violence when issued with a variety of recommendations. In this way, the essence of the discussions between observer states and states under review was on the measures that were in place once the crime had been committed. Whilst a focus entirely on ensuring measures are in place for addressing violence when it has already been carried out is problematic in itself, the more pertinent problem here is that the discussions between states on domestic violence can be described as static and mechanical. This is because observer states largely instigated discussions on laws and policies that were in place to ensure adequate protection once such violence had been carried out against the victim. This instigated a response by most states under review, who restated that laws and policies were already established in the domestic context to ensure appropriate measures were in place once the violence had been committed. The implication of this is that the states under review that provided such defensive responses failed to agree or commit to any actions or reforms as a result of being reviewed in the UPR process. For this reason, it can be argued that the fundamental objective of the UPR process to promote universality of human rights through a constructive dialogue can be questioned as the majority of the discussions held on domestic violence can be described as reporting existing policies and laws against domestic violence, rather than discussions on the issue and how further protection can be provided against domestic violence against women.

The second form of discussions on domestic violence was engaged in by a minority of states. Some states adopted positions which indicated a recognition that attitudes and beliefs embedded in the cultural norms may contribute to perpetuating or tolerance of domestic violence. For example, in the first cycle of review, seven observer states under the sixth category recognised this link between culture and domestic violence and suggested policies and reforms to be implemented to help discourage cultural norms that may contribute to domestic violence. Similarly, observer states issuing recommendations under the fifth category focused on suggesting incremental reforms, such an awareness-raising campaigns against domestic violence by engaging with relevant stakeholder groups. In this way, observer states suggested engaging in public awareness campaigns and engaging local community leaders to help discourage cultural practices to help implement laws against domestic violence. Similarly, 15 states under review provided an A5 response when issued with recommendations. The essence of these responses was that the states insisted that campaigns had been implemented to help raise awareness against domestic violence. These findings indicate that observer states issuing recommendations under categories 5 and 6, and states under review issuing responses under category A5 have adopted positions that resonate with aspects of the moderate cultural relativist position for two main reasons.[148]

The first is because the moderate cultural relativist position places emphasis on the significance of culture to an individual's perception and outlook of the world which has developed over a period of time.[149] Moreover, any reforms of negative attitudes must be undertaken in a gradual manner over a period of time, rather than expected to be precipitously eliminated. In this way, the minority of states in the UPR process recognised the significance of incremental reforms to prevent domestic violence in the first place. This was suggested by engaging in awareness campaigns and engaging in a dialogue with relevant stakeholders to help to discourage any cultural practices that may perpetuate domestic violence. The second reason for the suggestion that the minority of state positions resonate with the moderate cultural relativist position is one of the core beliefs of moderate cultural relativism is that reforms must be suggested in a culturally legitimate manner. One method of doing this is to encourage in an internal dialogue, within the culture itself, to reinterpret certain values that are inconsistent with human rights law to bring them into compliance with the current international human rights standards.[150] The fundamental aspect is that the internal dialogue must be undertaken by individual actors and groups within the culture itself to avoid the appearance of 'dictation by others'.[151] The nature of these suggestions is reflected in the statements made by some states during the discussions of domestic violence, who suggested that awareness-raising campaigns and constructive dialogue with relevant stakeholders must be carried out within the culture itself. In this way, the nature of the positions adopted by both observer states and states under review suggests that some state positions indicated an affiliation with the moderate cultural relativist position.

The implications of the minority of states that showed evidence of the moderate cultural relativist position in the discussions of domestic violence are twofold. First, there is a recognition amongst states, albeit in a small number, that there is a need to prevent domestic violence from occurring in the first place. In order to do this, deterrence through legislative measures is not enough. Therefore, what is required is that the individual and collective group attitudes that may perpetuate and tolerate domestic violence needs to be reformed.[152] In this way, the discussions on domestic violence focused on the need to reform attitudes within societies that are unconsciously embedded through cultural norms to prevent domestic violence in the first place. In addition, by adopting aspects of the moderate cultural relativist position, there was evidence of the discussions being moved away from merely ensuring that appropriate laws and policies were in place to ensure victims were supported and perpetrators punished; to moving towards focusing on methods to prevent such violence from occurring in the first place. In this way, it can be argued that when states in the UPR process affiliated to a moderate cultural relativist position, the dialogue on domestic violence was more fruitful.

In contrast, in the second cycle there was a dramatic decline in the subject of cultural norms being included in the discussions held in relation to domestic violence. For instance, only in the review of Cote d'Ivoire was a recommendation issued to implement measures with the aim to discuss cultural norms that perpetuate domestic violence. In fact, the recommendations that focused on implementing awareness-raising campaigns clearly steered away from any direct mention of discouraging cultural norms that may perpetuate the acceptability or normalisation of domestic violence. Therefore, unlike the first cycle of review where there was some evidence of a more nuanced understanding and discussions of how to address the issue of domestic violence and take full advantage of the dialogical nature of the UPR process; in the second cycle of review, the discussions were largely surface level, whereby focus of the dialogue was largely on the laws and policies that were recommended to be in place to address the issue, and the states under review referring to the existing policies in place. In this way, in the second cycle of review, there was no evidence of states aligning with the position of the moderate cultural relativist positions to fully take advantage of the nature of the UPR process to undertake more nuanced and issue-specific actions to improve the situation of women's rights in relation to domestic violence.

Overall, the majority of the recommendations issued in relation to violence were accepted, therefore indicating at least a formal consensus to the elimination of domestic violence. However, an analysis of the discussions held on the issue revealed that the majority of the states simply focused on the laws and policies that were to be implemented to ensure perpetrators were punished and victims acquired the necessary support. In other words, the focus was on addressing the aftermath of such violence. In addition, the responses by states under review simply reiterated the detail of laws and policies that were already in place to address domestic violence. There was evidence of a minority of states adopting a position that resonated with aspects of the moderate cultural relativist position. Both observer states and states under review recognised the importance of preventing domestic violence in the first place by encouraging a form of internal discourse to discourage cultural norms and practices that may perpetuate domestic violence. In conclusion, there was no evidence of states adopting a strict universalist or a strict cultural relativist position during the discussions on domestic violence.

However, despite the lack of polarisation between universalism and relativism on the issue, there was a clear lack of states engaging in fruitful dialogue. This is because discussions largely focused on implementing laws and policies to address such violence once it had already been committed.

Conclusion

The focus of this chapter was to present the findings on the nature of discussions held when the issue of violence against women was discussed during state reviews in the UPR process. More specifically, the exploration focused on the manner in which states adopted positions and attitudes during discussions on the issue to gain a fuller insight as to how the UPR process operates.

The exploration for this part of the investigation revealed that the express assertion of universalistic nature of violence against women was stagnated. This is because this investigation found that no observer made any reference to international human rights norms when issuing recommendations during the reviews of states on the issue of marital rape and honour killings. This means that when the two issues were discussed during state reviews, no express reference was made to any international human rights norms. When the issue of domestic violence was raised, a total of 14 member states were issued with recommendations to comply with the international human rights norms on the issue.

The findings of this investigation also revealed that the universality of international human rights norms was expressly challenged in relation to marital rape. The states under review adopted positions which challenged the reforms suggested on marital rape on the grounds of national sovereignty, and from a strict cultural relativist perspective. Unfortunately, neither of these positions were held accountable for by the observer states in any counter statements, despite evidence of some of these challenges being raised during the interactive dialogue stage, and not the time restricted HRC plenary session. By contrast, no express challenges to reforms were made from a cultural relativist perspective on the issue of honour killings or domestic violence. What is interesting to note here is that in both honour killings and domestic violence there were no observer states that issued recommendations that made express reference to culture and suggestions to eliminate it.

Aside from the issue of marital rape, no other states expressly adopted positions which affiliate with aspects of the strict cultural relativist position. In addition, as noted above there was no evidence of observer states issuing recommendations from a strict universalist position. Therefore, in the absence of polarised positions between universalism and relativism, together with the large number of states participating in the debates on violence against women, one would have presumed that there was room for a fruitful dialogue on issues of violence against women during state reviews. However, this was not evident in the discussions held. For instance, in relation to honour killings, states have expressly and implicitly detached the cultural influences that underpin honour killings. This has resulted in states underappreciating the reasons why such killings are carried out in the first place whereby the underlying motivation of the crime is the culturally conceptualised notion of honour, and the underlying reason to control the women's behaviour and sexuality is not raised in discussions during state reviews.[153] Instead, the focus of discussions in relation to honour killings and marital rape was on implementing legal provisions against both issues. For this reason, a lack of moderate cultural relativist positions by states has meant that discussions have been restricted to legal provisions to deal with the perpetrators of such crimes rather than discussing the core issues at stake. By contrast, in relation to domestic violence, there was some evidence of the appreciation of moderate cultural relativist positions by both states under review and observer states. This means that there was some evidence of discussions on reforming cultural norms and attitudes that contribute to perpetuating or tolerating domestic violence. However, this formed the minority of discussions. This is because, like the discussions on honour killing and marital rape, the states focused on the laws and policies in place to ensure perpetrators were punished and victims protected. Thereby the focus was on implementing laws once the crime had been committed.

In conclusion, the findings of this exploration reveal that the universalist assertions in relation to violence against women were stagnated. There were no states that expressly adopted a strict universalist position. In addition, despite a specific declaration on violence against women, and numerous reiterations of the issue in treaty jurisprudence, it was striking to note that there were no references to international norms in relation to marital rape and honour killing during state reviews. Also, there was evidence of some states adopting positions that resonated with a strict cultural relativist challenge in relation to marital rape, but not in relation to honour killing and domestic violence. Finally, whilst the moderate cultural relativist position was recognised in a minority of state reviews in relation to domestic violence, no such evidence of states adopting attitudes that resonate with the moderate cultural relativist position was evident in marital rape and honour killing. Therefore, overall, there was a lack of fruitful discussions in all three issues in the UPR process.

Notes

1   Radhika Coomaraswamy and Lisa Kois, 'Violence against women' in Kelly D Askin and Dorean M Koenig (eds), *Women and International Human Rights Law* (Volume 1, Transnational Publishers Inc 1999) 178.
2   UN General Assembly, 'Declaration on the Elimination of Violence against Women' (20 December 1993) A/RES/48/104.
3   UN Committee on the Elimination of Discrimination against Women, 'CEDAW General Recommendation No. 19: Violence against Women (1992) para 11. See also UN Human Rights Committee (HRC) 'CCPR General Comment No. 28: Article 3 (The Equality of Rights between Men and Women)' (29 March 2000) CCPR/C/21/Rev.1/Add.10, para 32; UN General Assembly, 'In-depth Study on All Forms of Violence against Women: Report of the Secretary-General' (6 July 2006) A/61/122/Add.1, para 80.

4 www.unwomen.org/en/what-we-do/ending-violence-against-women/facts -and-figures, accessed 28 August 2019.

5 Radhika Coomaraswamy and Lisa Kois, 'Violence against women' in Kelly D Askin and Dorean M Koenig (eds), *Women and International Human Rights Law* (Volume 1, Transnational Publishers Inc 1999) 190.

6 Ibid. 179.

7 Ibid. 190; See also C Watts and C Zimmerman, 'Violence against Women: Global Scope and Magnitude' (2002) 359 *Lancet* 1232; Lisa Aronson Fontes and Kathy A McCloskey, 'Cultural issues in violence against women' in CM Renzetti, J L Edleson and RK Bergen (eds), *Sourcebook on Violence against Women* (2nd edn, Sage Publications) 162–164.

8 P Werbner, 'Veiled Interventions in Pure Space: Honour, Shame and Embodied Struggles among Muslims' (2007) 24 *Theory Culture Society* 161. See also Aysan Sev'er and Gökçeçiçek Yurdakul, 'Culture of Honor, Culture of Change: A Feminist Analysis of Honor and Killings in Rural Turkey' (2001) 7 *Violence against Women* 964, 965.

9 UN Committee on the Elimination of Discrimination Against Women, 'CEDAW General Recommendations Nos. 19 and 20, adopted at the Eleventh Session' (1992) A/47/38, para 24 (r) (ii); UNGA 'Working towards the Elimination of Crimes against Women Committed in the Name of Honour' (July 2002) A/57/169, para 34. UN Human Rights Committee (HRC) 'CCPR General Comment No. 28: Article 3 (The Equality of Rights between Men and Women)' (29 March 2000) CCPR/C/21/Rev.1/Add.10. U.N. Doc., para 31; UN General Assembly, 'Working towards the Elimination of Crimes against Women and Girls Committed in the Name of Honour' (10 February 2005) A/ RES/59/165.

10 UN General Assembly Resolution 'Working towards the Elimination of Crimes against Women Committed in the Name of Honour' (2001) A/RES/55/66, para 4.

11 UNGA. 'Report of the Special Rapporteur on Violence against Women, Its Causes and Consequences, Rashida Manjoo' (2012) A/HRC/20/16, para 87; UN Committee on the Elimination of Discrimination against Women, 'CEDAW General Recommendation No. 19: Violence against Women' (1992) para 11.

12 UNGA, 'Working towards the Elimination of Crimes against Women Committed in the Name of Honour' (July 2002) A/57/169, para 3–7. See also Phyllis Chelser, 'Worldwide Trends in Honour Killings' (2010) *Middle East Quarterly* 3, 10, www.unfpa.org/swp/2000/english/ch03.html, accessed 28 August 2019.

13 See GM Kressel, 'Sororicide/Filiacide: Homicide for Family Honour' (1981) 22 *Current Anthropology* 141–158; Purna Sen, '"Crimes of honour", value and meaning' in Lynn Welchman and Sara Hossain (eds), *'Honour': Crimes, Paradigms, and Violence against Women* (Zedbooks 2005) 46.

14 Purna Sen, '"Crimes of honour", value and meaning' in Lynn Welchman and Sara Hossain (eds), *'Honour': Crimes, Paradigms, and Violence against Women* (Zedbooks 2005) 47; UN Commission on Human Rights, 'Report of the Special Rapporteur on Violence against Women, Its Causes and Consequences, Ms. Radhika Coomaraswamy, Submitted in Accordance with Commission on Human Rights Resolution 2001/49: Cultural Practices in the Family That Are Violent towards Women' (31 January 2002) E/CN.4/2002/83, para 18.

15 Recep Dogan, 'Different Cultural Understandings of Honor that Inspire Killing: An Enquiry into the Defendant's Perspective' (2014) *Homicide Studies* 12, http://hsx.sagepub.com/content/early/2014/03/12/1088767914526717, accessed 28 August 2019.

16 UNHRC, 'Afghanistan' (20 July 2009) A/HRC/12/9, para 39.
17 UNHRC, 'Syrian Arab Republic' (24 January 2012) A/HRC/19/11, para 104.8.
18 UNHRC, 'Iraq' (15 March 2010) A/HRC/14/14, para 47.
19 UNHRC, 'Jordan' (3 March 2009) A/HRC/11/29, para 77.
20 Ibid. para 56.
21 Ibid.
22 UNHRC, 'Report of the Working Group on the Universal Periodic Review Syrian Arab Republic: Addendum Views on Conclusions and/or Recommendations, Voluntary Commitments and Replies Presented by the State under Review' (6 March 2012) A/HRC/19/11/Add.1, page 2.
23 UNHRC, 'Albania' (4 January 2010) A/HRC/13/6, para 21.
24 UNHRC, 'Jordan' (3 March 2009) A/HRC/11/29, para 56.
25 UNHRC, 'Iraq' (15 March 2010) A/HRC/14/14, para 71.
26 Ibid. para 48.
27 UNHRC, 'Pakistan. Addendum' (25 August 2008) A/HRC/8/42/Add.1, para 15.
28 UNHRC, 'Iraq' (15 March 2010) A/HRC/14/14, para 11.
29 UNHRC, 'Jordan' (3 March 2009) A/HRC/11/29, 56.
30 UNHRC, 'Turkey' (17 June 2010) A/HRC/15/13, para 39.
31 UNHRC, 'Oman' (24 March 2011) A/HRC/17/7, para 90.36.
32 UNHRC, 'Pakistan. Addendum' (25 August 2008) A/HRC/8/42/Add.1, para 15.
33 UNHRC, 'Iraq' (15 March 2010) A/HRC/14/14, para 48.
34 UNHRC, 'Turkey' (17 June 2010) A/HRC/15/13, para 49.
35 UNHRC, 'Oman' (24 March 2011) A/HRC/17/7, para 39.
36 UNHRC, 'Report of the Human Rights Council on Its Twenty-Sixth Session' (19 September 2014) A/HRC/26/2, para 373.
37 Abdullahi Ahmed An-Na'im, 'The role of "community discourse" in combating "crimes of honour": preliminary assessment and prospects' in Lynn Welchman and Sara Hossain (eds), *'Honour': Crimes, Paradigms, and Violence against Women* (Zed Books 2005) 70, 71.
38 Ibid. 71.
39 See GM Kressel, 'Sororicide/Filiacide: Homicide for Family Honour' (1981) 22 *Current Anthropology* 141–158.
40 Recep Dogan, 'Different Cultural Understandings of Honor That Inspire Killing: An Enquiry into the Defendant's Perspective' (2014) *Homicide Studies* 12, http://hsx.sagepub.com/content/early/2014/03/12/108876791452 6717, accessed 28 August 2019.
41 UNHRC, 'Jordan' (3 March 2009) A/HRC/11/29, para 56.
42 UNHRC, 'Pakistan. Addendum' (25 August 2008) A/HRC/8/42/Add.1, para 15.
43 Abdullahi Ahmed An-Na'im, 'The role of "community discourse" in combating "crimes of honour": preliminary assessment and prospects' in Lynn Welchman and Sara Hossain (eds), *'Honour': Crimes, Paradigms, and Violence against Women* (Zed Books 2005) 73.
44 Ibid. 72.
45 Ibid. 74.
46 Ibid. 76.
47 UN Commission on Human Rights, 'Integration of the Human Rights of Women and the Gender Perspective Violence Against Women Report of the Special Rapporteur on Violence against Women, Its Causes and Consequences, Ms. Radhika Coomaraswamy' (March 1999) E/CN.4/1999/68, para 18.

48 RK Bergen, *Wife Rape: Understanding the Response of Survivors and Service Providers* (Sage Publications 1996) 11–36; M Pagelow, 'Adult Victims of Domestic Violence' (1992) 7 *Journal of Interpersonal Violence* 87.
49 UN Committee on the Elimination of Discrimination against Women, 'CEDAW General Recommendation No. 12: Violence against women' (1989); UN Committee on the Elimination of Discrimination against Women, 'CEDAW General Recommendation No. 19, Violence against Women' (1992), para 24 (b).
50 UN Committee on the Elimination of Discrimination against Women, 'CEDAW General Recommendation No. 19, Violence against women' (1992), para 24 (e); UN General Assembly, 'Eliminating Rape and other Forms of Sexual Violence in all Their Manifestations, Including in Conflict and Related Situations: Report of the Secretary-General' (4 August 2008) A/63/216, para 4.
51 UN Committee on the Elimination of Discrimination against Women, 'CEDAW General Recommendation No. 19, Violence against Women' (1992), para 24 6(b) (e); See also, UNGA, 'Report of the Fourth World Conference on Women, Beijing' (4–15 September 1995) Sales No. E.96.IV.13, para. 124 (a), article 4.
52 See LR Eskow, 'The Ultimate Weapon? Demythologizing Spousal Rape and Reconceptualizing Its Prosecution' (1996) 48 *Stanford Law Review* 677.
53 See Peggy Reeves Sanday, 'The Socio-Cultural Context of Rape: A Cross-Cultural Study' (1981) 37 *Journal of Social Issues* 5; C Renzetti, J Edleson, Jeffrey and RK Bergen, *Sourcebook on Violence against Women* (2nd edn, Sage Publications 2010) 155.
54 Owen D. Jones, 'Sex, Culture, and the Biology of Rape: Toward Explanation and Prevention' (1999) 87 *Cal. L.R.* 827, 840 (1999). See also Peggy Reeves Sanday, 'The Socio-Cultural Context of Rape: A Cross-Cultural Study' (1981) 37 *Journal of Social Issues* 5; C Renzetti, J Edleson, Jeffrey and RK Bergen, *Sourcebook on Violence against Women* (2nd edn, Sage Publications 2010) 155.
55 UNHRC, 'United Arab Emirates' (12 January 2009) A/HRC/10/75, para 74(c).
56 UNHRC, 'Denmark' (11 July 2011) A/HRC/18/4, para 106.36.
57 UNHRC, 'Hungary' (11 July 2011) A/HRC/18/17, para 73.39.
58 UNHRC, 'Slovenia' (15 March 2010) A/HRC/14/15, para 98.23.
59 UNHRC, 'The Netherlands' (13 May 2008) A/HRC/8/31, para 41.
60 UNHRC, 'Canada' (3 March 2009) A/HRC/11/17, para 23.
61 UNHRC, 'The Netherlands' (13 May 2008) A/HRC/8/31, para 18.
62 UNHRC, 'Brazil' (22 May 2008) A/HRC/8/27, para 100.61
63 UNHRC, 'France' (3 June 2008) A/HRC/8/47, para 44.
64 UNHRC, 'Portugal' (4 January 2010) A/HRC/13/10, para 61.
65 UNHRC, 'United States of America' (4 January 2011) A/HRC/16/11, para 80.3.
66 UNHRC, 'Hungary, Addendum': (14 September 2011) A/HRC/18/17/Add.1, page 4.
67 UNHRC, 'Kuwait' (16 June 2010) A/HRC/15/15, para 78.
68 UNHRC, 'Malaysia' (3 March 2009) A/HRC/11/30, page 5.
69 UNHRC, 'Eritrea' (4 January 2010) A/HRC/13/2, para 51.
70 UNHRC, 'United Arab Emirates' (12 January 2009), para 74 (c).
71 UNHRC, 'Report of the Human Rights Council on Its Tenth Session' (9 November 2009) A/HRC/10/29, para 429.
72 UNHRC, 'Brunei Darussalam' (4 January 2010) A/HRC/13/14, para 84.
73 UNHRC, 'Bahamas' (7 January 2009) A/HRC/10/70, para 9.
74 UNHRC, 'Singapore' (11 July 2011) A/HRC/18/1, para 48.

75 UNHRC, 'United Republic of Tanzania' (8 December 2011) A/HRC/19/4, para 85.62 and 86.36.
76 UNHRC, 'Hungary' (11 July 2011) A/HRC/18/17, page 4.
77 UNHRC, 'Armenia: Addendum Views' (13 September 2010) A/HRC/15/9/Add.1, para 21.
78 UNHRC, 'Oman, Addendum' (3 June 2011) A/HRC/17/7/Add.1, page 6.
79 UNHRC, 'United Republic of Tanzania: Addendum' (12 March 2012) A/HRC/19/4/Add.1.
80 UNHRC, 'Report of the Human Rights Council on Its Nineteenth Session' (24 May 2013) A/HRC/19/2, para 382.
81 UNHRC, 'Botswana' (22 March 2013) A/HRC/23/7, para 19.
82 UNHRC, 'Bahamas' (22 March 2013) A/HRC/23/8, para 31.
83 UNHRC, 'Tanzania' (14 July 2016) A/HRC/33/12 para, 78.
84 UNHRC, 'Report of the Human Rights Council on Its Thirty-Second Session' (14 November 2016) A/HRC/32/2, para 163.
85 UNHRC, 'Ghana' (13 December 2012) A/HRC/22/6, para 76.
86 UNHRC, 'Report of the Human Rights Council on its tenth session' (9 November 2009) A/HRC/10/29, para 429.
87 UNHRC, 'Brunei Darussalam' (4 January 2010) A/HRC/13/14, para 84.
88 UNHRC, 'United Republic of Tanzania, Addendum' (12 March 2012) A/HRC/19/4/Add.1, paragraph 382.
89 UNHRC, 'Yemen' (5 June 2009) A/HRC/12/13, para 48.
90 UNHRC, 'Bahamas' (7 January 2009) A/HRC/10/70, para 9.
91 Hilary Charlesworth, 'Human rights as men's rights' in Julie Peters and Andrea Wolper (eds), *Women's Rights, Human Rights: International Feminist Perspective* (Routledge 1995) 106–110. See also section 2.3.4.
92 Berta Esperanza Hernandez- Truyol, 'Human rights through a gendered lens: emergence, evolution, revolution' in Kelly D Askin and Dorean M Koenig (eds), *Women and International Human Rights Law* (Volume 1, Transnational Publishers Inc 1999) 32.
93 Lucinda Joy Peach, 'Are women human? The promise and perils of "women's rights as human rights"' in Lynda Bell, Andrew Nathan and Ilan Peieg (eds), *Negotiating Culture and Human Rights* (Columbia University Press 2001) 159.
94 Peggy Reeves Sanday, 'The Socio-Cultural Context of Rape: A Cross-Cultural Study' (1981) 37 *Journal of Social Issues* 5.
95 A An-Na'im, 'Islam, Islamic Law and the dilemma of cultural legitimacy for universal human rights' in Claude E Welch, Jr. and Virginia A Leary (eds), *Asian Perspectives on Human Rights* (Westview Press 1990) 46–48.
96 Abdullahi An-Na'im, 'The Rights of Women in International Law in the Muslim Context' (1987) 9 *Whitter Law Review* 515.
97 United Nations Centre for Social Development and Humanitarian Affairs, 'Strategies for Confronting Domestic Violence: A Resource Material 7' (1993) UN Doc. ST/CSDHA/20.
98 UN Committee on Economic, Social and Cultural Rights, 'General Comment No. 14: The Right to the Highest Attainable Standard of Health' (Art. 12 of the Covenant) (11 August 2000) E/C.12/2000/4, para 27; UN Committee Against Torture, 'General Comment No. 2: Implementation of Article 2 by States Parties' (24 January 2008) CAT/C/GC/2 para 18; UN Committee on the Elimination of Discrimination against Women, 'General Recommendation No. 19: Violence against women' (1992), para 9.
99 UN General Assembly, 'Domestic violence' (14 December 1990) A/RES/45/114; UN General Assembly, 'Declaration on the Elimination of Violence against Women' (20 December 1993) A/RES/48/104, para 6.

100 Ibid. See also UN Committee on the Elimination of Discrimination against Women, 'CEDAW General Recommendation No. 19: Violence against Women' (1992).
101 www.unwomen.org/en/what-we-do/ending-violence-against-women/facts -and-figures, accessed 31 August 2014.
102 Barbara Burston, Nata Duvvury and Nisha Varia, Justice, *Change and Human Rights: International Research and Responses to Domestic Violence* (International Center for Research and Women and the Centre for Development and Population Activities 2002).
103 Joan Fitzpatrick, 'The use of International Human Rights norms to combat violence against women' in Rebecca Cook (ed), *Human Rights of Women: National and International Perspectives* (University of Pennsylvania Press 1994) 562.
104 Ibid.
105 UNHRC, 'Federated States of Micronesia' (4 January 2011) A/HRC/16/16, para 61.26.
106 UNHRC, 'Canada' (3 March 2009) A/HRC/11/17, para 36.
107 UNHRC, 'Sao Tome and Principe' (16 March 2011) A/HRC/17/13, para 60.
108 UNHRC, 'Kazakhstan' (23 March 2010) A/HRC/14/10, para 92.
109 UNHRC, 'Albania' (4 January 2010) A/HRC/13/6, para 48.
110 UNHRC, 'Portugal' (4 January 2010) A/HRC/13/10, para 93.
111 UNHRC, 'Federated States of Micronesia' (4 January 2011) A/HRC/16/16, para 37.
112 UNHRC, 'Saint Kitts and Nevis' (15 March 2011) A/HRC/17/12, para 16.
113 UNHRC, 'Report of the Human Rights Council on Its Fourteenth Session' (23 October 2012) A/HRC/14/37, para 592.
114 UNHRC, 'Kuwait' (16 June 2010) A/HRC/15/15, para 62.
115 UNHRC, 'Syrian Arab Republic' (24 January 2012) A/HRC/19/11, para 36.
116 UNHRC, 'Hungary' (11 July 2011) A/HRC/18/17, para 21.
117 UNHRC, 'Papua New Guinea' (11 July 2011) A/HRC/18/18, para 40.
118 UNHRC, 'Kazakhstan' (23 March 2010) A/HRC/14/10, para 65.
119 UNHRC, 'Maldives' (4 January 2011) A/HRC/16/7, para 66.
120 UNHRC, 'Tajikistan' (12 December 2011) A/HRC/19/3, para 36.
121 UNHRC, 'Nauru' (8 March 2011) A/HRC/17/3, para 36.
122 UNHRC, 'Slovenia' (15 March 2010) A/HRC/14/15, para 44.
123 UNHRC, 'Liechtenstein' (7 January 2009) A/HRC/10/77, para 37.
124 UNHRC, 'Argentina' (13 May 2008) A/HRC/8/34, para 17.
125 UNHRC, 'Cape Verde' (12 January 2009) A/HRC/10/81, para 48.
126 Equatorial Guinea; Moldova; Kyrgyzstan; Madagascar; Palau; Switzerland; Costa Rica.
127 UNHRC, 'Russian Federation' (3 March 2009) A/HRC/11/19, para 67.
128 UNHRC, 'Cape Verde' (12 January 2009) A/HRC/10/81, para 48.
129 UNHRC, 'Croatia' (4 January 2011) A/HRC/16/13, para 91.
130 UNHRC, 'Denmark' (11 July 2011) A/HRC/18/4, para 58.
131 UNHRC, 'Iceland' (16 December 2011) A/HRC/19/13, para 39–41
132 UNHRC, 'Vanuatu' (4 June 2009) A/HRC/12/14, para 30.
133 UNHRC, 'Cyprus' (4 January 2010) A/HRC/13/7, para 78.
134 UNHRC, 'Marshall Islands, Addendum' (4 March 2011) A/HRC/16/12/ Add, page 2.
135 UNHRC, 'Albania' (4 January 2010) A/HRC/13/6, para 48.
136 UNHRC, 'Kazakhstan' (23 March 2010) A/HRC/14/10, para 65.
137 UNHRC, 'Mongolia' (4 January 2011) A/HRC/16/5, para 52.
138 UNHRC, 'Georgia' (16 March 2011) A/HRC/17/11, para 54.
139 UNHRC, 'Norway' (4 January 2010) A/HRC/13/5, para 98.

140 UNHRC, 'New Zealand, Addendum' (7 July 2009) A/HRC/12/8/Add.1, page 6.
141 UNHRC, 'Iraq' (15 March 2010) A/HRC/14/14, para 46–48.
142 UNHRC, 'Vanuatu' (4 June 2009) A/HRC/12/14, para 30.
143 UNHRC, 'Timor-Leste' (3 January 2012) A/HRC/19/17, para 62.
144 Ibid. 50.
145 UNHRC, 'Gambia' (24 December 2014) A/HRC/28/6, para 107.
146 UNHRC, 'Iceland' (19 December 2016) A/HRC/34/7, para 105.
147 UNHRC, 'Kuwait Addendum' (4 June 2015) A/HRC/29/17/Add.1
148 K Schooley, 'Cultural Sovereignty, Islam, and Human Rights – Toward a Communitarian Revision' (1994–1995) 25 *Cumberland Law Review* 651, 682.
149 C Geertz, *Interpretations of Cultures* (Basic Books, 1973) 49; A An-Na'im, 'Problems and prospects of universal cultural legitimacy for human rights' in An- Na'im and Deng (eds), *Human Rights in Africa: Cross Cultural Perspectives* (Brookings Institution 1990) 333.
150 A An-Na'im, 'State responsibility under International Human Rights Law to change Religious and Customary Law' in Rebecca Cook (ed), *Human Rights of Women: National and International Perspectives* (University of Pennsylvania Press 1994) 175.
151 Abdullahi An-Na'im, 'The Rights of Women in International Law in the Muslim Context' (1987) 9 *Whitter Law Review* 515.
152 Joan Fitzpatrick, 'The use of International Human Rights norms to combat violence against women' in Rebecca Cook (ed), *Human Rights of Women: National and International Perspectives* (University of Pennsylvania Press 1994) 562; Barbara Burston, Nata Duvvury and Nisha Varia, Justice, *Change and Human Rights: International Research and Responses to Domestic Violence* (International Center for Research and Women and the Centre for Development and Population Activities, 2002).
153 UN Commission on Human Rights, 'Report of the Special Rapporteur on Violence against Women, Its Causes and Consequences, Radhika Coomaraswamy' (21 January 1999) E/CN.4/1999/68/Add.3, page 7, para 18.

Bibliography

An-Na'im A, 'The Rights of Women in International Law in the Muslim Context' (1987) 9 *Whitter Law Review* 515.
An-Na'im A, 'Islam, Islamic Law and the Dilemma of Cultural Legitimacy for Universal Human Rights' in Claude E Welch, Jr. and Virginia A. Leary (eds), *Asian Perspectives on Human Rights* (Westview Press, 1990).
An-Na'im A, 'Problems and Prospects of Universal Cultural Legitimacy for Human Rights' in AA An- Na'im and FM Deng (eds), *Human Rights in Africa: Cross Cultural Perspectives* (Brookings Institution, 1990).
An-Na'im A, 'State Responsibility Under International Human Rights Law to Change Religious and Customary Law' in Rebecca Cook (ed), *Human Rights of Women: National and International Perspectives* (University of Pennsylvania Press, 1994).
An-Na'im A, 'The Role of "Community Discourse" in Combating "Crimes of Honour": Preliminary Assessment and Prospects' in Lynn Welchman and Sara Hossain (eds), *"Honour": Crimes, Paradigms, and Violence against Women* (Zed Books, 2005).
Bergen KR, *Wife Rape: Understanding the Response of Survivors and Service Providers* (SAGE Publications, 1996)

Burston B, Duvvury N and Varia N, *Justice, Change and Human Rights: International Research and Responses to Domestic Violence* (International Center for Research and Women and the Centre for Development and Population Activities, 2002).

Charlesworth H, 'Human Rights as Men's Rights' in Julie Peters and Andrea Wolper (eds), *Women's Rights, Human Rights: International Feminist Perspective* (Routledge, 1995) 106–110.

Chelser P, 'Worldwide Trends in Honour Killings' (2010) *Middle East Quarterly* 3, 10 <https://www.unfpa.org/swp/2000/english/ch03.html> accessed 28 August 2019.

Coomaraswamy R and Kois L, 'Violence against Women' in Kelly D Askin and Dorean M Koenig (eds), *Women and International Human Rights Law* (Volume 1, Transnational Publishers Inc, 1999).

Dogan R, 'Different Cultural Understandings of Honor that Inspire Killing: An Enquiry into the Defendant's Perspective' (2014) *Homicide Studies* <http://hsx .sagepub.com/content/early/2014/03/12/1088767914526717> accessed 28 August 2019.

Eskow LR, 'The Ultimate Weapon? Demythologizing Spousal Rape and Reconceptualizing Its Prosecution' (1996) 48 *Stanford Law Review* 677.

Facts and Figures: Ending Violence against Women <http://www.unwomen.org/ en/what-we-do/ending-violence-against-women/facts-and-figures> accessed 28 August 2019.

Fitzpatrick J, 'The Use of International Human Rights Norms to Combat Violence Against Women' in Rebecca Cook (eds), *Human Rights of Women: National and International Perspectives* (University of Pennsylvania Press, 1994).

Geertz C, *Interpretations of Cultures* (Basic Books, 1973).

Hernandez-Truyol EB, 'Human Rights through a Gendered Lens: Emergence, Evolution, Revolution' in Kelly D Askin and Dorean M Koenig (eds), *Women and International Human Rights Law* (Volume 1, Transnational Publishers Inc, 1999).

Kressel MG, 'Sororicide/Filiacide: Homicide for Family Honour' (1981) 22 *Current Anthropology* 141–158; Purna Sen, '"Crimes of Honour", Value and Meaning' in Lynn Welchman and Sara Hossain (eds), *'Honour': Crimes, Paradigms, and Violence against Women* (Zedbooks, 2005).

Pagelow M, 'Adult Victims of Domestic Violence' (1992) 7 *Journal of Interpersonal Violence* 87.

Peach JL, 'Are Women Human? The Promise and Perils of "Women's Rights as Human Rights"' in Lynda Bell, Andrew Nathan and Ilan Peieg (eds), *Negotiating Culture and Human Rights* (Columbia University Press, 2001).

Renzetti C, JL Edleson and RK Bergen, *Sourcebook on Violence against Women* (2nd edn, Sage Publications, 2010) 155.

Sanday RP, 'The Socio-Cultural Context of Rape: A Cross-Cultural Study' (1981) 37 *Journal of Social Issues* 5.

Schooley K, 'Cultural Sovereignty, Islam, and Human Rights- Toward a Communitarian Revision'(1994–1995) 25 *Cumberland Law Review* 651.

Sev'er A and Yurdakul G, 'Culture of Honor, Culture of Change: A Feminist Analysis of Honor and Killings in Rural Turkey' (2001) 7 *Violence against Women* 964.

Sen P, '"Crimes of Honour", Value and Meaning' in Lynn Welchman and Sara Hossain (eds), *'Honour': Crimes, Paradigms, and Violence against Women* (Zedbooks, 2005).

UN Commission on Human Rights, 'Integration of the Human Rights of Women and the Gender Perspective Violence Against Women Report of the Special Rapporteur on Violence against Women, its Causes and Consequences, Ms. Radhika Coomaraswamy' (March 1999) E/CN.4/1999/68.

UN Commission on Human Rights, 'Report of the Special Rapporteur on Violence against Women, its Causes and Consequences, Radhika Coomaraswamy' (21 January 1999) E/CN.4/1999/68/Add.3.

UN Commission on Human Rights, 'Report of the Special Rapporteur on Violence against Women, Its Causes and Consequences, Ms. Radhika Coomaraswamy, Submitted in Accordance with Commission on Human Rights Resolution 2001/49: Cultural Practices in the Family that are Violent Towards Women' (31 January 2002) E/CN.4/2002/83.

UN Committee against Torture, 'General Comment No. 2: Implementation of Article 2 by States Parties' (24 January 2008) CAT/C/GC/2.

UN Committee on Economic, Social and Cultural Rights, 'General Comment No. 14: The Right to the Highest Attainable Standard of Health (Art. 12 of the Covenant)' (11 August 2000) E/C.12/2000/4.

UN Committee on the Elimination of Discrimination against Women, 'CEDAW General Recommendation No. 19: Violence against Women' (1992).

UN Committee on the Elimination of Discrimination against Women, 'CEDAW General Recommendation No. 12: Violence against women' (1989).

UN Committee on the Elimination of Discrimination against Women, 'CEDAW General Recommendations Nos. 19 and 20, adopted at the Eleventh Session' (1992) A/47/38.

UN Committee on the Elimination of Discrimination against Women, 'General Recommendation No. 19: Violence against Women' (1992).

UNGA, 'Report of the Fourth World Conference on Women, Beijing' (4 September 1995) Sales No. E.96.IV.13, para. 124 (a), article 4.

UNGA, 'Working Towards the Elimination of Crimes Against Women Committed in the Name of Honour' (July 2002) A/57/169.

UNGA, 'Report of the Special Rapporteur on Violence against Women, Its Causes and Consequences, Rashida Manjoo' (2012) A/HRC/20/16.

UN General Assembly, 'Domestic Violence' (14 December 1990) A/RES/45/114.

UN General Assembly, 'Declaration on the Elimination of Violence against Women' (20 December 1993) A/RES/48/104.

UN General Assembly, 'Working Towards the Elimination of Crimes Against Women and Girls Committed in the Name of Honour' (10 February 2005) A/RES/59/165.

UN General Assembly, 'In-Depth Study on All Forms of Violence Against Women: Report of the Secretary-General' (6 July 2006) A/61/122/Add.1.

UN General Assembly, 'Eliminating Rape and Other Forms of Sexual Violence in All Their Manifestations, Including in Conflict and Related Situations: Report of the Secretary-General' (4 August 2008) A/63/216.

UN General Assembly Resolution, 'Working Towards the Elimination of Crimes Against Women Committed in the Name of Honour' (2001) A/RES/55/66.

UNHRC, 'Argentina' (13 May 2008) A/HRC/8/34.

UNHRC, 'The Netherlands' (13 May 2008) A/HRC/8/31.

UNHRC, 'Brazil' (22 May 2008) A/HRC/8/27.

UNHRC, 'Pakistan. Addendum' (25 August 2008) A/HRC/8/42/Add.1.

UNHRC, 'France' (3 June 2008) A/HRC/8/47.
UNHRC, 'Bahamas' (7 January 2009) A/HRC/10/70.
UNHRC, 'Liechtenstein' (7 January 2009) A/HRC/10/77.
UNHRC, 'Cape Verde' (12 January 2009) A/HRC/10/81.
UNHRC, 'United Arab Emirates' (12 January 2009) A/HRC/10/75.
UNHRC, 'Canada' (3 March 2009) A/HRC/11/17.
UNHRC, 'Jordan' (3 March 2009) A/HRC/11/29.
UNHRC, 'Malaysia' (3 March 2009) A/HRC/11/30.
UNHRC, 'Vanuatu' (4 June 2009) A/HRC/12/14.
UNHRC, 'Yemen' (5 June 2009) A/HRC/12/13.
UNHRC, 'New Zealand, Addendum' (7 July 2009) A/HRC/12/8/Add.1.
UNHRC, 'Afghanistan' (20 July 2009) A/HRC/12/9.
UNHRC, 'Report of the Human Rights Council on its Tenth Session' (9 November
    2009) A/HRC/10/29.
UNHRC, 'Albania' (4 January 2010) A/HRC/13/6.
UNHRC, 'Brunei Darussalam' (4 January 2010) A/HRC/13/14.
UNHRC, 'Cyprus' (4 January 2010) A/HRC/13/7.
UNHRC, 'Norway' (4 January 2010) A/HRC/13/5.
UNHRC, 'Eritrea' (4 January 2010) A/HRC/13/2.
UNHRC, 'Portugal' (4 January 2010) A/HRC/13/10.
UNHRC, 'Iraq' (15 March 2010) A/HRC/14/14.
UNHRC, 'Slovenia' (15 March 2010) A/HRC/14/15.
UNHRC, 'Kazakhstan' (23 March 2010) A/HRC/14/10.
UNHRC, 'Kuwait' (16 June 2010) A/HRC/15/15.
UNHRC, 'Turkey' (17 June 2010) A/HRC/15/13.
UNHRC, 'Armenia: Addendum Views' (13 September 2010) A/HRC/15/9/
    Add.1.
UNHRC, 'Federated States of Micronesia' (4 January 2011) A/HRC/16/16.
UNHRC, 'Croatia' (4 January 2011) A/HRC/16/13.
UNHRC, 'Maldives' (4 January 2011) A/HRC/16/7.
UNHRC, 'Mongolia' (4 January 2011) A/HRC/16/5.
UNHRC, 'United States of America' (4 January 2011) A/HRC/16/11.
UNHRC, 'Marshall Islands, Addendum' (4 March 2011) A/HRC/16/12/Add.
UNHRC, 'Nauru' (8 March 2011) A/HRC/17/3.
UNHRC, 'Saint Kitts and Nevis' (15 March 2011) A/HRC/17/12.
UNHRC, 'Georgia' (16 March 2011) A/HRC/17/11.
UNHRC, 'Sao Tome and Principe' (16 March 2011) A/HRC/17/13.
UNHRC, 'Oman' (24 March 2011) A/HRC/17/7.
UNHRC, 'Oman, Addendum' (3 June 2011) A/HRC/17/7/Add.1.
UNHRC, 'Denmark' (11 July 2011) A/HRC/18/4.
UNHRC, 'Hungary' (11 July 2011) A/HRC/18/17.
UNHRC, 'Papua New Guinea' (11 July 2011) A/HRC/18/18.
UNHRC, 'Singapore' (11 July 2011) A/HRC/18/1.
UNHRC, 'Hungary, Addendum' (14 September 2011) A/HRC/18/17/Add.1.
UNHRC, 'United Republic of Tanzania' (8 December 2011) A/HRC/19/4.
UNHRC, 'Tajikistan' (12 December 2011) A/HRC/19/3.
UNHRC, 'Iceland' (16 December 2011) A/HRC/19/13.
UNHRC, 'Timor-Leste' (3 January 2012) A/HRC/19/17.
UNHRC, 'Syrian Arab Republic' (24 January 2012) A/HRC/19/11.

UNHRC, 'Report of the Working Group on the Universal Periodic Review Syrian Arab Republic: Addendum Views on Conclusions and/or Recommendations, Voluntary Commitments and Replies Presented by the State Under Review' (6 March 2012) A/HRC/19/11/Add.1.

UNHRC, 'United Republic of Tanzania, Addendum' (12 March 2012) A/HRC/19/4/Add.1.

UNHRC, 'Ghana' (13 December 2012) A/HRC/22/6.

UNHRC, 'Report of the Human Rights Council on Its Fourteenth Session' (23 October 2012) A/HRC/14/37.

UNHRC, 'Botswana' (22 March 2013) A/HRC/23/7.

UNHRC, 'Bahamas' (22 March 2013) A/HRC/23/8.

UNHRC, 'Report of the Human Rights Council on Its Nineteenth Session' (24 May 2013) A/HRC/19/2.

UNHRC, 'Report of the Human Rights Council on Its Twenty-Sixth Session' (19 September 2014) A/HRC/26/2 para 373.

UNHRC, 'Gambia' (24 December 2014) A/HRC/28/6.

UNHRC, 'Kuwait Addendum' (4 June 2015) A/HRC/29/17/Add.1.

UNHRC, 'Tanzania' (14 July 2016) A/HRC/33/12.

UNHRC, 'Report of the Human Rights Council on Its Thirty-Second Session' (14 November 2016) A/HRC/32/2.

UNHRC, 'Iceland' (19 December 2016) A/HRC/34/7.

UN Human Rights Committee (HRC), 'CCPR General Comment No. 28: Article 3 (The Equality of Rights between Men and Women)' (29 March 2000) CCPR/C/21/Rev.1/Add.10. U.N. Doc.

UN Human Rights Committee (HRC), 'CCPR General Comment No. 28: Article 3 (The Equality of Rights between Men and Women)' (29 March 2000) CCPR/C/21/Rev.1/Add.10.

United Nations Centre for Social Development and Humanitarian Affairs, 'Strategies for Confronting Domestic Violence: A Resource Material 7' (1993) UN Doc. ST/CSDHA/20.

Watts C and Zimmerman C, 'Violence against Women: Global Scope and Magnitude' (2002) 359 *Lancet* 1232; Lisa Aronson Fontes and Kathy A McCloskey, 'Cultural Issues in Violence against Women' in CM Renzetti, JL Edleson and RK Bergen (eds), *Sourcebook on Violence against Women* (2nd edn, Sage Publications 2011).

Werbner P, 'Veiled Interventions in Pure Space: Honour, Shame and Embodied Struggles among Muslims' (2007) 24 *Theory Culture Society* 161.

7 One Step Forward, Two Steps Back? A Reflection on UPR Process and the Wider Implications

Introduction

The name of the human rights monitoring mechanism itself, the Universal Periodic Review (UPR) process, provides an indication of its inherent universalistic tendencies. As explained in the first chapter of this book, the claim of universality of the UPR process is based on two fundamental grounds. The first is the universal applicability of the process. At the time of writing, two cycles of the UPR process have been completed, and the third cycle of review has commenced. One of the profound achievements of the process is the full participation of all UN member states to date; this gives strong grounds to suggest that the aim of 'universal applicability' of the UPR process has so far been fulfilled.[1] The second claim of universality of the UPR process is more normative in nature and is grounded in its establishing resolution which defines the aim of the process to 'promote the universality, interdependence, indivisibility and interrelatedness of all human rights', based on an interactive dialogue and equal treatment.[2] In this way, the principle of universality is given effect by employing a comprehensive set of international human rights norms, in order to monitor the states' human rights records and engage in a dialogue to recommend processes and policies to improve the protection of human rights norms in the domestic context. This normative aim of giving effect to the principle of universality of international human rights law was at the heart of this investigation. The aim was to answer: has the claim of promoting and protecting the universality of human rights been met, or challenged, during state reviews in the first two cycles of the process, with a specific focus on women's rights issues? In answering this question, this investigation employed the most enduring and sophisticated scholarly debates on international human rights law between universalism and cultural relativism. These debates were used as a framework not only to aid understanding of the discussions being undertaken at the UPR, but also to analyse the debates held during state reviews, and assess the wider implications of this investigation in the context of international human rights law, more broadly.

The aim of this chapter is to draw to together the overarching themes that were uncovered during this investigation and to begin to construct a picture of the nature and character of this process, and how it operates in practice at the end of two complete cycles. In analysing the core findings of this investigation, the chapter aims to discuss some of the possible implications this unique, innovative, and possibly the most significant monitoring mechanism the UN has implemented to date has had. This chapter is divided into two main parts. The first part will discuss the themes that were uncovered in this investigation, based largely on the theoretical framework that has underpinned this study; the scholarly works on the debates of universalism and cultural relativism. The section will discuss how such debates materialised in the interactive dialogue during state reviews, and assess whether the fundamental aim of implementing the principle of universality has been met in the first two cycles of review. The second part of this chapter will present the themes of practices and approaches that were adopted by state representatives, and analyse the possible implications, together with suggesting recommendations to ensure that the ambitious and commendable aims of this monitoring process are achieved going forward in future cycles of review.

The Debates between Universalism vs Cultural Relativism, and Everything in between; in Practice

The interactive dialogue session at the UPR process is the 'core element of the entire process'.[3] The session is a platform to bring together the plethora of information and data that has been collected for the review, which form the foundations of the questions and recommendations that will be put forward to the state under review. This platform provides the opportunity to utilise the benefits of the soft law method of improving human rights protection in the domestic context, through effectively sharing and learning best practices of human rights policies and strategies from across the globe. The cooperative approach that sits at the heart of the process aims to achieve compliance with the international human rights law through positive encouragement, assistance, and incentives,[4] and recommend changes and reforms to be undertaken in an incremental manner to improve the human rights protection on the ground. As Elvira Domínguez Redondo has noted, one of the successes of a political and cooperative process such as the UPR is that controversial human rights issues can be raised and addressed on an international platform, which was proved correct as states utilised the interactive dialogue session to raise contentious issues. Whilst there may be geopolitical patterns in the groups of states that were issuing the recommendations to states, the focus here will be on the nature of the discussions being held in light of the aim of the process of implementing the principle of universality. One of the most profound and overarching findings of this investigation was that it provided evidence that the enduring debates of universalism and cultural relativism are not confined to the scholarly works of academia. In fact, to this date, elements of the positions that affiliate with universalism and cultural relativism are reflected in the dialogues held on international human rights law. Indeed, the interactive dialogue process provides a unique platform for such dialogues to be undertaken on by state representatives, which uncovered an array of positions being adopted by states that affiliated with the two positions to varying degrees.

Reaffirming a Degree of Universality in Most Women's Rights Issues

The findings of this investigation reveal that observer states, when undertaking state reviews, adopted positions that were comparable to the normative universalist perspective during the discussions of all the issues, aside from honour killing and marital rape. However, the degree of universalism that was evident in the positions adopted by observer states varied depending on the particular women's rights issue that was discussed. For example, during the discussions of domestic violence, abortion, access to health care services, and forced and early marriages, some observer states made express reference to the relevant international human rights laws and suggested that the state under review complied with its international obligations in relation to the particular issue.

By comparison, when the issues of female genital mutilation (FGM), polygamy, and inheritance were the focus of discussions during state reviews, there was evidence of some observer states adopting positions that were comparable with the strictest form of universalist positions being adopted. In these instances, observer states expressly recognised that the issues were subject to be influenced and informed by cultural norms, and that the practices in relation to the issue should be eliminated. Thus, similar to the strict universalist position, states whilst recognising the existence of cultural diversity, insisted that the universal implementation of international human rights law should transcend any cultural boundaries and particularities.[5] In fact, there is reason to suggest that the express mention of the relationship between culture and the practice in question, before suggesting to eliminate it, gives reason to imply that the observer states suggested that the cultural norms that condoned such practices should also be eliminated.

This investigation has found that when states under review were issued with a recommendation by observer states that adopted aspects of the strict universalist position, it was notable that all the responses by the states under review were subdued as states did not provide any further comments; or, were defensive, by referring to existing laws and policies in the area. The strict universalist position, just as the extreme form of cultural relativism has been subject to rigorous criticism. Whilst universalists do not necessarily deny that cultural norms may be different, the belief is that the similarities between human beings should prevail over any cultural particularities when it comes to human rights.[6] It is this very disposition adopted by strict universalists that exposes it to criticism. The feminist legal anthropologist, Marie-Benedicte Dembour argues that exclusively relying on universalism is likely to breed moral arrogance as 'it excludes the experience of the other'.[7] In fact, the culture has a huge impact in the shaping of individuals and societies that develop and evolve over time.[8] Not only are the theoretical criticisms of strict universalism credible but the outcome of the adaptation of this position by observer states in practice in the UPR process adds weight to the merit of this criticism. Over the two cycles, when observer states adopted a position that affiliated with the strict universalist position, the states under review provided a subdued or a defensive response, which is contrary to the aim of the UPR process of engaging in a cooperative and constructive discussion of human rights issues. This ultimately means that no concrete outcome or commitment that was expressly agreed by the state under review as a result of the discussions on FGM, inheritance, and polygamy were reached in the two cycles of reviews when such recommendations of a strict universalist nature were being issued to states under review. This shows that not only are there theoretical and moral reasons to challenge a strict universalist position, but, in practice, the adoption of such a position in a human rights dialogue, on an international human rights law platform leads to far from a fruitful and meaningful outcome.

It is worth mentioning that one of the most striking findings of this investigation was that when the issues of honour killing and marital rape were being discussed over the two cycles of reviews, observer states refrained from expressly referring to international human rights norms when suggesting recommendations to the state under review. Therefore, during the discussion of these two issues, no observer states expressly adopted positions that were comparable to the strict form of universalism, despite the inherent relationship with cultural norms with such practices. In the first instance, one may explain this on the lack of a specific international human rights norm in relation to marital rape and honour killing, which may have influenced the lack of reference by observer states during state reviews. However, this explanation can be questioned as the issues of inheritance, polygamy, and FGM also lack any specific international human rights norms; despite this, observer states still adopted strict universalist positions when reviewing states' records. Whilst it cannot be concluded with any degree of certainty as to why states refrained from adopting an express normative universalist position when reviewing states on honour killing and marital rape, it is clear that states are more sensitive to expressly raising the universal nature of women's rights against honour killing and marital rape during state reviews than any other women's rights issues examined. This shows that despite the aim of the UPR process to promote the universality of all human rights, some observer states evidently refrained from expressing this normative claim of universality when two of the women's rights issues were the focus of discussions during state reviews.

Despite this ambitious aim, the discussions held amongst states in relation to the selected women's rights issues over the two cycles provides evidence that the degree of universalism that is adopted by observer states when undertaking the review varies depending on the issue that is the focus of discussions.

A Cultural Relativist Challenge in the UPR Process

One of the themes that were uncovered from the findings of this investigation was that states adopted positions in the UPR process that expressly challenged the aim of the process to give effect to the principle of universality of human rights in its work. This challenge was based on states using the relationship between culture and the particular issue as foundation to justify the non-acceptance of the recommendations to reform practices with the aim to address the human rights issue. For instance, during the discussions of polygamy, the states of Burkina

Faso, Chile, Tanzania, Ghana, and Libya used religious and cultural norms to justify the continuance of polygamous marriages over the two cycles of review. The universality of women's rights to equality in relation to inheritance was also challenged by the Solomon Islands and Libya on the basis that inheritance norms were governed by established traditional and religious practice. In addition, reforms in relation to marital rape were challenged by the United Arab Emirates and Brunei Darussalam. In more implicit terms, Mali and Liberia challenged the reforms concerning FGM on the basis that the practice was deeply embedded in culture, and therefore the states could not accept the suggested reforms.

The theoretical criticism of the strict cultural relativist position has been widely documented in a number of scholarly writings. The most profound example being that such a disposition presumed a static and bounded interpretation of culture, which does not recognise any form of change or development of such cultural norms, whether that comes from within the culture or external to it.[9] It is this extreme view of variations between cultural norms that leads to the complete dismissal of transcultural dialogue that is often used to deflect any kind of criticism of external sources, and to justify intolerable practices.[10] These criticisms can be projected on the states that adopted positions of strict cultural relativism, as they refused to accept recommendations to reform based on cultural norms and values. Aside from the moral and theoretical criticism, the adoption of these positions in practice, in the UPR process, has profound detrimental implications for the protection of women's rights, as well as the process itself.

When states adopted the strict cultural relativist positions, the implicit dismissal of the impossibility of a transcultural dialogue on cultural norms by those external to the culture had a resounding effect. For instance, when the strict cultural relativist position was adopted in the UPR process, it was notable that no observer states held any state to account when the suggested reforms on the selected women's rights issues were challenged based on strict cultural relativist grounds. Considering that one of the most profound laudatory characteristics of the interactive dialogue session is the discussions and instantaneous feedback, together with opportunities to hold states to account in the adoption of the Final Outcome Report in the Human Rights Council (HRC), no observer states utilised the cooperative and dialogic nature of the review to issue counter statements to hold the state to account for the challenge based on strict relativist grounds. This resounding silence on the part of the observer states posed a serious challenge to the universalist nature of the international human rights norms in relation to women's rights issues. Being a peer review process, the onus of ensuring that the principle of universality of human rights norms are met falls squarely on the responsibility of state representatives. Whilst the incremental and soft governance nature of the UPR process is at the heart of process, this unchecked direct challenge to the universality posed from a strict universalist position seriously jeopardises the aims and objectives of the review process. In this way, it can be observed that whilst it is laudable that the UPR process is used as a platform to raise controversial issues, which may not necessarily be raised elsewhere, such lines of dialogues were essentially drawn to a close when the strict cultural relativist position was being advocated. Contrary to the position adopted by the observer states, this opportunity should have been utilised to check the position of the states under review, and continue the dialogue in the spirit of the aims of the UPR process in unpicking the position that was being advocated, whilst engaging in a dialogue for gradual change and reforms on the issue in question. Thus, this lack of initiative by the state representatives in response to the strict cultural relativist position suggests that there was a missed opportunity to facilitate a dialogical response to the strict cultural relativist position on an international platform; more significantly for the UPR, it fractures one of the most fundamental objectives of the review process which is to engage in a constructive and cooperative dialogue on the human rights issues with the aim of promoting universal human rights.

The Implications for the Polarised Debates in Practice

As discussed in Chapter 2 of this book, the scholarly debates between universalism and cultural relativism have largely moved away from the polarised extremes and adopted a nuanced and sophisticated middle ground, which itself has been subject to profound literature; this investigation finds that such a polarisation continued to bear fruit in human rights dialogues that occurred in the UPR process. However, the implications to women's rights issues being discussed amongst the polarised extremes of universalism and relativism is profoundly evident in the discussions held between some states in the two cycles of review.

   The most significant implication is that when states adopted positions that affiliated with the strict universalist and strict cultural relativist positions, the findings show that the nature of the discussions on the particular issues have largely been oversimplified. The reason for the oversimplified discussions can chiefly be explained because at the core of both strict universalism and strict cultural relativism, the observer states and states under review have, explicitly or implicitly, presumed the traditional conceptualisation of culture.[11] This is the belief that culture is a static, homogenous, and bounded entity which cannot be influenced by any norms or beliefs external to the culture itself.[12] This interpretation of culture is evident in the position adopted by observer states which affiliate with the strict universalist position during the discussions of the issues. In a practical example, observer states that adopted a universalist stance to criticise polygamous marriages failed to acknowledge that those that are sympathetic to such marriages often hold deeply embedded views that such marriages are legitimised on cultural and religious grounds.[13] As such, suggestions to simply eliminate such practices that are condoned by culturally held beliefs is not a plausible or a helpful recommendation. Polygamous marriages are a function of sociopolitical alliances and a source of prestige, power, and influence.[14] In this way, observer states restricted the discussions to employing culture to suggest elimination of such marriages, rather than engaging in discourse to address the deeper underlying reasons as to why such marriages are undertaken in the first place. Similarly, when states responded by justifying the marriages on cultural grounds they overlooked multiple complex issues in relation to culture and such marriages. To name a few, states defending such marriages overlooked a number of complex issues. These include the pressing issue of gender inequalities in the apparent consent obtained for such marriages; the concern of women being unfaithful to their religion and being ostracised should they object to such marriage structures;[15] and the possibility of suppression and marginalisation of the voices of women in such marriage structures.[16]

In both cases when culture was used as a foundation to criticise or defend practices, states under review and observer states failed to consider if, and how, the cultural norms that influence the sympathetic attitudes towards the practice can be reformed and reinterpreted in a manner that would be accepted by the states under review. It has been argued earlier in the book that the presumption of a traditional conceptualisation of culture leads the discussions, in relation to the relevant women's rights issues, to be 'caught in various outdated approaches to "cultural contact" within which a rigid 'us' and 'them' dichotomy is constantly reproduced, and from which there seems to be no apparent escape'.[17] This is most evident in the discussions held in relation to some women's rights issues in the first two cycles of review. State representatives, through having positions that affiliate with a strict form of universalism or cultural relativism, have resulted in more important issues in relation to women's rights remaining unexplored and somewhat blocked from being materialised in the discussions during state reviews.[18] For instance, when observer states adopted a position from a strict universalist perspective, the suggestion by the observer states to simply eliminate the practice shows that the states have underappreciated the complex role that cultural norms play in the continuance of the practice, which have been developed and reaffirmed over a period of time.[19] In a similar way, when the strict cultural relativist position was exercised by states under review in relation to women's rights issues, this position overlooked the 'politics of culture' itself, whereby cultural norms, values, and representation are subject to a constantly contested political struggle between those who want to legitimise their power and those that want to challenge the status quo to address grievances.[20] In this way, states that have introduced arguments from a strict cultural relativist position veil pertinent issues such as: who represents the claimed cultural beliefs, the internal politics of the culture, and the representation of the voices and concerns of those women whose rights are violated.

This shows the implications of discussions undertaken by states when the strict universalist and strict cultural relativist positions are adopted in isolation of each other. Some states during the discussions of women's rights issues adopted two polarised positions; one which used culture as a basis of criticism when adopting a strict universalist position, and the other using culture to justify the rejection of reforms in relation to women's rights issues. These polarised positions restricted deeper underlying issues in relation to the cultural influences of the practice from being brought to the centre of discussions during state reviews. For this reason, it is posited that where states adopted the extreme polarised positions of universalism and relativism, the reviews of the states were conducted at a surface level, as complex issues that question the foundations of the strict universalist and cultural relativist position were simply ignored when the positions were introduced during the discussions.

The marginalisation of contentious and controversial issues being discussed in the UPR process is unfortunate. This is because the cooperative and discursive nature of the UPR process provides a unique platform to engage on controversial issues in relation to human rights. The findings of this investigation questions one of the points of optimisms of the review process; the opportunity it provides for raising contentious issues in relation to human rights.[21] Whilst in scholarly writings, the polarised debate between universalism and relativism is one that is largely confined to history, in the practice, conversations in relation to polygamy give reason to suggest that it continues to exist in some instances of discussions in relation to international human rights law. As a result, the problematic implications of such polarised discussions are applicable in the modern day discourse on human rights on the international forum in relation to some women's rights issues.

Mediating a Middle Ground in Practice

Despite the polarised positions adopted by some states on the UPR process, there is evidence to show that some states adopted approaches that affiliated with the more nuanced middle ground between the extreme forms of universalism and cultural relativism, described as a moderate form of cultural relativism. This was evident in both the positions of the observer states and states under review during the discussions of FGM, forced and early marriages, domestic violence, and honour killing over the two cycles of review. The states, during the discussions, began by, expressly or implicitly, recognising the relationship between the women's rights issue in question and the culture. The states then moved on to show an appreciation of reforms which affiliated with An-Na'im's suggestion of engaging in an internal dialogue, within the culture itself, to help discourage the cultural attitudes towards the practice which are inconsistent with international human rights norms. It was evident from the statements that the ultimate aim was to suggest reforms to protect women's rights issues in a manner that would be accepted by the communities and societies that hold views contrary to the protection of women's rights in relation to the particular issues. In this way, the essence of the states' positions were comparable to the core beliefs of the moderate cultural relativist position, which is to ensure that the current formulation of rights is more acceptable and better implemented in various cultures, by ensuring that the reforms are suggested in a culturally legitimate manner.[22]

What becomes apparent from the discussions held amongst states that adopted positions that resonated with the moderate cultural relativist position is that the states adopted a modern conceptualisation of culture. This is a belief that culture has porous boundaries and its values and norms are subject to influence and reforms over a period of time.[23] This is reflected in the positions adopted by states that affiliated with the moderate cultural relativist position because whilst the states recognised that the women's rights issues may be inherently associated with culture, the states appreciated that reforms to the cultural attitudes can be undertaken in a gradual and incremental manner. This indicates that states adopting a position that affiliates with the moderate cultural relativist position have shown an understanding of the nature of culture itself whereby values and norms that justify cultural practice are developed over a period of time, and thus cannot be eliminated in a precipitous manner.[24]

The implications of states adopting positions that affiliate with the moderate cultural relativist positions have been that aspects of the discussions on FGM, forced and early marriages, domestic violence, and honour killing were evidently more fruitful. This is primarily because states have recognised the relationship between culture and the women's rights issue and have then shown an appreciation of implementing reforms to help discourage cultural norms and attitudes that may perpetuate the violation of women's rights in relation to the women's rights issues. This has often resulted in more core issues in relation to the reasons behind the continued violations of women's rights issues being drawn to the centre of discussions. Issues such as cultural barriers and norms that women may face when seeking protection of their rights in relation to these issues were drawn to the centre of discussions. This can be contrasted with the use of culture by the strict universalist and strict cultural relativist position, whereby states used the notion of culture to either criticise or challenge reforms in relation to women's rights issues, and where discussions were largely oversimplified.

Room for Improvement? The Practices and Approaches Adopted at the UPR Process

Carrying the burden of the largely criticised mechanism of human rights monitoring that operated under the Human Rights Council predecessor – the Commission, the UPR process was laden with expectations to undertake the task of universal applicability, and give effect to universality of rights in its work through a unique interactive dialogue session as part of the review. Indeed, a number of the UPR process' high expectations have been met. The process boasts a universal participation to the process from all the UN member states during its decade of existence which itself, is a remarkable achievement. In addition, the UPR process has added a practical value to the system of human rights at the United Nations as it provided an invaluable opportunity for all member states of the United Nations to participate in a dialogue of international human rights law and policies, and raised awareness of how human rights norms are being implemented in different countries. This provides a unique opportunity to share and support best practices in improving the implementation of human rights norms in the domestic context. The opportunity given to observer states to raise any issue during the state under review, regardless of whether the state had formally ratified a human rights treaty has been fully utilised by the observer states. For instance, as this investigation has revealed, observer states have raised issues in relation to women's rights norms in relation to states, despite the state under review formally having submitted reservations to the Women's Rights Convention.[25] Thus, the UPR process has provided a platform whereby peer states can bring areas of concern in relation to human rights protection to the attention of the states. In this way, all member states of the United Nations are united in a shared and collaborative project of improving human rights through the UPR process. This very character of the process is in sharp contrast to the Commission's human rights monitoring mechanism which had been shaped by 'naming and shaming'. In fact, even where states under review have directly rejected recommendations, and provided an explanation, the UPR process has uniquely hosted a dialogue on an international stage and highlighted areas of genuine normative disagreement amongst states on the interpretation and implementation of international human rights law on an international platform. This means that the process has provided an invaluable normative value to the identification and development of international human rights norms.

The peer review nature of the process was naturally going to inherit an element of politicisation in the manner of which it operated. However, as Cowell, Milon, and Redondo suggested, the political and cooperative nature of the UPR process facilitated the raising of controversial issues in the interactive dialogue sessions in the UPR process. The issues in focus in this investigation clearly show that observer states were not coy in holding states under review accountable for issues that were not only traditionally perceived as controversial, but also shared an inherently complicated relationship with culture. Going further, Redondo suggested that the political and cooperative nature of the UPR process will apply pressure on the states to increase compliance and commitment to improving human rights concerns in the domestic context. This investigation reveals that the overwhelming majority of recommendations distributed in relation to the women's rights issues selected for this study, were accepted by the states under review. This means, that at least formally, the states under review have agreed to comply with the suggested reforms made during their state reviews at the UPR process. Indeed, there is an argument to suggest that this formal commitment could be beneficial to the civil society and other human rights institutions as it can be utilised to apply pressure to implement the accepted recommendations made during state reviews in the UPR process. For instance, it is very difficult for states to publicly commit to human rights norms through accepting or issuing recommendations, and then to justify their own non-compliance to these very norms.[26]

However, the aim of this investigation was to look beyond the numbers between the accepted and noted recommendations, to the nature of the actual discussions held in the interactive dialogue. Over the course of this investigation, there have been recurring strategies that have been adopted by states under review and observer states, which, as a combination, has manifested as a clog in achieving the overarching aims and objectives of the UPR process. Below, a description of these strategies are discussed, together with an analysis of possible implications of these strategies that are considered in light of the aims and objectives of the process. The section will conclude by providing recommendations for averting these approaches that undermine the aims of the process.

Approaches and Positions Adopted by the States under Review

As mentioned above, one of the aspects of the UPR process that warrants it as a unique and innovative development was its interactive dialogue sessions, which form a fundamental part of the review process. The aim of this core aspect of the process is to provide members states with the opportunity to undertake a dialogue on the human rights issues and concerns, and suggest appropriate recommendations based on these discussions. However, some of the approaches and positions adopted by the states under review over the two cycles provide strong grounds to suggest that this fundamental aim of the UPR process is, currently, being seriously undermined in four different ways.

First, and most significantly, over the course of this investigation, one of the most prominent forms of responses to recommendations has been accepting or noting recommendations, without any further comments. Naturally, when the recommendation is being accepted by the states under review, there may be reason to be optimistic and presume that the state is in agreement with the recommendations issued. Whilst this may be the case in some instances, there is reason to suggest that the remaining silence on acceptance of recommendation may not be so benign or a productive outcome. For instance, the failure to provide a clear response by the states under review means that whilst the recommendations are accepted, it is not clear how they will be implemented in practice in the domestic context. As a result, any progression on the implementation of recommendation will be difficult to monitor, but in addition, it gives reason to doubt whether any substantial or comprehensive reforms will be implemented to better guarantee the rights for women. This is problematic because the unique character and purpose of the UPR process is for peers to engage in a dialogue over pertaining issues, and the silence in response to recommendation defeats the very purpose of the UPR process. The implication of the silence is that it is difficult to gauge out the state's position on the issue and the commitments that the state is willing to make, so that it can be reviewed in the domestic context by stakeholders, but also in the next cycle.

This lack of clarity is more conspicuous and problematic in those circumstances where the states simply note the recommendation. An example of where remaining silent in response to a recommendation is apparent is in the reviews of Iraq in relation to honour killings. In the first cycle, Iraq noted the recommendation to enact or reform laws on honour killing without any further comments.

Strikingly, in the previous cycle, the delegate of Iraq was issued with the same recommendation, to which Iraq responded with noting the recommendation, however, adding that the ministry was working towards the abolition of the penal code which permitted mitigating circumstances for the crime. Disappointingly this was a missed opportunity as in the second cycle, the state noted the recommendation, and provided no explanation, and unfortunately, there is no follow up on the approach adopted by Iraq in the dialogue session. In these cases, the line of dialogue on the human rights issue of concern closed, and is thereby difficult to hold accountable for the reasoning behind the position that is adopted by the state under review. In addition, there is no particular commitment that the state under review has made in relation to the concerns being raised in relation to the issue in the next cycle of review. More profoundly, when states under review note the recommendation and fail to provide any other comment, and it remains unchallenged on the UPR process, this position can be used on other platforms by the state under review to gravitate, normalise, and justify their positions on the issue.

To avert these drawbacks in the forthcoming cycles of reviews, the most ambitious recommendation would be to remove the opportunity for states to accept or note a recommendation during their reviews, without an explanation. In this way, the states are compelled to provide reasoning behind their response to the recommendation, which itself can be criticised by other states under review and civil society movements. In addition, this would also expose the states under review to directly respond to the recommendation being issued, and make commitments on how the issue is going to be addressed in the domestic context, in the responses provided. Alternatively, the onus ought to be placed on the observer states to apply pressure on the states under review to issue more detailed explanation when the state under review chooses to accept or note a recommendation without any further comments. Ultimately, the adaptations of these practices will contribute to fulfilling the ultimate aim of the UPR process to engage in an interactive dialogue in the process of monitoring human rights records of states.

The second practice that was commonly adopted by the states under review was that of states referring to existing measures, whether law or policy, that were already in place. For example, the majority of discussions held in relation to marital rape over the two cycles focused on states under review referring to existing laws and policies that were in place. This pattern was a prevalent position adopted by the states under review in relation to the issues examined. The implication of this position is that the state under review has failed to adopt any new commitments or policy initiatives to ensure better protection of women's rights and that the protection is continually developed and improved. In fact, the reference to existing policies would suggest that there is a fair possibility of the lack of any further initiatives being taken in the domestic context to provide better protection of rights. In this way, unfortunately, there is little in terms of substantial outcome from the UPR process, whereby the states have expressed commitments to reforms or to implement new practice to better guarantee the protection, when this position is adopted by the states under review as a result of being reviewed in the UPR process.

Another approach that was adopted by states under review was often issued during the discussions where the state under review perceived the issue as controversial and strongly disagreed with the positions adopted by the observer states issuing the recommendation. In such cases, a number of states under review used national sovereignty as an explanation for not accepting the position and recommendation that was issued by the observer states. For instance, this was the most frequent form of response, when a state declined to accept a recommendation on the issue of abortion in both cycles of review. The implication of states adopting a position is, arguably, a more confrontational challenge to international norms than those that are justified on cultural grounds. This is because a justification of the non-acceptance of recommendations based on state sovereignty can be considered as being more definitive in nature, and arguably indicates a non-negotiable position adopted by the state in question.

Finally, there were some instances whereby the states under review provided a response that was inherently ambiguous in nature, which was unrelated to the recommendation being issued. As a result, the state under review used this strategy to deflect the recommendations that were being issued to them. For example, on the issue of women's rights in relation to inheritance, the states of Greece and Madagascar both accepted the recommendation that action should be taken to address religious and cultural barriers that impede women's right to inheritance. However, what is striking is that the responses issued by both states have focused entirely on the domestic legislation that is already in place, or will be implemented, to address the issue. In this way, rather than responding to how such cultural barriers that impede will be addressed, the states under review chose to focus on the existing laws that were in place. In this way, the states under review adopted an ambiguous approach to deflect the suggested reforms that were issued to the state under review in relation to women's rights to inheritance. In another example, in relation to the issue of abortion, the delegate of Rwanda noted a recommendation to implement incremental reforms towards abolishing the criminalisation of abortion. In response, whilst noting the recommendation Rwanda stated the recommendation requested 'legal protection and guarantees are already in place and actively implemented'.[27] In this way, despite the recommendations themselves being incremental suggestions in nature, both states justified not accepting the recommendation by referring to existing laws on the issue in the domestic context. This, of course, does not demonstrate that the laws adequately permit abortion and are in compliance with the international norms on the issues in relation to women's rights, but in fact simply state that the issue is being regulated by law in the domestic context. Finally, the state of El Salvador insisted that such changes would require a public dialogue on the issue. This response is unusual, particularly as the recommendation is to initiate such dialogues in the domestic context.

Approaches and Positions Adopted by the Observer States

Whilst one of the most fundamental aspects of the UPR process is its interactive dialogue session, it is difficult to overstate the significance of the auditing process prior to the state review itself. The observer states have, at their disposal, reports submitted by UN bodies, civil societies, as well as a report submitted by the state itself. Therefore, the observer states have at their disposal a catalogue of information to draw from when issuing recommendations. However, over the two cycles of reviews, it emerged that observer states, in each of the issues being examined, often issued recommendations that were exceptionally generic and vague in nature. For example, in relation to access to health care services, observer states instructed states under review to ensure that women were provided with adequate access to health care services. In these instances across the different women's rights issues being discussed, states did not make any references to the state's international obligations in the suggestions made, or provide any specific guidance as to the laws or policies that should be implemented. Despite being largely accepted by the states under review, the issuance of these recommendations is problematic as its generic nature means that the states under review are not directed to implement any specific and significant policies in the domestic context to ensure that women are provided adequate protection of their right to access health care. Going further, the lack of a clear and detailed set of actions in these recommendations means that despite the wide ranging acceptance, it is difficult to measure the extent to which the recommendations have been implemented both in the national and international context, and in particular, the future cycles of the review process. This position adopted by observer states gives gravity to Charlesworth and Larking's suggestion of 'ritualism' on the review process, whereby recommendations and acceptance of them are made on a purely 'tick box' basis, rather than with a genuine intent to hold states accountable on the issue and to bring about reforms.[28] The concerning aspect of this is that the nature of these recommendations formed an overwhelming part of the discussions held on the issue over both cycles, which gives strong reasons to question the constructive and productive nature of these discussions on these issues, and whether reforms will be made for change in the domestic context.

If the ambitious aims of the UPR process to give effect to universal rights and improve human rights in the domestic context are to be met, then the confidence and creditability of the UPR process must be developed into the third cycle. For this goal to be facilitated, the role of the observer states during the state reviews is pivotal. The observer states should utilise the political nature of the process to suggest reforms that build upon the recommendations of the previous cycle, to ensure that the recommendations are more specific, rigorous, and measurable in nature. This requirement becomes particularly apparent in light of the emergence of the findings that reveal states have maintained the same position over both cycles of review in relation to the issues such as FGM, abortion, and honour killings. For this reason, observer states should draw upon the data that is available in the reports and utilise diplomatic strengths to place pressure on the state under review to provide more specific, rigorous, and possibly measurable responses to the incremental reforms taking place to eradicate the practice. Observer states need to hold states directly accountable when states under review issue responses that are not related to the recommendations issued, or when the responses are ambiguous in nature. This naturally does not mean that the practices undertaken under the Commission's monitoring mechanism of 'naming and shaming' are adopted. Rather, the platform of the UPR process that is inherently cooperative in nature is utilised to undertake a line of dialogue that is encouraging and supporting, as well as rigorous, challenging, and informed by the data that is available. The role of the observer states can be utilised here to challenge the position advocated by the states under review, or ask for further clarity or explanation as a follow up question from the initial question being asked. Naturally, this will require the observer states to be more courageous in their role on a largely diplomatic platform, together with additional time to be dedicated to the interactive dialogue. Going further, in some instances, a more carefully constructed line of dialogue may be required to be channelled by the observer states to issue less ground-breaking reforms in order to continue to keep an open and diplomatic dialogue with the state under review in relation to the issue of contention. The aim here will be to strive for incremental reforms to be undertaken by the state under review. Indeed, reforms being implemented in a gradual and incremental manner are at the very heart of the nature of the UPR process.

Conclusion

As the title of this chapter suggests, the findings of this investigation reveal that whilst there are many reasons to laud the prospects of this human rights monitoring process that has existed for over a decade, there are aspects to this process that give grounds to suggest reforms and further reflection on what the UPR process actually is are required, as well as on the role and purpose the greater infrastructure of international human rights law has. This chapter has provided a discussion of the overarching themes that have emerged as part of this investigation. The first section of this chapter discussed the themes uncovered as part of the broader theoretical framework of this study. It concluded that the core aim of the UPR process of giving effect to the universality of rights is variant dependant not only on the issue at stake, but also the state representatives that undertake the review. This section illustrated how, despite the polarised debates between universalism and cultural relativism largely being relegated to history in the scholarly work; in practice, these polarised debates continue to exist in international human rights discussions undertaken in the UPR process. The section discussed the implications that such a polarised debate had on the state reviews over the two cycles and for the UPR process. The second part of this chapter revealed the findings of this study on the practical approaches and positions that states had adopted during state reviews. The section discussed the implications the positions, whether in the forms of actions or omissions, that states have adopted impact the effectiveness of the review process. Based on the findings of the study, the section also suggests recommendations to be implemented in the future cycles to facilitate in meeting the overarching aims and objectives of the process.

This chapter notes some of the profound ways that the UPR process has fulfilled its aims not only as a process, but making a mark as a significant contributor in the monitoring of human rights at the United Nations. However, despite this, the chapter concludes that the study reveals that the positions adopted by some states under review in the UPR process to avoid accountability in relation to women's rights issues that are perceived to be contentious, coupled with the rather underwhelming role that the observer states have played over the two cycles of review gives reason to suggest these positions adopted by states leads to a rather superficial level of discussions being held during state reviews. Lines of dialogues on pertinent and pressing women's rights issues during state reviews have been drawn to a close; in some instances due to deflecting and defensive tactics adopted by the state under review, and in other instances due to the lack of initiatives taken by observer states to undertake more detailed and rigorous discussions during the state reviews. At the outset, it is clear that the success of the UPR process mechanism cannot be measured by immediate implementation of reforms, and rather changes and reforms are likely to be slow and evolutionary in nature. Whilst the success of the review process, primarily due to its nature, cannot be measured solely by the reforms being implemented immediately, the argument here is that there is a missed opportunity in lack of fruitful discussions being held in the two cycles of review that can potentially be used as building blocks to engage states under review in a serious and reformative dialogue on the issue in the future. At worst, the unchallenged positions of the states under review can be used as justification for not accepting recommendations may be used as ammunition to reaffirm the states' position to decline to undertaken reforms on the issue in the other international forums, as well as in the domestic context. The reflections and recommendations provided in this study of the first two cycles provides significant food for thought and adaptations in the approach for state representatives in the future cycles of the review process.

Notes

1 UN General Assembly, 'Human Rights Council' (15 March 2006) A/RES/60/251. para, 5 (e).
2 A/HRC/RES/5/1, para, 3 (a).
3 Björn Arp, 'Lessons Learned from Spain's Practice before the United Nations Human Rights Reporting Mechanisms: Treaty Bodies and Universal Periodic Review' (2011) 15 *Spanish Yearbook of International Law* 1, 13.
4 E Domínguez Redondo, 'The Universal Periodic Review – Is There Life beyond Naming and Shaming in Human Rights Implementation' (2012) 4 *New Zealand Law Review* 673, 685.
5 R Sloane, 'Outrelativising Relativism: A Liberal Defence of the Universality of International Human Rights' (2001) 34 *Vanderbilt Journal of Transnational Law* 527, 553.
6 LS Bell, AJ Nathan and I Peleg, 'Introduction: culture and human rights' in LS Bell, AJ Nathan and I Peleg (eds), *Negotiating Culture and Human Rights* (New York 2001) 5.

7 Marie-Benedicte Dembour, 'Following the movement of a pendulum: between universalism and relativism' in Jane Cowan, Marie-Benedicte Dembour and Richard Wilson (eds), *Culture and Rights: Anthropological Perspectives* (Cambridge University Press 2001) 58.

8 R Falk, 'Cultural foundations for the international protection of human rights' in A An-Na'im (ed) *Human Rights in Cross Cultural Perspectives* (University of Pennsylvania Press 1995) 59; A An-Na'im, 'Introduction' in A An-Na'im (ed), *Human Rights in Cross Cultural Perspectives: A Quest for Consensus* (University of Pennsylvania Press 1995) 4.

9 X Li, *Ethics, Human Rights and Culture: Beyond Relativism and Culture* (Palgrave Macmillan 2006) 9–10. See also, Lynda Bell, 'Who produces Asian identity? Discourse, discrimination, and Chinese Peasant Women in the quest for human rights' in L Bell, A Nathan and I Peleg (eds), *Negotiating Culture and Human Rights* (Colombia University Press 2001) 27.

10 T Spaak, 'Moral Relativism and Human Rights' (2007) 13 *Buffalo Human Rights Law Review* 73, 75; Thomas Khun, *The Essential Tension: Selected Studies in Scientific Tradition and Change* (University of Chicago Press 1979) 290.

11 X Li, *Ethics, Human Rights and Culture: Beyond Relativism and Culture* (Palgrave Macmillan 2006) 9. See further 2.3.1.

12 Ibid.

13 Javaid Rehman, 'The Sharia, Islamic Family Laws and International Human Rights Law: Examining the Theory and Practice of Polygamy and Talaq' (2007) 21 *International Journal of Law, Policy and the Family* 108, 115.

14 Fidelis Nkomazana, 'Polygamy and Women within the Cultural Context in Botswana' (2006) 92 *Scripture* 265, 269.
   C Geertz, *Interpretations of Cultures* (Basic Books 1973) 49.

15 F Raday, 'Culture, Religion, and Gender' (2003) 1 *International Journal of Constitutional Law* 663–675.

16 Fidelis Nkomazana, 'Polygamy and Women within the Cultural Context in Botswana' (2006) 92 *Scripture* 265, 269.

17 Ann-Belinda Pries, 'Human Rights as a Cultural Practice: An Anthropological Critique' (1996) 19 *Human Rights Quarterly* 289. See also C Geertz, *Interpretations of Cultures* (Basic Books 1973) 49.

18 Ibid. See also, Robert Ulin, 'Revisiting Cultural Relativism: Old Prospects for a New Cultural Critique (2007) 80 *Anthropological Quarterly* 803.

19 A An-Na'im, 'Problems and prospects of universal cultural legitimacy for human rights' in An- Na'im and Deng (eds), *Human Rights in Africa: Cross Cultural Perspectives* (Brookings Institution 1990) 333.

20 Ibid.

21 Frederick Cowell and Angelina Milon, 'Decriminalisation of Sexual Orientation through the Universal Periodic Review' (2012) 12 *Human Rights Law Review* 341, 346.

22 A An-Na'im, 'Problems and prospects of universal cultural legitimacy for human rights' in An-Na'im and Deng (eds), *Human Rights in Africa: Cross Cultural Perspectives* (Brookings Institution, 1990) 332.

23 Sally Engle Merry, 'Human rights law and the demonization of culture (and anthropology along the way) (2003) 26 *PoLAR* 55, 67.

24 A An-Na'im, 'Toward a cross culture approach to defining international standards of human right: the meaning of cruel, inhuman or degrading treatment' in Abdullahi An-Na'im (ed), *Human Rights in Cross Cultural Perspectives: A Quest for Consensus* (University of Pennsylvania Press 1995) 23.

25 Whilst Malta expressly made references to its reservation on the issue to the women's rights treaty, and thereby insisted that it was not subject to any international human rights obligations on this matter.

26 R Chauville, 'The Universal Periodic Review's first cycle: successes and failures' in Hilary Charlesworth and Emma Larking (eds), *Human Rights and the
Universal Periodic Review: Rituals and Ritualism* (Cambridge University Press
2014) 89; Valentina Carraro 'The United Nations Treaty Bodies and Universal
Periodic Review: Advancing Human Rights by Preventing Politicisation' (2017)
39 *Human Rights Quarterly* 943, 967.

27 UNHRC 'Rwanda Addendum' (10 March 2016) A/HRC/31/8/Add 1,
para 12.

28 H Charlesworth and E Larking (2014) 'Introduction: the regulatory power of
the Universal Periodic Review' In H Charlesworth and E Larking (eds), *Human
Rights and the Universal Periodic Review: Rituals and Ritualism* (Cambridge
University Press 2014) 23.

Bibliography

A/HRC/RES/5/1

An-Na'im A, 'Problems and Prospects of Universal Cultural Legitimacy for Human
Rights' in AA An- Na'im and FM Deng (eds), *Human Rights in Africa: Cross
Cultural Perspectives* (Brookings Institution, 1990).

An-Na'im A, 'Introduction' in A An-Na'im (ed), *Human Rights in Cross Cultural
Perspectives: A Quest for Consensus* (University of Pennsylvania Press, 1995).

An-Na'im A, 'Toward a Cross Culture Approach to Defining International Standards
of Human Right: The Meaning of Cruel, Inhuman or Degrading Treatment' in
Abdullahi An-Naim (ed), *Human Rights in Cross Cultural Perspectives: A Quest for
Consensus* (University of Pennsylvania Press, 1995).

Bell L, 'Who Produces Asian Identity? Discourse, Discrimination, and Chinese Peasant
Women in the Quest for Human Rights' in L Bell, A Nathan and I Peleg (eds),
Negotiating Culture and Human Rights (Colombia University Press, 2001).

Bell LS, Nathan AJ and Peleg I, 'Introduction: Culture and Human Rights' in LS Bell,
AJ Nathan and I Peleg (eds), *Negotiating Culture and Human Rights* (Columbia
University Press, 2001).

Carraro V, 'The United Nations Treaty Bodies and Universal Periodic Review:
Advancing Human Rights by Preventing Politicisation' (2017) 39 *Human Rights
Quarterly* 943.

Charlesworth H and Larking E, 'Introduction: The Regulatory Power of the Universal
Periodic Review' in H Charlesworth and E Larking (eds), *Human Rights and the
Universal Periodic Review: Rituals and Ritualism* (Cambridge University Press,
2014).

Chauville R, 'The Universal Periodic Review's First Cycle: Successes and Failures' in
Hilary Charlesworth and Emma Larking (eds), *Human Rights and the Universal
Periodic Review: Rituals and Ritualism* (Cambridge University Press, 2014).

Cowell F and Milon A, 'Decriminalisation of Sexual Orientation through the Universal
Periodic Review' (2012) 12 *Human Rights Law Review* 341.

Dembour M, 'Following the Movement of a Pendulum: Between Universalism and
Relativism' in Jane Cowan, Marie-Benedicte Dembour and Richard Wilson (eds),
Culture and Rights: Anthropological Perspectives (Cambridge University Press,
2001).

Geertz C, *Interpretations of Cultures* (Basic Books, 1973).

Khun T, *The Essential Tension: Selected Studies in Scientific Tradition and Change*
(University of Chicago Press, 1979).

Li X, *Ethics, Human Rights and Culture: Beyond Relativism and Culture* (Palgrave Macmillan, 2006).

Merry S, 'Human Rights Law and the Demonization of Culture (And Anthropology Along the Way)' (2003) 26 *PoLAR* 55.

Nkomazana F, 'Polygamy and Women within the Cultural Context in Botswana' (2006) 92 *Scripture* 265.

Pries A, 'Human Rights as a Cultural Practice: An Anthropological Critique' (1996) 19 *Human Rights Quarterly* 289.

Raday F, 'Culture, Religion, and Gender' (2003) 1 *International Journal of Constitutional Law* 663–675.

Rehman J, 'The Sharia, Islamic Family Laws and International Human Rights Law: Examining the Theory and Practice of Polygamy and Talaq' (2007) 21 *International Journal of Law, Policy and the Family* 108.

Sloane R, 'Outrelativising Relativism: A Liberal Defence of the Universality of International Human Rights' (2001) 34 *Vanderbilt Journal of Transnational Law* 527.

Spaak T, 'Moral Relativism and Human Rights' (2007) 13 *Buffalo Human Rights Law Review* 73.

Ulin R, 'Revisiting Cultural Relativism: Old Prospects for a New Cultural Critique' (2007) 80 *Anthropological Quarterly* 803.

UN General Assembly, 'Human Rights Council' (15 March 2006) A/RES/60/251.

UNHRC, 'Rwanda Addendum' (10 March 2016) A/HRC/31/8/Add 1.

Conclusion

The Universal Periodic Review (UPR) is an intriguing and ambitious development in the monitoring of international human rights law at the United Nations. Described as having the potential 'to promote and protect human rights in the darkest corners of the world',[1] the UPR process carried a burden of expectations and great optimism as it operated under the new Human Rights Council, following the demise of the Commission. The peer review process was designed to give effect to the principle of universality on all international human rights norms through a unique interactive dialogue system. Indeed, the UPR process has gathered sufficient and significant merit over the two cycles and over a decade in existence. To begin with, the process boasts a universal participation of all UN members to the review process for over a decade of its existence. Further, it has provided a unique platform for all state representatives of the United Nations to engage in dialogue in the interpretation and implementation of international human rights norms, as well as raise awareness of how human rights norms are implemented in the domestic context throughout the globe. The UPR process is a soft global governance mechanism, whereby states have come together on a periodic basis with the sole intention to further the promotion and protection of the universality of human rights law through collaborative and positive support and encouragement. Without taking away the gravity of these positive traits that have become accustomed to the practice of the UPR process, the findings of this investigation reveal that the attractive simplicity of giving effect to the universality of human rights in the UPR process veils a complex web of issues that the state representatives in the process itself, are confronted with during state reviews. A detailed analysis of the discussions held between states in the review process has emphasised the protruding complexities that are faced when state representatives attempt to marry diplomatic strategies and performance with the embedded complexities with the interpretation implementation of universal human rights norms through an interactive dialogue on an international platform.

In answering the research question of this study, the findings of this study reveal that despite the process' egalitarian principles, whereby the aim of the review is to treat all states equally using highly formal and rigid procedures, the principle of giving effect to the universality of rights is contingent on the composition of state participants that undertake the review, and the human rights issue that is being discussed. Naturally, this means that the extent to which the embedded universalist claim of promoting all human rights norm is met will vary not only between state reviews, but also, within the lines of dialogue in relation to the specific human rights issue itself. In the same way, the study reveals that the extent of the challenge from a degree of cultural relativism will similarly vary depending on the state being reviewed and the human rights issue at stake. Consequently, despite the universalist claims that are embedded in the fundamental aim of the UPR process of promoting universality of all human rights norms, and, indeed, in the name of the process itself, the findings of this project give reason to question the overarching universalist aims and principles on the basis that the nature of each state review is unique in nature as it will be formed depending on the participants of the state review and the human rights issues discussed.

The findings of this investigation also reveal that the challenge of universality from a cultural relativist perspective is prominent in practice during state reviews in the UPR process. As discussed in the first chapter of this book, the challenge posed by the theories of cultural relativism to the universality of human rights is a significant one due to the similarities of the theoretical foundations of both studies. The findings of this project not only add weight to the significance of the cultural relativist critique of international human rights law, but the context in which the position was adopted shows how profound the theory is in practice. For instance, states adopted the strictest form of cultural relativism to challenge the universality of human rights on an international human rights platform at the UN in a process which repeatedly asserts its aim of promoting the universality of all human rights. In addition, the strict cultural relativist position was raised in a setting where one may have anticipated that state representatives would have exercised a diplomatic attitude in light of the international and political pressure that it imposed on the UPR process due to its inherent political nature. Therefore, despite the repeated assertion of the universalist aims of the UPR process, and the review process being subject to an international spotlight, it was striking to note that states expressly challenged reforms to comply with international women's rights on an international platform such as the UPR process, rather than remain silent on the issue. This gives reason to suggest that some states perceive the UPR process to be more than a monitoring mechanism, and more of a platform to express discontent with some international human rights norms in relation to women's rights issues.

Leading from the express challenge from a strict cultural relativist position on the platform of the UPR process, what was also striking to note was that the states themselves were not held accountable for their challenge to the universality of international women's rights. This silence by the observer states in response to an implicit or explicit challenge to the universality of human rights norms from a strict cultural relativist perspective in the UPR process has much wider ramifications. Naturally, it is acknowledged that any meaningful change cannot be binary in nature e.g. either that it is occurring or not. Indeed, the very nature of the UPR process is that change occurs over a period of time, through consensus initiatives, whereby reforms happen in a slow and evolutionary manner.

However, on this very basis, the discussions and dialogue held in the UPR process are immensely significant in nature since its substance can potentially be used a catalyst to feed into the momentum or movement to bring about reforms in the domestic context. For instance, the discussions and the commitments made in the UPR process can be used by civil society and human rights institutions as material and leverage being gathered to put pressure on the state in question to develop and shape reforms to address human rights concerns. If the UPR process is truly going to acquire creditability as was envisioned, then the nature of the discussions held carry enormous significance for the civil society movement, who can use it to apply pressure for compliance in the domestic context. For this reason, a sustained and unchecked challenge from a strict cultural relativist position expressed in the UPR process at best closes a dialogue on issues that are essential to be discussed using a platform like the UPR process. At worst, an unchecked challenge from a cultural relativist perspective, that is remained unchallenged, can potentially be used by the state under review as a point of reference to continue to refuse to undertake reforms to improve human rights protection in the given area of concern. It has been argued in the literature that the outcomes of the UPR process can potentially be significant enough to be considered as contributing to the international human rights law itself. However, if such gravity and importance are given to those outcomes where states show evidence of consensus on international human rights protection, then similar grave concern should be raised when states challenge the universality of international human rights norms on the UPR process.

The continuation of this unchecked challenged to universality in fact risks jeopardising the fundamental aims of the UPR process of giving effect to the principle of universality in its work and operation. This in itself feeds into the criticisms of the United Nations as being a body that is riddled with bureaucracy, and often unsuccessful in responding to member states that challenge and fail to fulfil their international human rights obligations. Leading from this, if a challenge from a strict cultural relativist position is expressed in a sustained manner in the third cycle and beyond, and the observer states remain silent and refrain from holding the state to account, then this could result in having wider ramifications to the universality of women's rights protection. This is primarily because an unchecked challenge to the universality of women's rights on an international platform such as the UPR process, may in fact undermine the universality of the particular women's rights obligations when raised on different platforms, whether that be on UN treaty bodies, where advocated by NGOs, or in the national jurisprudence.

Overall, the discussions held over the two cycles of review have revealed that the polarised debates between universalism and cultural relativism have been relegated to history in the scholarly world and this polarised debate still continues to materialise in international human rights discourse, in practice. As discussed in Chapter 2, many academics have criticised this polarised manner of discussing international human rights law. Providing practical evidence for these criticisms, this investigation has revealed how this polarised debate between universalism and cultural relativism in the conceptualisation and implementation of human rights that have been relegated to a distant past in the academic literature, in fact, are still prominent and profound in practice and have had a negative impact on striving to achieve the aims and objectives of the UPR process. The states representatives that have often adopted positions that have aligned with the extreme universalist and relativist positions have led to a surface level dialogue in relation to women's rights issues that have been averse to bringing complex issues to the focus of discussions during state reviews. The oversimplified nature of debates that have resulted from states adopting polarised extremes of either universalist or cultural relativist positions during debates has significantly contributed to substantive commitments being made by states under review during review process.

This investigation primarily recommends that a greater sense of responsibility is to be placed on observer states undertaking the state reviews to draw upon the vast amount of data and reports that are generated as part of the review process. Employing this data, more informed and detailed recommendations need to be issued to ensure a line of dialogue that holds that the state under review is held accountable. In addition, moving away from oversimplified debates, the observer states should be required to instigate detailed discussions on controversial human rights issues on this accommodating platform of the review process, in a manner that is more affiliated with the moderate form of cultural relativism. The platform of the UPR process provides a unique opportunity for encouraging and supporting states to implement universality of human rights norms, through the process of cultural legitimacy. Beyond this, the study also recommends that the observer states need to be more proactive in challenging and presenting counter arguments during state reviews, when representatives adopt positions in relation to suggested reforms that affiliate with a strict form of cultural relativism.

The required reform in the nature of discussions held in the UPR process is not only significant for the creditability for the review itself, but also because the discussions and the recommendations held on a particular issue can be used as advocacy tools by civil society and other stakeholders for policy dialogue and social change. The political momentum that is generated at the UPR process, through the discussions and recommendations, can initiate or facilitate avenues for participation by a range of stakeholders in the domestic context. The statements made by representatives in the interactive dialogue session can be used in the national coordination, planning, and monitoring for the promotion and protection of human rights issues in the domestic context. In this way, the nature of discussions held at the UPR process becomes critical in the development of the direction and tone of any social, cultural, and policy reforms on the ground. As it currently stands, at the end of the second cycle of review, the lack of substantial commitments and outcomes that resulted from the often superficial nature of discussions held in the UPR process feeds into the criticisms of the United Nations, more generally, as being a body that is riddled with bureaucracy, and as often unsuccessful in responding to member states that challenge and fail to fulfil their international human rights obligations. The book stresses that addressing the shortcomings of the UPR process is essential to avoiding irrefutable damage to the process' creditability, and avoiding the very destiny of the abolished Commission. More broadly, there is a strong investment required in addressing the concerns raised as part of this study to prevent adding fuel to fire of the existing criticisms of the United Nations' previous poor track record because of falling short of successfully monitoring states' actions in fulfilling their obligations under international human rights law. The failure to address this problem risks significantly damaging the principles of global social cohesion in the promotion and protection of human rights, which form one of the founding pillars of the purpose of the United Nations.

These conclusions provide a significant contribution to enhancing the understanding of how the UPR process operates in practice by providing a unique insight into the manner in which discussions are undertaken during state reviews. Whilst these conclusions can be significantly grounded on the findings of this project, what cannot be overlooked is that one of the obvious limitations of this study is that it focuses on only nine out of the 52 human rights issues that were raised in two cycles of the UPR process. It cannot be denied that the UPR process is a huge mechanism that produces numerous documents, and as a result, a full understanding of the UPR process is not the work of one project, but rather an ongoing project of research in itself. Nevertheless, the findings of this investigation are significant because they provide reasons to suggest that there is a serious and significant challenge being raised to the universalist claim of the UPR process from a cultural relativist perspective during state reviews in the first two cycles of review. It has been argued in the literature that the outcomes of the UPR process can potentially be significant enough to be considered as contributing to the international human rights law itself. However, if such gravity and importance are given to those outcomes where states show evidence of consensus on international human rights protection, then similar grave concern should be raised when states challenge the universality of international human rights norms on the UPR process. On this basis, it seems essential to undertake further exploration of the UPR process with a particular focus on the universalist claim of the review process, and the significant and serious challenge raised by states from a cultural relativist perspective to the universality of other international human rights norms. If nothing else, this is particularly necessary as a sustained and unchecked challenge to the universality of international human rights norms on an international platform like the UPR process could potentially have wider ramifications for the international human rights infrastructure itself. Such research seems particularly apt as the third cycle of this innovative review process draws to a close.

Note

1 https://news.un.org/en/story/2007/03/211752-human-rights-council-opens-session-ban-ki-moon-says-world-watching, accessed 20th October 2019.

Index